MW00669251

MEDITATIONS OF
GLOBAL FIRST PHILOSOPHY

SUNY series in Western Esoteric Traditions

David Applebaum, editor

MEDITATIONS OF GLOBAL FIRST PHILOSOPHY

Quest for the Missing Grammar of Logos

Ashok K. Gangadean

Cover photo: ©Erik Reis/iStockphoto

Published by
State University of New York Press, Albany

For information, contact State University of New York Press, Albany, NY
www.sunypress.edu

Production by Diane Ganeles
Marketing by Michael Campochiaro

Library of Congress Cataloging-in-Publication Data

Gangadean, Ashok K., 1941–
    Meditations of global first philosophy : quest for the missing grammar of
logos / Ashok K. Gangadean.
        p. cm. — (SUNY series in western esoteric traditions)
    Includes bibliographical references and index.
    ISBN 978-0-7914-7605-5 (hardcover : alk. paper)
    ISBN 978-0-7914-7606-2 (pbk. : alk. paper)
    1. First philosophy. I. Title.
    BD331.G2735 2008
    110—dc22

                                                                            2007052986

                        10   9   8   7   6   5   4   3   2   1

Dedicated to ((LogoSophia))

Contents

Acknowledgments

The meditations of this volume were composed over the past decade and certain portions have appeared in part or in modified form in prior publications or public presentations. I wish to acknowledge the following:

1. An abridged version of Chapter 1 appeared as "The Quest for the Universal Global Science" in *The Philosophy of Seyyed Hossein Nasr The Library of Living Philosophers* Volume XXVII, ed. Lewis E. Hahn, Randall E. Auxier, and Lucian W. Stone, Jr., Open Court 2001.
2. Portions of Chapter 2 appeared as "The Quest for the Primal Word" in *PARABOLA*, 20:3, August 1995.
3. A modified form of Chapter 5 appeared as "Dialogical Awakening in the Global Evolution of Cultures" (pp. 335–356) in *Doors of Understanding: Conversations on Global Spirituality in Honor of Ewert Cousins*, ed. Steven L. Chase, Franciscan Press 1997.
4. An earlier version of Chapter 6 appeared as "The Awakening of Primal Knowledge" in *PARABOLA*, 22:2, Spring 1997.
5. Selected portions of Chapter 7 appeared as "Dialogue: The Key to Global Ethics" in *PERSPECTIVES* (Journal of the World Business Academy), December 1997.
6. An earlier version of Chapter 8 appeared as "Meditative Reason and the Holistic Turn to Natural Phenomenology" in *Analecta Husserliana* Vol XLVII *Heaven and Earth and In-Between in the Harmony of Life*, (ed) A. T. Tymieniecka, Kluwer Academic Publishers, 1995.
7. A modified version of Chapter 9 appeared as "Masao Abe and Nishida's Logic of Place" in *Masao Abe: A Zen Life in Dialogue*, ed., Donald W. Mitchell, Charles Tuttle Press, 1998.
8. A version of Chapter 10 appeared as "Logos of Dao: The Primal Logic of Translatability" in *Asian Philosophy*, Vol. 12, No. 3, 2002.
9. An abridged version of Chapter 11 appeared as the Foreword in *The End of Suffering: Fearless Living in Troubled Time*s, Russell Targ and J. J. Hurtak, Hampton Roads Publishing, 2006.

I am grateful for support from the Faculty Research Fund of Haverford College and for assistance in preparing the manuscript from my Administrative

Assistant, Andrea Pergolese. My Student Assistant, Paul Bisceglio (Haverford Philosophy Major, class of '09) did an excellent job in working with me on completing the Index. Finally, I am most grateful for the gracious assistance of the Editorial Staff of SUNY Press in the final production of this book.

The Missing Global Evolutionary Drama

There is one truth so powerful that if we had the courage to encounter it together it would change our lives forever and lift us to the next stage of human evolution. This truth has been emerging throughout history and has matured to such a point that if we did face this truth, our individual and collective lives would take a significant step toward well-being and flourishing, but if we fail to come to terms with it the current global crises and unsustainable trends that threaten our survival as a species may well grow worse. So we are in the midst of an ultimate evolutionary drama that is global in scope and centuries in the making. In this drama our survival is at risk—we are all directly involved in one way or another in this historic event, and we have a direct say in how it will play out. Each of us has a choice in what comes next, and it all turns upon authentically awakening to this truth.

This historic truth is very simple. It is the truth that logos is real, that logos is the living foundation of all existence, the unified field of reality itself, the moving power of evolution. Logos is the source of all truths, the common ground of all religions and cultures, and it energizes all human experience. This logos is the very process of reality, and all history has been the story of the emergence of logos in the human condition. It has been said in modern times that if God is dead, anything goes. But it also is true that if logos lives, is real, then everything changes and our self-understanding requires radical revisioning.

But the authentic encounter of this truth is at once the easiest and most difficult thing in the world, for there is not a moment of life wherein this truth of logos is not present, available, and expressing itself. Since logos is revealed in every pulse of experience, it should be the most natural thing in the world to awaken to a direct and an immediate encounter of logos. Yet in the slow and painful evolution of consciousness and cultures, it is evident that powerful forces in human thought and cultures have continued to eclipse the truth of logos. For this reason the historical drama of logos rising, which is at the core of human evolution and ultimate concern, has not been clearly seen. And the failure or incapacity to process this truth has blocked and distorted our essential human nature and has caused abysmal human suffering.

So we face a challenge from the start. The single most important factor for our survival is awakening to this missing story of the emergence of logos, which requires the awakening of the global mind. But the single most important barrier to seeing this deeper evolutionary drama is the predominance of old dysfunctional patterns of thinking that make it virtually impossible to see and process this missing global story. How are we to break this cycle and rise to the global mind that brings the story of logos into focus? Of course we are already living this drama, already deeply involved in this awakening event. But it takes special efforts now to jump-start this vital process of rising to the missing historical drama. It takes a higher technology of thinking to process this missing truth of logos. As this higher form of mind awakens, our true human nature blossoms, and our lives flourish. We need to find a creative way to bring this story out.

This missing story of human evolution makes it apparent that every important advance in human cultures has been a breakthrough in the emergence of logos. But at the same time this drama reveals that there is a force in human life that has worked to conceal, suppress, displace, and deform the presence of logos. It is the pervasive and potent influence of this counterforce in human evolution that makes it so difficult to realize the truth of logos and that has produced suffering and devastation in the human condition. It is this counterforce in human thought that has brought humanity increasingly to the brink of extinction and self-destruction.

Nevertheless we also are in a most exciting and promising moment in our evolution. The relentless and irrepressible emergence of logos has moved us to the brink of an amazing breakthrough in individual and corporate human life—it is the awakening of the global mind through the dialogical revolution in our lives. All evolution has moved humanity to the threshold of an enlightened recognition of logos, and this comes to fruition with the individual and collective awakening of the global mind. Thus we now need to focus our attention and experiment on this dialogical awakening that opens the global mind.

As the global mind awakens, we begin to see that we humans have been evolving through the ages under the powerful influences of two great polar forces. A recurring theme in the global evolution of cultures is that all history has been a struggle between two competing paradigms or models of what it means to be human—a struggle between the egocentric human nature and the emerging dialogical human being. From a variety of perspectives in religious life, scientific life, and cultural evolution in general, it has been seen that human evolution has been moving through the ages from an egocentric culture to a dialogical form of life.

This emergence of dialogical culture is seen to be accelerating on a global scale, and the collision and confrontation of the two visions and practices of human life are now at a critical turning point. Human life is in the midst of a deep civil strife on all levels between the egocentric forces in human nature and the forces of dialogical awakening. This is the core drama at the heart of the many forms of cultural crisis that are now quite evident. As we now bring out this missing evolutionary drama, we see that humans are in the midst of a profound evolutionary transition from egocentric life to dialogical life. Our human form, our very essence, has been in a transition from egocentric beings to dialogic beings.

While egocentric culture leads increasingly to separations, divisions, localizations, strife, and polarizations in all aspects of daily life, the emerging dialogical way of life enhances communication, globalization, creative encounter, compassion, and mutual nurturing and care for self and others and for the ecology. How we manage this dialogical turn in global culture and in our own lives is all important for our survival and sustainability. As the dialogical turn emerges and intensifies, the egocentric counterforces also peak, bringing even deeper fractures, stresses, and fragmentations in all aspects of cultural life. The stakes get higher in our evolutionary drama as the opposing forces in everyday life intensify to the breaking point.

We now face a deep cultural crisis that has been building for centuries. And unless we can rise to a clear vision of the deeper evolutionary drama—the missing story of logos—we will not truly understand the nature and magnitude of the existential crisis we now face. So our survival and well-being turns on our awakening to the truth that logos is real, and this supreme global truth comes to focus with our realization that egocentric life is a disaster.

We have evolved to the critical point at which becoming more fully aware of the missing drama of logos is now the key to our survival. But we face an impasse that we must get around—the story of logos on which our well-being turns requires the deeper integral and dialogical thinking of the global mind. And this form of thinking has been blocked and discouraged by the predominant forces of egocentric thinking in all aspects of our lives. How do we stand back from these inhibiting and fragmenting forces? Can we really overcome the overwhelming forces of egocentric culture and experimentally enter the thinking of the awakening mind? We need to find a creative way to break the cycle.

One powerful way to intensify the awakening mind is to cultivate deeper dialogical encounters. Something remarkable happens in our being as we activate the dialogical turn and participate in deeper global vision. Awakening to this dialogical turn in evolution affects every aspect of our lives—our inner well-being, our relations with others, our capacity to negotiate fundamental differences in our shared cultural space, and our ability to honor and cultivate the human and natural ecology. It is through this dialogical awakening that the global mind ignites and helps us see and live the deeper truth of logos. The egocentric forces in cultural evolution have kept humanity in localized languages, partial and fragmented vision, artificially bounded experience, and forms of discourse that block access to the global truth of logos and hence to the realization of our true human essence.

But in dialogical awakening we are able to stand back from our particular cultural orientation and localized historical situation and truly enter into other cultural worlds and forms of life and encounter them from within. Something astounding happens in this dialogical awakening as we rise to a higher global perspective between worlds. As our experience expands and deepens in a global context between diverse cultural and religious worlds, between diverse perspectives and worldviews, the rational power of mind expands, and we begin to see the unmistakable pattern of global evolution of human life through the emergence of this higher dialogical consciousness.

So the missing evolutionary story of logos arising through global evolution in the human condition becomes accessible to us as we enter the global mind through deeper dialogical encounter. The awakening global mind realizes a higher power as it rises to the global perspective and overcomes the dysfunctional technology of the egocentric mind. The global mind has a deeper and more powerful access to the process of reality. Everything now turns on our capacity to advance to this higher technology of global minding. We shall now see that all of the important advances in cultural evolution have been moving us toward this more effective way of processing reality.

Human evolution has made clear that recognition of logos essentially requires a revolutionary advance in mind, a dramatic advance from the egocentric mind to the dialogic or global mind. And this advance in how we mind is the blossoming of our human nature as dialogical beings. So the evolutionary drama has brought us to an exciting and a dangerous brink. It is exciting because it is now within our power and reach to awaken to the global mind, to realize our true nature as dialogical beings. And this awakening to logos brings well-being and human flourishing. Or we may persist in egocentric ways of being that violate logos, distort reality, and are devastating to human flourishing. It all turns on how we now choose to conduct our minds, individually and corporately.

So let us experiment together as we now seek to tap the dialogical energy and enter the higher processes of the global mind. Let us see if we can get a preliminary sketch of this deeper missing drama of logos, the story of human evolution. All sorts of obvious questions erupt at the same time: What is this "logos"? Where does it come from? Why should we humans be concerned about this alleged missing scenario of history? Why should deeper knowledge of logos be the key our survival and flourishing? And what is this "global mind"? Why does our survival and well-being turn upon the "awakening" of mind? Why should how we "mind" be so important in our lives? What is this "egocentric" mind? What are these alleged two great forces working through human evolution and supposedly bringing us to the current "existential crisis"? Why is the egocentric mind such a "disaster" in human evolution? Are we humans not essentially egocentric?

Are we really in a "deep" cultural crisis? Is our survival really threatened? Is this not a bit overly dramatic? And if there is a "deep" evolutionary crisis, then why should an awakened "knowledge" of logos be the key to our survival? How can the "awakening" of the global mind make any real difference to the practical problems we humans now face? Is our "human nature" really in a deep evolution and transformation? What does it mean to say that we are essentially dialogical beings? What is this "dialogical turn"? Why is it so important in our evolution? These are just some of the questions that immediately come to mind. They need to be addressed, and they are so interconnected that we should now try to address them as a whole as we experiment in bringing out the missing story of logos.

The Emergence of Global Logos: The Awakening

We are in the midst of an amazing event that is global in scope and centuries in the making. It is the awakening of the global mind, the emergence of a higher form of life in human evolution. This event has been accelerating through the ages and has now reached an unprecedented critical moment in which our future survival and sustainability are hanging in the balance. There-fore, how we respond to the historic challenge before us will surely determine the fate of human life here on earth.

This awakening has been playing out in the heart of human evolution itself. Although the evidence of this emergence of the human form surrounds us in all aspects of cultural life, it has been painfully difficult, almost impossi-ble, to see it clearly in its full global form. But if we are able to stand back and get some critical distance from our particular cultural orientation and histori-cal situation, and truly enter into other cultural traditions, and authentically encounter, both from the outside and the inside, diverse religious worlds and alternative worldviews, then something astounding begins to come into focus. A new and higher dimension of reality and experience becomes available. As our experience expands and deepens in a global context between diverse cul-tural and religious worlds, between diverse perspectives and worldviews, we begin to see the unmistakable pattern of the evolution of human life in the emergence of a higher dialogical consciousness.

Through this living encounter with alternative worlds and perspectives new possibilities open, and we begin to see deeper patterns in human evolu-tion and in the human condition itself. In authentic living between worlds it becomes clear that there is and must be a deep common ground generating diverse worlds, holding worlds together, and enabling us to live and move between worlds. This common origin of multiple worlds is of course already at the heart of any world, but it comes to the fore more dramatically in its global form when we venture into the space between worlds. Living between worlds opens a higher dialogical dimension of reality that allows us to see that diverse worlds arise out of a common reality and are expressing a common evolutionary drama.

In this global dimension the most dramatic disclosure is that there is a fundamental reality or origin generating diverse worlds and expressing itself in all directions in and through these multiple worlds. Deeper reflection on this common origin of worlds, this generative principle of reality and existence, reveals that human life across cultures and traditions gravitates to, and arises out of, this common origin and strives to manifest and express its presence. Diverse religions, worldviews, philosophies, and cultural forms have all sought to express this moving principle of reality in one way or another. The rich expressions of this reality principle are so wide ranging that it has been virtually impossible to see that these expressions are indeed alternative expressions of one and the same reality. The greatest minds in human evolution across cultures and religious visions have somehow known that there must be a common origin underlying all realities. But the local forces in their worldviews and the states of evolution of their languages, discourse, and technologies of mind have worked against the clear global articulation of this truth.

Over the past 3,000 years (to focus on a significant moment in this story of Logos), through the heroic efforts of the highest creative minds, and through the continuing evolution of the human condition, it is more possible now to rise to a global vision and expression of this common moving principle of all realities. It would be helpful here to introduce a global name for this common origin of worlds. Let us call this fundamental moving force "Logos." The very fact of having this global name will facilitate a deepening of the global vision and articulation of the drama of human evolution.

Logos, as a candidate for the primordial global name, is so profound in its presence, as the origin of all worlds and as the moving principle of all realities, that it is prior to all the more localized names that have emerged in historical evolution. And yet it is this Logos that is being named and approximated by the diverse traditions of religions, philosophies, and cultural narratives that have evolved over the ages. Logos is the primal Word, the Living Spirit, the Unifying force of Nature, the field of Infinite Consciousness, the embodiment of material universe; it is Language, Thought, World . . . all realized in a higher global dimension.

When we approach Global Logos through the diverse cultural traditions that have striven to express Logos, we gain new and deeper access to this origin of all realities and evolutionary narratives. One of the most striking revelations is that all historical evolutions are essentially the expression of Logos and the emergence of Logos in the human condition. Logos is revealed as the generative principle of all realities—the reality principle itself—the moving force of all natural, historical, and cultural evolutions. Indeed, reality is seen to be a dynamic and creative process of the embodiment and emergence of Logos—the evolutionary process itself. And when we approach this moving principle of reality through the richly diverse narratives of reality that have experimentally evolved through the ages, it becomes apparent that this evolutionary drama of the emergence of Logos in history is the essential factor in all cultural forms of life.

In fact, this Idea of Logos is so powerful, deep, and overwhelming that to think it, to come to authentic awareness of its global scope and force, changes everything. And we shall see in our global exploration that Logos is an Idea whose time has come.

This supreme Idea of Logos cannot be thought in the way we customarily think. To approach Logos we must rise to a higher form of thinking, evolve to the global way of minding. The global perspective of Logos involves a higher way of perspective making, and this calls for the awakening of the global mind. So the Idea of Logos and the awakening of the global mind are essentially connected, and one cannot come forth without the other.

As we rise to the global dimension of Logos and enter the awakening mind, a higher reality between worlds comes into view. In this global perspective we can see clearly for the first time the remarkable evolution that has been proceeding on a global scale through the centuries. In this historical drama the greatest revelation is that Logos is real. The ultimate insight into cultural evolution across diverse worldviews, religious traditions, and philosophical narratives is that Logos is a living reality.

In this global perspective it becomes clear that all of the great religious and philosophical teachers across the cultures were in one way or another expressing this truth of Logos. In a remarkable plurality of visions and vocabularies, the historic teachers all express the living truth of Logos and contribute to an evolving and emerging global language of Logos. In this global evolution it begins to come into focus that there must be an ultimate origin and presence that generates all cultures, all worlds, and all forms of life.

The great teachings of the ages, when placed in this global emergence of Logos, concur that human reality is a function of how we conduct our mind and discourse. The disclosure of Logos, as we have suggested, is inherently tied to how we think, to the way in which we conduct our mind. As we reflect on the evolution of cultural life over the past 3,000 years, we may see the unmistakable pattern that the right approach to Logos calls for a profound paradigm shift in how we think, and with this the overcoming of habits of mind that have produced disastrous consequences in the human condition.

The historic teachers of Logos have seen that the egocentric ways of minding have not only eclipsed and repressed open access to Logos but have positively and actively caused ongoing devastation and suffering in the human condition. So one of the great lessons of the global perspective of cultural evolution is that the egocentric mind and its technology of thinking is an adolescent stage in human development that has been a primary cause of human suffering and existential pathologies. When the diverse cultural, religious, and philosophical traditions are rightly placed in the evolutionary drama of Logos, their higher global significance is released, and we begin to see their common diagnosis that egocentric thinking is a human disaster and that a higher technology of thinking that is centered in Logos is the common prescription for well-being.

In fact, the truth of this global evolutionary drama could not be seen clearly because of the dominance of the egocentric way of being human and of culture making. But if we can step back from the pernicious influence of this form of life and rise to the global dimension of Logos, we may readily see that all historical or cultural evolution has been the confrontation and interplay between the cultural forces of egocentric life and the counterforces of the historic emergence of Logos with its rise to the awakening of the global mind and global culture. In this drama it is impossible to exaggerate how deeply the influence of egocentric culture has repressed and deformed the clear vision of this global emergence of Logos. We shall see in detail how egocentric thinking has worked systemically against the recognition of the greatest insights of the teachers of Logos through the ages.

If we are able to step back from egocentric thinking and enter the ways of the global mind, then we may more readily see how and why this supreme event of Logos is the greatest moving force in the human condition and a direct moving force in historical developments.

PART 1

The Emergence of Global First Philosophy

Our Dimensional Shift to Global Reason and the Missing First Discipline

PROLOGUE: QUEST FOR THE MISSING GRAMMAR OF GLOBAL LOGOS

The emergence of Global First Philosophy (GFP) is just one expression of a profound and an unprecedented dimensional shift in the technology of consciousness that has been millennia in the making and that calls for a radical revisioning of every dimension of our human condition. This emergence becomes more evident when our rational consciousness dilates to its mature global form as we cross into the more expansive rational space of a global perspective across and between diverse worldviews, traditions, and disciplinary perspectives. In this awakening of the global mind and the activation of its global lens, certain astounding findings, patterns, and dynamics in the evolutionary drama of our maturing human form become evident that are not readily apparent when we are lodged within our more localized perspectives, disciplinary orientations, and lifeworlds.

When we enter the global perspective across and between diverse worldviews, perspectives, and disciplinary orientations, it becomes immediately apparent that all through the ages on a planetary scale there has been a perennial and relentless quest, attraction, and irrepressible urge in human consciousness to name, encounter, and enter the space of that which is First, Originating, Infinite, Primal, and Ever Present. As a global lens dilates in and through this simultaneous holding together of diverse First Narratives, a deeper encounter with Reality becomes possible. In this expanded horizon, it becomes evident that there is a Primal First yet to be Named in its *global* disclosure, which is and must be the common Originating Source of all possible worlds, and which awaits excavation and narration in a yet-to-be-articulated First Discipline. This is the frontier of *Global First Philosophy*.

1

DILATING A GLOBAL LENS:
A DEEPER ENCOUNTER WITH REALITY

As our rational capacity to process reality matures and we are more able to step back and gain critical distance from our relatively localized perspectives, worldviews, and disciplinary orientations, a global lens dilates as we cross into the more expansive rational space whence our diverse worldviews co-arise and play out in a global dialogue and evolutionary dialectic. A global perspective enables us to hold multiple diverse worldviews together in an integral and a "*hologistic*" consciousness that is genuinely interperspectival and "*holoperspectival*," and this activates and brings forth a *dimensional* shift in our capacities for thinking, experiencing, languaging, living, being, and processing Reality.

When, for example, through our awakened global power of reason we are able simultaneously to enter internally and hold together in integral awareness certain diverse classical worldviews, teachings, or first narratives, for example:—the classical teaching of the Chinese *Tao*; the Vedic Hindu discourse of *Aum* and *Brahman*; the Madhyamika Buddhist teaching of radical Emptiness (*Sunyata*); the classical Greek philosophical reflections on the *Primal Logos* through the teachings of Heraclitus, Parmenides, Socrates, Plato, and Aristotle, as well as the profound biblical revelations of *Yahweh* in our Judaic origins, or the scripts on the life and teachings of Jesus with their reflections on the *Infinite Spirit* (God), and the *Christ* (the Logos made Flesh), nor yet again on the Moslem teachings of *Allah* as the one true Primal Name; and so on, just to scan a few exemplars from a vast repertoire, certain global patterns, dynamics, and hitherto unnoticed megatrends in the evolution of consciousness become manifest.

CROSSING INTO THE SPACE OF GLOBAL REASON

As we enter this expanded space of global reason, a deeper emergent consensus across and between diverse worldviews and traditions comes into relief, and certain global patterns that we shall begin to explore in a moment become evident that could not as readily be seen from the lens of our more localized worldviews and perspectives. The expanded vista of GFP enables us to realize that "*What-Is-First*" is essentially *global in scope and power*, is an *Infinite, hence, Global Logos*, that must be the originating source, ground, and foundation of all possible worlds, words, phenomena, cultures, religions, philosophies, narratives, disciplines, perspectives, fields of research, and forms of life. It should be clear that in this context the term *global* resonates in its ontological sense as holding for all possible worlds: lifeworlds, worldviews, religions, cultures, perspectives, narratives, language forms, philosophical grammars, ideologies, cosmologies, logics, disciplines, forms of life, and so on. "Global" here captures the full boundless scope of the Infinite First, hence, hologistic, integral, dialogic, and all encompassing.

THE MISSING FIRST DISCIPLINE

This hitherto missing First Discipline of *Global Logos* helps us realize that *What-Is-First* is and must be an *Infinite Force Field* that extends and presides in every detail as an Integral and Hologistic Unified Field of Reality. And although this *Global* dimension of Infinite Logos was always already inscribed, implicit, and sometimes even hinted at, within our repertoire of diverse First Narratives, it took millennia of evolution and development in our collective human enterprise to arrive at its present moment of unprecedented ignition, articulation, blossoming, and fruition. In crossing into the "global age," as we now enter the twenty-first century, the evolutionary process presided by this Infinite Global First has arrived at the cusp of a truly magnificent maturation of our human form as global rational beings, as the long-emerging Global First Discipline self articulates as the global space of reason and discourse blossoms.

A further disclosure of this global turn is the uncovering of a missing *Primal Logic or Universal Grammar* of Global Logos, which reveals why each and every item within the Infinite Field of Logos essentially encodes and reiterates the infinite dynamic of this Infinite Primal Force. In this light it is little wonder that our diverse traditions across the planet through the ages would in one way or another both express this Logos and also strive in quest of reaching it and realizing its highest self-expression and fulfillment within this boundless, ever-dynamic, and unfolding Integral Field of Being and Existence that is the interwoven web of our Universe.

So one of the astounding disclosures of GFP is that *What-Is-First*, the Primal Logos, is Global and Infinite in its Presiding Presence, and that this Infinite Force Field rules and makes its Presence felt in every detail, at the micro and macro levels and dimensions of Objective Reality. The fact that diverse worldviews, traditions, and disciplinary orientations throughout the evolution of cultures and consciousness are actually symptoms or effects of a more vastly pervasive universal dynamic inscribed in every pulse of existence is just plain common sense in the global vision of the First Discipline.

OUR WORLDS ARE MIND-MADE:
THE TECHNOLOGY OF MIND

This fact that there is a missing global first narrative with its disclosure that **Global Logos is Real, ever Present, and Presiding** encodes, implies, and brings with it a vast network of allied astounding and reality-shifting findings. One such remarkable global truth in the emergent consensus across our diverse traditions of First Narratives, for example, is that **we are as we mind**—that we humans play a direct causal role in cocreating our living realities. One of the striking disclosures of GFP is this recognition that how we conduct our mental life—**our technology of minding**—in making our selves, our experience, and our lifeworlds is of the highest importance in shaping our human condition.

In this light it may be said that the supreme technology is not to be found in our remarkable inventions of machines, or electronics, or telecommunications, or the harnessing of digital or nuclear power, and so on, for these are all *effects* of the remarkable "ontologistical" powers of mind. Rather, **the ultimate technology is the technology of mind**—of how we conduct our consciousness in cocreating our worlds and shaping our living realities. This is a presiding and decisive factor in determining the state of our human condition.

Certain of our great traditions through the ages have noticed and accentuated, for example, that when we conduct our minds in egocentric or monocentric patterns of thought and world making this produces all kinds of polarities, dualities, fragmentations, artificial divisions, incoherencies, and alienations and is the source of all kinds of rational and existential disorders, dysfunctions, and pathologies on intrapersonal, interpersonal, cultural, and institutional levels. Thus to the extent that "egomental" patterns in the technology of mind dominate our lives, we would naturally expect to find the cumulative deleterious egomental effects manifested in all aspects of the resulting cultural worlds. In what ensues, it will become quite apparent that the full spectrum of global crises that humanity faces today, threatening our sustainability and survival as a species, is the direct cumulative effect of millennia of culture making dominated by egomental malpractice.

In contrast, diverse first philosophies, particularly those that have taken the lead in pioneering and developing meditative or integrative technologies of natural reason, have insisted and demonstrated that egomental minding is a primary source of human disorders and existential suffering in its diverse forms, made clear that when we conduct our consciousness in hologistic, nondualistic, integrative, and global dialogic patterns that flow with the objective interconnected dynamics of Reality, human well-being and flourishing result. In a moment we take a closer look at precisely how and why egomental minding, and its limited and distorted form of "reason," constitutively and proactively generates pathological polarities, rational and hermeneutical deformation, phenomenological and epistemic fragmentation, and existential alienation in the lifeworlds it produces.

THE GLOBAL TURN IN RATIONAL
TECHNOLOGY STILL IN THE OFFING

First we should notice that several alter-narrative strands are simultaneously opened before us, and we need to break through and suspend the usual linear narrative line of thought and open holo-narrative space to let these multiple narrative lines co-arise and shed light on one another. One strand or theme is that there is no getting around *What-Is-First*—this lead theme has of course already been haunting our narrative in its subliminal presence even before this particular narrative unfolding began.

Second, we need to pause to see why diverse traditions through the ages have instinctively and consciously gravitated to *What-Is-First* and recognized its Infinitude in all dimensions, hence its infinite Unity and Unitive Force Field in its Boundless Diversity. And of course we also are co-tracing the themes of the global turn in rationality and hermeneutical life, the emergence of the missing Global First Discipline, and its long-awaited global logistic, grammar, or technology of mind. So let us hold these alter-themes together as these diverse narrative strands weave a higher dimensional narrative.

This consensus feature of The First reveals that It must be One, all pervasive, always presiding. But this latent theme still hit certain walls and barriers in the technology of discourse and awaited its full global maturation and flowering. So even as this question of the "technology of mind" as being of supreme importance began to surface in diverse first narratives across the planet, the logistical techno-logic of this Primal Field remained eclipsed by the more localizing and particularizing forces of cultural grammars and traditions and thus **the Global Face of *What-Is-First*** awaited its moment in the evolutionary process, which of course is always driven by the emergent forces of this ever-presiding Infinite Force Field.

Indeed, it may be said that the irrepressible emergent force of this global (and, of course, cosmic) First has been the evolutionary driver of the unfolding human condition and all discourse and cultural life. In this respect it is apparent that the lead event in our ever-evolving human condition is this event-horizon of the full global-cosmic emergence of *What-Is-First*: the self-expression of this Infinite Force Field. In a real sense it may be said that the lead event in our rational and hermeneutical development through the ages is this headline event of Global Logos emerging and blossoming in our human condition in its full global form.

As we now trace the unfolding of this presiding theme throughout the development of cultural discourse and human evolution, it would be good to be mindful of this theme of **the emergence of the global grammar of The First** and of course of **the global logistic or technology of mind** that opens the access code to this primal grammar of the Infinite Word. In a real sense it might be suggested that significant breakthroughs in tapping this hitherto missing access code to the global technology of mind via the explication of the global grammar of the Primal Field would have stunning consequences for revisioning our human enterprise. And one narrative strand that we shall trace is the theme of why it is that despite the great teachings of diverse first philosophies and sacred narratives through the ages, which warned against the pathologies of egomental minding, these patterns have continued to dominate our human situation.

TOWARD THE GLOBAL TURN
IN THE TECHNOLOGY OF MIND

Holding these multiple alter-narrative strands simultaneously in mind, let us probe more deeply into this all-pervading presence of *What-Is-First* and its presiding event-horizon. This will help us get closer to making a truly dimensional shift in rational praxis as we enter the global space of The Primal Field and tap the global grammar of this Infinite Word.

PRIMAL JOURNEY INTO WHAT-IS-FIRST:
ENCOUNTERING GLOBAL LOGOS

Every impulse in our universe, every pulse of life, every vibration of energy, and every motion of particles will both express *What-Is-First* and gravitate through itself toward this Infinite Force Field, which always already overflows it. This holodynamic of Primal Reality reiterates itself recursively, hologistically, and it issues forth as the perceived universe. This is the primal context in which all thought, all consciousness, all life, all intelligence, and all evolution unfold. Finding our way through our cultural constructs into this Sacred Space of Infinite Presence is the journey into GFP.

It is little wonder, then, that every expression of consciousness and every reflection on experience and existence gravitate simultaneously out of and toward this Infinite Presence to discover that it has been ever-present. And certainly, before this Primal Force Field is "divided" and "broken" by human conventions into separations of "philosophy", "science," "religion" . . . and all of our other conventional names, this Original Word, ever unbroken and unbreakable by human artifice, is the space of a Primal Narrative Drama that encodes the story of human evolution and the playful unfolding of our universe.

The evidence of this Primal Story of the Infinite Word is so evident and manifest in every human act, in every cultural event, that it is easy to overlook and almost natural to ignore, forget, or lose sight of this ever-present source of life and existence. It is just because we humans, and everything else in our universe, are so filled and overflowing with this Infinite Force and Energy, this Infinite Presence, that we fail to recognize or remember "it" as we go about our business of living, seeking meaning and truth and surviving in the world.

Nor is it surprising that our diverse cultures across the planet and throughout our evolution have in one way or another found ways to thematize and bring this Infinite Presence and Force Field to articulate consciousness, for when we stand back from our more localized orientations and perspectives and expand into the vista of a global perspective across worldviews, it is immediately clear that our diverse traditions have sought to name and narrate this Primal Force Field and recognize it as our organizing principle and supreme priority. But hitherto we awaited a truly global grammar, logic, logistic, rational, and narrative space to access, receive, and encounter this Primal Field of Reality in its truly global form.

DIVERSE PRIMAL ALTER-NAMES FOR THIS FIRST

Whether in the Judaic origins in approaching *Yahweh*, or the early Chinese questing of *Tao*, the Hindu Vedic science of *Aum*, or the Buddhist radical emptiness in naming this Primal *Sunyata*, or, again, the Christian primacy of *God* and *Christ*, or the Moslem calling out to *Allah*, the early Greek *Logos*, the ongoing quest for the fundamental grammar of thought, or even the quest of modern science to discern the ultimate stuff of the universe, cosmic origins, or the grand unified field of the universe . . . the list goes on and the pattern is clear. These diverse and perennial quests for Primal Origin are signs, symptoms, and *effects* of being always already situated within the Primal Infinite Force Field that accommodates and incorporates all of these diverse "First Names" and infinitely more names without bound.

One remarkable fact of our situatedness in this Infinite Presence is that each and every "item" in this Primal Domain, each person, every individual, every being or event, will participate in this Infinite Web and will reiterate within itself this infinite potential. That each person, for example, encodes the infinite dialectic within itself, is a stunning disclosure that has nonetheless been recognized and acknowledged over and over by our great traditions, even if it has been often too much for us to process, face, or accept. The Christian (especially Quaker) formula that God is within each person, for example, and the Hindu teaching that the true Self, the Atman, is one with and nondifferent from Brahman, the Infinite Primal Presence, are just two prominent instances of this global finding and trend.

APPROACHING A GLOBAL NAME AND
TECHNOLOGY OF MIND: ((GLOBAL LOGOS))

This overwhelming truth is just one tip and strand of a range of world-changing findings that become evident when we expand our rational capacities in crossing into the deeper dimension of this global perspectivity across and between diverse worldviews and narratives of *What-Is-First*. One such finding, of course, is that *What-Is-First*, being Infinite, is Infinite in every possible dimension, thus Boundlessly Global in all directions—the Global Word, Global Grammar, Global Technology of Mind—and manifesting the universal power of a Global Name for all possible worlds, grammars, perspectives, disciplines, cultures, ideologies, and forms of life.

NO ((GLOBAL NAME)) OR
((GRAMMAR)) HAD EMERGED

We have suggested that *What-Is-First*, being constitutively Infinite in every way, in every dimension, modality, category, or kind, is thus inherently hologistic, undivided, and global in our special ontological sense. This finding has been echoed in widely diverse first narratives on a global scale through the ages, yet these narratives remained relatively localized and idiosyncratic even as each naturally purported to be a universal grammar expressing and naming this Infinite First. So in the global perspective across such first narratives, we find a variety of "First Names" (several just mentioned in the foregoing) but no truly ((global name)) had yet emerged and no clearly ((global grammar)) articulated or clarified.

And in my forty-year adventure in exploring the foundation of first philosophy, in seeking a truly global grammar and fundamental logistic for natural reason, I was led inexorably to introduce certain basic notations to help make explicit and articulate the hitherto dormant global dimension of language, thought, experience, and philosophical grammar. The notational clarification and advance at once helped me see and bring out that the egomental space of discourse had its own generic logic, formal dynamics, and grammar (irrespective of a particular worldview or ideology), and that the transformation into the hologistic and integral dimensions of Mind, Word, and World likewise had its global or universal grammar, its integral dynamics, and holistic logistic. This was a "discovery" or "clarification" of the highest order that enabled me to see and understand the profound shift in technology of mind from the polarized rational space of egomental mind and word into the global space of the Infinite Word. This needs some elaboration.

MY EXPERIMENTAL JOURNEY INTO THE ((GLOBAL GRAMMAR OF LOGOS))

My early training and research was in the foundation of logic and ontology in the Anglo-European traditions of analytic philosophy and the philosophy of language. In my doctoral dissertation, I focused on a comparative exploration of the logical paradigms of Aristotle and Frege and on certain fundamental issues in logic and ontology concerning time, truth, and the ontological status of the future. My study focused on the logistical and theoretical powers and limits of the two great competing paradigms for philosophical logic, and in the end I reached a disturbing impasse in finding that the two competing paradigms for the fundamental logic of consciousness and organon of philosophy seemed to repel each other, to be constitutively incompatible and irreconcilable, yet each appeared to have vital contributions to the philosophical understanding of the space of reason and the logic of language and meaning.

My early exploration in the foundation of logic and ontology—vital concerns for first philosophy—led me to encounter a fundamental polarization at the heart of rationality and the logic of consciousness. And if logic (as the science of thought and reason) itself was polarized across incompatible competing paradigms, then this did not bode well, to say the least, for the coherence of rationality and the discourse of philosophy. If the science of logic is polarized at its core, then it appears that rationality itself is polarized and broken at its core, which would have disastrous consequences for philosophical discourse, human inquiry, and of course for our existential condition and cultural discourse. So this was a most disturbing finding that precipitated a philosophical crisis. My instinct and intuition were that natural reason was, indeed, fundamentally coherent, and that there must be a deeper level at which this polar split could be overcome.

It was at that time that I traveled to India for the first time and began a systematic encounter with Indian philosophical thought, diverse first narratives, and experienced what I would later call "meditative reason." When I entered the philosophical discourse of classical Hindu and Buddhist texts, a new horizon opened that enabled me for the first time to gain a deeper critical understanding of the rational space in which I was raised and educated and conducted my philosophical research.

Since my philosophical education was situated in the rational space from early Greek thought (Socrates, Plato, Aristotle) through the contemporary Anglo-American analytical traditions, as well as the European Continental traditions, my philosophical life unfolded within the logical and hermeneutical dynamics of predication and the rational space of philosophy as this evolved through the ages from the logic of Aristotle through the modern and postmodern developments of the analytical and Continental traditions of rationality and evolving discourse.

I will not go into details here. This exploratory journey has been presented in some detail in my earlier books, especially *Meditative Reason: Toward Universal Grammar* and in my forthcoming volume, *Time, Truth, and Logos: Quest for an Integral Global Logic.* My early philosophical research certainly made me keenly aware of the vital importance of philosophical grammar and the logistic of thinking, but I had not yet arrived at the key idea of a "technology of minding." It took over twenty years of intensive continuing experimentation and development to arrive at this opening and another fifteen years to further develop and test the new logistic technology in explicating the global space of integral natural reason and the missing ((First Discipline)).

One key advance in my crossing into the space of GFP was my "discovery" of a missing global grammar of *What-Is-First* and the experimental introduction of special logistical notation to tap, excavate, and make explicit this **fundamental Logic of Logos**. With the formulation and clarification of these universal dynamics of the Unified Field, I also was able to discern and articulate the generic logic of egomental minding as well. The notational devices I innovated to mark these two fundamental technologies of mind enabled me to accelerate in clarifying these two contrasting, though related, dimensions of rational and hermeneutical life. For me, the introduction and use of these notational devices played a key role in the breakthrough of the missing fundamental grammar. This is presented more fully in Part 2.

On this occasion I wish merely to give a quick sense of my encounter with the dynamics of meditative reason and its radical critique of egocentric thinking, or what I would later call "egomental" minding. For the meditative critique, whether in the Hindu or Buddhist philosophical traditions of first philosophy, both detected the dynamics of egocentric minding and, despite their apparently competing philosophical narratives, both concurred that the form of consciousness that may be called "egocentric," which was organized around the posit of a separately existing "thinking subject" entertaining phenomena appearing to it as an "object of thought," was highly problematic, inherently lodged in patterns of polarization, pernicious unsolvable dualisms, fragmenting dynamics, and artificial constructs that were all cut off or alienated from the alleged primal field of integral reality.

Indeed, one of Hindu thought's essential findings is that the "self" that was posited in this egocentric rational space is an artificial entity that was cut off from the true Self that is boundlessly integral and essentially woven into the Unified Field of objective reality. Buddha's essential finding is that the egocentric self is the source of existential pathologies and suffering and was a construct of the egological structure and dynamics. Buddha's great awakening as a first philosopher turned on seeing deeply into the dialectics of the egocentric technology of mind and discerning rational therapeutic patterns for rehabilitating the egocentric addictive patterns into a nondualizing flow with the fundamental Dharma or Law inscribed in the Unified Field, wherein all items mutually constituted one another in a boundless dynamic co-arising.

So in both the Hindu and Buddhist traditions of first philosophy, the key advance into coherent rationality turned on discerning the dualizing dynamics of egomental mind and prescribing powerful rational strategies and therapies for breaking the egocentric barrier and maturing into holistic and integrative dynamics of hermeneutical life.

Of course this powerful encounter with the rational therapies of Indian first philosophies opened a vast new frontier in my continuing inquiry into the foundations of logic, ontology, and natural reason. I realized for the first time that there was such a thing as egocentric thinking, and I was both stunned and delighted to understand how and why egomental minding inherently self-polarizes and generates deep dualisms and polarities in all aspects of the life-worlds and hermeneutical productions that "egominding" generates.

I now understood why my earlier research into the foundation of natural reason and my search for a coherent logic of natural language ended in the profound split and polarization of logic itself across the polar paradigms of Aristotle and Frege. I experienced a rude awakening that jolted me into a new critical awareness of the logical space in which I had been proceeding all of these years. Could it be that the rational space in which I was raised and educated—the space of predication—in its evolution from Aristotle through Frege and beyond was lodged within a deep structure of egomental minding? Was I experiencing the polarizing and dualizing dynamics of egomental reason? A new dimension opened in my research and teaching, and it took twenty-five years of continued intensive inquiry to answer these and related queries with the publication of *Meditative Reason: Toward Universal Grammar.*

SOME INNOVATIVE NOTATIONS TO MARK AND CLARIFY THIS GLOBAL TECHNOLOGY: FUNDAMENTAL STEPS IN MY ENCOUNTER WITH ((GLOBAL LOGOS))

Global Space Opens and Deeper Patterns Emerge

With this life-shifting encounter with these "Eastern" versions of "first philosophy," a new expanded frontier in the rational enterprise opened. At that time there were several fundamental questions, themes, and issues that preoccupied me, but I had not yet seen their essential convergence. A key focus was my ongoing quest to become clear on the foundation of rationality, for the fundamental logic of natural reason and of natural language. Another was the concern of developing a coherent "first philosophy" in the domain of deep ontology and its perennial concern to understand and process the language of Being and its grammar of Reality.

These concerns of the foundation of ontology naturally raised profound issues concerning worldviews, especially the nature of rational discourse or the possibility of dialogue or transformations across or between diverse worlds. It was clear in the space of comparative ontology that there were fundamentally diverse worldviews, which disclosed Reality differently, in fact so differently that it was a challenge to understand the possibility of discourse between worlds. The field of philosophy had not yet adequately addressed these issues of how worldviews were formed or the nature of transformations between widely variant worlds.

Yet these issues were as fundamental as they were urgent in the human condition for cultural discourse and personal relations as humanity faced the challenges of globalization in entering the modern world. But these two clusters of ultimate concerns—the foundation of logic/rationality and its quest for the fundamental grammar of thought, together with explorations in the foundation of ontology and the concerns of understanding the grammar of being and discourse between worlds—would converge in the expanded space of first philosophy.

Indeed, we shall see that diverse strands of "ultimate" or foundational concerns in the diverse domains of philosophy become essentially linked as we probe more deeply into the dimension of global first philosophy. For example, inquiries into the foundation of Logic turned out to be profoundly linked to ultimate issues of Ontology, and these in turn would naturally connect to foundational inquiries into the ultimate ground of Knowledge (Epistemology) or into the foundations of Ethics, or questions concerning the nature of the Self (Self-Knowledge), and so on. These would all turn out to be essentially convergent in the ever-deepening explorations of first philosophy.

Emergent and Convergent Patterns

The reason for this fundamental convergence, of course, is the disclosure within the expanded global perspective between worldviews and philosophical traditions that *What-Is-First* must be a Primal, Infinite, Boundless Presence. Over the decades, as my explorations across diverse worldviews, traditions, and dimensions of philosophy expanded on a global scale and I became saturated in widely diverse philosophical paradigms and narratives, certain striking patterns alluded to earlier became pronounced.

Is There a Convergent Primal First?

One such megatrend, as suggested, is the glaring feature that diverse philosophical narratives across the planet and through the ages seem to gravitate inexorably to some Primal First. It appears that there is an emergent "consensus" that such a "First" must be Infinite in every possible way. But even this alleged idea of "Infinite First" is problematic and possibly fraught with all sorts of systemic ambiguities and equivocalities across diverse worlds and narrative contexts. Whether diverse first narratives name its First candidate as *Yahweh* or *Aum* or *Logos* or *Tao* or *Being* or *Sunyata* (Absolute Emptiness) or *Christ/God* or *Allah* or *Energy, Nature,* or *Unified Field* . . . it is not at all clear that these alternative "Primal Names" must or do in fact indicate or express the same "First." Nevertheless, prima facie, the very idea of "Infinite" triggers a profound and potent logic that has a life force of its own, and this is what the innovation of GFP heightens and manifests.

The Missing Technology of Global First

What will become increasingly compelling as we proceed is that the primal logic of the First, being Infinite, is infinitely unitive, univocal, univocating, and at the same time generative of boundless diversity that it nevertheless supports and sustains within its boundless unifying power. So the supremely potent Idea of Infinite First entails a Primal Unifying Force Field that constitutively holds all possible diversity, including diverse first narratives and alternative first names, within its unifying jurisdiction. The Primal First, in its Infinitude, inherently plays out in an ever-presiding dynamic of Unity-in-Diversity and Diversity-in-Unity.

However, this primal dynamic that pulsates throughout every fiber of Reality at the micro and macro dimensions cannot be processed or discerned in the mundane precritical patterns of thought that are dominated by egomental minding. The logic of the Infinite Force calls forth a technology of minding that opens to and flows with the infinition force of the Global First. It appears that this infinition technology of minding, though tapped and hinted at over millennia by our great teachers, awaited more complete explicitation with the emergence of the global grammar through its global lens and the global turn in rationality.

Technology of Minding as a First Concern

Indeed, this question of the appropriate technology of minding becomes all-important in approaching the Infinite First and the development of GFP. If we begin lodged in the patterns and dynamics of egomental minding, then we will find ourselves already situated in fragments, divisions, separations, systemic ambiguities, and primal polarizations across worlds that constitutively violate the infinite integral rational space of the First.

For example, when we commence our queries from the egomental rational space we are already in divided fields of logic versus ontology versus epistemology versus ethics, and so on, so the query into the First is already taken as divided into diverse domains and hence alternative first narratives. First philosophy in ontology seeks primary Being, while first philosophy in logic seeks the primal laws of thought, while first philosophy in epistemology seeks the ultimate grounds of knowledge, and so on. Thus the disciplines of Being, Thought, Language, Knowledge, and the like are already divided. And the diverse domains of Mind versus Word versus World are already presented as severed independent fields.

Whereas when we approach the Infinite Primal First in the appropriate integral or hologistic rational calculus, the Global Face of the First reveals that the Infinite Word is already filled with Infinite Consciousness and saturates the World—so there is an original convergence, inseparability, or co-arising of MindWordWorld: each co-expresses and co-constitutes the other to manifest an original, unbroken, boundless Continuum.

And of course the moral of this story is that in approaching *What-Is-First*, the cardinal principle is **First Things First**: the technology of minding must be commensurate with the global dynamics of what is being minded—with the hologistic dynamics of the Infinite First. So the question of the technology of minding is a first order of business when it comes to inquiry (dialogic encounter) into the First. And to presume egomental minding as pre-given is to beg the fundamental questions. We shall now see that a driving force in the evolution of our human condition has been this incredible drama to find the access code to the Infinite First, which turns essentially on activating this integral technology of mind.

First Things First: The Driving Force of Evolution
The Great Quest for Global Logos:
The Mysterious and Elusive Access Code

With this in mind, let us now resume our lead story of the great global quest for *What-Is-First*.

((Logos)) as a ((Global Name)) for ((Infinite First))

Realizing, then, that we are in this self-referential spiral process of mindfully calling on the higher rational space of the Global First, even as we make our way into this dimensional mind shift, let us proceed in an accelerated way through our global lens to scan the mind scape of our remarkable human evolutionary journey. One of the ironies of this global drama is that although the Global Infinite First is the presiding force field playing out throughout our evolution, an explicit "global name" has not yet emerged to hold the open common ground for the rich spectrum of first names emerging over millennia across the planet.

The full flowering of a ((global name)) co-arises with the explicit emergence of the ((global grammar)) of the ((Infinite Word)). In this remarkable co-emergence, it becomes clear that the ((Infinite First)) must be ((global)) (which of course here also means "cosmic" and "infinitely universal") in every way, in every possible aspect or dimension. One of the key innovations that arose along the way over decades of radical inquiry was to nominate "Logos" as an effective logistic candidate for this awesome role and to introduce special "logistic notation" to mark this dimensional shift into the Logosphere: ((. . .)), hence ((Logos)). In what follows I give a brief, compressed sketch of this historic crossing into the global rational space of ((Logos)).

((LOGOS)) AS THE LEAD EVENT
IN OUR COSMIC EVOLUTION

Once we truly encounter this ((Infinite First)) in its ((global disclosure)), the astounding megatrends and evolutionary patterns alluded to earlier come into relief. It is immediately clear that this Infinite First is the source and resource of all possible names and forms and items, indeed, of the foundational space or field wherein anything whatever may appear and be. Thus this ((Infinite First)) must be the ((Infinite Word . . . Name . . . Sign . . . Symbol . . . Sound . . . Utterance)), so all language flows from this source. But this ((Infinite Word)) is filled with all dimensions of Reality . . . every conceivable category is always already originally co-constituted in this ((Boundless Word Power)): thus it is also ((Infinite Mind)), ((Thought)), ((Consciousness)), ((Knowing)) . . . so ((Word)) and the full spectrum of (((Mind)) mutually constitute one another as ((Mind-Word)); again, this ((Original Word)) issues forth as ((Primal Source = Force = Cause . . .)), and the ((Primal Space of Reality)) is thus already manifest in this ((Infinite Word)), thus forming the primal continuum of ((MindWord-World)) . . . which is the ((Primal Field of Reality)) . . . the ((Logosphere)).

This ((Logosphere)) is naturally the ((Infinite Power or Force)), which being Infinite, is ((Infinitely One)) = ((Infinite Unifying Force Field)) of the Boundless Cosmos, and this is the Primal ((Unified Field)) of the Universe. But this ((Unifying Force)), the Primal Force of the Universe Itself, must be Infinitely Present in every iota or item of the Universe, so it is in this profound sense that ((Logos)) presides in every event or moment. This of course ((implies)) that Infinite ((Unity)) manifests in boundless original ((Diversity)), and so the ((SpaceTime)) of the ((Logosphere)) extends infinitely in boundless Alterity, Multiplicity, and Diversity, held together in boundless ((Relations)), ((Relationality)), and ((Connectivity)) in the Unified Field.

We begin to see the Infinite Potency of the ((Primal Onto-Logic)) of this ((Infinite Word)): It shows itself as ((Holistic)), as ((Unity in Diversity)), as ((Infinite Being)) in Boundless ((Dynamic Interplay)) as ((Being = Becoming: Infinite Dynamic Process)), as the ((Event Continuum of the Cosmos)). Thus the ((Mind Power)) or ((consciousness)) that minds itself, minds this very dynamic Process of the Logosphere, must itself issue in a Logic or Logistic that both expresses and reflects the Holistic structure and dialectic of ((Existence)). This is the ((Hologistic Logic, Technology, Calculus)) of the ((Infinite Word)).

So when ((mind power)) monitors itself in the very dynamic hologistic (self-referential, recursive) process that constitutes the fabric of the ((Event Continuum)) of Reality, we see that this primal technology of consciousness flows in sync with the lawlike order of this ((Cosmic Flow)). From this preliminary play of the ((Infinite Word)), we should have a better ((Idea)) of how and why the Lead Event of Existence is the ((Event of Logos)) playing itself out in a cosmic evolutionary drama. This is why every pulse of human evolution, of cultural development, of the evolution of ((Discourse)), the unfolding a maturation of ((Natural Reason)), of the developing technologic of consciousness, of the emergence of the mature and whole ((human form)) constitutively unfolds as integral to this leading ((Cosmic Event of Logos)). And the ((Narrative History)) of this Global Event is yet to be fully articulated—the hitherto missing Story of ((Global Logos)).

PRELIMINARY SKETCH OF
OUR EVOLUTIONARY STORY

In this light we may now take a highly compressed look through the ((global lens)) of our continuing evolutionary drama—the global emergence of our ((human species)). As we scan our philosophical, rational, and cultural development on a planetary scale over, say, the past three millennia, certain striking patterns become evident. We are in a better position now to resume our earlier story line of making a dimensional shift into the global rational space of Logos.

Given the presiding ((Logos Event)) we have just introduced and the disclosure that the Infinite First is self-expressing in every possible event, it is not surprising to see evidence of this ((global emergence)) throughout the evolution of our cultures on a planetary scale. Put succinctly, ((Logos)) is the Presiding Primal Premise of all Being, Existence, Reality, Rationality, Experience, Discourse, and Cultural Evolution. This is the presiding force in the hermeneutical processing of all processes, events, and developments. The Infinite Presence of the ((Logosphere)) makes its presence felt in every moment of life and experience.

STAGES IN THE TECHNOLOGY OF MIND

As we now proceed to scan the evolution of thought through our global lens across worldviews and traditions, it becomes apparent that a natural stage in the development of human rational consciousness is to focus on the screen of awareness wherein the world and experience presents itself to us in naïve pre-critical appearance. This is the space in which commonsense experience, rationality, and discourse naturally appear, and philosophical thought emerges. Philosophical reflection seeks to make sense of things in quest of wisdom and initiates its reflective activity on this screen of everyday appearances.

As we now scan diverse traditions of such reflection, we find different philosophical responses to this naïve space of thought and discourse. What becomes clear is that in the dawning of philosophical thought, it appears that there is a powerful gravitation of such inquiry toward *What-Is-First*. In the early Greek tradition, for example, philosophy is born with the attempt to find and articulate the Logos (speech, word, thought, discourse, language, mind, reason, theoria) and give an account of First things—of Being, of primal Causes, of the ultimate stuff of the universe, of the Arche or Principles making sense of things, ordering the world, and disclosing unity and unifying forces for the vast diversity disclosed in experience.

THE SPACE OF PREDICATION: THE SCREEN OF BEING, THOUGHT, AND EXPERIENCE

The early reflections of Parmenides and Heraclitus, for example, follow this path, and the refinement of such a quest for wisdom is taken up by Socrates, Plato, and Aristotle. It is with the brilliant articulation of the latter three in particular that the space of reason and the logic of consciousness reach a new threshold as the science of reason and logic is born. Clearly Socrates was consciously preoccupied with First things, and Plato's philosophical grammar sought to map out the mind scape of rational consciousness and to initiate the grammar of Being, a blueprint for making sense of experience and world.

In this early birthing of the language of reason (of Logos), Plato instinctively gravitated to "form," "essences," and "universals" in the articulation of *What-Is-First*. In his narration through deep dialogues, and via the voice of his teacher Socrates, Plato followed the path of awakening wisdom and rationality to see that there must be some ultimate Source or Universal Form of all forms, which is the rational light itself and the source of all intelligibility—the ground of truth and being. But in the fundamental blueprint laid down by Plato, it appeared that there was a profound divide in the space of discourse between the space of everyday appearances (the world of experience) and the unchanging space of universal forms and essences, which made the world possible and illuminated experience with its rational light. There appeared to be a deep split between the world of universal eternal forms and the particular things and experiences of everyday life: a split between Being and Existence, between Soul and Body.

And his protégé, Aristotle, accelerated the birthing of "first philosophy" in developing the grammar of Logos in the form of Ontology—the fundamental first science of Being—as well as the initiation of the science of Logic—the fundamental dynamics and laws of thought. In a way both "sciences" were alter forms of "first philosophy," since both purported to articulate the formal deep structure of all possible experience. It was Aristotle who explicitly ignited the formal science of Logic and the grammar of Being in the space of predication. In this birthing of first philosophy—both in terms of Ontology and Logic—Aristotle built on the unfolding blueprint for rational space bequeathed by his mentor, Plato, and he sought to find deeper coherence by bridging the two worlds in reconciling the realm of Being and Becoming, of Soul and Body, of Reason and Sense. So in more explicitly inaugurating the rational shape of the space of predication, Aristotle launched the enterprise of first philosophy and the grammar of Logos in the European traditions.

PREDICATION AND RATIONAL FORM: A BIRTHING OF FIRST PHILOSOPHY

In this classical Greek articulation of the fundamental Logos, the birth of the philosophy of Rationality (Rationalism) presumed, interestingly, that there was some primal union or isomorphism between Thought and Being—and Reason is the union in which these two primal dimensions mutually reflected one another. In this context Predication is the rational space of discourse in which to think is to predicate:

To join a logical subject and predicate in the formation of a unit of intelligible thought—something that can be true or false—

< S is or isn't P >.

For example, "Socrates is wise," or "Rain is falling," or "I am hungry."

Aristotle brilliantly showed that the fundamental laws of thought were at the same time the primal laws of being. A given subject must be either P or not- P. And since the space of thought is the space of being, the fundamental inquiry into Being (the inquiry of first philosophy, since for Aristotle Being is First and Primary in every sense), the ultimate quest for Being, will naturally focus on the ultimate subject of Predication—the primary logical subject.

Aristotle conjectured that the ultimate inquiry into Being would play out in finding the ultimate logical subject(s) of predication. And the being, essence, and identity of things (beings) would be constituted in their empredicated locus within the space of predication. What a thing is is revealed in the configuration of predicates that constitute it, which reveals its unique "identity." So the birth of science—the inquiry into the truth and being of things—proceeds within the space of predication—the space of reason.

EVOLUTION OF GRECO-EUROPEAN THOUGHT UNFOLDS WITHIN PREDICATION

The space of predication became the focal point for philosophical inquiry, and over the ensuing centuries the spotlight for reflective thought and the unfolding of discourse riveted on dynamics within this predicative space. It is no exaggeration to say that the space of predication provided the dialectics and dynamics of rationality and thus embodied the logistics or technology for discourse, experience, and culture making. As we fast-forward through the centuries in the unfolding drama of first philosophies, we find our great philosophical visionaries and geniuses morphing, revising, renovating, and reworking the lens of rational consciousness through which the world and experience make their appearance. We find our gifted philosophical teachers designing and redesigning the space of reason and the dynamics and structure of predication, as diverse alternative blueprints or narratives of reality, diverse worldviews, are proposed for making sense of things, for revising experience and initiating cultural revolutions and profound paradigm shifts in world making.

As we scan the creative innovations of key thinkers through the centuries as the European story unfolds—from Aristotle through St Augustine, St. Thomas, Francis Bacon, Copernicus, Newton, Locke, Descartes, Berkeley, Spinoza, Hume, Leibniz, Kant, Hegel, Nietzsche, Frege, Husserl, Russell, Wittgenstein, Pierce, Einstein, Heidegger, Sartre, Quine, Sommers, and Derrida, to mention a few prominent exemplars—we witness a remarkable morphing of the lens of rationality, experience, and culture making in an everchanging dialectic of predication. Which is not to say that these vastly diverse thinkers accepted the space of predication with its dynamics of rationality as the appropriate scene for culture making and self-production.

On the contrary, we shall see in what follows that the space of predication has been enormously plastic and revisable as these great grammarians of reality and rationality introduced their world-changing renovations. Rather, the point is that the ongoing drama of alternate proposals and narratives of first philosophies—for making sense of things and for self-making—took the space of predication, in all of its variety and variability, as a point of departure, even for radical deconstruction or transcendence.

Indeed, we shall see, as our scan of diverse traditions of first philosophy expands further in a moment that the locus of the "thinker" or the "thinking subject" to whom and for whom the space of predication is presented, and which we may represent as follows,

"I"		**< S is or isn't P >**
(thinking subject)	v	(screen of appearances)
		(object of thought)

becomes the focus of intense philosophical concern. This thinking self or subject outside the "box" of predicative space, which is, so to speak, the screen of awareness in which experience and the world are processed as an "object of thought," becomes a hot spot for diverse alternative narratives of first philosophy.

WHY "GRAMMAR" IS A KEY TO FIRST PHILOSOPHY

In any case, it becomes clear that the space of predication as a locus of rationality and discourse, in one way or another, is a focal point for the unfolding drama. In this compressed scan, it is truly remarkable that through the centuries there has been a relentless quest to decode the deep grammar of thought as an access code to *What-Is-First*—in a sense, the "holy grail" of First Philosophy or, to use another metaphor, the "DNA" of rational consciousness and the structure of Reality. This quest to articulate the fundamental grammar of thought—the logic of language and consciousness—had been a driving force and a preoccupation in the unfolding story. And the complementary quest to discern the grammar of Being—of primary being, the grammar of existence—as well as the quest for the ultimate grounds of Knowledge—is profoundly interwoven and co-driven by the same presiding ((Logos Event)).

For example, Descartes sought to uncover the missing universal grammar, and Leibniz had visionary dreams of disclosing the *"charcteristica universalis"*—a logistic calculus of thought that would reveal the missing logical code of thought and reality. Frege sought to capture the grammar of thought in his "Concept Script," as Russell and Wittgenstein ignited the twentieth century Anglo-American analytical revolution in suggesting that Frege had finally tapped the missing universal grammar of language and thought. It is clear that the stakes are high in this quest for the fundamental grammar that would reveal the deep structure of thought, language, rationality, and reality—highly relevant to the enterprise of First Philosophy.

The perennial sense is that in tapping the fundamental grammar of thought, we would be significantly closer to the code for the rational structure of discourse and reality—the mysterious script of ((Logos)). And the grammar of thought is clearly First in the sense that it constitutes the conditions for all other disciplines and narrative forms that presuppose and proceed within this grammar or rational space. The grammar of thought (the logic of language) rules and presides over whatever particular content or subject matter is being thought or narrated. And the presumption for First Philosophy is that if and when we have the rational form of thought or language, we thereby have the key to discerning the content or particular subject matter that shows up in and through this presiding form. So the "Platonic" insight and blueprint, suggesting that **Form presides over Content**, seem to be deeply imprinted in the enterprise of First Philosophy. And of course the analogue for us is that ((Logos)) is the Infinite Primal Form (Unified Force Field) that rules and presides over all possible content, situated and arising within its cosmic field, though, as we shall soon see, not in the old egomental hierarchical sense.

SCANNING MEGATRENDS IN EASTERN AND OTHER TRADITIONS OF FIRST NARRATIVES

Interestingly enough, when we turn our ((global lens)) toward Eastern and other traditions of first narratives, we naturally find the same gravitation of awakening thought to the Infinite First. Earlier, when I spoke of my journey to India and my early encounter with the classical Hindu and Buddhist traditions of First Philosophy, I mentioned that I experienced an awakening shock in becoming aware of deeper dynamics and chronic problems concerning the space of predication in which I was raised and educated. Indeed, the quest for authentic coherence and connectivity in these Eastern explorations of rationality was equally preoccupied with the space and dynamics of naïve predication but saw the philosophical journey into wisdom and enlightenment as liberation from being uncritically ensnared within the "predication box." This encounter with meditative critique, what I later recognized as meditative rationality, jolted me in a rude awakening from my prior dogmatic "rational" trance.

EGOMENTAL PREDICATION AND MINDING TECHNOLOGY AS PROBLEMATIC

The Hindu tradition of First Philosophy, as we saw, focused on the proper encounter with Aum, the sacred symbol for the Infinite First, the Infinite Word that is the source of all names and forms. In this richly developed deep ontology of the Infinite First, we find in the early Vedic teachings a meditative focus on the overpowering truth of Brahman, the Infinite Unifying Presence, which is the ground and source of all that is or could be. As the philosophical grammar of Brahman developed and unfolded over the centuries, it is clear that this is a classic articulation of ((Logos)).

Over millennia, as this amazing tradition unfolded, we find diverse sophisticated schools of analytical logical investigations, the development of subtle and powerfully transformative sciences and technologies of Yoga—all designed to assist the maturing Self in its awakening journey into union and communion with Brahman/Aum. The journey of wisdom, of first philosophy, of becoming rationally awakened, enlightened, and connected to Reality, with Brahman—((Logos))—essentially turned on meditative technologies of consciousness that assisted the Self in extricating itself from reification and self-objectification and self-identification within the space of egomental predication.

The naïve and uncritical self—**the ego subject**—that naively accepted at face value the screen of predication as disclosing the world, reality, and the self—this tradition of first philosophy would be exposed as being lodged in existential suffering, bondage, and primal ignorance. The rationally awakened or enlightened Self, the Atman, is the true Self, which through radical meditative critique and transformative technologies is able to recenter itself in Yogic communion with *What-Is-First*, Brahman. So, here, "first philosophy" is the philosophical liberating therapy of becoming an authentic Self beyond the naïve enclosure of egocentric predication. And the great *Yoga Sutra* text of Patanjali presents the science-technology of Yoga Philosophy at full force in recognizing that Yoga is the quieting of naïve ego predication, and the awakening of the higher yoga technology of minding—the meditative art/science—bringing forth the integral Self in its union and communion with Aum/Brahman. It all turns on moving from a fragmented technology of minding to the integral meditative technology.

KRISHNA HELPS ARJUNA AWAKEN
TO HIS EGOCENTRIC MINDING

We mentioned earlier the classic Hindu text, *Bhagavadgita*, wherein Lord Krishna, as the embodied voice of Aum, is engaged in a therapeutic deep dialogue with Arjuna, a warrior on the battlefield about to enter a fratricidal war with his kin. Arjuna can be seen as an exemplar of the naïve precritical egocentric self whose life has reached a deep existential (identity) crisis, and whose worldview is in a meltdown as it self-deconstructs and implodes—a predictable radical collapse of meaning. This classical text unfolds in a powerful transformative dialogue in which Krishna (who speaks from the higher domain of Aum) helps Arjuna gain critical awareness of his egocentric condition and rise out of his cave of ignorance into a new path of awakening critical rationality. Krishna, speaking from the higher dimension of Aum, from the integral calculus of meditative reason, instructs Arjuna, the egomental self, to first become aware of the dynamics of his thought process, to realize that how he is minding is directly shaping his existential condition—the scene of his polarized fratricidal war and, of course, his existential despair—that the outer polarization of violence mirrors an inner war and polarization between his uncritical egocentric self and his higher unrealized Self.

Of course Arjuna has only known the rational space of his naïve consciousness—the everyday space of predication in which he was raised, and in which he processed himself and others and his world. So it is natural and inevitable for him to receive and process Krishna's words within his own logical space and technology of minding. He is not aware, yet, that this will distort and deform the meaning and intent of Krishna's rational therapy, and that he will get even more confused listening to Krishna's instructions. This confusion, as Arjuna enters the path of awakening rational therapy, drives the deep dialogue between Krishna and Arjuna chapter after chapter.

But Krishna naturally understands that Arjuna is misappropriating his meditative words spoken from the higher dimension, and proceeds, step by step, to educate Arjuna in the art/science of Yoga, focused on the technology of minding. Krishna helps Arjuna become critically aware of his ego-minding as a prerequisite to rising into a higher meditative technology that comes as Arjuna prepares to dilate his "Third Eye" and enter the dimension of Aum/Brahman and through this rationally awakened Self to behold Reality in its Integral and Holistic Form. This journey peaks in Chapter 13, where Krishna and Arjuna have become deep dialogue partners and Arjuna is ready to enter the higher integral epistemology of Integral and Nondual minding.

SHANKARA MAKES EXPLICIT
THE NONDUAL TECHNOLOGY

In our continuing compressed scan through the unfolding of Hindu First Philosophy, we find a historic development in the contributions of Shankara in the seventh century A.D., building on centuries of continued refinement of Vedic wisdom. The more informal deep dialogue of the *Gita* presumes the "nondual" discourse of Krishna's voice and speech, but Shankara's more formalized articulation of "Advaita Vedanta," in his great *Brahma-Sutra Commentary*, marks another global moment in the unfolding dialectic of First Philosophy. In this remarkable work, Shankara brings to more explicit articulation the essential nondual nature of the discourse of Brahman and the essence of Vedic wisdom.

In this breakthrough we find a relentless distinction drawn between the egocentric dynamic of minding and the nondual nature of discourse of *What-Is-First*. However, what has not yet emerged, and what is of highest importance, is the recognition and clarification of the profound logical grammar of this Primal Field of Brahman. Rather, Shankara is so naturally preoccupied with drawing the line of differentiation between the fallen dualistic (egocentric) process of minding and the awakened nondualistic and Unifying force of Infinite Brahman that he appears to reduce all differentiation and individuation, multiplicity, plurality, and diversity to the egocentric dimension, and he insists that in the true "higher Reality," there is no differentiation, that all individuation is mere appearance due to the constitutive ignorance of egomental minding.

It would take a few more centuries of the unfolding dialectic of the discourse of Yoga and Brahman and self-realization to recognize that in the sacred space of Brahman, in enlightened awakened rational consciousness, there is a deeper form of individuation, process, evolution, and diversity in the fabric of Reality. These vital insights begin to emerge in the twentieth century in the remarkable advances of Sri Aurobindo. When we soon switch our ((global lens)) to the unfolding dialectic of first philosophies in the European and Western drama, we will see an analogous pattern of evolution and development unfolding there as well.

But for the moment we notice that from the informal deep dialogue of the *Gita* through the amazing advances of Shankara we begin to see a fundamental distinction between the naïve egomental dimension of minding and the radical shift into the non-dualistic rational space of the discourse of Brahman. We see a global spotlight focused on the technology of minding and the vital importance of being clear on the life-and-death difference between minding in the egocentric space of naïve "reason" and the awakened integral technology of meditative reason. In one way or another, it appears we humans need to become critically aware of the ways of our everyday patterns of minding as being of the highest importance. Our welfare and well-being turns on this awakened awareness.

BUDDHA'S RADICAL CRITIQUE
OF EGOMENTAL MINDING

As we now expand the scope of our global lens to take a deeper look at the astounding breakthrough into the discourse of *What-Is-First* that came with Buddha's awakening, we find an intense spotlight focused on the existential pathologies that come with being uncritically entrapped within egomental forms of minding. Buddha's contribution to GFP confirms the vital importance to our human enterprise of paying full attention to our technology of consciousness. Buddha is a first philosopher of the highest order whose philosophical journey took him deeply into the workings of naïve predication where he found the source of human existential malpractice—the source of human pathologies. His great awakening and articulation of the "Four Noble Truths" is a global event that opened new dimensions for our human conscious evolution. As a deep ontologist, Buddha saw precisely how and why naively producing our selves within the objectifying space of ego predication—making our selves as entities, as beings, as logical subjects of predication—entraps us within a dangerous and deadly dialectic and chronic vicious cycle.

Buddha's Four Noble Truths (I would suggest, "Global Truths") expressed a deep diagnosis of the cause of our human existential pathologies and a power prescription of how to rehabilitate our technology of minding to truly flow with the Boundless Open Space of Primary Being (Sunyata/Emptiness), wherein everything mutually flows in profound coherence and connectivity into the wordless (hence Wordfull) space of *What-Is-First*.

Buddha saw that naïve precritical reason was habitually addicted to egomental patterns that cut us off from being in harmonious flow with Objective Reality. The Four Global Axioms may be stated as follows:

1. Egomental existence is chronically pathological and the source of suffering.
2. This existential malpractice has a primary cause: It is egomental minding, and it is attachment to (naïve identification with) this egoized self that is the cause.
3. We have a choice—we can stop this addiction to egomental minding and rehabilitate our minding to true coherence and connectivity—to awakened rational life. We can let go of this egoized self and enter the Flow.
4. The rational therapy that will enable us to rehabilitate our technology of minding is the eightfold path—new integral habits of mindful minding that come through constant attention to Right Judgment, Right Intention, Right Understanding, Right Action, Right Livelihood, and so on.

Buddha's diagnosis and prescription as a deep ontologist (first philosopher) is obviously a radical critique of precritical egomental minding, living, and being. His global insight is that we should get out of the ego-rational space in which we get stuck in ideologies, worldviews, beliefs, predications, metaphysics, and the contention of battling worldviews. Buddha wanted a radical end to doing egocentric metaphysics and to focus instead on the rational therapy of liberating the Self (the no self). For this reason he wished to focus on ending the human existential suffering that comes from rational

ignorance rather than to engage, or even appear to engage, in egomental theorizing and ontologizing in the screen of predication.

In this spirit Buddha taught that as we practiced mindfully the meditative
rationality outside the box of egomental predication, we enter ((Objective Reality)), wherein everything is profoundly interactive, no "things," no "beings," no
reified "entities" or "events" could enter. This is the dimension of the "no self,"
the place of radical "co-arising" of all things, entering the sacred space of Indra's
Infinite Dynamic Holistic Web of Relations, which is the dynamic of the
Global Dharma—the universal law of co-arising, the Moral Law of deep compassion, where every "no self" experiences its essential "co-arising" with Other
"no selves" in this awakened boundless drama of true living. This is the space of
Sunyata (radical emptiness, zero-ness), the place of radical co-arising and relationality—the place of dynamic relativity = relationality.

NAGARJUNA BREAKS THE
EGOMENTAL PREDICATION BARRIER

Alas, despite Buddha's radical first philosophy and prescription for rational
awakening, the technology of discourse—of thinking, speaking, interpreting,
listening, processing language, making experience, and self-production—
remained steeped in the predicative dynamics and dialectics. After all, as we
saw with Krishna and Arjuna, and with the advances of Shankara, the objective space of language use, the common marketplace of discourse, had not yet
been taken to the next horizon or dimension of minding. Buddha's teaching
(as was Krishna's) was presented, it seemed, in the everyday space of language,
of predication, which is where the technology of discourse had evolved.

So even a radical story, such as Buddha's or Krishna's or Shankara's, is
apparently being presented in the common space of language, thought, and
interpretation. It is quite natural for interpreters of Buddha's radical message
to process it in the only space of language and thought that was available or
known: the common rational space of objectified predication. It seemed
inevitable, despite the best intentions, to be faithful to Buddha's teaching, to
continue to use this old predicative technology to process the teaching, which
ironically focused on abandoning this inherently tainted space of discourse.

Indeed, as this compressed global scan across teachings and traditions
will suggest, this continuing situation concerning the state of development of
the technology of discourse will continue to haunt the human condition on a
planetary scale through the ages, and despite great global moments when
teachers would make profound breakthroughs beyond the egomental predicative space, their teaching would inevitably and inexorably be "downloaded"
(hence deformed) within this inadequate hermeneutical space.

In this light, Nagarjuna's magnificent contribution to Global First Philosophy is nothing short of miraculous. He enters the scene in the second century A.D., after Buddha's teaching had been codified by the Elders for over 500 years. How do we present the **content of Buddha's teaching** of the "no self" and of "radical emptiness" and of the boundless "co-arising of everything" within the available naïve, or even sophisticated, egomental predicative space? There appears to be no avoiding this primal fallacy (which is yet to be explicitly recognized and named), and it is not surprising that in the early School of the Elders the teaching of Buddha is presented within the predicative technology. The Buddha's teaching of "no self" is developed in sophisticated narratives that render his radical first philosophy within the dialectics of predication. If the "self" is not the logical subject of predication, not an object or a reified entity, then it is natural to jump over the "is" (< S is/isn't P >) to the Predicate space to seek the no self: could it then be a bundle of predicates? Radical qualities having no being or duration? Clusters or bundles of qualities that make up the field of Reality? Such continuing "metaphysical" speculations abound.

PREDICATION POLARIZES
AND SPAWNS DEEP DUALISM

Apparently this is what was happening, and Nagarjuna saw through this futile move and sought to radically deconstruct the naively constituted space of predication and its inherently dualizing, polarizing technology of consciousness and discourse. The brilliance of Nagarjuna as a rational dialectician was shown in his recognition that the Teaching of Sunyata could not be presented or processed in the space of objectifying predication, neither favoring the space of the logical subject nor the space of the logical predicate. He noticed the larger repeating megapattern of polar splits spawned by the logic of naïve identity that rules in the space of predication. Later we will explore this dynamic more deeply to see precisely how and why egomental predication spawns deep dualisms, and how and why it generates rational and existential pathologies in the human condition. For this occasion it is not appropriate to go into details about Nagarjuna's great breakthrough concerning the technicalities of egominding.

Let us focus on the big global picture: Nagarjuna's genius was in developing a radical rational dialectic to demonstrate that if we took the naïve egomental logic of identity at face value and played it out with excruciating rigor and impeccable logical critique it would self-deconstruct and reveal its inner absurdity and incoherence. His great *Karikas* is a global classic of analytical critique of the highest order wherein he introduces his radical "Fourfold

Negation": "Not P," "Not not-P," "Not P-and-not-P," and "Not P-or-not-P."
In playing out his radical method relentlessly, he helps us experience the
implosion and radical deconstruction of the egomental "rational" space.

When the disciplined student works through this radical dialectic rigorously, she or he experiences the emptiness of naïve predication, and the futility
of seeking to live, interpret, understand, judge, speak, think, and process "self"
in this "irrational" logical space. The successful student becomes critically
awakened in discovering that egomental predication, which alleges to be self-
contained and self-sustaining, instead collapses under its own weight (or lack
thereof), and then the student recognizes that language, thought, discourse,
experience, and the everyday world can only make sense and flow in the space
of Emptiness, the space of *What-Is-First*. The strategy of this rational therapy
is thus essentially one of first philosophy—to realize and experience directly
and immediately the truth that the Unified Field of Reality ((Emptiness)) is
the ground and source of all proceedings of the universe.

So in some clear historic sense, Nagarjuna's radical ((dialectic)) carries
forth the Buddha's teaching into the space of ((Sunyata)) and makes it clear
that human flourishing cannot proceed within the egomental space of predication. It should be noted that Nagarjuna inaugurated and practiced a radical
form of awakened "postmodern deconstruction." But he saw this radical rational critique as not merely leaving us with the rubble of the imploded space of
ego predication but took this as an essential step in Buddha's rational therapy
of moving beyond the bondage to the restricted and reified space of predication into a deeper liberated rational space of ((Emptiness)) where we can realize the truth of Buddha's first philosophy and break the addiction to egomental minding. What is the rational form of this open space of *What-Is-First*?
Does it have a logic? Is there a higher order form of "predication" that does
flow with objective reality, meaning, and truth? Is there a logistic or technology of mind for this awakened rationality? These, of course, are vital concerns
of GFP. We will take these up in greater depth later.

The radical deconstruction practiced by Nagarjuna (carried forth
through the centuries via the globally influential Madhyamika—Middle
Way—School he founded) is not an end in itself but is a vital first step in
preparing the way to take the next key step in the open sacred space of ((Sunyata)). Soon we will see that what has in the twentieth century been called
"postmodern deconstruction" could be seen as positing radical deconstruction
as an end in itself, perhaps suggesting that the only space in which we can be
in discourse is within this tainted egomental technology, as if this egomental
rational space is the only space we have, or could have—clearly not so!

To the extent that "contemporary" deconstruction philosophy is lodged
in egomental dogmatism, it naturally ends in nihilism and self-deconstruction. In contrast, the classical form of meditative deconstruction ushers the

diligent student into higher dimensions of open rational space where she or he flows in the ((Dharma)) of objective reality—in the primal space of radical First Philosophy. This is where we become fully Rational, Moral, and Cognitive beings, the space of becoming Human. But it should be noted that Nagarjuna's dialectic does not proceed explicitly to suggest that there is a primal ((Logic)) of the space of Radical Emptiness, primal rational space. Nor does he seek to begin the excavation of this Logic of Sunyata. This would take centuries to come to explicit articulation in the amazing innovations of Nishida, the founder of the modern Kyoto School of Japanese Zen, which evolved out of the heritage of Nagarjuna (more on this later).

OTHER TRADITIONS AND
NARRATIVES OF FIRST PHILOSOPHY

Before proceeding to focus our fast-forward scan on certain selected contributions to the enterprise of GFP in the evolving European traditions, let us pause a moment and dilate our ((global lens)) more widely. Although we have focused thus far on classical origins of first philosophies in the early Greco-European and Indian traditions, we began with the suggestion that widely diverse traditions across the planet have rich traditions of first philosophy, and they too struggle with profound issues of coming into authentic encounter with *What-Is-First*.

We could, for example, go deeply into classical Chinese origins and discuss the developments in the Grammar of Tao, or we could explore the rich alternatives presented over millennia in so-called indigenous wisdom traditions—traditions in African thought, or traditions of First Nations in the North American heritage, to mention one or two exemplars. It is important to realize that once we get out of the compromised and reductive space of ego-mental rationality, there are profound alternative modalities of authentically encountering *What-Is-First*, alternative modalities that feminist philosophy, for example, has recognized and articulated, modalities in diverse art forms, such as music, dance, literature, mytho-poetic forms of cultivating expanded awareness, and so on. So the enterprise of first philosophy can take diverse forms, boundless alternative pathways into the space of *What-Is-First*. For example, the diverse narratives and modalities of the great "mystical" voices and visions through the ages may be seen as obvious alternative attempts to celebrate, encounter, express, or enter into communion with ((Logos)).

Certainly, as I shall now suggest, diverse religious or spiritual forms of life, which may not "officially" be considered "philosophical narratives," may nonetheless be potent, effective, and authentic alter-forms of encountering *What-Is-First*. Indeed, I have suggested that the Infinite Force Field of

((Logos)) permeates ever pulse of experience, discourse, and life. In this light it should be clear that ((Logos)) is not the "Logos" of egomental space that may have been dominated by "male"-oriented forms of patriarchical reason but is the higher order Infinite ((Logos)) that also is fully ((Sophia)), beyond egomental gender polarity, beyond "Eurocentric" modes of rationality, and so on.

The global ((Logos)) is holistically gendered and overcomes the diverse forms of prejudices that are now well documented in twentieth-century critiques of what we are calling "egomental rationality," the compromised spaces of egocentric logos. So although we are highly selective in the inventory of voices queried and explicitly thematized here, we do so with caution, and we are quite mindful of the vast diversity of alternative narratives, art forms, and even disciplinary perspectives we might incorporate if we had greater time and space. Indeed, we shall see later that the development of scientific method may be seen as an integral moment in the unfolding drama of the universal quest for ((Logos)) and the fundamental concern of advancing the cognitive modalities of encountering objective Reality and developing more effective technologies of minding. But for now let us refocus our global lens and follow one of the main narrative strands before us—the amazing struggle through the ages to deal with overcoming the dogmatic restrictions of egomental minding in the perennial quest to awaken genuine global rationality.

THE CONTINUING STRUGGLES WITH EGOMENTAL DISCOURSE OVER MILLENNIA: JUDAIC, CHRISTIAN, AND ISLAMIC ORIGINS—FIRST NARRATIVES

Let us refocus and resume our power scan to follow certain megatrends in the unfolding drama over millennia. In keeping with the caution just registered concerning opening the doors to a wider scope of alternative first narratives, it is interesting to reflect a moment on the fundamental struggles of our three biblical traditions to come to terms with *What-Is-First* in Judaic, Christian, and Islamic origins. We have suggested that the call to *What-Is-First* permeates every pulse of existence, experience, consciousness, and discourse. So it is natural to find evidence of this in our great "religious" (first narratives) traditions. Indeed, we have opened the box to see that through the ((global lens)) quite diverse narrative forms also are alter-first narratives, even if the more exclusivist name "first philosophy" may seem to exclude them, or their vital contributions. In this spirit we take a quick glance at these three unfolding first narratives.

Of course all three religious first narratives take their common origin within the Abrahamic faith—and are all "religions of the Book." It is strikingly clear that the founding of the Judaic faith is precisely the call of the Infinite First—Yahweh—to the people of Israel, indeed, to the "Global Israel." That the scared script of this Infinite First should call out to be recognized as One, as supremely First, and the primal origin of the Universe, is axiomatic for GFP. The primal instruction or command of this ((Word)) to humanity, always to honor and prioritize Yahweh as being first and foremost in all things, is an immediate corollary in this Sacred Logic of ((Logos)). In this light we may naturally see the heroic struggle of Abraham as still another global exemplar (as with Arjuna's classic struggle, for example) of the agonizing twin pulls of one's egocentric self and one's faithful response to the call of the Infinite First.

In this paradigmatic drama that tests his being to the core, Abraham has to decide whether his personal agenda and priority, reflective of his egomental worldview, symbolized here as his attachment to his beloved son Isaac, should command his interests over and above the call of the Infinite Word to always put First Things First. And of course Abraham's decision, in another classic global moment, to honor the call of Yahweh as having highest jurisdiction, even if it means sacrificing one's personal (egocentric) agenda and priorities, is paradigmatic in the context of first philosophy. It appears that some such test of (Rational) Faith in what is higher and the requirement to place what is First and Higher above one's subjective egocentric agenda is a global call to the human condition that reverberates and echoes through our great Faiths, and in fact throughout our human condition for all worldviews. Clearly it is the choice Arjuna is called upon to make by Krishna, and the pathway to liberation taught by Buddha. In a way it is the Rational Faith in the living truth of one's higher Self in its communion with *What-Is-First*.

Needless to say, this theme of sacred sacrifice and the continuing struggle with the egomental human condition is central in the global breakthrough performed by Jesus. As the Judaic grammar connects to the Hellenistic language of Logos in the birthing of early Christian discourse, Jesus is seen (in the Gospel of John) as being the **Logos-made-flesh**—the incarnation of the Infinite First in the human form. This Gospel is another classic First Narrative that begins: "In the Beginning is the Logos." And from the point of view of deep ontology or first philosophy, it is easy to make the move from the "condition of sin" as separation from the Infinite Logos to the alienation from *What-Is-First* in the egomental space of predication. The ontology of "sin" in terms of first philosophy is the existential condition of being separated from and alienated from *What-Is-First*, from ((Logos)). And the perennial human concern is that of moving out of egomental alienation into authentic encounter with ((Logos)).

In this light we may see the essence of the global significance of the event of Jesus as Christ as precisely our perennial struggle to overcome the pain, suffering, and pathology that inevitably come from the egomental mentality and form of life and the radical awakening and transformation to a higher Christ Consciousness that reconciles us with Logos in our ontological transformation of "Resurrection" into a higher form of integral life. And here again the global pathway of first philosophy, in moving from the dualistic, alienated life to the integral, nondual discourse of awakened Christ Consciousness, is perfectly modeled by Jesus.

As a model of the resurrected or cognitively awakened human—being a nondual bridge of the alienated finite and the infinite—we begin to see a pattern echoed across diverse traditions of first narratives. The global breakthrough of the first philosophy of Jesus is the teaching that in Christ Consciousness we must live the Law, the Dharma, beyond the script that is inscribed or reified in "stone," or written in objectified form in egomental predication. The Script of Logos, The Word of God, is seen to be scripted in a higher dimension beyond the egomental writing tablets of objectified content or reified mind. In this light all of the "miracles" and dimensional shifting rituals introduced by Jesus as Christ may be seen as transformations from the egomental life into the higher dimension of being in direct encounter with the Infinite Thou—a classic transformation of GFP.

But here again there has been a chronic pattern of "downloading" the Higher Sacred Script of Logos, as well as the life and teachings of Jesus as Christ, into the egomental space of discourse, with disastrous consequences. Just consider for a moment the possibility that the Sacred Script of Logos or of the Christ cannot be rendered or processed in the dualizing technology of egomental reason. What if the literal rendering of biblical script requires the higher integral technology of discourse of *What-Is-First*. And what if the Life, Teaching, and Sacrifice of Jesus are precisely modeling and making this point for humanity? What if God and the Word of God cannot be captured and rendered appropriately within our egomental box of predication? Yet this seems to be the emergent consensus of GFP across the planet.

These global points are echoed in the unfolding of Islam through the teachings of the Prophet Mohamed, and as developed over centuries by diverse eminent voices and first narratives that spawned the rich mystical Sufi traditions. True to the Abrahamic faith, which Islam takes as a premise, the name "Islam" means "surrender to Allah," taken as the True Name of the Infinite First. Here again we find the core theme of first philosophy of honoring *What-Is-First* above all else, and surrendering the alleged independent self-existence of the egoized self to live in a deep, authentic encounter with the Infinite First.

In this context we may regard the mystical work of philosophical poet Rumi as another paradigmatic development of first philosophy, which points in the direction of our global concerns. We also may regard the remarkable development of Kabbala in the Jewish mystical tradition as seeking to decipher the hidden mysterious script and thus open the way to a global grammar of the Infinite First. Similarly, of course, the discourse of Christian mystical writings is rich and varied in contributions to the discourse of the Infinite First and embodies ongoing attempts to overcome the alienating barriers of egomental mind, life, and discourse. In any case, these three global exemplars are powerful witnesses to the ongoing global struggle to overcome the barriers of egomental separation and fragmentation and advance into more authentic encounters with the Infinite First.

THE STRUGGLE TO OVERCOME EGOMENTAL "REASON": HERACLITUS TO DERRIDA

In building on these megatrends of first narratives through the ages, let us focus our ((global lens)) in a power scan of certain remarkable developments in the evolution of rationality from early Greek thought to contemporary times. We shall now see certain astounding patterns unfolding through the centuries in keeping with dynamics we have already noticed on a more global scale. This will be invaluable in preparing the way for our dimensional shift into the missing integral technology of Global Reason.

We shall now "fast-forward" to certain key recurring dynamics in the perennial struggle to overcome the chronic restrictions and barriers of egomental minding through the centuries. I earlier suggested in the context of GFP that the Infinite Force Field of ((Logos)) makes its presence felt in every conceivable happening. This presiding influence of the ((Logos Event)) situates all events within its Field and pulsates in every moment of experience and consciousness. I now trace this continuing subliminal influence as it inexorably leads and guides the evolution of reflective consciousness in the continuing quest for coherent rationality through the centuries. This is the presiding "telos" that generates, attracts, impels, and drives the evolutionary event toward the awakening of global reason and the global mind.

THE SUPERIMPOSITION AND CONFUSION OF DIFFERENT DIMENSIONS OF LANGUAGE

We have noticed thus far that there has been an ongoing struggle in the human condition to become critically aware of the workings of naïve egomental minding, and to mature beyond the alienating, polarizing, and fragmenting dynamics inherent in this stage of our rational development and technology of discourse. Perhaps the lead point thus far in our journey is the lesson that the technology of discourse (thinking, consciousness, language, world making) is of utmost importance in our struggle to become integral rational beings. We also have noticed the trend that the ever-present pull to encounter authentically the script of *What-Is-First* seems invariably to become ensnared in the more familiar technology and dynamics of everyday language with its egomental patterns of objectified predication.

URGENT EVOLUTIONARY NEED FOR
HIGHER INTEGRAL TECHNOLOGY

As awakening reflective consciousness gains access to and touches into the primal rational domain of Logos, wherein it naturally gravitates, it seems to have no choice but to resort to the egomental dynamics of predicative discourse to express itself. But we have seen the irony, the futility, if not the tragedy, involved in this "translation" or rendering. So a driving force in the evolution of awakening rationality has been precisely to make room, renovate, or open higher fresh space to render adequately the "thoughts" and "insights" that flow from the higher integral dimension of the Infinite First. It appears that this higher dimension of the grammar of ((Logos)) is fused with or superimposed upon the predominant and familiar everyday technology of language with all of its trappings. And of course this confusion or conflation is highly problematic: there is a profound dissonance and disconnect between the pull of Logos toward awakened integral reason and cognitive life, on the one hand, and the inherently disintegral dynamics inscribed within the fragmenting technology of egomental minding and the naïve use of everyday language, on the other.

TREMENDOUS EVOLUTIONARY
PRESSURE TO OPEN HIGHER SPACE

One focal theme is to trace the attempts to renovate the techno-script of language and the grammar of thought to find a more suitable philosophical grammar to access and express the rational power of this ((Primal Domain)). In a real sense a presiding theme in the perennial quest to encounter Logos ((Objective Reality)) is the quest to advance the technology of discourse to a higher, more adequate form for the processing of our awakening rational life. One of the great lessons in our evolutionary drama is that the discourse of integral, hologistic, awakened reason cannot be rendered in the disintegral and polarizing script of everyday, precritical, egomental language. So there is tremendous evolutionary pressure to access and articulate the higher dimensional script of Logos, and thus to "disambiguate" and "de(con)fuse" the superimposition or fusion of the two contrasting (though intimately related) dimensions of language and discourse. Our well-being and welfare, and even our survival, turn on this.

THE GREAT PHILOSOPHICAL DRAMA: QUEST FOR THE GLOBAL CODE OF REASON

Let us now use the power of our ((global lens)) to hold together in one synoptic vision the evolutionary drama and developments from Heraclitus to Derrida, from early Greek origins of Logos first narratives through the contemporary scene as we now enter the ((global age)) in the twenty-first century. In this breathtaking vista, we nevertheless find remarkable megatrends through the ages as we hold together these vastly diverse philosophical narratives with their widely variant worldviews. We have already noticed the deep trend in egomental predication to polarize and spawn deep dualisms. And we witnessed Nagarjuna's diagnosis of this inherent tendency in egomental "reason" and his heroic attempt to break this barrier in opening the "middle way." Here, too, through the centuries we find analogous patterns of recurring or repeating cycles of polar swings and dualizing dynamics.

RECURRING POLARIZING CYCLES

The mutual repulsion of "is" versus "isn't," the wedge between the "logical subject" and the "predicate," the space between the often absent "thinker" and the preoccupation with the objectified "screen" of predication—the object of thought or experience, all conspire to feed and energize the repeating dynamics of polarization, chronic dualizing, and dysfunctional dueling and discommunication across and between competing philosophical narratives that battle for dominance or exclusive dominion over the precious space of predication.

While the pre-Socratic first philosophers, Parmenides and Heraclitus, launch their magnificent deep grammars of reality and disclose a primal split, Socrates enters the scene seeking to mediate the apparent polarization in discourse, to save Knowledge and Reason in mediating a middle way. While Parmenides traces the power of "is" and ends in the grammar of "Absolute Eternal Non-Changing Being," Heraclitus shows equal philosophical genius in privileging the priority of "isn't" and follows it to its logical and ontological conclusions in the radical grammar of Becoming (beyond the fixity of "being"). One voice of "reason" finds "Absolute Being" the fundamental truth of *What-Is-First*, while the other finds "Absolute Becoming" the ultimate truth of Primal Reality. The first finds process, change, and becoming mere "appearance" or illusion, while the other finds being, static identity, or any form of fixity illusory and mere appearance. The ultimate truth of "is" appears to repel and be repelled by the fundamental truth of "isn't." And the fundamental law of "reason" appears to be "either is or isn't."

Of course, if the investigation of reason itself rigorously carried out (as these two philosophical geniuses allege), then reason itself appears to be self-divided, discoherent, self-contradictory, and inadequate as an *organon*, instrument, or medium of reliable knowledge. And in the unfolding drama, over time it begins to become clear that the grammar of "is" seems to line up a range of allied fundamental concepts or building blocks on one side that appears diametrically opposed to the polar cluster of basic ideas allied with "isn't":

Allied with "IS": Being, One, Self-Identity, Sameness, Unity, Nonchanging, Eternal, Undivided, Essence, Universality . . . (Absolute Presiding Unity);

While, Allied with "ISN'T": Becoming, Radical Change, Nonfixity, Difference, Other, Many, Multiplicity, Diversity, Nonessence, Particularity . . . (Absolute Presiding Diversity).

Of course this polar split is the very one noticed by Krishna as he instructs Arjuna in the grammar of egomental "reason" and that Nagarjuna discovers and exposes in its generic form in his gallant attempt to open the middle way.

The inner tension and ongoing battle between "is versus isn't" would recur through the centuries and manifest in all sorts of ways—for example, Kant finding inherent "antinomies" within reason, or Hegel seeking to save Reason through a radical revision of Logic, which seeks to reconcile "is-and isn't" in his historic or evolutionary dialectic of Infinite *Geist* (Infinite Spirit) presiding and unfolding in historical process. In this megatrend it is no accident that the deep cultural swing from "modernism" to a historical moment of "postmodernism" in the latter part of the twentieth century may be seen as a latter-day power showdown between the tendencies of Unity/Universality (Foundations, Transhistorical, Unified Truth, Essence), which are encoded in the culture of "modernism," on the one hand, and the counterforces of Otherness, Diversity, Change (Nonessence, Particularity, Multiplicity, Perspectivism, Ethnicity, Localism, Historicality), which are encoded in the discourse and culture of "postmodernism."

In some deep sense then the ongoing polar war between the split forces in egomental reason appears to recur, writ large, through the ages. The crisis in reason faced by Socrates as he risked (and gave up) his life to counter the forces of relativism and sophistry to save Truth and Knowledge is still urgently before us today as global citizens in the twenty-first century seek to find nonreductive global and unifying truth, knowledge, and universal values across our widely diverse cultures and worlds that honor deep diversity, individuality, and particularity. It is quite clear that mere fragmented or disconnected diversity that privileges difference or otherness at the price of real unity and common ground across our diverse worlds is not viable or sustainable in our globalized world—a ((global village)) of diverse worldviews.

Nor, of course, is the polar opposite tendency to privilege Unity or Universality over Diversity and Individuality viable as a basis for sustainable rationality or global culture. So it appears that the dialectic of Unity and Diversity, Is and Isn't must find the creative "middle way" of co-arising in the higher mediating dialogic and coherent powers of Natural Reason. And, of course, this is the pathway into the ((Rational Powers of Logos)). It is here in the powerful dialectic of infinite connectivity that we shall find the long-sought-for primal meeting point of Unity-in-Diversity and Diversity-in-Unity, wherein both ((Unity and Diversity)) are primitively co-given and mutually constitutive on one another. This, we shall see, is the deep dialogic fabric of the hologistic unified field.

But this quick flash-forward from Heraclitus to Derrida, who both seem to concur in the priority of Difference and Multiplicity over Identity and Unity, is just a hint of a long and laborious dialectic that has been played out on a global scale through the ages. So let us slow down a bit in this ((power scan)) to get a little more flavor of the details of the drama without losing sight of the larger megatrends. In this first power scan let us go over the larger terrain and focus on major "headlines," so to speak, as the centuries unfold.

POLAR PARADIGMS OF PLATO AND ARISTOTLE

While Socrates initiates radical critique and models the rational life of living dialogue in the quest for Self-Knowledge, his brilliant protégé, Plato, brings these dialogues to life in the rational quest for Knowledge, Truth, and Wisdom. It appears that both see the naïve precritical life, which accepts experience, language, and cultural life at face value, as living in mere appearance and in a certain rational sleep of forgetfulness, a life of mere belief, opinion, and ignorance. Whereas the life of critical reason, of philosophical inquiry, activates the dimension of the Soul and the grammar of Reason, which rises into a higher dimension or world of essences and universal forms.

For Plato this journey into awakening reason culminates in a profound unitive encounter with the ground and source of Rational Light, the primal Logos, the First, deeper than Being and Truth, their very source. This fundamental Logos is the ground of thought, the light of Reason itself, and the generative source of all forms, all being, all discourse, all existence. So in a real sense in inaugurating his fundamental grammar of Reality, Plato apparently favors Parmenides in siding with ultimate Unity and Being, and he finds the language and experience of Becoming, Change, and Multiplicity lodged in the "lower" mentality of precritical, everyday beliefs, opinion, and appearance.

So a blueprint is inaugurated by Plato for the rational life, for Knowledge, for Truth, for Reality, and for the Self, which places Unity over Diversity, Universality over Particularity, Soul over Body, Being over Becoming, and Reason over the Senses, and a fundamental dualism comes into relief even as Plato seeks to solve the dilemma of the polar split between the first philosophies of Parmenides and Heraclitus. His attempt to salvage Reason, Knowledge, and Wisdom comes at the price of another polar split or dualism across the fault line of Being versus Becoming.

Plato's ingenious protégé, Aristotle, builds on his teacher's foundations but finds the deep split between the "two worlds" incoherent and unacceptable, even counterintuitive. So he seeks a radical revision in the grammar of reason and first philosophy bequeathed by Plato and seems to defy all "logic" in what is alleged to be a higher synthesis of Being and Becoming, Soul and Body, Form and Matter, Universal and Particular, and so on. And as mentioned earlier, it was Aristotle who almost single-handedly launched the science of Logic and the discipline of "first philosophy" in his historic clarification of the laws of predication, rules of inference, and primacy of Being.

Ironically, though, in seeking to heal the split in the grammar of reality left by Plato, Aristotle seems to favor analytic diversity, finding many senses of "is," and he ultimately finds a fundamental polarity between theoretical reason and practical reason: between reason as it deals with eternal and non-changing truth in the life of *a priori* reason (the life of Theoria), in contrast to the reason as it deals with matters of action, where time, change, choice, and decision are involved, the life of action and praxis. So the rational life hits a fault line between two kinds of virtue, two forms of rational life that call out for reconciliation in an integral rational existence—Theoretical versus Practical Wisdom.

So while Plato seems to favor a unitive and an integral rational life where to know the good is to do the good (highest knowledge is linked to right action), Aristotle seems to favor an analytic division of kind between two forms of rational virtues and analytical diversity in the grammar of being. Of course we are here simplifying and looking at the bolder strokes and trends. And it is fair to say that between the contrasting first philosophies of Plato and Aristotle, we are in some sense given a blueprint or road map in the quest for Reason that will recur through the ages as the European drama in the quest for the grammar of *What-Is-First* plays out. For example, as the centuries unfold and Christian discourse develops with the confluence of the Judaic biblical script and the Logos of Hellenistic thought, we find powerful alternative grammars being forged in the lifework of St. Augustine and St. Thomas. The former uses the template of Plato's grammar of *What-Is-First* to develop a Platonic Christian grammar, while the latter brings forth and adapts the brilliant innovations of Aristotle to launch Christian discourse in a new Aristotelian direction that now dominates the Medieval or Scholastic period.

We emerge from this Scholastic period, where the logic and grammar of Aristotle are predominant, and we enter the "modern" period, with the amazing work of thinkers such as Locke, Berkley, and Hume, who inaugurate a new Empiricist approach to philosophy, and first philosophers such as Descartes, Spinoza, and Leibniz, who seek to modernize the grammar of reason and open a new age of Rational Enlightenment. Again, we are taking bold steps and leaps in this power scan, but as we shall now see, the plot thickens as an unprecedented dramatic stage is set for the revolutionary innovations of Kant in another great pivotal moment.

ANOTHER POLAR SPLIT:
TWO COMPETING STRANDS OF FIRST PHILOSOPHY

As we pick up the unfolding drama, we find radical beginnings of different sorts with Locke in the British empiricist tradition and his significant counterpart, Descartes, in the Continental rationalist tradition on the other side of the English Channel. There is a sense during this fertile seventeenth-century period that a new age is being born and that deep stress points and polarities are in the air. With the dramatic rise of the Catholic Church, with its awesome political power and authority, the forces of Faith versus Reason vie for center stage and presiding power. This is another deep dualism of egomental life that haunts the evolving culture—two incompatible modes of making commitments of affirmation and belief within the egomental predicative space. It also is a fertile period in which the political philosophy of democratic values is advancing in leaps and bounds, and all tied in with the enterprise of first philosophies. More on this later.

With innovative thinkers such as Francis Bacon, we begin to see the emergence of a new form of critical inquiry and the overcoming of dogmatic authority that will eventually develop as a new and an unprecedented evolving grammar of scientific inquiry and the enterprise of modern science. Names such as Copernicus, Galileo, and Newton make major contributions to "Natural Philosophy" as the enterprise of science as an emergent, applied, alternative first philosophy advances.

It becomes apparent as this drama unfolds that the enterprise of empirical science comes with new critical attitudes of rational inquiry, which are grounded in a philosophical worldview with its particular versions of first philosophy, and cognitive or epistemic attitudes. And it also is clear that the old fault lines between knowledge by Reason versus knowledge through our Senses, between *a priori* knowledge and the beliefs and perceptions we form through the embodied life of the senses, *a posteriori* continue to haunt philosophical discourse. We are following here with keen interest our central concern of the fate of egomental reason and its polarizing dynamics in the space of predication.

Indeed, Locke inaugurates one vital opening to the (techno)logic of scientific minding when he boldly wipes the slate clean, suggesting that with birth the mind is a "blank tablet" free of "innate" ideas or rational content. The long-held belief that Reason furnishes us with *a priori* knowledge independent of sense experience is rejected as mere dogma of rationalism. We suggest that this skepticism about the power of "reason" to provide "innate ideas" that correspond to objective reality is actually the appropriate recognition that "egomental reason" has no such unilateral power, and anyone who so alleges should give up this pretension. This bold stroke is, of course, of keen interest to our primary concern here of paying strict attention to the technology of minding as being vital in the rational enterprise. And Locke will have set in motion a powerful dialectic that will play out in the first philosophies of Berkeley and Hume and set the stage for a dramatic turn in the innovative work of Kant.

But, of course, Descartes also was keenly interested in the right method of minding (our conduct of mind) as being all-important for the rational enterprise. And in stark contrast to Locke, he continues the earlier "Rationalist" attitudes and commitments as he gives primary attention to the issue of the rigorous method of minding. So between Locke and Descartes, two alternative procedures are inaugurated for the right conduct of mind in pursuing our rational life, each presenting a very different first philosophy.

Regarding the origin of mind, consciousness, language, and experience, Locke claims that Reason provides no content, and he insists that all ideas on the tablet of consciousness (space of predication) must come through our Senses. While Descartes, in his *Discourse on Method*, insists that when we use our rational faculty with analytic and intuitive rigor, all Ideas that are "clear and distinct" to the (*a priori*) light of Reason must be true and disclose objective Reality. So we are presented with starkly contrasting first narratives concerning the origin of ideas and the power of reason in the encounter with Reality, and so another dramatic polarity emerges as this early modern drama unfolds.

The "Rationalist" first philosophy privileges "Reason" as being paramount in the rational enterprise, while the contrasting "Empiricist" first narrative privileges the "Senses" as being paramount in funding our ideas in the space of predication. Of course it becomes evident that terms such as *reason, senses*, and *ideas* are systematically equivocal across these competing first narratives, and we continue to be haunted by profound issues of real communication, translation, and communication across and between such polarized and competing philosophical grammars.

It appears that both "paradigms" share a presumed common deep structure of positing the "knowing subject" on one side, and the field of objective reality—the object of knowledge—as external to and independently presented to this subject. The fundamental challenge of "knowledge" is to bridge this deep divide in achieving the supposed "intimacy" of cognition, between knower and known. One paradigm suggests that Reason provides the needed link across this deep dualism through *a priori* Ideas that are innate in consciousness. The other paradigm alleges that our senses bring us *a posteriori* in direct touch with this external "Other," the external world, which is supposedly independently posited or given. So the challenge for epistemology is to explain how this deep dualism is overcome in the intimate relation of cognition. Again, we seek a plausible bridge or common ground across this dual divide.

DESCARTES' CRUCIAL MEDITATIVE
EXPERIMENT: A TEST CASE

In fact, Descartes' bold philosophical experiment presented in his historic work *Meditations on First Philosophy* is explicitly self-conscious about the enterprise of first philosophy. It opens up new possibilities in meditative minding and marks a clear turning point in the rational enterprise. Indeed, Descartes' experiment is a test case for us, since on our reading we find that he does, indeed, break out of the egomental predicative box in opening and venturing into the meditative dimension of first philosophy. But it takes the ((global lens)) or expanded capacities of ((global reason)) to see this clearly.

DESCARTES' BREAKTHROUGH
TO MEDITATIVE REASON

Descartes' experiment is profoundly relevant to our central theme concerning the perennial struggle to break free of the barriers of egomental predication in the quest for *What-Is-First*, for in his first-person meditative voice, it appears that he does make the classic crossing into the integral (nondual) space of meditative reason, and yet he himself seems to falter and fall back into the scholastic technology of egomental (dualistic) predication in presenting his breakthrough meditative insights. Ironically, he himself seems to be caught in the fatal "fusion" (con-fusion) of the two dimensions of discourse and naturally seems to speak his insights in the technology of egomental predication, thus leaving himself open to the typical (mis)readings of his breakthrough moments. He has become infamous as the "father of modern dualism" and as espousing a "mechanistic" view of the universe.

If we follow rigorously Descartes' meditative experiment, unprejudiced by the dogma of egomental minding, then we more readily see that there are peak moments where he does, indeed, perform the meditative breakthrough into the nondual dimension of integral reason. I suggest that when we follow his meditative pathway and his declared findings carefully, rigorously, and sympathetically, it becomes evident that his text can only make sense if read meditatively, and not through the egomental lens.

DESCARTES BREAKS THE
DUALISTIC EGOMENTAL BARRIER

We will pursue this line further in some depth later. But for now, as we continue to follow the bold strokes in pursuit of the main drama, let us remember that when Descartes entered his thought experiment of radical doubt to see if there was any thought, belief, or predication that he was constrained by the light of Reason to hold as absolutely certain and necessarily true that every conceivable predication could be placed in philosophical doubt. In fact, it is a classical moment in meditative critique when the rigorous meditative thinker discovers that any and every predication in the egomental space of reason could be tainted with doubt, precisely because there is a fundamental separation (another deep dualism) between the subject who is thinking, and the predicative screen, the predicative box in which our beliefs and our encounter with the external world are constructed and presented.

When Descartes introduced the hypothetical possibility of an "evil deceiver" controlling his mind and tricking him into affirming with certainty a predicative content in the objectified space of predication, he was in fact raising a classic concern of the meditative traditions that found the chasm between the thinker and the object of thought in the egomental space of predication suspect and problematic, and always taking a radical risk of corrigibility in interpreting the thought item presented to it in this objectified predicative space. It is the dualistic separation and severance between the knower and the known that opens legitimate space for philosophical doubt, and the perpetual possibility of mistaken interpretation, judgment, affirmation, and belief. The deep dualism between knower and known opens up the space for this radical doubt in egomental life.

CARTESIAN NONDUALITY:
"I AM" IN THE MEDITATIVE VOICE

In this meditative critique, it is precisely when Descartes exits (deconstructs) the egomental screen of dual predication and ventures more deeply into the nondual dimension of meditative reason in the awakening of "I am," "I think" . . . now spoken in the meditative voice . . . that he touches his potentially monumental breakthrough. Ironically, we find that it is this historic breakthrough to nonduality that is most revealing, rather than the more customary ego-ridden reading of the Cartesian villain who is blamed for saddling modern culture with deep dualism and alleging to find the ultimate foundation of knowledge within the egomental voice. While our **meditative** reading discerns a heroic Descartes who opens nondual rational space for first philosophy, on the one hand, the oft-repeated "mantra" of egomental interpreters finds, on the other, a Cartesian culprit whose name within this culture of scholarship has become synonymous with "dualism" and even ego-ridden "foundationalism."

I am not, of course, suggesting that Descartes clearly and unambiguously understood that he had moved beyond the egomental voice and entered into a deeper dimension of meditative reason. On the contrary, my main point is that this tradition of first philosophy had not yet charted the nondual dimension of meditative reason, nor articulated the integral and hologistic technology of discourse in contradistinction to the egomental technology of dualistic predication. So Descartes himself apparently felt that he had only the familiar and entrenched "scholastic" predicative logical space in which to express his amazing new ((insights)), which naturally get lost and seriously deformed in such "translation." And in appearing to continue to use this egomental space of discourse, he naturally left himself open to the egocentric (mis)reading of his voice, which has now become engraved into our collective consciousness over the centuries.

A careful reading of his voice, in his own terms, will reveal that Descartes himself felt a certain rational shock when he uttered his now infamous *cogito*—"I think, I am." He realized that this was a new experience, a new encounter with mindful consciousness and thinking, indeed, with his primal Self, which he never had before. And it is clear that he was now out of the egomental predicative "box," since he realized immediately that he "knew not" what this "I" was. He said, "That I am is certain, but what I am, I know not," which was truly a remarkable moment in the evolution of first philosophy—a deep and direct meditative encounter with his primary being, with his meditative Self, which potentially opened a new chapter in radical existentialism. And this is truly a global moment, since this very insight and advance is axiomatic and commonplace in the classic meditative first philosophies alluded to earlier.

What immediately follows in this unprecedented breakthrough could have been a dramatic turning point for his cultural traditions. He proceeds in his bold meditative experiment rigorously to probe and fathom this new "I am" that he discovers, to enter a perhaps even more amazing discovery—that he was in a direct encounter with Infinite Being as his meditation inexorably leads him to another classic finding, that within the "I am" the "Infinite Thou" is already present, given, and disclosed. And he himself declared in his equally infamous "proof of the existence of God" that as certain as he was in his own primary being, in "I am," he was now even more certain and confident that "Infinite Being" IS, and that this was truly the ground and foundation of his "I am," and of true Rational Light, hence of culture, ethics, truth, common sense, and authentic religious and scientific life.

We shall soon see when we seek to bring out more explicitly the missing hologistic technology of integral reason that in fact the "I am . . . God is" forms a primal unit in the more primitive nondual "I⟸⟹Thou" relation. But in the more customary egomental and dualistic reading of this potentially monumental moment in Descartes' experiment, he is seen as alleging to prove within the egomental predicative space (which he had clearly just abandoned) that "exist" is a necessary attribute or predicate of God or Infinite Being. And once we place Descartes' meditative discovery and grounding for first philosophy back in the egomental predicative space, the alleged proof is easily taken apart, and what is in fact an ingenious breakthrough moment for the culture and for the rational enterprise is eclipsed, turned around, and Descartes is again made to appear as a philosophical buffoon and laughingstock for thinking that he could or did prove that "Infinite Being must be," as a necessary predicative truth.

Whereas, in fact, in the dialectics of meditative reason there is a nondual immediacy or intimacy between the "Idea of *What-Is-First*" and its overwhelming existential Presence. As we shall soon see in the dimension of Meditative Reason, this inseparability of the holistic "Idea" of Infinite Being from its Presence is axiomatic, and a natural and an inevitable starting point for GFP.

And, in fact, in this integral dimension of reason there is likewise an immediate existential intimacy between the primal utterance "I am" and one's Primary Being, so "Word⟸⟹Consciousness⟸⟹Being" will meet in a primal union and continuum. So the test case of Descartes meditative experiment supports our narrative line and its corollary that the absence of an explicit nondual or hologistic grammar for the integral dimension of the Infinite First inhibits and blocks the clear explicit expression of vital insights and discoveries in the encounter with *What-Is-First*. Having to resort (or appear to resort) to the dualistic technology of egomental predication as the only linguistic game in town and the sole and exclusive legitimate space for rational discourse has undermined the advancement of our rational enterprise and, indeed, our highest and best human interests and welfare.

SHIFTING THE SPOTLIGHT TO THE "THINKER" OUTSIDE OF THE PREDICATIVE SCREEN

Jumping ahead a bit in this power scan of the unfolding drama, we shall see that the monumental opening to "transcendental reason" initiated by Descartes in his meditative experiment does get picked up, at least in part, down the road by Husserl, who inaugurates the new area of Phenomenology and opens the way to further radical disclosures of Existential thought developed by his eminent protégés, Heidegger and Sartre. For as Husserl opens new dimensions in the rational enterprise with his vital pioneering exploration in Transcendental Logic, and in the critical shift in minding technology of Phenomenology, he initiates this historic turn with his early work *Cartesian Meditations.*

With this opening a new spotlight focuses on the presence and role of the "thinker" outside of the content of the predicative box, which is a witnessing presence, a proactive interpreter and judge, and a participating force in shaping what appears on the predicative screen. But this fundamental shift in the spotlight from the content of predicative space to the dynamic and formative influence of the thinking subject outside of the predicative screen takes a giant step with the revolutionary work of Kant.

THE CONTINUING STRUGGLE WITH DEEP DUALISMS: DESCARTES TO KANT

In setting this dramatic stage for the innovations of Kant, let us step back and resume our central strand of thought in opening the polar pathways initiated anew by Locke and Descartes. We shall now, again in bold strokes, rehearse some key factors in the polar streams that issued from the new openings initiated by these innovative thinkers. The twin polar narrative lines of Empiricism and Rationalism are in effect competing alter-first philosophies that would each mature and peak revealing another stark (dualistic) contrast, thus ripening and setting the context for Kant's revolutionary revisions in the enterprise of first philosophy—his "Copernican revolution" in the rational enterprise. So this dramatic development may be seen as still another exemplary illustration in our lead story, suggesting that the ever-present Infinite Force continuously influences and impels forth the evolution of rational consciousness from ego-mental dualism toward higher-order coherence, consistency, and rational unity.

ANOTHER DEEP DUALISM:
RATIONALISM VERSUS EMPIRICISM

As we now focus our scan from Locke and Descartes to Kant we witness another great moment in our evolutionary story of the struggle to overcome the inherent polarizing forces of egomental reason with its chronic pattern of spawning recursive dualisms in all directions and at all levels. The earlier fault lines in the rational enterprise that haunted the amazing first philosophies of Plato and Aristotle continue to recur through the centuries and are picked up in still another round in the unfolding dialectics of Rationalism versus Empiricism, which Kant sought to resolve in his radical turn. The ancient tensions between Being versus Becoming, Universal versus Particular, Mind versus Body, the role of Reason versus the role of the Senses, of *a priori* Concepts versus *a posteriori* Percepts, between the knowing subject and the object known, and so on emerge in a heightened form. And we shall see that the driving force moving this dialectic is the deep drive in rational awareness to overcome incommensurable dualisms and mature into a higher integral coherence, consistency, and completeness, and that Kant's heroic attempt to break this pattern and elevate the bar of rational discourse to new heights in breaking the egomental barrier only resulted in a new deep dualism.

As we pick up this drama in the innovations of Locke and Descartes we notice that there appears to be a common deep structure in the two lineages with the knowing subject posited on one side of a fault line and the object of knowledge (or experience) presented and lodged in the space of predication on the other. There is a presumed mutual independence between the Knower and the Known, and the task of first philosophy is to develop a narrative to explain how the Knower can truly know this independently given Object of knowledge. The ancient stratagem of "rationalism" is to allege that the chasm between the knower and the known is bridged by primal ideas innately inscribed in reason that somehow correspond with external or "objective reality." Presumably there must be some common ground or primal link between these *a priori* "ideas" implanted in our rational faculty and the externally presented world.

POLAR PARADIGMS OF FIRST PHILOSOPHY

Of course it is precisely this "dogma of rationalism" that is radically rejected by Locke when he breaks with this tradition, wipes the slate clean, and announces that there are no such *a priori* ideas innate in reason and insists that our senses provide us with the ideas that link us to the posited external empirical world. So in this bold move Locke initiates a paradigm or lineage that privileges the senses over reason in funding our experience and potential knowledge of the independently presented field of reality. Naturally the first philosophy that plays out in the "rationalist" tradition involves a philosophical grammar or narrative that presented a profoundly different worldview than the one that emerges in this "empiricist" tradition.

And these radically contrasting narrative fields or worldviews are so polarized that it appears that the basic terms or concepts of one lineage are incommensurable with the philosophical vocabulary of the other. For example, the terms or building blocks of each worldview—*reason, senses, knower, knowledge, ideas, experience*—take on radically different meanings in the two narrative traditions. So we begin to see a recurrence of primal polarizations or dualisms at all levels: a split between the knower and the known, between the thinker and the screen of predication in which objects of experience appear, between thinking and the content of thought, between mind and matter, between the logical subject and the predicate, and also, on the macro level, of the polarization in philosophical worldviews themselves. Of course this raises challenging issues concerning the possibility of rational discourse between these polarized paradigms of discourse.

THE "THINKER" OUTSIDE OF THE PREDICATIVE BOX

Keeping in mind this omnipresent recurrence of dualities and polarities from the micro through the macro levels, let us jump in for a quick tour through these two unfolding parallel lines of first philosophy as the dualistic plot thickens, setting the stage for Kant's radical intervention. Here it should be noted that the locus of the "thinking subject" outside of the space of predication still remains relatively inconspicuous for both lineages, even though each privileges a different "faculty" in weaving its first narrative. On the one hand, the rationalist tradition naturally takes the power of Reason in the thinking subject to be the main cognitive link with the external field of Reality, while the empiricist lineage accords the faculty of sense experience as the primary mode of linking us to this presumed objective reality. So in both cases there is a key "relation" privileged between the "thinker" and the field of reality that is presented within the predicative "box" that is the object of consciousness for the thinker, and both seem to focus primary attention within the predicative space in developing its philosophical narrative.

THE DRAMA AND DIALECTIC
WITHIN THE PREDICATIVE SPACE

Both polar paradigms seek to play out their stories within the space of predication. On the one hand, for the classical rationalist tradition the resource of reason alleges to provide the fundamental building blocks of experience and world—such as the category of "substance" (the locus of being, essence, unity, identity) for the objects of experience, and for Aristotle the quest for the primary being of things focuses on the ultimate logical subject of predication. So the contrasting empiricist tradition, in radically rejecting this resource of reason as providing such information, must find some other way to account for the appearance and ongoing identity of objects as presented in the space of predication. Thus the fundamental categories of experience, such as substance, causality, space, and time, must now be explained in terms of the ideas originating in the data of the senses, from percepts and not rational concepts. But in jumping across the deep divide between these two traditions, all terms radically shift in signification. Words such as "substance" or "causality" mean one thing for the rationalist narrative, and quite another for the empiricist lens. We face here a polarity of worldviews—another fundamental dualism.

As we now focus our global lens on this remarkable dialectical drama, we find that both traditions emphasize and struggle with one of the fundamental dualisms, that of "mind" versus "matter." In Locke's narrative of experience, grounded in the language of the senses, we find that he proposes two kinds of substance—mental (mind) and physical (matter). He assumes or alleges that in taking the ideas derived from our senses as primary, we find two fundamental kinds of substance in the narrative of reality—one that grounds mind, consciousness, thinking, and ideas (mental substance) in contrast to a presumed independently existing external material world—the domain of physical objects grounded in material substance that is outside of the sphere of mind or thought. At the same time, as we switch our focus to the groundwork laid by Descartes in his "modernized" version of the classical rationalist story, it appears that he too finds two fundamental kinds of substance—mind (thinking substance, not extended in space) and body (extended material nature in space and time). So, mindful of the systemic ambiguity in all of these key terms across the divide of these two unfolding worldviews, let us observe how this dialectical drama unfolds.

On the one hand, Locke initiates a new philosophical narrative that privileges the senses and demotes the role of "reason" in the formation of experience and our encounter with reality. And presuming the radical independence of the thinker (perceiver), on the one hand, and the object of experience (perception), on the other, Locke's challenge is to explain precisely how the thinking "substance" comes to contact and know the independently given "material substance" posited as appearing in the space of predication. So the primal dualism between the knower (outside the space of predication) and the known (presented within the predicative zone) becomes replicated and projected in the basic dualism of mental and physical substances within the screen of predication.

We find Locke struggling to build a credible story of how perception and the data of our senses can jump across the chasm of the dual domains of mental and physical realities without the assistance of "reason" providing an *a priori* link or bridge. Since for him sense perception is the primary source of "ideas," and of our link with the external material world, we find him finessing a primary dual distinction between "primary" and "secondary" ideas that will be fundamentally challenged by Berkeley and Hume as they seek to carry his first philosophy to deeper coherence and consistency.

Both Berkeley and Hume advance this inner dialectic within the "empiricist" story in welcoming and accepting Locke's radical starting point—that the mind is a blank tablet at birth, that reason provides no "innate ideas" that link us to the external world, and that the senses are the primary source of our "ideas" and of our link to the independently given external world. However, Berkeley challenges Locke's postulation of two kinds of substances (mental and physical) and develops a powerful critique to show that Locke's dualism of mind and matter is untenable, incoherent, undermining of common sense, and a dangerous dogma also undermining our spiritual, moral, and cognitive life, leading us into paradoxes and ultimately landing us in nihilism.

BERKELEY'S RADICAL REJECTION OF "MATERIALISM" AND LOCKE'S DUALISM

Berkeley's critique (as in his classic text *Three Dialogues between Hylas and Philonus*) turns precisely on the incoherence of bridging the chasm between the domain of mental life and the independently given domain of external physical reality. Indeed, in seeking to carry Locke's first philosophy to deeper coherence Berkeley presses his premises to the radical position that "*to be is to be perceived*," his now infamous principle of "idealism" that suggests that only "mind" and "ideas" exist (spiritual substance), and that "material substance," as posited independently of perceiving consciousness, is incoherent, untenable, and vacuous, and it leads to nonsense. Berkeley's ontological principle is of course important for first philosophy, suggesting that reality, being, existence, or world is essentially mind related, and that what is known has some vital grounding in the constitution of the knower.

Quite pertinent to our lead story, that *What-Is-First* presides in all situations and drives the historical dialectic beyond dualisms to higher-order coherence, Berkeley proceeds to show that "ontological idealism" is the only coherent story that saves common sense, and that this first philosophy immediately leads to the conclusion that an Infinite Mind (God) actively holds and sustains all of our ideas (percepts, perceptions) and saves our common sense worldview that assumes that the "perceptual objects" we experience, and that essentially will need a perceiving mind to exist, continue to exist when we (the contingent, finite perceivers) are not present to actively perceive them.

So Berkeley purports to save the empiricist starting point of Locke by rejecting his dualistic worldview that posits an independently existing material (physical) world and seeks to demonstrate an alternative first philosophy that is grounded in Infinite Spirit, vindicates our common sense worldview of an independently existing perceptual world, decisively favors philosophical idealism, and radically rejects the worldview of materialism and the primal dualism that comes with it. In so doing, Berkeley introduces some radical revisions in our language or grammar of experience, for example, proposing that the immediate objects of perception (percepts, sense data, ideas) given to our consciousness are the "things themselves." In his modification of everyday language, it appears that technically the immediate data of our senses—percepts or ideas—are the perceptual objects themselves.

In fact he suggests that the philosophical belief in "material substance" as sustaining the perceived world leads to atheism and breaks our direct link to Infinite Spirit and thus with the true foundation of existence, common sense and knowledge. So his philosophical revision alleges to solve the incoherent dualism of Locke's starting point, to vindicate philosophical Idealism, to discredit ontological Materialism, and to reveal a spiritualized first philosophy of mind, spirit, and ideas. And since, strictly speaking, the immediate data of our senses (percepts, ideas) present fleeting atomic or discrete "ideas," "percepts," or "sense data," having no connection or relations, he recognizes that our everyday perceptual "objects" are really "constructs" from our perceptual data, and that the names that we give objects that might suggest ongoing substantial continuity or existence are just "conventions" of speech rather than indicating "unified substances" that objectively exist.

BERKELEY'S IDEALISM—INFINITE SPIRIT AS THE GROUND OF COMMON SENSE

Berkeley's "Idealism" comes with the price tag of "Nominalism" that affirms that only particular immediate objects of perception exist, and that all "general names" are only "conventional names." For example, what we may call a "cherry" is really a bundle of ever-changing sensual data, wherein what is seen, touched, smelled, and tasted is a fleeting, independent (atomic) entity or unit that happens to cluster as it does because it is so arranged by the Divine Mind that sustains it. And here we see one fallout from the rejection of "reason" as providing the *a priori* building blocks of experience, such as "substance." Strictly speaking, "substance" is never perceived, never presented to our senses, hence it must be a mere conventional name only and not an objective reality.

Nevertheless, while Berkeley presses Locke's first philosophy to deeper coherence in seeking to overcome his ontological dualism of mind and matter, his Idealism, which rejects any independently existing "material substance," still appears to cling to "mental substance," to "mind," which appears to give ongoing, "substantial weight" to the perceiver, thinker, knower. The knowing or perceiving "self" (presumably both outside and within the predicative space) appears to have a continuing substantial mental or spiritual being. And Hume will take Berkeley to task precisely in this lingering vestige of the rationalistic, old school, dogmatic metaphysics.

HUME'S RADICAL CONCLUSIONS:
WE ARE PASSIONAL BEINGS

Interestingly, Hume takes the dialectical baton from Berkeley and presses his predecessors more radically, taking Locke's starting point and Berkeley's revisions to their full and ripened outcomes. He builds on Berkeley's revisions of Locke and finds that he does not go all the way in also rejecting "mental" or "spiritual" substance. As mentioned, Berkeley radically rejected "material substance" but held onto "mental substance," both in the Infinite Spiritual Substance of God or Divine Being, as well as in the more localized finite substance of the thinking or perceiving "self." But Hume was relentless in pressing the empiricist starting point to full and ultimate conclusion in finding that we strictly never have any "percept" or "idea" of substance, not of "God" nor of the "self." So not only is there no "material substance" existing independently of Mind or Spirit, but more radically, there also is no "mind substance," no "substantial self," and we have no idea or percept of "God" as Infinite Substance. So in this he moves into new territory beyond Berkeley and seeks to find the true basis of our everyday worldview beyond a reliance on the "Divine Mind."

In the language of the senses, we strictly perceive only discrete fleeting items, percepts, the original source of all of our "ideas." These fleeting "atomic" units have no "duration" and can only be "associated," never "related," in the sense suggested or assumed in rationalistic "dogma." Hume did not hesitate to draw the radical conclusion (already hinted at by Berkeley) that all things are really ever-changing "bundles" of discrete and associated percepts— so, ostensibly, we never, strictly speaking, perceive everyday common sense "objects" or a substantial "self" or a continuously enduring object that is the referent of "I." This startling conclusion, that there is no substantial "self," was of course already noticed in early Buddhist first philosophy, albeit in a very different worldview and critical context.

What appears to be driving Hume's remarkable first philosophy is the explicit recognition that the primary data of our senses, including our internal percepts, are fleeting in duration and "atomic"(radically distinct and independently given units) in their being. Here, again, within the space of predication, these fleeting "objects" of perception appear not as substantial logical subjects but rather as predicates, as qualities that more naturally take the predicate position. And since "Reason," in this newly emerging legacy of Locke and Berkeley, is in some sense empty of content and impotent to supply real or objective relations, links, or connections between the primary "atomic" data of the senses, he did not hesitate to draw the conclusion that at best the atomic percepts of experience are radically discrete and have no perceivable "connection" or intrinsic "relation" but rather are "associated" in a loose "external" psychological link in the experience of the perceiver.

This finding is of course potentially devastating for the "rationalist" enterprise that presumes that causal relations are rationally grounded in the fabric of reality. And it makes a world of difference whether causation expresses a real *connection* between phenomena or indicates a mere *association* in our subjective experience. Our understanding of "science," indeed, of common sense experience, turns on this. It appears that the grammar of the senses, strictly speaking, when stripped of the pretensions of *a priori* "reason," finds no real "connection" or "common ground" in objective reality. When we set aside these presumptions of "reason," and we set aside all alleged *a priori* or innate "ideas" or "categories" and "relations," we enter a new frontier of accounting for everyday experiences and beliefs.

Indeed, this radical shift from the primacy of Reason to the primacy of the Senses marks a deep worldview shift in the nature of the human being, rejecting the classical "dogma" that we are "rational beings" to the new empiricist worldview in which we are truly "passional beings." In his relentless analysis and phenomenology of experience and "knowledge," based on the "association of ideas," Hume finds that our everyday beliefs are not, after all, grounded in the power or resources of Reason but rather in our primal Animal Faith, in our feelings, sentiments, and passions. And of course this radical shift beyond the old dogmatism of "rationalism" marks a new era in the self-understanding of the human being as well as the cognitive enterprise. In his first philosophy Hume clarified a new problematic, which centers on "the problem of induction." On what grounds do we move from a perception or an association immediately given in experience to some future possibility not immediately given? Hume inquired into the basis of this "inferential leap," which we are constantly making in everyday life, and he found that it was not based on reason but rather on subjective psychological associations and "animal faith."

In the former world of rationalism, it was presumed that reason was the ground of our cognitive commitments and everyday beliefs or conjectures regarding the future. But since for Hume reason is not capacitated to provide real links between the immediate ideas of the senses, we had to give up, for example, the dogma of "causal connection" and instead countenance the associative idea of "constant conjunction" or mere juxtaposition together with psychological conditioning or habit formation. In this scenario, science turns out to be discerning the constant conjunctions in our experience as these lead to the formation of our beliefs. "Induction" is not based on "Reason."

In this philosophical grammar, "causation" is not a real, rational connection between items but an association of ideas together with habit formation through the contingencies and vagaries of experience. And in reaching this unprecedented conclusion Hume opens a new vision of the human being and the true ground of our beliefs and cognitive claims—it is our animal nature—animal faith—that capacitates us to live in the everyday world, not reason. So with Hume's remarkable revisions, the empiricist starting point initiated by Locke and developed by Berkeley reached its mature conclusion. As our story unfolds we will notice again and again that whenever we have "atomic units" (as we apparently face constantly in egomental reason), it appears that "relations" between such independently constituted and given units are highly problematic.

Thus Hume was definitely on to something profound and perennial here. And following our lead theme, it appears that he gravitated outside of the space of predication into the dynamics of "animal faith" and our embodied passional nature to find the grounds of our everyday beliefs. It appears that some deep dialectic has been driving this self-revising dynamic as the drama unfolds, and as we shall soon see Kant reports that his encounter with Hume's first philosophy jolted him from his rationalistic "dogmatic slumbers." We have suggested that the ever-present powerful influence of the Primal Field that surrounds and situates all egomental predicative spaces works to deconstruct the artificial constructions of the egomental mind and seeks to resolve chronic dualisms in lifting our discourse to higher ground in quest of unifying forces. But before we get into Kant's amazing innovations, let us first rehearse the remarkable developments on the rationalistic side of this great dialectical drama.

DESCARTES TO LEIBNIZ—
THE RATIONALIST DIALECTIC UNFOLDS

We now switch the focus of our ((global lens)) to the dialectical developments of the rationalist story as this unfolds from Descartes through Spinoza and Leibniz as the context is prepared for Kant's entrance. Let us remember as we now jump from the empiricist narrative to the rationalist grammar of Descartes that we are in very different universes of discourse, different worldviews and philosophical grammars that use basic terms in systemically ambiguous ways. The "reason" that is demoted and marginalized in the empiricist narrative is not at all the same "reason" that funds the discourse of Descartes, Spinoza, and Leibniz, nor the same rational power that is at the heart of the rationalist enterprise, as articulated by Plato and Aristotle. Keeping this in mind, let us move with Descartes as he is keenly attentive to the "method of minding" and the innate *a priori* "ideas" that the clarified power of reason reveals. Descartes continues the classical tradition of reason as being inscribed with fundamental forms and content that disclose true reality. Earlier we suggested that in his analytical method of clarifying these ideas of reason, he finds as an axiom that all "clear and distinct ideas" must be true and correspond to objective reality.

THE DEEP DUALISM OF THE "EGOMENTAL" DESCARTES

We also suggested that in Descartes' meditative turn to first philosophy, he encountered himself as a Primal Thinker outside the space of predication, and he performed a monumental service to our common philosophical enterprise. But, alas, in presenting his unprecedented meditative breakthrough, he hit the old walls of egomental predicative space with its egomental logistic (or technology of discourse) and was impeded in his expressive power to present his historically vital insights and advances in an adequate way. We suggested too that this meditative reading of Descartes' experiment shows that he broke with the dualizing patterns of egomental mind, and he crossed into a "nondual" rationality that we touched upon earlier and will explore in greater depth soon. But for now let us go with the customary egomental and "dualistic" Descartes that appears to be stuck in a deep and chronic "mind versus body" dualism.

In provisionally playing along with this dualistic reading of Descartes, it appears that Descartes also struggles with another version of the mind/body dualism that plagued Locke's empiricist narrative. We saw with Berkeley a classic stratagem to overcome this dualism by privileging Mind and Ideas (Idealism) and "reducing" "Matter" and "Physical Nature" to the domain of Consciousness. The materialist solution of this dualism, of course, is to go the other way and privilege the primacy of Matter and "reduce" the discourse of mind, ideas, and consciousness to Material Nature (Materialism). But a dualistic ontology is one that simultaneously affirms the mutual independence of the domains of both Mind and Matter.

The dualistic reading of Descartes suggests that he is such a dualist, and he struggles with the same kind of ontological paradoxes faced by Berkeley and Locke in seeking a bridge and common ground or existential mediating link between these alleged radically independent realities. For Descartes the challenge focuses on explaining how one and the same Self or Person (Thinking Subject) also can be one with "his" Body, where there is a constant back-and-forth causal interaction between Mind and Body in every act of perception (external matter modifying the consciousness of the thinker) or volition and action (in which the will, as a causal agent of the thinker, ostensibly moves our material bodies or other material things in every conscious action). The mysteries of the Mind/Body Problem suggest that the Thinking Agent (self) must be an ontological unit (individual), and yet must be composed of two distinct natures or essences, hence must be a dual or composite entity. Descartes clearly struggles with these classic problems (also explicitly faced by Socrates in Plato's *Phaedo*) in his Sixth and final Meditation.

At this point we are focusing on the larger picture as we prepare to move to Spinoza, as this historical dialectic unfolds, so we will not get into details. But it is important to remember how Descartes lands in his "modern" version of the Mind/Body dualism and rediscovers and reaffirms this classic dualism already found in Plato's thought. Again, Ontological Dualism (in one version) is the position that there are two radically independent and irreducible domains of reality—Mind and Matter—that play out in diverse local dualisms—Soul/Body, Consciousness/Physical Nature, and so on. These two ontological domains (types of being) disclose two worlds that exhibit different natures. One problem is seeking to understand or explain how an embodied person can participate in these two domains of reality, engage in causal interactions between them, hence be a bridge or common ground, and yet be a composite (dual) entity rather than an individual or ontological unity. In this way the thinking subject is the site of a troubling paradox, the very one that Berkeley sought to resolve in his move to Idealism.

Let us remember how Descartes allegedly arrives at his ontological dualism. In his bold and unprecedented meditative journey into first philosophy, he presses his experiment in radical (methodical) doubt and finds that all predications are suspicious and could in principle be doubted. He then appears to make the startling "discovery" out of the predicative box that in being a conscious thinker he must be, exist, even if he has no predicative information about this newly encountered "thinking subject." So his first ontological discovery or "proof" is that "I am," his primal thinking (prepredicative) Self exists. And in this radical space of meditative thinking (which is new to him) he then discovers that Infinite Being must be, and he claims to "discover" this Infinite Other, this Primal Presence inscribed within him, and that if he exists as a finite and contingent being, then this implies all the more the Presence of a boundless, Infinite Being causing and sustaining him and the source of his rational light. Thus his first ontological finding is that "I am," and the next discovery that immediately follows is that "Infinite Being must be," so his expanded discovery is "I am ⟸⟹ Infinite Being must be," taken as a unit. This Dialogical Unit is the primal starting point.

The key here is that he finds he can be or exist in this radical space of primal thinking without any predication of being embodied or having a material nature, at least at this point in the experiment. So far he only discovers anew himself as a radically thinking subject outside of the former space of predication. Ostensibly, at this point, the former categories of "mind" and "matter" are set aside, not applicable to his newly discovered meditative self outside of the predicative space where these former ontological categories, distinctions, and dualisms arise. Having discovered the source of his "rational light" arising from this newfound intimacy with Infinite Being, he vows to remain relentlessly in this sanctuary of rational perspicuity and proceed with extreme caution to see if he can discover any other truths.

Again, remaining in this meditative zone outside of the older space of egomental predication, he seeks to discover if he could encounter his embodied self, whether he also could "prove" that 'bodies exist," not only his own but other external bodies that he formerly encountered in material or physical nature. And in his "infamous" moves in the Fifth and Sixth Meditations, he claims to reach his third great ontological discovery—that "Bodies Exist." But he is clear that in some important sense "Thinking" or "Consciousness" is primal and first, and the existence of Body and Physical Nature is a subsequent discovery. A key aspect of this third ontological discovery is that material nature exists independently of consciousness or his thinking nature, and it is the bridge or common ground provided by the Infinite Light of Reason that empowers the thinking subject to move in certitude to encounter the independent existence of body or material nature, yet without breaking the essential "continuum" between thought and matter. Within the awakened rational Light, thought touches the external material world through the awakened senses without a breach. This is the key.

THE CARTESIAN DUALISTIC PARADOX

So it is at this point in the final (Sixth) Meditation that Descartes struggles to reconcile some fundamental ontological findings that resist reconciliation: that he knows himself as a purely "thinking being" capable of existing independently of being embodied (so far, this is a primal version of "idealism"); next, that he can now affirm with assurance that he also is embodied; that his Body exists (along with material nature); further, he finds that he is quite intimately linked in ongoing mutual interactions between his Mind and Body (suggesting that he is one integral unit). He wishes to show that the idea of "immortality" does make sense, thus, that he is capable of disembodied existence, so this ontological finding is vital. Yet he also acknowledges that he forms some kind of primal unity with his body, which must be the case to explain the most common occurrences of everyday experience. Here he faces the perennial problem of finding *existential relations* between *atomically discrete kinds of being*—the dualistic problem. So his version of the Mind/Body problem is that, on the one hand, he (his embodied Self) must be *a composite entity* participating in two ontologically distinct and independent natures, and, on the other hand, at the same time, these two natures must be in an intimate causal interaction, which implies that he also must be *an ontological unity*, an individual. Apparently he is not able to reconcile these two polar findings.

SPINOZA'S ATTEMPT TO SOLVE THE DUALISTIC DILEMMA

As with Descartes, Spinoza is keenly attentive to the method of minding and of the importance of the rigorous clarification of ideas in this rationalist tradition. In this he shares the sentiment that Reason has the power, *a priori*, to touch and disclose objective Reality, so Reason and Reality are in some primal communion. He advances the classical rationalist narrative and inherits the dualistic challenges bequeathed by Descartes, his immediate predecessor. It appears that he accepts the pathways and findings of Descartes, but, as the dialectic goes, he finds certain deep dualisms in Descartes' first philosophy that he takes to be incoherent, inconsistent, and therefore unacceptable. For example, in the tradition of Parmenides, he finds that the primal idea of "substance" (being, existing in itself) implies a Primary Being that is Infinite, Self-Caused, Boundless, and One. He therefore finds the idea of a "finite substance" fatally flawed and self-contradictory, since being "finite" entails existential (ontological) dependency on Infinite Being for its being. Yet it appears that Descartes affirms in his ontology two kinds of substances—finite being (finite substance) (e.g., his "I am," his Self, which is presumably "finite") and Infinite Being (Infinite Substance) (God, *What-Is-First*), which alone is Self-Existent and radically self-caused in its being. This deep dualism of finite being versus infinite being needs to be resolved, as well as the other dualisms of Mind versus Matter that we just explored.

SPINOZA'S RADICAL MONISM— "THERE IS ONLY ONE SUBSTANCE"

To save the salvageable findings of Descartes' first philosophy, Spinoza took unprecedented steps in radically revising and renovating the space of

predication to innovate a more consistent and comprehensive first philosophy. The classical "Aristotelian" space of predication suggests that the ultimate logical subject is the locus of "primary beings," the individual *ousia*, or
substances, making up reality. This "ontologic" over centuries evolves into
the "Scholastic" logic of the schools and is naturally inherited and used by
Descartes as the logistic to express his meditative insights. It is this predicative space that shapes the European cultural lineage and mentality over
centuries that Spinoza radically renovates. He apparently agrees that the
place of the logical subject taken to its primal limit is the locus of "Substance," but finding that this primal concept of first philosophy entails that
there can be only "One Substance," namely, Infinite Being, since this First
Being alone can truly be "self-existent," "self-caused," needing no other to
be. In carrying out this finding to its full ontological conclusion, he finds
that there can be only one true Primary Being and one true logical subject
of predication, and he calls this Infinite Being "God" or "Substance" or
"Nature" (multiple alter-primal names).

INFINITE NAMES, ATTRIBUTES, AND NARRATIVES OF *WHAT-IS-FIRST*

This, of course, is a radical revision in a number of ways. It recognizes that there
can be only one "Substance," that it must be Infinite, that it must have Infinite
Names, Infinite Attributes, and even Infinite Alternative Narratives. This is
immediately implied in being "Infinite"—boundless in all directions and
dimensions, yet Absolutely One, Unified and Integral. As he carries out this
renovation of the space of predication, Spinoza shows that our ordinary customary ways of thinking and predicating are flawed and need to be revised to be
made consistent with his findings of first philosophy. Most striking is his suggestion that the ordinary "things" or "objects" of everyday experience that we
might mistakenly take to be "substances" and "logical subjects" of predication are
actually modifications of the one true Logical Subject—which is "Substance =
God = Nature." This, in effect, means that from the point of view of genuine
first philosophy, the ordinary objects and individuals of everyday (or even philosophical) thinking and speech are actually modifications or predications on
"Infinite Substance." Further, this radical ontology also implies radical revision
for the grammars of theology, since it implies that "God" has infinite alter-
names—including "Substance" and "Nature," among boundless possibilities.
God is Material nature. This Spinoza finding shook and shocked the predominant worldview when it was presented, for suggesting that "Nature" is an alter-
name for Infinite Being carried radical implications, such as that God also is
"Material nature," not just "Infinite Spirit." Indeed, Spinoza, in his amazing text

Ethics, presents his rigorous "pure axiomatic science" of "Infinite Substance" in seeking to rectify the inconsistencies in the Cartesian ontology, indeed, of the prevalent narratives of the "Infinite First." Spinoza argued that Infinite Substance, having Infinite Attributes, would accommodate the attributes of Consciousness or Thinking (the language of "mind"), as well as the attributes of Extension in Space (the language of Material nature, Body or Matter).

SPINOZA'S SOLUTION: INFINITE
SUBSTANCE FULLY MIND, FULLY MATTER

This latter suggestion was scandalous and was seen to place Spinoza in the domain of blasphemy—the "outrageous" and dangerous suggestion that Infinite Being is Infinitely Embodied and perfectly expressed in the alter-narrative of Material Nature. Although he was clear that Infinite Being had Infinite Attributes (and Narratives), he alleged that we humans are limited and can apprehend this Infinite Substance under two equally alternative grammars or languages— the language of "Mind" (Thinking) and the language of "Body" (Extension). The key to this remarkable conjecture is that the Infinite Logical Subject was the common unifying locus that could receive, accommodate, and incorporate these two alternative narratives and radically independent domains of Consciousness and Material Nature. In this radical move Spinoza seeks to solve the Mind/Body dualism in discerning objective reality—Infinite Substance—to be rich enough to unite radically diverse categorical domains or narrative forms.

The chronic split between two kinds of substance (located in the ultimate logical subject) is now removed in discerning the Infinite Unity of the sole true primal subject—Infinite Being. But the dual split shifts to two alternative grammars of Reality that apparently have no direct intimate cross-link or relations located in the Predicate or Attributes of this Reality. Ostensibly, this Primal Infinite Subject is deep enough to be a common "referent," a common ground, for boundless alternative narratives or fundamental dimensions. But this presumed "common ground" underlying radically diverse alter-narratives remains a mystery of first philosophy awaiting explanation or understanding. There remains a deep dualism between the two polar narratives.

A DEEP DUALISM OF TWO GRAMMARS OF REALITY

In making this move to "Ontological Monism," within the space of predication, now radically reconceived and renovated, Spinoza sought finally to resolve the chronic dualisms that haunted and plagued the traditions of first philosophy, and Descartes' first philosophy in particular. However, it must be noted that this ingenious "solution" (of Monism) to the ontological dualism in objective reality only lands Spinoza in another deep dualism—the dualism of alternate grammars, languages, or narratives of reality, for he insists that the two distinct languages of experience that we humans have access to—the grammar of Mind and the grammar of Matter—are perfectly adequate for expressing or representing the Reality of Infinite Substance.

The distinct Infinite Attributes or Dimensions of "Infinite Being" receive and accommodate multiple (nonrelated) alternative narratives. So we are still haunted by now another form of the deep dualism between the domains of Mind and Matter—now focused on these dual grammars or languages of Reality. This pattern appears to recur throughout history—the attempt to patch up and resolve one form of deep dualism seems to cause a "burst" or "rupture" at another site of first philosophy within the predicative space. If the dualism is not in objective reality (indicated by the logical subject) then it appears to rupture into a dualism in the discourse of reality (here indicated in the place of the predicate or fundamental attributes). And so our dialectical drama persists.

LEIBNIZ'S INTRIGUING FIRST PHILOSOPHY: MONADS

The continuing attention to finding the right method of conducting our rational powers in the conduct of our mind continues in the ingenious contributions of Leibniz. It is well known that he sought for a universal calculus of consciousness, a *charisterica universlis*, a universal grammar of concepts, that would clarify our rational discourse and provide an instrument or organon for first philosophy. And just as Hume sought to reach a deeper coherence in amending and revising the innovations of his predecessors, Leibniz likewise introduces some remarkable innovations in the grammar of first philosophy to resolve ongoing perceived inconsistencies or inadequacies in the first philosophies of Descartes and Spinoza. The apparent dualism at the heart of Descartes's narrative and the counterintuitive revisions proposed by the grammar of Spinoza spurred Leibniz onward to innovate a more coherent and natural first philosophy that did not go to these extremes. And, of course, he sought to solve the continuing deep dualism bequeathed by Spinoza in proposing two incommensurable and radically independent and unrelated languages of reality.

A PLURALISM OF INFINITE MONADS
(SPIRITUAL ATOMS)

The Monism of Spinoza—the suggestion that there is only one true Substance or Logical Subject, and that the "objects" of ordinary experience and language are actually "predicates" or modes of being predicated on this one Absolute Unified Substance, seemed to call out for a more intuitive narrative that squared with the common sense features of our daily experience. So Leibniz sought a creative way to hold onto vital advances of Spinoza while accounting for the radical plurality and multiplicity in objective reality. One key insight of Spinoza's, as we saw, is that the ontological idea of "substance" implies a self-caused independent being that has infinite potential. But while for Spinoza this idea implied a Monism leading to one Ultimate and Absolute Substance (Infinite Being), Leibniz introduced the radical idea of a boundless infinitude of such primal substances and suggested that they were "spiritual atoms": monads. We are of course more familiar with material "atoms" (dating back to the first philosophy of Democritus in ancient Greek ontology), but this idea of a "spiritual atom," each of which is a primary substance, existent in itself, seems tantamount to proposing a pluralism of infinite beings or substances. In this way Leibniz innovated a new spiritualized atomism as the language of first philosophy.

But in this radical innovation Leibniz was apparently touching certain features that were important in crossing into the grammar of GFP, to which we shall soon turn. He captured Spinoza's insight that a true "substance" must be self-caused and express the infinite within itself. And this is precisely the constitution of each "Monad"—each spiritual atom, being a primary substance, expresses all reality, infinitely, within its inner self-constituted space. But he did not hold back from another stunning finding, that such independently existing "atoms" could have no "relations" or "connections" with other substance-atoms. So he intuited that each monad expresses the entire universe within its inner space, so that there were "internal relations," but at the same time had no "windows" and had no discernible external relations with anything else beyond itself—they were self-contained windowless monads. In this he echoed, by analogy, similar findings of Hume, that the "atomic items" of sense perception had no connections or relations other than mere "association" or a loose, contingent juxtaposition with each other. So even across diverse philosophical grammars it appears that "atomic units" have problems having or sustaining real external relations or connectivity with other atomic units. I will pursue this issue later.

Needless to say, this bold and daring innovation of the monad may have solved certain aspects of the chronic dualism, only to introduce new mysteries and counterintuitive implications that defy our common sense intuitions. For example, Leibniz had to explain the apparent pluralism and materialism seen in the everyday world, in everyday experience and language, by suggesting that the diversity of appearance depends on the associations and clustering of the boundless (and bondless) monads. Clusters of monads that were smooth, subtle, and high energy appeared as mind and consciousness and soul, whereas the clusters that were more gross and hence low energy showed up as material things. So in this proposed resolution of the classical Mind/Matter dualism,

Leibniz in a clear sense privileged the side of Mind and Spirit in his monadic atoms and sought to explain material objects in terms of derivative features of the association of these monads. We have not yet touched upon the lurking question of the being and status of Divine Spirit—the unique "monad" of Infinite Being (God), and so on.

MONISM VERSUS PLURALISM: POLAR FIRST PHILOSOPHIES

Again, just as Spinoza had to fall back on certain "mystical" parallel coordinations between the two languages of reality, Leibniz likewise had to posit some kind of "preestablished" harmony and coordination between these radical monads that each expressed the universe internally but had no external connectivity. One may wonder whether there is a creative way to salvage the best insights of Spinoza's Monism as well as the important advances of Leibniz's radical Pluralism. The challenge of Monism is to give a credible account of the appearance and reality of multiplicity and diversity in the world. And the counterpart challenge of Pluralism is to give a viable account of the profound pull to Unity given in the presiding infinite domain of *What-Is-First*. In any case, we see the continuing dialectical drama of dualism and polarization in the narratives of first philosophy.

From the dawn of first philosophies we have seen the recurrent tensions within the space of predication between substance versus no substance, between the pull of the primary logical subject versus the pull of the primacy of the predicate, the tensions between the force of "is" versus the force of "isn't," between the primacy of Identity versus the primacy of Difference, the primacy of Mind versus the primacy of Matter, and the battle between the pull to Unity versus the pull to primal Plurality. Could it be that Primal Reality exhibits features of Spinoza's Monism as well as Leibniz's Pluralism—Unity-and-Plurality? Could it be true that in the structure of *What-Is-First* there is both primal Unity *and* primal Diversity? We will soon pick up this suggestion, but for now as we keep our focus on the unfolding drama, we find with Leibniz that the inner dialectic of the rationalist story has matured, and the stage is now set for unprecedented mediation and renovations in the radical revisions of Kant.

KANT'S REVOLUTIONARY TURN IN FIRST PHILOSOPHY

We have been anticipating our arrival at the Kantian moment in this drama, and hinting that there was a monumental turn in Kantian first philosophy.

Now that the dramatic stage has been set with the ripening of the inner dialectical development of both the Empiricist and the Rationalist strands, it is time to focus our ((global lens)) on Kant's innovations. Again, to keep with the larger megatrend that is unfolding, we shall stay with the bold strokes and not get into details at this point. In this larger picture it is important to remember now that these two great strands or streams involve very different worlds, worldviews, and philosophical grammars. This means, of course, that the terms used in the Empiricist narrative are not to be confused with the use of "similar terms" in the Rationalist philosophical ecology. For example, we have seen that the nature and power of "reason" are very different for the two languages or paradigms, and we must exercise great caution as we seek to jump from one domain to the other. So too with key terms such as *causality, sense experience*, and so on.

The fact that the two narrative traditions use key terms in systemically diverse or equivocal ways helps us see the enormous challenge that Kant faces in bringing them into rational discourse, mediation, possible synthesis, and radical revision. In his earlier career Kant was raised within the rationalist traditions, and he reports that his encounter with Hume's teaching jolted him and "awoke him from his dogmatic slumbers." He openly acknowledges that Hume's radical narrative shook his world and both stimulated and challenged him to answer Hume's skeptical doubts concerning the rationalist understanding of causality and other fundamental building blocks of experience. Hume's piercing critique shook Kant into realizing that the older rationalistic metaphysics, with its claim to have innate or *a priori* knowledge of reality independently of the contribution of sense experience, was now bankrupt, and was based on metaphysical dogma. At the same time he found that the results, arrived at by Hume in taking Empiricism to its natural outcome, show that this polar extreme was also problematic, if not bankrupt as well, and there were dogmas of Empiricism as well. Something had to give. We have noticed that when faced with fundamental dualism, the pressure of the Unified Field calls us to higher ground to resolve such polarizations.

KANT'S "COPERNICAN" REVOLUTION IN FIRST PHILOSOPHY

Kant was deeply saturated in both philosophical narratives and noticed that as different as they were, they shared a common deep assumption about the relative positions of the knower and the known—both assumed that the Knower stands on one side of the divide and the space of what is Known is independently given on the other. This fundamental dualism of Knower/Known has been presented earlier in the partitioned distance between the Thinking Subject outside of the predicative space, on the one hand, and the Object of thought or experience as rendered within the objectified space of predication, on the other. It was Kant's judgment that this deep dualism between Knower and Known was the shared presumption ("dogma") that led to the philosophical bankruptcy of both polar extremes. And he sought to find a higher critical synthesis to rework the mind scape of discourse, and in so doing to irrevocably shift the focus of primary attention from the dual dynamics within the predicative "box" to the locus of the constitution and creative role of the Thinking Subject or Knower outside of this predicative space, and its powerful role in shaping what appeared on the "screen of experience."

THE ROLE OF REASON AND THE SENSES IN EXPERIENCE: "SYNTHETIC *A PRIORI*"

A key innovation introduced by Kant that changes the discourse and grammar of first philosophy was his clarification of what was perhaps "unthinkable" in the polar narratives of Rationalism and Empiricism, namely, the presiding power of "synthetic *a priori* judgments." While the earlier rationalistic metaphysics presumed that Reason could know objective Reality in itself *a priori* through its pure concepts (innate ideas), this was now rejected as dogma by Locke and Hume in their empiricist critique. In this empiricist thinking "Reason" could not give us knowledge of the world, and in its predications or thoughts it could merely play with meaning relations between ideas, which originated from the data of the senses. So there was a fundamental dualism between two kinds of predications—those made through our rational powers (meaning relations between ideas: analytic predications) and those made through the information of our senses (synthetic predications).

THE DUALISM OF ANALYTIC VERSUS SYNTHETIC PREDICATIONS

In this grammar there was a dualism between *analytic versus synthetic predications* (and the judgments we make in affirming or denying such predications). Thus our mental life was divided between these two kinds of predications, and with this *a dualism between a priori judgments and a posteriori judgments*: all *a priori* predications (grounded in reason) were merely "analytic," expressing meaning relations between ideas and giving no new "factual" information about the world, while all *a posteriori* predications were synthesized through the intuitions of our senses—synthetic predications—and provided the only access to the contingent facts of the world. The ancient polar split then between Reason and Senses continued to play out in this fundamental dualism between analytic and synthetic predications. Any *a priori* predication could only be analytic, and any synthetic predication could only be *a posteriori*. The former had logical necessity, while the latter was merely contingent and lodged in probability. Each originated from different faculties, different domains of thought or consciousness.

Reason alone *a priori* (for the empiricist ideology) could yield only "analytic" predications, while all judgments and predications that reached out to touch the world through our Senses were synthetic and *a posteriori*. Therefore, in this empiricist worldview, the very idea of a "synthetic *a priori*" predication was in effect a "category mistake," inconceivable, unthinkable, and impredicable. And yet it was precisely here that Kant found the key to breaking out of the polar split between the polar extremes of both traditions. He alleged that to make sense of everyday experience there had to be "synthetic *a priori*" predications (judgments), and the breakthrough to his new philosophical narrative turned on showing and explaining how this hitherto "inconceivable" form of predication is not only possible but absolutely necessary to make sense of our discourse—a key to his transcendental first philosophy.

For example, Kant claims that the judgments of mathematics (arithmetic and geometry) are "synthetic *a priori*," not merely "analytic," as Hume thought. Also, laws of "causality" (cause-and-effect relations) that make "science" possible also were "synthetic *a priori*," not merely contingent "*a posteriori*" predications. So Kant had to open a higher mediating rational space that could lift up the key findings of both the Rationalist and Empiricist first philosophies and leave their dualistic incoherencies behind. He had to show how "synthetic *a priori*" predications/judgments were possible and give a new account of the ontological categories or building blocks of experience (such as Space, Time, Cause, and Substance). He suggested that they arose in the dynamic constitution of the "Thinker," which thus conditioned and structured whatever appeared upon the screen of predication—the place of all appearances. And here it is clear that Kant sought to mediate and bridge the polarized worldviews across the two great grammatical traditions of first philosophy.

THE KANTIAN CRITICAL TURN:
HOW THE THINKER SHAPES WHAT IS THOUGHT

To bridge the deep dualisms across and between these polarized worldviews of Rationalism and Empiricism, Kant made a bold and an unprecedented move. He suggested that the only way to explain how there could be "synthetic *a priori*" truths of experience was to break the old dualism between the Knower and the Known shared by both camps. In the scientific spirit of trying a revolutionary hypothesis, he proposed that what appeared in the space of predications was inherently dependent upon (and conditioned by) the constitution of the Thinker (Experiencer/Knower).

Kant, himself a scientist, suggested that we could learn an important lesson from the sciences and bring this to philosophy, for one of the great virtues of science is that when a model, paradigm, or conceptual framework is clearly not working, there comes a point where a shift in the paradigm to a new theoretical space, a new hypothesis, can bring stunning progress. A good example of this is the shift from the Ptolemaic model of the solar system, which placed the earth at the center, to the Copernican model, which placed the sun at the center. He argued that such a radical shift in the conceptual space of philosophy was now called for, given the apparent bankruptcy of both polar paradigms of first philosophy.

His radical (but also intuitive) suggestion was to now see the Object of experience appearing in the space of predication to be already filtered through and thus taking on the form and imprint of the Thinking Subject, who shapes the content of all experience—a "Copernican" revolution in philosophy. This opens up a new horizon in critical thinking, since it requires us to become self-conscious and critically aware of the lens of the mind and the makeup of the thinking subject, as this materially shapes our world and our experience: to "experience" is to "interpret"—the "hermeneutical turn" in philosophy. The interpretive lens of the "thinker" shapes all "content."

CONCEPTS WITHOUT PERCEPTS ARE EMPTY

This revolutionary revision, it appeared, made it possible for Kant to overcome the deep dualism between the Knower and Known and to now find a vital continuity and bridge between the two: what appears to us in our experience, since it is shaped by what we bring to the scene, makes it possible for us to imagine anew how we could find "synthetic *a priori*" truths (laws, dynamics, principles) in the content of our experience and the world as it appears. This new paradigm of the essential *a priori* link between the Knower and the Known, between the Thinker outside of the space of predication, and the Objects of experience as they appear within the predicative space, enabled Kant, it seemed, to solve other derivative dualism that haunted the tradition since the time of Plato, namely, the apparent alienation of Reason and the Senses (Mind and Body) in our experience and cognition.

PERCEPTS WITHOUT CONCEPTS ARE BLIND

The Rationalist tradition held that the pure concepts or ideas of Reason linked us to Reality independently of the Senses. The "ideas" or "percepts" we gained through our bodily senses only provided vague images that were not trustworthy in making contact with Reality. In contrast, as we have seen, the Empiricist grammar held that only the objects of sense experience genuinely made contact with the external world, and the "ideas" of Reason were copied from these (the originals), the concepts of Reason and the percepts of the Senses polarized and competed for primacy. But now with his revolutionary shift that makes the "synthetic *a priori*" a living reality Kant found an essential continuum, common ground, and mutuality between Concepts and Percepts. It now appears that both Reason and the Senses make an essential contribution in our link to the World—and Kant sums up this insight in a memorable formula: Concepts without Percepts are empty, and Percepts without Concepts are blind. So we find a "dialogic" mutuality between the two in making experience possible. Both Reason and the Senses make an essential contribution collaboratively to what appears to us on the screen of predication.

CLIPPING THE WINGS OF "KNOWLEDGE" TO MAKE ROOM FOR RATIONAL FAITH

In making his radical revision and proposed solution to the old deep dualism, Kant clearly sided with the Idealist move that makes the world of experience dependent in some essential way on the subjectivity of the Thinker. But he sees his philosophy as breaking with the earlier dogmatic forms and being a more advanced "critical idealism." In making these amazing and dramatic revisions in the space of first philosophy, Kant realized that a profound shift had taken place—that whatever shows up in the space of predication is never Reality itself (the "thing in itself") but only *things as they appear*. The object of experience is the object of appearance (phenomena), not direct Reality itself (noumena).

Kant's great contribution was to go beyond Hume in showing how we *can* have genuine knowledge (science) of what appears in experience, but at the same time making clear that such "knowledge" is of what appears, not of "reality in itself." So the ancient hope or expectation that we humans can know Reality in itself is now to be decisively given up. Kant also lays down a fundamental challenge for all future "metaphysicians" (first philosophers) who would allege to know Reality as it is to answer his critical challenge. In making this radical move Kant says in a poignant remark that he had to "clip the wings of knowledge to make room for faith." Thus the Rationalist dream or dogmatic pretension of having direct access to Reality as it is in itself, he thought, is forever dissolved, since knowledge applies only to things as they appear to us on the predicative screen of experience.

A NEW DEEP DUALISM IN KANT'S FIRST PHILOSOPHY: NOUMENA VERSUS PHENOMENA

In assessing the major contributions of Kant to the rational enterprise and the project of first philosophy it is important to note that in apparently "solving" some of the chronic deep dualisms in rationality Kant appears to follow the megatrend of seeming to solve one area of polarization only to fall into another deep dualism. In clipping the wings of knowledge to make room for Rational Faith, Kant draws a fundamental line between things as they appear (in the space of predication)—"phenomena," and things as they are in themselves, "noumena."

His stricture is that we humans have no cognitive access to noumena— our predicative (conceptual, linguistic) powers are inherently restricted to phenomena, and we have no such direct access to noumena. In this he seems to be in company with many mystical traditions that allege that the highest Reality or Truth is beyond words, language, and speech and must be countenanced in deep silence. But this is particularly troubling in Kant's case, since he wisely sees that there is and must be a "Self" beyond the predicative box—our noumenal self—that is the moral agent who alone has true autonomy, freedom, and dignity.

THE PHENOMENAL SELF VERSUS THE MORAL (NOUMENAL) SELF: ANOTHER DEEP DUALISM

This is where "Rational Faith" enters. Kant saw that the "self" that appears in the space of predication, like all objects of experience, falls under the causal laws of nature, hence is not the Free Agent that is autonomous and exercises moral choice and decision making. So in his subsequent critical writings, in which he clarifies the philosophical foundations (first philosophy) of Moral Consciousness, he finds that this primal ambiguity in the life of the "self," the phenomenal self that appears and the noumenal self that is in itself but does not appear, saves the possibility of our moral life. This is the frontier of "Rational Faith," which is the ground of our moral life.

We cannot "know" this Moral Self, but we do have direct access to this Noumenal Self in being the Moral Agent exercising volition or will, and this is the dimension of Rational Faith, beyond "knowledge." In clarifying this

Noumenal Moral Agent and its domain of "Ought"—the Categorical Imperative—we find lurking another deep dualism—between the dimension of Ought (Value) and the dimension of "Is" (Fact) disclosed in the space of objectified predication. Of course certain troubling paradoxes lurked here, for example, in the causal interactions and intentional relations between the Will of the Moral Agent and the facts of embodied phenomenal life and causation in the realm of action. When we exercise such "Free Will," we move our bodies in the causal realm, in the phenomenal world. How is this possible?

This Noumenal Self, the "self" outside the space of predication, and beyond egomental language, concepts, and knowledge, is found to be the source of our deep worth and ultimate respect, never to be treated as an "object" but as a Person, as a free, autonomous, Moral Agent, as an end-in-itself. Kant was brilliant in discerning this true Moral/Rational Agent, whose Will . . . Goodwill, is of supreme worth. Of course we are familiar with this "I am" that is "pre-predicative," not an object within the space of predication. We suggested earlier that all of the intense focus on "Eastern" meditative traditions of first philosophy recognized this "pre-predicative" "I am" as the true Self, and as the key to becoming mature, integral, rational (moral) beings, becoming fully human, becoming free. We shall soon see that the missing grammar of *What-Is-First*—the grammar of Logos—will make accessible and give words and primal speech power to this "noumenal" Self, the awakened, integral language already tapped and spoken by our great integral teachers who spoke the grammar of Logos.

We hinted earlier that Descartes, in his meditations on first philosophy, also touched this "I am" when he broke free from his egomental voice. What is most interesting in our journey into GFP thus far is noticing this continuing struggle to overcome the dualizing effects of the egomental predicative space, and the rise into a more holistic and unifying dimension or rational awakening beyond the objects of predication, which for Kant is the space of "appearance." In shifting primary attention to the "Self" outside of the predicative space, Kant clearly enters a dimension and horizon that has been of keen interest to the enterprise of GFP. So a guiding question for us after Kant is: Is there an expanded integral rational space and lens of awakened consciousness wherein true Reality may ((appear)) and be disclosed?

AFTER KANT: THE STRUGGLE WITH
EGOMENTAL RATIONAL SPACE CONTINUES

We have taken some time tracing certain major developments from Descartes to Kant to get a more textured sense of the continuing struggle with the dualizing forces of egomental reason and the gallant attempts to move discourse beyond the enclosed, restrictive, and inherently fragmenting predicative space. But now let us fast-forward our global lens, intensifying the pace of our scan of major developments after Kant as we prepare the way for crossing into the dimension of Global Reason and GFP. The great innovative thinkers we shall now briefly mention all perform remarkable experiments that contribute to crossing into the space of Global Reason.

There were such amazing continuing developments after Kant—the stunning innovations of Hegel, as he sought to renovate the space of discourse after the great Kantian experiment and challenge; an ingenious attempt by Hegel to make the space of predication work with a bold new dialectical logic and a first philosophy of Absolute Geist (Infinite Spirit), unfolding in the process of history in an evolutionary drama (Dialectical Idealism); but then we see the megatrend continue in the polar narrative of Marx (Dialectical Materialism), where Marx "stands Hegel on his head" and suggests that the material forces of our human condition are the primary ones in determining our historical dialectic and destiny; and we are aware, of course, of the vast political and social revolutionary implications of the rise of "Communism," as Marx's ideology became a blueprint for a cultural revolution in the twentieth century.

We see an increasing great shift and preoccupation with the nature and constitution of the Thinking Subject outside the screen of predication. We find Nietzsche exposing the subjectivism of egomental "reason" and opening our eyes to "perspective," the eyes of the beholder, the importance of will and power in our discourse and worldviews, to a new consciousness of perspectivism and perspectivity in the "rational" enterprise and quest for truth and authentic moral agency; and in his scathing critique of Christian culture and the "slave mind" or "herd mentality," he dares to speak the unutterable words "God is dead," suggesting that the "God" of egomental mind and of cultic life is not truly God (*What-Is-First*).

We encounter a new frontier opening simultaneously with the pioneering work of Husserl and Frege—each dramatically renovated the space of discourse and the continuing quest for the fundamental grammar of thought and consciousness; we see Husserl pick up the "Cartesian Meditations" and open a new lens of consciousness as the "I am" breaks free from the prejudices of the egomental lens and becomes a deeper "meditative" witness to what appears in the space of predication; we find a bold new adventure into "transcendental logic" as the new discipline of "Phenomenology" opens and new first narratives of "Existentialism" come forth in the innovative work of Sartre and Heidegger, eminent protégés of Husserl.

We see Heidegger focus primary attention on the "Thinking Subject," calling for a deeper analytic of "Dasein" and dramatically reversing the spotlight of first philosophy from what appears in the predicative "box" to this pre-predicative "being there" of this Thinker/Experiencer; we hear from Heidegger a scathing critique of the classical and evolving European tradition of first philosophy going back to Plato that placed "Sein," "Being," in the objectified box as (ontologically) being our first concern and first in every sense, prior to the "being there" of Dasein, outside of this apparently benighted space; and with his "Copernican revolution" in first philosophy, placing the narrative of Dasein as coming before and shaping the space of "Sein," we open the space for Existentialism to place "existence" before "being" or "essence," as another deep dualism becomes articulated.

We see, further, with the rise of Phenomenology/Existentialism in the pioneering work of Sartre, Camus, and others, that this pre-predicative "I am," stripped of names, forms, essence, and predications, is a primal "Nothing," a mere "open variable" (an "X," a "nothing," rather than a "something"), having to make a primal existential choice in the exercise of radical freedom in shaping its "life," its "existence," its "identity," its "being," and naming its "essence" in an ultimate self-creative act in coming to authentic Existence—a new chapter in first philosophy; in his picking up the turn of phrase "If God is dead, anything goes," this marks another wiping clean the slate of the predicative space, reversing the prejudices of first narratives that dogmatically privileged "Being," stripping it of any pre-fixed "essence" and "essential predications" to open a new horizon of "Nothingness" as being a primary concern for first philosophy.

At the same time, as Frege seeks to realize the great dream of a "universal grammar" in the perennial quest for tapping the grammar or logistic of thought, we see that he also wipes clean the slate of predicative space, and he radically renovates it in his historic *Bregriffschrift* (1879)("Concept-Script") with a new grammar of predication that builds upon the hypothesis of "atomic propositions" as the units of thought; in his rejection of the "Aristotelian" paradigm of predication, which shaped the European philosophical and cultural imagination and traditions of first philosophy through the ages, he boldly initiates and inaugurates what would ignite and unfold as the Anglo-American Analytic tradition.

So as Russell discovers Frege's results and makes them accessible to the English-speaking world, his protégé, Wittgenstein, accelerates this new twentieth-century revolution with his *Tractatus*, which rewrites the script of first philosophy; and as this amazing revolution unfolds throughout the twentieth century, we find new polarized lines drawn, and the "Continental" tradition initiated by Husserl appears not to be in mutual, rational dialogue with this emergent "Anglo-American Analytic" school; we find, for example, Frege challenging Husserl for seeking to ground logic within the apparently "subjective" or "psychological" reality of the Thinker, and in seeking unprecedented "rigor" in the logistic of predication to refocus primary attention to the predicative content within the ratio-logical space of predication and propositional think-ing; and the fault lines of chronic polarizations continue to haunt the discourse of philosophy throughout the past century; we now see a polarizing of the pull to the locus and constitution of the Thinker versus the pull to the propositional content presented in the predicative space—a powerful focus on the Object or Content of Thought.

As we step back farther and dilate our ((global lens)) a bit to see the ongoing, chronic megaswings over the centuries from Aristotle to Frege and beyond, we can see more readily how these competing logistics of rational consciousness spawn polarizations and play into chronic deep dualisms: for as Russell clarifies the philosophical logic introduced by Frege, we begin to see that the primary logical subject becomes a mere "this" a purely referential "X" devoid of any predicative or conceptual content; since Frege's model of pred-ication, analogous to the language of mathematics, enforces a strict split or dualism between the "predicate" (which presents the "concept") and the logi-cal subject (which, unlike Aristotle's primary *ousia* presents a variable "x," which plays a role in the formation of a proposition); as all of this plays out, we see another polarization emerge between the primary logical subject, which Russell calls a referential "this" (devoid of Concept information), which becomes the primary logically proper name; so we find across these two great paradigms of logic a polarity between the nature of the primary logical sub-ject, which of course is of special interest for first philosophy; in one paradigm the primary subject of predication is an "S," a thing with inherent essence and conceptual/catgorial content, while in the other model the ultimate primary logical subject is an "X," a "this" ostensively presented in a pure referential act devoid of conceptual or predicative content. In Frege's mode of "predication" there is a deep dualism between the logical subject and the "predicate"—between "concept" and "object."

We also begin to see as this drama unfolds that Aristotle's logic, as expanded and renovated by Sommers in the latter part of the twentieth cen-tury, develops a powerful logic or calculus for the classical space of predica-tion, which now presents a viable alternative to the Frege and post-Frege logistic of the Analytic Movement. Through Sommers we see that while Aris-totle's logical paradigm is sensitive to the formation of sense in forming pred-ications, the Frege instrument is more designed for the logic of reference and the truth condition (rather than sense conditions) in the formation of predi-cations or primary propositions; so in the deepest philosophical grammars of thought, we find a polar split in the instrument (organon) of first philosophy, one focusing on categories and sense formation, the other focusing on refer-ence and truth-conditions as primary for the analysis of meaning and lan-guage; the former takes "terms" to be the primary units of thought in the space of predication, while the latter takes "atomic propositions" as the primary units of thought and meaning, and these two great paradigms seem to repel one another in a deep dualism.

Through our expanded ((global lens)) we can even see patterns connecting through the centuries and across divided traditions that appear to echo one another—we see the deep polarity concerning the primary logical subject—Aristotle and Sommers suggesting that it is an "S" (something with inherent essence or character), while Russell and Quine see the primary logical subject to be an "X" that is attained through pure "reference" devoid of "sense," reminiscent of Sartre's radical subject that is a mere "X," a Nothing, stripped of essence or inner characteristics; of course this reminds us of the primary subject of the meditative mind that finds in the "I am" a radical "This" that is pre-predicative and devoid of any egomental predicative marks, names, or predicates, and so on. Our global lens also helps us see other recurring megapatterns in the larger picture. One interesting pattern is to notice how even within the career and life span of a "single" thinker, she or he can swing in a polar shift from one orientation to its polar counterpart; Wiggenstein and Heidegger are good examples of this. In his early career, Wittgenstein (in his *Tractatus* phase) was under the influence of Frege and an ideology that there could be one fundamental and essential pure logic or grammar of thought that could capture the logic of language and rational consciousness; this was the pull and presumption of a foundational and unifying logic or grammar that captured the essence of language; and in his early work he thought he had captured this fundamental logic, which he sought to present in strict mathematical and aphoristic fashion, believing that the essence of language and meaning was to picture the facts clearly; language, he thought, was an instrument designed to present facts, and he apparently believed that the logic introduced by Frege finally captured the Ideal Grammar of Language and Thought once and for all, and this was the ideal instrument of philosophical analysis; what could not be expressed in this logic was therefore literally and cognitively meaningless, as, for example, utterances of Ethics, Ontology, Theology, or first philosophy. As he concluded this powerful work, he announced, "Whereof one cannot speak, thereof one must be Silent," and he exited the scene of philosophy. But, interestingly, some years later he returned to a new and transformed scene and apparently realized that his youthful enthusiasm may have been somewhat misplaced, and in a more mature voice he took a polar swing from the earlier ideology of Unity, Essence, Foundation, and Ideal Language, over to the polar ideology of Difference, Plurality, Non-Essence, Non-Foundation, and Non-Ideal and a new sense of the multiplicity of logics and functions of natural language; the earlier ideology carried with it its attitude that everyday language is inherently flawed (inappropriate as an instrument of philosophy and clear thinking) and took on the project of reforming and revising language into its idealized pure form), whereas the later paradigm recognized boundless alternative functions of language (describing, prescribing, emotive, performative, etc., with diverse "language-games") and brought forth a new appreciation for the perfection of ordinary language and as being in perfect order just as it is. In both phases of his career he was instrumental in initiating a revolutionary movement in the discourse of philosophy; so in this "single" life we see an exemplar of a polar swing from Unity to Diversity, Identity to Difference, Essence to Non-Essence and Plurality, Foundations to Non-Foundations—a pattern that we noticed early in the game from the polarity between Parmenides (Unity) and Heraclitus (Difference); indeed, we shall soon notice that while Wittgenstein's earlier career was in the spirit and signature of what is now called "Modernism," his later work not only flowed in the spirit of "Postmodernism" but helped ignite and launch this moment in the continuing dialectic; needless to say, the polar swing from one extreme to the other does not complete the dialectical maturation of the movement to Global Reason. Instead we shall soon see that the continuing influence and pressure of the pull to Global Reason call for a deeper dialectical turn to a more holistic, integral, rational space that can accommodate both Unity and Diversity, both Identity and Difference, and this is clearly what is being called for in the twenty-first century.

Analogously, our ((global lens)), now focused on the early and later career of Heidegger, notices another interesting polar swing that is of interest to our global narrative, for while in his earlier career Heidegger succeeded in building on Kant's revolutionary shift of focus from the information within the predicative box to the presence of the Thinker outside this space, we now see that even this important step in critical consciousness remained under the influence of egomental discourse, since the insights and advances gleaned outside of the predicative space were being rendered and articulated within the predicative linguistic and conceptual space and unwittingly being deformed or undermined by its objectifying, dualizing, and fragmenting dynamics. So although Heidegger made the revolutionary move for first philosophy by alleging that the constitution of the Thinker—the subjective presence of Dasein—is the first order of business for first philosophy, his brilliant analytic of this existential Self was (as with Descartes, Kant, and others) processed within the predicative space and under its sway.

No wonder Heidegger abandoned his earlier project and, as with Wittgenstein, took a very different course in his later career as he moved more radically "On the Way to Language" now more in tune with the holistic and integral dynamics of the sacred space of *What-Is-First*; Heidegger went through what we would call a radical rational "inversion" or recentering into the meditative space of the "I am," which Descartes touched upon and opened but apparently could not sustain. So this later career of Heidegger not only shifts to the Dasein position outside of the egomental space, but he apparently took a deeper plunge into the open and boundless space of Primal Language, which he now speaks of as the "house of Being"; he speaks in new and "strange" inverted ways, for example, this "I am" finds herself or himself in a Space, a Region, a dimension in which the space acts upon her or him—"that which regions," and so on.

He also speaks now from a deeper "Dasein," more like the meditative "I am" in which all of the earlier metaphors and tropes shift to a deep dialogic and participatory phenomenology, wherein the thinking subject arises within and experiences a deep interconnectivity to Self and the surrounding Ecology, now liberated from the artificial containment of the predicative containers. Here we begin to get a new paradigm of Truth (as unconcealment and disclosure, *gelassenheit*) and our mindful encounter with the Other, whether Object of knowledge or of aesthetic appreciation, enters an open epistemic dimension where we stand open before whatever is presented to allow a primal and more authentic encounter. It is in this spirit that he makes his passionate and heart-felt plea in his famous "Inaugural Address" (his *Discourse on Thinking*) in the maturity of his career—that we are "Meditative Beings" as he warns that this truth is of highest importance in facing our human condition, since it is the ultimate concern of who we truly are and threatened by the inherent forgetfulness of everyday uncritical (objectifying) thinking; so here again we find within one first philosopher's journey a swing and maturation that opens the way to a deeper space of GFP as the relentless pull of *What-Is-First* moves the evolution of our discourse. We also might note in this "fast-forward" power scan of developments that certain key philosophers also were opening the way in alternative narratives; we are obviously skipping over many great innovative thinkers whose teachings reveal this larger pattern of the struggle to overcome the dualizing dynamics of egomental mind and who seek to open the pathways into the Integral Dynamics of Primal Discourse. For example, Martin Buber, Levinas, and Derrida might be naturally picked up on our radar screen as making key dialectical moves, but we are keenly mindful of the vital contributions of certain feminist thinkers in the latter part of the twentieth century, along with thinkers in the area of "non-Western" critique who open new understandings of African thought and worldviews that enrich and deepen our move into an expanded space of first philosophy.

With this in mind (of our vast omissions in this compressed scan), let us conclude this first round by noticing that Buber (in his *I and Thou*) is another key experimental moment as he seeks to make a fundamental distinction between two kinds of consciousness and ways of being—the "It-It" way and the "I Thou" mode of deep meeting and dialogic encounter. It is not hard to see that Buber recognizes that the objectifying space of egomental mind treats self and other as objects—"It," whereas our humane encounter of the Other as Person, as Presence, calls for a very different mode of relating, of meeting, and we suggest that he is here seeking the open humane space of Kant's Noumenal Self and Other, of Heidegger's meditative encounter with the "Other" and the primal space of deep interconnectivity that we have only begun to touch upon as the primal space of the "I am"; but, alas, Buber presents his findings in the same narrative space and dynamics of our shared predicative life, and we still await the explicit opening and crossing into the Integral and Deep-Dialogic Dimension of *What-is-First*.

Still in another related primal narrative, Levinas may be seen as helping to clarify the primacy of the Other (in his *Totality and Infinity*), where it is seen that the "Other" transcends the One, and this Presence of the Other becomes a fundamental factor in self-understanding. But we may close this initial scan by shifting to Derrida, whose life and work push the unfolding dialectic to a ripened form in arguing for the primacy of Difference and Alterity, and the full momentum of contemporary "postmodern" thinking comes into prominence in the latter part of the twentieth century; here we see a radical critique of the egomental tendency to privilege the One, the Self, Identity, Unity, and the full range of fundamental concepts aligned with such Unity and Identity. Instead we get a polar shift to privileging Difference, the Other, Alterity, and Multiplicity, and with this a radical practice of "deconstruction" of all of the "constructs" of egomental identity. We notice here that such radical deconstruction was already recognized by Nagarjuna centuries ago when he developed his radical dialectical critique of the egomental space of Identity versus Difference, "Is" versus "Isn't," and so on. Still, in Derrida's innovative work, as he develops his "Grammatology" he argues that there is a primal form of "Writing," a primordial dimension of Language in which "Difference" and "Alterity" and "Multiplicity are primary, rather than Unity and The Same"; for him this mark of primal "Difference" is the signature of "Writing," not in the ordinary sense in which there has been a polar war proceeding over centuries as to whether the "Oral" or the "Written" is primary, but a more primal space, perhaps reminiscent of the later Heidegger's place of "Language as the house of Being"; what is noteworthy here, and becomes vital for the dimensional shift to GFP is that this Primal Space of Language as Writing honors radical "Difference" as primary, not derivative. This reverses the dominant orientation that presumes that Unity is original, and that difference and multiplicity are derivative and come out of such "Unity," favoring the oral tradition of the Word over the Written, since, presumably, the former is taken as being closer to and stemming from consciousness. From this orientation of privileging Unity and the Oral tradition over Difference and the Written, it appears to be counterintuitive to reverse this order and claim that "Writing" is primary. Yet this is precisely what Derrida suggests, and we shall soon see that this is, indeed, a fundamental feature of the Space of the Primal Word. But in crossing into the Integral dimension of the Primary Word we no longer have to choose between Unity and Difference; rather, the space of the Infinite Word is powerful enough to honor both Unity-and-Difference as both Primal and cogiven together. But while we might see Hegel as a representative of the Modernist voice that gravitates to Absolute Unity (of Geist), Derrida may be seen as a polar Voice of privileging radical Difference as the presiding character of *What-Is-First*, reminiscent of the dialectics of Heraclitus or perhaps certain Buddhist deconstructive narratives after Nagarjuna. But we will pick these points up later.

Concluding Summary Reflection: Transition to Part 2
Reality Shifting Lessons from Our Journey
through the Evolution of Consciousness

This global scan of quite diverse traditions of First Philosophy through the ages has covered much ground, and it is timely to pause a moment to reflect on certain foremost themes that have emerged thus far. Through our ((global lens)) we have been able to discern striking recurrent patterns and megatrends across our diverse traditions in the perennial quest to encounter *What-Is-First*. As we open the way experimentally into the expanded space of GFP it has become clearer that *What-Is-First* must be an Infinite Presence that is the primal and presiding Force Field of the Universe. This Infinite Force is cosmic (and, of course, global) and thus situates and contextualizes all possible worlds, all possible forms of language, and all worldviews, narratives, perspectives, religions, cultures, disciplines, and forms of life.

The implications of this simple global truth are astounding, and we shall bring these more into the open as we enter Part 2. But in making this transition it is important to focus for a moment on perhaps the most striking disclosure in the foregoing exploration. Reviewing our diverse traditions through our global lens and its emergent global perspective, it is now more evident that this Infinite Presence exerts its ever-present influence on every possible aspect of existence, life, and experience. This is the presiding moving force in all moments, in all situations. And diverse traditions have responded to this Infinite Force in boundlessly diverse ways—the very quest for The First, the quest for Primary Being, the perennial quest for Unity and the Ultimate Origin of the Universe, the First Cause, the quest for Ultimate Knowledge and the foundation of Truth, the quest for coherence and the overcoming of polarizations, fragmentation and chronic dualisms, the quest for the primal logic of consciousness and the grammar of thought, the quest for the primal Word or Language, the quest for Meaning, Truth, Goodness, and Beauty, the quest for Primal Wisdom, for Radical Faith, the quest for Wholeness, Well-being and Happiness—the list goes on. At core, these are alter-versions of the same Primal, Holistic Quest that pulsates in every cell, atom, in every person, every life-form.

We shall soon see, if it is not already obvious, that our collective failure to activate our global lens, to awaken our global mind, and to rise into a truly global perspective has been a primary reason for the continued suppression or eclipse of GFP and the global encounter with Infinite Presence. The absence of a truly Holistic and Integral logistic or technology of consciousness allowed, by default, the continued apparent predominance of more localized, scattered first narratives, each of which purports to have universal scope and jurisdiction. In the rich strains of European lineages from Heraclitus through Derrida, as we have seen, the narratives are so diverse and multifarious that the glaring megapatterns and recurrent dynamics more evident via the global lens had not and did not yet come sufficiently into prominence or preeminence.

Yet we have seen as we scanned the amazing evolution of first narratives in the European traditions that the ineluctable call of *The Infinite First* and the diverse responses, as in the quest to reach Primary Being, struggled over centuries with the boundaries and limitations of the objectified space of predication—the barriers and boundaries of egomental mind and discourse. Our deep quest to realize our Primary Being, to express our true individuality and existential freedom, kept hitting the artificial walls and polarizing dynamics of the objectified space of egomental "reason." We witnessed the ingenious attempts to open higher space to encounter our authentic Self, Primary Being, True Reality, Meaning, and Truth—outside of the box of objectified thought and experience.

The diverse, competing first narratives each made compelling cases and spoke in more localized and idiosyncratic dialectics, even as they each sought to be a universal grammar, and this made it most difficult to connect the dots across their borders, to discern common ground, megapatterns, or common global insights into *What Is Primal*. Indeed, the mood and temperament of more recent "postmodern" narratives clearly favored the prioritizing of multiplicity and "difference" over oneness or "unity." Earlier "modernist" attempts from Descartes through Hegel and beyond, which sought deeper foundations or megapatterns in the evolution of consciousness and cultures, are dismissed as misguided and unfounded "grand" or "totalizing" narratives that we have, according to this perspective, gratefully outgrown. According to this orientation, we humans are invariably lodged in localized perspectives, in particularized historical situations, with specified local identities of all sorts, and in the ever-recurring polar war between Unity and Diversity the postmodern vote goes to Diversity with a decisive thumbs down to "Unity."

In the wide range of rich and diverse Eastern meditative traditions, we also find competing alter-narratives that likewise universalized from their own more local dialects and ontological mind fonts. Here too, for example, the ultimate insights into Infinite Brahman were not in any obvious way connected in common cause to the depth insights of the Buddhist middle-way path into Absolute Emptiness or Sunyata. Indeed, they saw themselves at odds, in competition, and presented their self-narration in this mood. So diverse were these powerful first narratives that even here the fundamental logistic or global grammar of Primal Logos remained eclipsed by more localizing forces. For these widely ranging meditative lifeworlds, strategies, and dialects, it was not clear whether there was a Primal Global Grammar of Meditative Reason, a deep Logic of Global Logos. Each assumed and presumed that it was the universal grammar of *The First*. It was even less obvious whether the widely variant first narratives of East, West, and diverse Indigenous traditions were alter-narratives of Global Logos, that they inherently shared any common concerns, common ground, or offered any common global insights into *What-Is-First*, into Infinite Presence.

Nevertheless, in the foregoing scan of developments over the ages through the global lens and across all borders, we have noticed certain striking recurring patterns, megatrends, and deep dynamics in the irrepressible quest for and call of Infinite Presence. Diverse meditative traditions converged on the depth insight that egocentric mind, with its artificial patterns of minding, is a primary source of existential disorders, fragmentations, chronic dualisms, and polarizations. And the predominant weight of these diverse meditative technologies suggests that the key to human flourishing essentially turns upon finding ways to overcome the pernicious fragmentation inherent in egomental life and to rise into a more awakened nondual technology of consciousness that brings us into a more authentic encounter with Infinite Presence, by whatever name it is called. In fact, the common deep structure of what we are now calling "egomental reason" was not fully discerned and brought forth in its full global disclosure.

Diverse brilliant and ingenious disclosures of "egocetric life" were brought to light, as we have seen, but they were not creatively connected to bring out the generic global form of this technology of mind. Nor was it made sufficiently clear how and why "egomental minding" is a primary generative source of chronic dualisms, addictive polarizations, pernicious fragmentations, and abysmal existential suffering. Even more importantly, the deep global grammar of Logos remained eclipsed, and it was not clearly seen whether the diverse nondual meditative strategies for overcoming egomental life arose from this global grammar and were alter co-expressions of the hologistic and integral forces of Infinite Presence. Rather, these two great alternative technologies of consciousness remained ambiguously and chaotically entangled, confused and superimposed upon each other in the sprawling and still inadequately uncharted ecology of everyday language. In the absence of the global lens and the dilation of our global mind, the generic nature of these two contrasting, though intimately related, technologies of consciousness and dimensions of language remained unarticulated, and the higher dimensional rational space of GFP remained dormant.

As we enter into Part 2 let us experimentally cross together into this long-sought-for passage into the hologistic space of Infinite Presence as we now move deeper into the expanded rational space of GFP and tap the amazing logistic power of the hitherto missing global grammar of Logos. We shall soon see that this unprecedented clarification of the two contrasting technologies of consciousness, and our deeper global access into the higher rational dimension of Infinite Presence, is a long, emerging, evolutionary step in the drama of our human emergence. Indeed, with the depth insights of GFP we shall see that our cultural sustainability and human flourishing now turn upon our becoming clear on the stark contrast yet intimate relation between these two technologies of mind and life. It becomes clear that the maturation of our human species essentially turns on our individual and collective crossing from the adolescent and dysfunctional patterns of egomental mind into the holistic integrity of the awakened global mind and the global grammar of Logos.

PART 2

Explorations in Global First Philosophy

INTRODUCTION: ENTERING THE
SPACE OF GLOBAL FIRST PHILOSOPHY

Perhaps one of the greatest lessons from our journey through the evolution of consciousness on a global scale is that entering the space of *What-Is-First* calls for a more potent technology of mind than our everyday patterns of processing life and a radical dimensional shift in how we conduct our consciousness. One simple yet overpowering global truth distilled from millennia of cultural experiments in the encounter with this Primal Force is that this First must be boundlessly Infinite in every possible way, and thus the original and originating source of all that is, of all that appears, in every possible dimension.

Global First Philosophy (GFP) is the missing *First Discipline* that rigorously thinks through and articulates the radical implications of this Primal Truth. One of the astounding lessons culled from centuries of philosophical experiments seen through our global lens is that "egomental" patterns of minding eclipse, distort, and deform any authentic encounter with this Primal Source of all existence, life, meaning, discourse, and truth. These earlier experiments toward First Philosophy teach us that the authentic encounter with our Primal Source is the highest priority for the human enterprise, and that a higher dimension of consciousness and language is called for in this all-important grounding.

DIMENSIONAL CROSSING INTO
INFINITE PRESENCE: GLOBAL LOGOS

These findings flow immediately from the truth that the Primal First is Infinite and hence Omnipresent. No truly "Global Name" has yet emerged for this First, and over the years I have found it helpful to use the Greek term *Logos* as a desirable candidate for this role. We shall soon see as we introduce a special notation for the higher dimensional discourse of Global Logos that this Primal Infinite Word needs to be explicitly marked to remind us that it can only be named, thought, or spoken in this highest dimension of consciousness and language. To appreciate this fundamental point, let us cross into this hologistic dimension for a moment for a preliminary encounter with Logos.

Certain recurring global axioms, which are self-evident to awakened global reason, immediately issue forth: Logos is Infinitely First in every respect, and it is Infinitely One, thus Infinitely Unifying. But this higher dimension, Unity, is saturated with Infinite Multiplicity, Alterity, and Diversity, so Unity and Multiplicity are both coprimal; Primal Logos is the Infinite Force that funds and generates all possible realities, all possible worlds, languages, perspectives, narratives, cultures, worldviews, disciplines, dimensions of experience, and forms of life. As such, everything in the Universe both arises out of this Infinite Force Field, and expresses it, gravitates to it, and is profoundly interconnected to its boundless dynamic web of relations. No item, no relation, is possible apart from this Primal Infinition Force.

As such, Logos is cosmic/global—the origin of all first narratives, cultures, religions, philosophies, disciplines; no item in the universe can stand on its own apart from this Logos, or apart from the infinite network of holistic relations permeating the cosmic field. No item or event is possible without it; no name, word, or form can be apart from this Infinite Word; no relation could emerge or be without its infinite relational power, so all possible relations, all possible logics, all possible thoughts, predications, or propositions inherently arise in its ever-present context; Logos, and its Infinite Force Field—the Logosphere—is the cosmic/global context that situates all possible appearances; in this light, Logos as the Infinite Force is the most potent force of the Universe that is ever-present and operative in all moments and in all events, presiding in all processes, hence the telic force of evolution in all of its forms.

In this synoptic preview of the Primal Logosphere, it becomes immediately evident that each fundamental name, concept, term, or field arises within this Infinite Word, which in its Infinite Unitivity forms a boundless and seamless Continuum of Interconnectivity—this is the Primal Field of Language—The Infinite Word—but in this Hologistic Dimension all primal concepts, categories, names, and forms coarise in its Primal Continuum: Word, Being, Mind, World, Substance, Matter, Space, Time, Cause, Relation, Event, Consciousness, Sign, Object. Each of these primal terms mutually permeates and constitutes the other; this Primal Word permeates and surrounds all possible appearances—Primal Mind, Consciousness, Cosmos, Nature, Energy, Matter. The Primal Word is Primal Consciousness, MindWord . . . Primal SpaceTime, Primal Matter, MindMatter, Primary Being, Tao, Aum, Allah, Yahweh, Brahman, Sunyata, Chi . . . so in this Hologistic Field, Mind-Word-World are originally inseparable and mutually coarise in one another, and so too throughout the Cosmic Continuum.

This Primal Infinite Word-Mind-Being-Event Continuum is unimaginable, unthinkable, inaccessible, unapproachable, inexpressible . . . via the finitized, artificially objectified, atomized, and compartmentalized forms of everyday language and thought forms that are severed from this Primal Continuum of the Logosphere. In this respect, the fundamental grammar of the Logosphere is of a different dimension of mind, word, and discourse from the artificial and culturally constructed grammars of the egomental mind, discourse, and worlds. Nevertheless, egomental "reason," worldviews, narratives, logics, and identities could not come into being or appear to persist and exist apart from the ever-Present and ever-Presiding Logosphere that funds it, sustains it, and makes its appearance possible. So although egomental lifeworlds and grammars may mistakenly take themselves to be self-constituted, radically independent, and self-sustaining, within their own terms, they are always nevertheless constituted in and through the boundless funding, resources, and endowment of this ever Present and Presiding Logosphere. No "egomind" has the power or capacity to stand outside and beyond the Infinite Presence of the Logosphere.

A PRIMORDIAL CONFUSION AND CHAOTIC AMBIGUITY ACROSS THESE DIMENSIONS

Nevertheless, despite the profound asymmetry and dimensional alterity between the Primal Grammar of the Logosphere and the artificial grammars of egomental cultures, worldviews, religions, logics, and disciplines, the failure of earlier emergent First Philosophies to clearly discern, clarify, name, articulate, and bring into explicit prominence the dimensional difference between them allowed by default an ongoing primal confusion, a sprawling chaotic ambiguity between these alter-dimensions. We have seen in our fast-forward journey through the genealogy of first philosophies the deep and ongoing struggle to disambiguate, disentangle, and reach lucid clarity in marking and discerning the contrasting dimensions and understanding their intimate relations. And we have seen how this failure to diagnose, name, and bring this dimensional difference in forms of discourse into explicit notational and symbolic clarity has contributed to continuing existential disorders, chronic dysfunction, and suffering in our human condition.

AN EVOLUTIONARY ADVANCE: DISTINGUISHING THE TWO DIMENSIONS OF WORD, MIND, AND LIFE

In this Logos light, it might be said that a lead telos or moving force in the evolving human drama is precisely this emergence in our globalized rational space of powerful explicit markers for these contrasting dimensions of discourse.

In the evolutionary drama of the Logosphere—the presiding event continuum of all events—the moving pulse and cutting edge of our evolutionary process is our individual and collective awakening of consciousness to Infinite Presence— the Infinite Force of the Logosphere both generates all items, encoding each with its seed and signature, and thus calling each in infinitely diverse ways to self-expression of *What-Is-First*. All evolutionary narratives arise from this Primal Event Continuum—the Event of all events—and are takes on the lead story of the Cosmic Drama. In this context it appears that a presiding telos in our human maturation is precisely this blossoming into the open of the missing grammar of Logos, of the emergence of the awakened technology of consciousness, bringing us into a more authentic mindful encounter with our awakened Self, with Infinite Presence.

EXPLICIT MARKERS FOR THE TWO CONTRASTING TECHNOLOGIES OF MIND

What-Is-First . . . Global Logos . . . is infinitely present and presides in every moment. This every-present Logosphere is the Primal Space of Natural Language, the grammar of all grammars, the depth sign of all possible signs and linguistic forms. And we have seen that this dimension of the Logosphere, the presiding Infinite Word (Logos, Tao, Aum, Yahweh, Allah, Christ, Sophia, Nature, Energy, Sunyata, Consciousness, MindWord, Language, SpaceTime, MindMatter, and so on) constitutes an infinite continuum wherein all of the fundamental categories of reality are mutually constituted in an infinite web of primal relations.

This primal dimension of Natural Language is a different dimension from the mind space of everyday language, culture, and consciousness. The simple truth of GFP is that all possible forms of everyday language, all expressions of egomental life, mind, and language, derive from and are funded by this primal grammar of Logos. But, as already suggested, when we are using everyday natural language, these two dimensions are fused, confused, and mutually superimposed on one another in a primordial and preconscious ambiguity, and a deep drive in the evolution of consciousness and discourse has been moving us and urgently calling for the disentangling of these alter-dimensions. We have arrived at a crisis moment in our evolutionary drama in which it is urgent to bring to explicit clarity the radical dependence of all forms of discourse on this primal grammar of Infinite Presence. So let us now introduce dimensional markers and simplified notation to disentangle and align the contrasting dimensions of mind and discourse.

((. . .)) MARKS THE DIMENSION OF THE
INFINITE WORD—THE ((GRAMMAR OF LOGOS))

Let us begin then with a primal marker for the space and semiology of the Infinite Word. We use **((. . .))—the ((Logos)) quotes, the Logos primal ((sign))**—to situate any word or sign or item in the infinite space of ((Logos)), and thus to tap and release its infinite potential as a ((logos sign)) within the ((mind-word continuum of Infinite Presence)). So any word ((X)) expresses the grammar of the Infinite Word and is thus dynamically interconnected to all other ((signs)) in the ((Primal Word Continuum)).

In this primal dimension of discourse the presence and mentality of the ((thinker)) is inseparable from the signifying power of the ((word)) uttered or the ((sign)) used. Thus crossing into this ((dimension)) of ((Infinite Word)) essentially invokes an awakened and a dilated ((mentality)) and holistic logistic = ((hologistic)) that is able to interface with the boundless ((infinition)) of ((Natural Language)). We shall soon see that when, for example, we ((mind)) ((speak)) within this ((hologistic mind-word dimension)), as in uttering ((I am)) . . . the ((consciousness)) of the thinker is essentially encoded within the ((spoken)) . . . ; again, when we say ((Time)) . . . this primal word touches all other ((words)) within the ((Word Continuum)) of Infinite Presence and essentially involves the awakened consciousness of ((primal temporality)). All ((moments)) meet and mutually co-arise in a boundless ((Now)) within this primal ((Time)). And, of course, the ((logistic of Mind)) is pervaded by this ((Time)): ((MindTime)) . . . and so on.

/ . . . / MARKS THE DIMENSION OF EVERYDAY
/LANGUAGE/ FINITIZED BY /EGOMENTAL MIND/

In contrast, let us mark off the space and discourse of everyday language by the use of **/ . . . / . . . the finitized words of egomental mind and culture— egomental /quotes/**. This linguistic and rational space of the egomental mind is governed by the law of /identity/, which treats each word or term or item as encoding its own meaning (self-identity) within itself. Thus, /time/ is differentiated from /space/ . . . /mind/ from /matter/ . . . and each from all other terms. And the locus and mentality of the /thinker/ is separated from the /content of the spoken/. Furthermore, each is severed from its immediate origination and dependency on ((Natural Language)).

Thus when we say /I am/ . . . this egomental /utterance/ is taken as independent of the /mentality/ and /logistic/ of the one who utters it; to say /I am/ is not the same as ((saying)): ((I am)). The /distinctions/ that are drawn and enforced within the /egomental logistic/ through its governing law of naïve /identity/ are not to be confused with the higher order ((distinctions)) and ((alterity)) that flow forth from the global ((Principle of Relativity)), which respects primal ((diversity)) without losing ((presiding unity)). Naïve /Identity/ fragments, while ((Integral Relativity)) heals.

Each of these dimensional markers shall become clearer with use in diverse contexts as our narrative unfolds. But in this initial stage of bringing them into the open, it is important to notice that **all /language/ is situated within ((Language))**:

$$((\ldots /x/ \ldots))$$

Every form of /language/ derives from, trades upon, and is situated within the presiding ever-present and presiding ((context)) of the ((Infinite Word)). This is an axiomatic disclosure of ((First Philosophy)). ((. . .)) dilates the ((global lens)) and is a ((dimensional shifter)) of our "being" and "minding," whereas / . . . / indicates the /egomental lens/ . . . /egomental consciousness/. . . . It should be noted in the aforementioned ((formula)) that if we drop off the / . . . / surrounding the "x" . . . its inner ((logos code)) is released, as it is found already ((situated)) within the ((x)). . . . And it may be said that the perennial evolutionary quest of ((First Philosophy)) is the maturation from /x/ to ((x)).

Another way to express the primordial confusion and chaotic ambiguity between the two dimensions spoken of earlier may be rendered as the collapse of ((. . .)) versus / . . . / into each other . . . as "language." There is an inherent primal indeterminacy and pernicious ambiguity within everyday "language"—with the conflation of ((. . .)), and / . . . / . . . any word or utterance could be cashed out in the context of ((. . .)) or / . . . /, and it is commonplace to engage in and treat "language" as standing independently of ((Language)). Indeed, this primal ((Word)) or space of ((Grammar)) is not discerned, and often not countenanced. "Language" is taken to be inherently /egomental/, /dualizing/, /discriminating/, even as its own deep structure is not recognized or brought into the open. This collapse and conflation is potentially (and historically) pernicious, since it allows the ((Script)) of ((Logos)) to be rendered in the egomental script of /man/. And the free-floating "ambiguity" lurking in everyday "language" occurs through this indeterminate and unwitting conflation of /x/ and ((x)), as shown in the ((. . . /x/ . . .)) disambiguating notation.

But now our logistical markers help bring out the simple axiomatic truth of GFP, that /language/ derives any meaning force it has from, and is essentially situated within, the ever-present and presiding domain of ((Language)):

$$((\ldots /language/ \ldots))$$

We can now picture in a simple and vivid way a common perversion wherein the egomental space of /language/ privileges itself as first and primary and renders (or "downloads") all insights of ((scripture)) or ((first philosophy)) to its culturally constructed egomental domain:

/ . . . ((infinite word)) . . . /

This is a fatal fallacy . . . a dimensional confusion . . . that is a matter of ((life)) and /death/. To /inscribe/ the ((Infinite Word)) within the domain and jurisdiction of the /finite word/ . . . within the /egomental/ space of discourse, is a primordial mistake that has persisted through the ages. The Infinite Word of ((Global Logos)) cannot be captured and inscribed within the finitized and egomental /word of ego-man/: /god/ is not ((God)); ((Global Scripture)) cannot be rendered within the /egomental script/, and the present advance in explicitly marking the contrasting dimensions of "language" and realigning them in their proper and appropriate mutual relation and jurisdictional asymmetry is an evolutionary advance of ((Global First Philosophy)).

As we shall see in what follows, this explicit marking off of the contrast and relation between the dimensions of mind, word, and life opens a higher space of rational, logical, and linguistic competence and literacy. At the same time, in becoming more critically aware of the ways and dynamics of /egomental reason/, we shall bring into the open how and why it severs us from ((connectivity)), eclipses ((*What-Is-First*)), and produces chronic human and existential fragmentation, discoherence, and dysfunction.

CROSSING MORE DEEPLY INTO THE ((DIMENSION OF THE LOGOSPHERE))

Before focusing our attention on the dimension of /egomental mind/ and its dysfunctional ways, let us place first things ((first)) and proceed more deeply into the ((dimension)) of ((Infinite Presence)). As we have seen, the quest for ((First)), for ((Logos)), essentially calls forth the ((hologistic)) minding process that we have called the ((awakened global mind)), with its ((global consciousness)). We can now see more explicitly why the /egomental mind/ must be left behind in our journey into ((First Philosophy)). ((Infinite Logos)) cannot be processed in the self-limiting discourse and /logistic/ of /egomental mind/. It may be said that this is one of the great ((lessons)) through the ages in the epic experiments to ((encounter)) ((Infinite Presence)).

Still, an effective way to bring out our present unprecedented crossing into the ((grammar of Logos)) is to play this ((primal dimension)) of ((language, mind, and reason)) over against the /egomental dimension/ of /discourse/. In this ((light)), it is apparent that the ((language of God)) is not the /language/ of /god/; the voice of ((Buddha)) is not the discourse of /Buddha/; the ((speaking)) of ((Krishna)) is not the discourse of /Krishna/; the /speech/ and /being/ of /Jesus/ is not the ((Logos made Flesh)) in the ((Life and Speech of Jesus)); the ((Space of Reason)) is not the /space of reason/; and so on.

((. . .)) AS THE INFINITE
HOLOGISTIC ((SIGN OF LOGOS))

Once we make the dimensional crossing beyond the artificial limits of /ego-mental mind/ and /language/ into the sacred space of ((Logos)), we experience a profound ((inversion)) in our orientation . . . no longer approaching ((logos)) and ((logosphere)) through the egomental /lens/ . . . but activating a higher order ((hologistic)) minding process and praxis that opens deeper pathways into the encounter with ((Presence)). Several of our great traditions of "First Philosophy" . . . Advaita, Madhyamika, Zen . . . as we have seen, recognize that this ((primal field)) is nondual through and through . . . and the egomental mind, with its logic of /identity/, cannot cross over. In the Buddhist Middle-Way discourse, this primal Buddha Field of Absolute Emptiness (empty, that is, of all /ego items/, all /ego identities/ melt away) is the place of ((Relativity)), where everything mutually connects to everything else ((co-arising)) in the ((infinite dialectics)) of ((dynamic process)).

The ((ontologic) of the ((Logosphere)) is incomparably different from the /objectified logics/ of /egomental reason/, which works on the naïve principle of /identity/; the former works on the ((Principle of Relativity)), while the latter is grounded in the /Principle of Identity/. It has been shown, as in the radical critique of Nagarjuna, that /Identity/ could not subsist without ((Relativity)) . . . and the variety of everyday egomental /logics/ all trade upon the ((logistic power)) of the ((Logosphere)) to gain the appearance of workability.

((LOGISTIC)) IS ALL-IMPORTANT:
((MENTATION)) MATTERS

Here it is timely to recall that "mentation," "mentality," or our mind-processing practices are all important in the texture of our discourse, in the fabric of our life, and in the nature of the lifeworld that we inhabit: **((we are as we mind))** is another global ((axiom)) of ((First Philosophy)), and I have used the word "logistic" to capture the technology of consciousness we are employing. In egomental discourse, we tend to focus on the /content/ of consciousness . . . in the objectified /box of predication/ . . . and not focus sufficiently on the "mental calculus" or "mind operating program" we are employing = ((logistic)). There is a powerful pull in /egomental minding/ to get riveted in the /objectified/ and /reductive/ space of its /content/ . . . and "logistic" gets /reduced/ to the /content/: /logic/ is divorced from ((logistic)). The /egomental/ mind operating system (its "logistic") becomes eclipsed in its obsession with its /content/: it cuts itself off from the ((logosphere)), loses self-critical awareness of its "logistic," and becomes taken up with the /content/ it generates.

One of the great lessons we have seen from the evolution of emerging ((first philosophies)) is that the /egomental logistic/, whatever its declared /logic/ or /ontology/, is not powerful enough to cross over into the ((hologistic)) mind space and mentation process called for in entering the ((Logosphere)). So as we now focus on the infinite logistic power of ((. . .)) it is important to see that genuine ((content)) can never be severed from ((hologistic)) mind processing: ((logic)) is constituted and disclosed in its ((logistic)); every "logic" is grounded in ((Logos)).

Let us ((experiment)) further in entering this ((hologistic)) minding praxis as we move more deeply into the ((deep ontology)) of the ((Logosphere)). As we cross over from /egomental logistic/ into ((Hologistic)), crossing from the artificial /logics/ of /egomental identity/ into the Primal Natural ((Logic)) of ((Relativity)), we experience in this profound ((inversion)) and ((reorientation)) in ((Logical Space)) a new ((situatedness)) in the ((Mind-Word Continuum of the Logosphere)). While in the prior /egomental rational life/ . . . the place where /I/ stands . . . the place of /my consciousness/ . . . is separated from the /objectified/ place of /language/, which in turn is in its own domain over against the space of the /world/ . . . so I /experience/ a disconnect between /I am/, /mind/, /word/, and /world/.

But in my new ((orientation)) I experience within the awakened awareness of ((I am)) the Presence of ((Primary Being)): ((I am . . . Awakened Consciousness, Existence . . . Being . . . Time . . . Infinite Presence, SpaceTime, and the Otherness of World . . . Universe . . . Cosmos . . . Matter . . . Other Beings)). In activating and entering this ((Hologistic)) MindPraxis . . . I immediately ((experience)) ((MindWordWorld)) . . . the Infinite Word is Infinite Being. This Infinite Word . . . permeates ((I am)) ((Mind)); this ((Word)) permeates all ((things)) . . . ((World)) and all the ((categories)) that constitute this ((World)) and awakened ((experience)).

In every ((power point)) I touch, say, ((Time)) . . . I find ((it)) permeates all other ((categories)) . . . including, my ((awakened awareness)) . . . not just the ((SpaceTime)) Continuum . . . but the ((Hologistic Continuum)) of the ((Integral Logosphere)). And here ((I am)) . . . my ((awakened conscious presence)) . . . is saturated with ((Time)) . . . and when I focus on ((Space)) . . . I find naturally that it pervades all other ((categories)). ((Mind)) touches ((Time)), ((Space)) . . . ((Matter)) discloses itself in ((MindSpace)) . . . so ((I am)) directly encounters an intimate ((touching)) of ((matter)) ((objects)) ((World)) . . . and so on.

Thus the ((Primal Continuum of the Logosphere)) . . . the ((Categorial Continuum)) . . . is a seamless ((hologistic continuum)) that teems in boundless ((diversity)); in this way the shift from /egomental logistic/ to the awakened ((hologistic continuum)) of Infinite Presence is truly a ((dimensional shift)) in Mind, Minding, Language, Discourse, Rationality, Hermeneutical Praxis, Cognition, Life, and Phenomenology of Experience; this dilation of life from /I/ to ((I)) is a dimensional shift in mind, life, being, consciousness, logistic, experience, language, discourse, meaning, knowledge, rationality, and truth. Here we find that the primal ((I am)) is truly ((I⟷Thou)) . . . the ((Other)) is always already inherently constituted in the ((One)), the ((Other)) constituted within the ((I)), and ((vice versa)).

The simple disclosure of ((Global First Philosophy)), in entering into ((Logosphere)) . . . the primal Field of Infinition . . . via the ((Hologistic MindPraxis)) . . . is that every ((point)) or ((locus)) or ((item)) in this ((infinite web)) encodes and expresses the ((infinite dialectic)) . . . any ((piece of the Logosphere)) . . . inherits, encodes, reiterates, and co-expresses the ((infinite dialectic)). There is that of ((Logos)) in every ((x)).

This ((global formula)) has astounding consequences for every conceivable aspect of our life, culture, and existence, for example, the primal ((I am)) . . . wherein I realize my ((primary being)) through deeper communion with ((Logosphere)) . . . is never /alone/ but encodes in its unique way all ((being)). While the /I am/ within its alleged /self identity/ stands alone in its presumed /atomic space/ . . . the ((I am)) is hologistic, hence always intrinsically interconnected to all ((Others)); any ((x)) is a ((dynamic network of relations . . . moments . . . events . . .)) . . . our ((being)) is ((relational)), and this opens a deeper ((dialogic)) space for all aspects of ((experience)) and ((knowing)):

((I⟷Other)) ((I⟷Thou))

In this hologistic dimension of living and minding the ((primary being)) of ((I am)) is ((I⟷Thou)) . . . we are ((dialogical beings)) . . . and this is key to understanding the deep structure of our ((moral consciousness)) and the ((moral law)): to tend to my ((Self)) is to tend to my ((Other)) . . . since the ((Other)) is already relationally implanted in ((me)), and ((I)) in ((It)). And in the primal ((intimacy)) of

((I⟷Other)) and ((Subject⟷Object))

a deeper epistemology, ethos, aesthetic, and cognitive depth will open. It is in this deep dialogical space that the open-minded knowing ((subject)) is able to encounter the ((Other)), the ((Object)) of ((knowledge)) as it truly ((is)).

In contrast, the deep structure of the egomental logistic presumes a separation between the /knowing subject/ and the /object/ that is presented in the /objectified space/ of /content/:

/ /I/ versus / Object/ / or /Knower/ versus /Object of Knowing/

and, of course, egomental /logics/ then further break down the /object/ in its favorite /subject-predicate/ font . . . whether Aristotle's, Hegel's or Frege's, and so on. In the egomental logistic there is a fundamental ontological space of separation between knowing /subject/ and /object/ known; whereas, in the ((integral dimension)) of the ((hologistc calculus)) the ((knower and known)) are mutually given in an open and intimate dialogic encounter:

((Knower ⟺ Object of Knowledge))

CRITIQUE OF /EGOMENTAL LOGISTIC/ WITHIN ((GLOBAL HOLOGISTIC))

Perhaps it is timely to pause in this excursion into the ((holistic dimension)) of the ((Logosphere)) and focus for a moment on the contrasting /egomental logistic/. But rather than severing the primal link between ((. . .)) and / . . . / . . . engaging them as if in separate rational spaces, we now place all /egomental logics/ within the ever presiding ((context)) of the ((Primal Natural Language of the Logosphere)):

((. . . / . . . / . . .))

This figure displays the global truth that the /egomental logistic/ with all of its possible /logics/ is essentially situated within the ((Logosphere)) out of which it arises. This ((figure)) sums up and displays the essence of ((Global First Philosophy)). Every ((fragment)) is ((fractal)), so to speak.

Nevertheless, the egomental mind arrogates its presumed independent logical space as if free-standing and self-constituted:

/ . . . /

This self-privileging of its logistic, language forms, and forms of life is the attitude of /egomentalism/. Despite the fact that it could not be, could not endure for a moment without the surrounding ((funding)) of the ((Logosphere)), it acts, whether intentionally or preconsciously, as if it has a life of its /own/, enjoying radical independence from ((Infinite Presence)). This turns out to be a deadly /original sin/ that sets in motion the debilitating and recursive dynamic of self-splitting, polarization, fragmentation, chronic dualism, and discoherence that violates ((Integral Rational Space)) and spawns chronic individual and collective dysfunction in the fabric of its /life/.

WHY /EGOMENTALISM/ SPAWNS CHRONIC DUALISM AND FRAGMENTATION

While recognizing, of course, that /egomental logistic/ and its /objectified logics/ could not arise or exist for a moment without the ((resources)) of the ever-present ((Logosphere)), let us proceed experimentally and for a moment tentatively accept its uncritical stance of being self-generating, self-constituting, and self-sustaining. In the rigorous critique of the ((Hologistic Calculus)) it becomes evident that the logics of /egomental identity/ are inevitably self-defeating, self-contradictory, and self-deconstructive. The mythos of this alleged radical rational independence [of ((Logos))] invariably turns in on itself and reveals its inherent incompleteness and dependence on ((Relativity)). All /logics of identity/ are inherently ((Incomplete)): this is the ((Global Incompleteness Theorem)), which we will take up later.

So with this caution let us delve for a moment into the depth of the egomental /logistic/ and /egomentalism/. As we have seen, an elementary and ((axiomatic)) disclosure of ((Global First Philosophy)) is that all possible words, words, logics, hermeneutical forms of life, all perspectives . . . are essentially ((situated)) within the ever-present and all-pervasive ((Logosphere)). We have depicted this simple truth in the earlier formulation:

$$((\ldots/\ldots/\ldots))$$

There is no stepping outside the jurisdiction and funding of ((Infinite Presence)), so we are always already surrounded by ((. . .)).

So the primordial rift or "severance" from ((. . .)), and the /self positing/ of /egomental mind/ from its essential dependence upon the resources of the ((Logosphere)) for its every breath, antecedes the subsequent fatal flaws of egomental /logistic/ and its absolute principle of /identity/:

$$/\ldots/$$

But this arrogated /mind space/ and /logical space/ need to be broken out more explicitly as we uncover the genealogy of its illicit self-positing: The usual naïve picture is that the locus of the /thinker/, the egocentric /I/ is on one side, usually preconscious, and over against /it/ is the egomental /screen of consciousness/, wherein all of its mental /contents/ appear:

$$/ \; /I/ \; v \; [\; /\text{not-I}/ \;] \; /$$

As the / . . . / space opens up within, we find the locus of the /thinker/ on the left side, and over against it within the [. . .] objectified content space is all that could appear to /it/—the /content/ of its consciousness. The next step in breaking this out is to see that the space of the egocentric thinker—/I/ may also be a /we/—a community of like-minded thinkers that shares in this logistic and its lifeworld; on the other hand, within the space of the [content screen], where all of its conscious attention usually is focused, the inner and outer worlds of its mental /objects/ appear:

[/content/]

This egomental [content] is what is more explicitly analyzed by the /logic/ to render the /logical structure/ of the /content of consciousness/.

As we have seen, in the classical Greek and Aristotelian logical traditions, the /thought content/ is found to be /predicative/ in nature, to /think/ is to /predicate/ . . . to join a /logical subject/ to a /logical predicate/:

/I-We/ versus [/S/ is-or-isn't /P/]

For the moment let us focus in on the predicative /content box/, where all of the action is for /egomental mind/. The "screen" of egomental mind marked off by [. . .] is the logical space in which all experience appears and is processed. The birth and development of /logic/ in the early Greek tradition, as we saw, emerged with the formal and predicative analysis of all /content/: "to think is to predicate," to join a logical subject with a logical predicate. All /information/ was naturally processed in this predicative logical structure. And since the /I/, the /self/ and all its inner world and mental states are likewise processed in this /egomental screen/, our inner world of "consciousness," or innermost /identity/, is externalized and processed within the /logistic/ . . . now reduced to /content/ . . . in the /objectified box of predication/. Our inner world of consciousness, and self-consciousness, is processed in the /egomental box/ and thus takes on its /rational form/.

Furthermore, it should be noted that whether a thinker-speaker was consciously aware of the predicative dynamic or not is not ultimately relevant for our present concern, for everyday people, living uncritically in their cultural language, naturally /objectify/ the /content of their experience/ and naively process the world and the content of experience through their cultural lens, through the egomental mind. Whether one had an "official logical theory" for this /content/ was not the point—what is relevant here is whether one was playing the /egomental game/ and lodged within the /egomental logistic/. One need not have a "logical" or "philosophical theory of "predication" or "objectification of content" to be living this /egomental logistic/.

Irrespective of a philosophical theory of how best to analyze the /content/ of thought and experience, the key point is whether one was living life and engaging in discourse through the egomental /lens/ and thus /objectifying/ the /content of consciousness/. The fundamental issue here is whether one is ensnared within the /objectifying/ and /reductive/ patterns of egomental /logistic/, for this is the primary source of polarization, fragmentation, dualizing, and the alienation from the ((connectivity)) of the ((Logosphere)). In our present ((thought experiment)) the essential factor in our rational critique of /egomentalism/ is to take it at its /word/, that it is /self-constituted/ and /self-sustaining/ and in no way illicitly taps the ((rational resources)) of the ever-present and surrounding ((Logosphere)) that permeates its every breath. Can the naïve and absolutized /law of identity/ (/"A" is "A"/) apart from ((Relativity)) hold its own and generate and sustain reason, language, consciousness, and fund /egomental worlds/? Is it the absolute /first principle/? the /primal law/ of ((Logos))?

/EGOMENTAL OBJECTIFICATION/: THE SOURCE OF CHRONIC DUALISMS AND DYSFUNCTIONS

Recognizing that very diverse logical analyses have been presented for the /content/ of egomental /thought/, Aristotle's analysis differs from Frege's, and these differ from that of Spinoza or Hegel, and so on. The key factor through our ((Global Lens)) is the deeper underlying /egomental logistic/. Our foregoing journey through the evolution of consciousness made clear that the core /egomental logistic/ has continued to dominate cultural life on this planet across vastly diverse worldviews and cultural traditions.

Once the breach and severance from the ((Logosphere)) is made, once the unsuspecting /mind/ enters the /egomental logistic/, and the further split is made between the /thinker/ and the /object of thought/ on the [screen of egomental mind], the harm is done. Even if one insists that the /egocentric thinker/ outside the /objectified screen of content/ and its /content/ are /related/ (e.g., insisting that one shapes the other), the /harm/ is still already done, since it alleges to be self constituted apart from ((The Hologistic Unified Field of Natural Language)). This egomental technology of consciousness appears to be a premature stage in our human development, which accommodates widely variant worldviews and alter-renderings of the /content/ of consciousness.

EGOMENTAL /POLARIZATION/ INSIDE THE /CONTENT BOX/

We have been suggesting that /egomental identity/ cannot get started without ((Relativity)). Even if we focus on the identity of the alleged /thinker/

outside the /predicative box/, the presumption that it has its inner /identity/ is fatally flawed, for ostensibly it is already using its /egomental logistic/ and its foundation in /identity/ to posit itself as the thinker-with-identity . . . having ongoing logical and ontological coherence and consistency through /time/ . . . having /self-identity/. With ((rigorous critique)), it is already apparent that this would-be /thinker/ in its posited /identity/, and any /identity/ for that matter, is vacuous without the funding of ((Relativity)) and the resources of the ((Logosphere)).

THE /LOGISTIC OF IDENTITY/ IS FATALLY FLAWED

But, again, in the spirit of carrying forth our ((experiment)), let us provisionally grant /identity/ and enter the /egomental content box/. Even before we enter this /objectified screen/ of egomental /logistic/ we sense that we are already in a ((deep dualism)). Not only has the /egomental thinker/ severed from direct connectivity with its ((rational ecology)), with its surrounding ((Logosphere)), but there is now the further deep dualism of the severance of the /thinker/ from the /objectified screen/: the /thinking subject/ from the /object of thought/.

Our meditative critiques touched on earlier through the centuries have given great attention to this /subject/ v /object/ dualism, which is a primal symptom of the original splitting off from ((Communion with Logos)), from ((Relativity)). For no /relation/ could arise apart from the presiding ((Law of Relativity)), which makes all "relations" possible, and once the identity of the /thinker/ is posited independently of its /content/, also posited independently, the abyss between them is found to be unbridgeable. The ((fact)) is that any /identity/ that alleges continuous reiteration through time is already tapping the ((rational power)) of the ((hologistic)). Indeed, we, in this very ((experiment)), could not be engaged in "thinking" without ((Relativity)).

CHRONIC DUALISM WITHIN
THE EGOMENTAL SCREEN

Nevertheless, with this ((primal insight)) in ((mind)), let us, for the moment, go into the predicative screen, within the /egomental box/ of /objectified content/. Let us take up the "Aristotelian" experiment in "first philosophy" and play out his /predicative/ scenario for the rational and ontological analysis of the /content/ of what /appears/.

[/S/ is or isn't /P/].

The logical structure of the space of /thought/ is that the logical /Subject/ is positively or negative connected to the /Predicate/. Already we are in the game of /Identity/: The /identity/ of the /Subject/ is presumed: **"S is S," and more generically, "X is X."**

We have already noticed a primal problem in this alleged /law of identity/, which is taken as the absolute /first principle/ of thought and being in the Aristotelian /logistic/. The first appearance of "S" is posited as self-constituted and self-perpetuating, as /self-identical/ and recursively reiterating itself. But, for now, we are looking the other way to allow this to pass. Naturally, the second occurrence of the "S" needs to be /identical/ with the first occurrence, in addition to housing its own "univocity" and self-identity. What if the first occurrence of /S/ is equivocal or multivocal, even indeterminate, rather than univocal? What are the conditions that make any /sign/ "univocal" and "determinate"?

In whose /consciousness/ is this /law of identity/ being /articulated/, received, processed, or interpreted? And is his or her consciousness univocal and continuous? What if it is not? How could any /thought/ or /thinker/ get started? How could any /sign/ allege /self-identity/ and having the /relation of identity/ with itself in the two iterations? As this ((drama)) unfolds we shall soon see that the space of everyday discourse, wherein this formulation of the /law of identity/ is being posited, may already be indeterminate, spanning diverse worldviews and alternative logics wherein any /sign/ is originally lodged in radical indeterminacy and multivocity across worldviews. Could it be that in the space of everyday language, any and all signs are in flux and indeterminate across /worldviews/, /egomental lens/, and /perspectives/? How does one get a coherent formulation of the alleged fundamental /law of identity/? Unless we presume ((univocity)) in the thinker, in the signs, and in the ((content)), how can /identity/ get started? Well, never mind. Let us forget all that and proceed.

Once naïve /egomental identity/ is granted, the polar dynamic of /either-or/ is launched: If /A is A/, then +A displaces −A: either A or not-A; not both A and not-A . . . so immediately the simple posit of /identity/ plays out into two allied theorems: the law of excluded middle: "Either A or not-A," and the foundational law of "noncontradiction": "Not both A and not-A." And this dynamic playing out into the structure of /predication/, /S is either P or not-P/, /S cannot be both P and not-P/, and the fundamental structure of logic and ontology, is launched. This logical /law of thought/ somehow also reflects the structure of /Being/: The logical /subject/ mirrors the ultimate items of reality /Substance/ and the logical /predicate/ indicates /Attributes/

/Logic/:   **/S is either P or not-P/.**
/Ontology/: **/Substance/ either has an /Attribute/ or not.**
               A /Thing/ cannot both be and not be.

So the technology or logistic of /predication/ at once yields the laws of thought and reasoning, and also presents the structure of reality, the ontological laws of /being/. In his historic launching of /First Philosophy/, Aristotle, in his brilliant *Metaphysics*, declares that the ultimate question, "What is Being?," is in effect the question, "What is the ultimate subject of predication?" = "What is Substance?" . . . and the game is on. So the quest for the ultimate subject of predication will ostensibly open the way to /primary beings/.

In this logical and ontological space of /predication/, governed by the absolute law of /Identity/, the space of /rationality/ and /discourse/ is launched, and the rest is /history/. Aristotle discerns certain fundamental /categories/ from this structure, and thus the alphabet of ontology, the building blocks of reality, and intelligible grammar of thought are inaugurated.

Here, as we follow the polar structure within the /logistic of identity/, every /Predicate/ has a polar structure: +P/−P: visible/invisible, colored/colorless, married/unmarried.

In general, +P and −P taken together = /P/, and this indicates a deeper domain that proscribed all its possibilities; /P-and-unP/ taken together indicates /contrariety/.

When we take both polar pairs together as one /concept/, we get a deeper "category" or domain of the field of /Being/: /Colored/, /Married/, /Visible/: so being /Colored/ is an all-encompassing /category/ that spans all possible "colors," including what is "uncolored" or "colorless."

These building blocks mutually exclude one another, each indicating a primary /Domain/ of existence. So /Space/, /Time/, /Cause/, /Substance/, /Motion/, and so on are such fundamental /categories/, fundamental /Attributes/, that belong to the primary /things/ that exist.

Aristotle is clear that /Substance/ is the primary /category/, and all others are /Attributes/ that can only exist in and through belonging to /Substances/. So everything in Reality is either a /Substance/ or an /Attribute/, and the primary /beings/ are /substances/, the ultimate /logical subjects/ of /predication/: the calculus of /thought/ mirrors the /ontological calculus/. The /polar/ structure permeates each locus within /predication/: the primary /Subject/ is not only an /individual/ but a /type of being/: /Socrates/ indicates a primary being but is at the same time a /kind/ of being, /Person/ or /Human/, and the logical sign that joins the /Subject/ and /Predicate/ also is a polar operator: is-or-isn't.

/Socrates/ is or isn't /wise/.

One lurking /deep dualism/ is precisely bridging the /divide/ between the /Subject/ and the /Predicate/, /Substance/ v /Attribute/, not to mention the /presumed isomorphism/ between the domains of /Logic/ and /Ontology/. We shall not take time to go into details here. Can a /substance/ inhere in itself independently of its /attributes/? Given that each has its own inner /identity/, how can each "blend" and come together to form a unified "thought" or "being"? While the /law of identity/ encodes each item in the field with its independent "atomic" identity, these need to be ((blended together)) by a powerful ever-present ((force)) that unites them appropriately either to form coherent ((thoughts)) or to become embodied in ((individual things) or ((events)). Any presumed /relation/ needs to be accounted for by the /egomental logistic/, and this will invariably lead to ((Relativity)) = ((Relationality)). By making the two dimensions of discourse explicit with our ((. . .)) v / . . . / notation, and by stripping the logic of /identity/ of any presumed ((rights)) to tap and exploit the ever-present ((Logosphere), we begin to see that /Egomental logic/ unravels, falls apart, and cannot sustain itself: **/Identity/ presupposes ((Relativity))**.

How does this governing principle of /identity/ tap this ((relational power))? How can it account for this ((unifying force))? Could it be that /egomental mind/ and its logic of /identity/ is presuming that a unifying and relational ((power)) beyond the /atomizing/ and /polarizing/ force of /identity/ is working behind the scenes and underground to hold the /atomic units/ together? Is strict /identity/ sufficient to account for the unifying forces that hold the fabric of existence together in ((deep connectivity))? In this quick flash into the workings of /Predication/ as the logistic of /Identity/ we begin to see that each /category/ or building block of /reality/, standing in its own /identity/, has a certain /atomic/ independence of all else, and yet each must come together in deep logical and ontological ((connectivity)) to form coherent ((thoughts)), to show themselves as genuine ((individuals)), and to flow in the dynamic ((web of holistic events)).

The /dual/ and /polar/ structure pervades the /logic of identity/, and the /egomental logistic/ somehow assumes that the divisive and splitting force of /identity/ can nevertheless overcome the /polar/ dynamics of objectified /predication/. Given the radical plurality, multiplicity, and mutual exclusivity of /categories/, how can they "come together" to constitute a genuine primal "individual"? Aristotle struggles gallantly with these and related issues, but they are left dangling and have haunted the traditions through the ages, still unresolved. When /identity/ is taken strictly and rigorously in its own terms, independently of the ((Rationality of Relativity)), it appears to fall apart at the ((seams)), and the /relational power/ of the /is/ or /isn't/ is not powerful enough to pull it off.

CHRONIC DUALISMS IN EGOMENTAL LOGISTIC

Furthermore, within this egomental /screen/, vastly diverse /worldviews/ or /ontologies/ are possible—as the alphabet of radical /categories/ and /types/

that get "organized" into a worldview gets deployed and rearranged, alternative worlds emerge, and it must be remembered that the terms, concepts, and categories that configure in a world get their identity and meaning within that world context, so as we shift world contexts into diverse /ontologies/, the identities and meanings of the /categories/ shift. For example, when certain primal /categories/ such as /matter/ and /mind/, /time/ and /space/, /motion/ and /energy/, /consciousness/ and /number/ . . . and many others . . . get moved around in new patterns, different worlds arise; if /matter/ is taken as the presiding organizing category, we get a world of /materialism/; if /consciousness/ /mind/ or /spirit/ presides, we get a very different world of /idealism/; if /matter/ and /mind/ are both given priority and are equally independent, we get /dualism/, and so on. The world of /materialism/, as we have seen, is profoundly different from the world of /idealism/.

But these fundamental /categories/ shift in /identity/ and /meaning/ across world contexts, so "matter" in /materialism/ is not the same as "matter" in /idealism/, and there is a systematic ambiguity of terms across worlds. We cannot presume "univocity" in the meaning of terms as we shift worlds. When, for example, Einstein rearranged the categories of /space/ and /time/, /matter/ and /energy/, beyond the Newtonian worldview, we get a different /Universe/, and the constitutive categories shift: the "space-time" continuum of Einstein's ontology is not the same as these terms in Newton's world. Still, the question of how separated /categories/ and /types/ become ((organized)) and ((reorganized)) into worlds haunts us. /Egomental Identity/ is certainly not powerful enough to account for such profoundly organizing and connecting forces. Just presuming or positing such ((connectivity)) will not do, certainly not when we are engaged in the enterprise of ((First Philosophy)) and the ((Foundations of Reason, Ontology, and Logic)).

Looking back for a moment on our earlier fast-forward movement through the evolution of consciousness and diverse /first philosophies/ through the ages we encountered recurrent deep dualisms in almost every aspect of evolving worlds. The /mind/ v /body/ dualism was just a tip of the egomental iceberg—we found recurrent tensions between polar splits in all directions: /finite/ v infinite; /sense/ v /reason/; /faith/ v /reason/; /one/ v /many/; /individual/ v /community/, /universal/ v /particular/; /unity/ v /plurality/; /identity/ v /difference/; /form/ v /content/; /essence/ v /existence/; /reason/ v /passion/; /is/ v /ought/; /fact/ v /value/; /a priori/ v /a posteriori/; /analytic/ v /synthetic/; /subjective/ v /objective/; /private/ v /public/; /inner/ v /outer/; /substance/ v /attribute/; /temporal/ v /eternal/; /being/ v /becoming/; /absolute/ v /relative/ . . . to mention a few; and we have not yet mentioned the deep polar splits between /worldviews/, /religions/, /cultures/, /ideologies/, /disciplines/, and so on. We will take these up in a moment.

/EGOMENTALISM/ IS THE SOURCE OF CHRONIC FRAGMENTATION AND PERSISTING DUALISM

The main point here is to notice that the /deep dualisms/ that have haunted our human condition through the ages are not just "technical" or "theoretical" problems of philosophy—they are lived, existential predicaments that abound in the life of the people across cultural and religious worlds. What has not been sufficiently clear is that the /egomental logistic/, with its practice of /objectified identity/, is the generative core that spawns chronic deep dualisms in all directions.

Through our ((Global Lens)) we can now see more deeply into the originating source of chronic /dualism/, /polarization/, fragmentation/, /discoherence/. It is clearer now that /egomentalism/, with its /objectifying screen/ and inadequate first principle of /identity/, atomizes and isolates everything it /touches/ and trades underground on ((relational power)) to shore up the surface appearance of these /atomic fragments/ being nevertheless ((related)) to one another to get /reason/, /thought/, /meaning/, /truth/, /objects/, /world/, /experience/ . . . ((going)). Without thus tapping the ((Logosphere)) and the genuine ((first principle)) of ((Relativity)), /egomental life/ cannot work. The very coherence and presumed univocity of the thinker, and thought process, is, of course, also taken for granted.

Yet these dualisms show up in the lifeworlds that appear on the /objectified screen/ of /egomental reason/, so it is easy to overlook the common generative source of chronic dualism. The disconnect between the /egomental logistic/ or technology of consciousness in /egomental life/ and the /content/ that shows up in the /objectified box/ feeds and perpetuates the blind spot that holds us captive. The lure of naïve /identity/, which purports self-sufficiency while it illicitly taps and trades upon the ((rational resources)) of the ((Logosphere)) and ((Relativity)), sinks humanity even farther into the vicious cycle of chronic /egomentalism/. The ((presence)) and ((praxis)) of ((consciousness)) always permeates and co-arises with its ((content)): being ((mindful)) of this primal ((continuum)) is ((rational therapy)) for the chronic polarizing of /egomentalism/. And, of course, this is a focus of ((Global First Philosophy)).

DIVERSE WORLDVIEWS ON THE EGOMENTAL SCREEN: CLASH OF CULTURES AND WORLDS

We have suggested that /egomental logistic/ is widespread in the human condition and is generic across all kinds of borders—cultures, religions, first philosophies, ideologies, and disciplinary perspectives. We have seen in the foregoing that many of our diverse great visionary teachers through the ages and across traditions have sought to help people become more critically aware of the /egomental/ condition and its pernicious consequences for the ((quality of life)). But we also have seen that the pull of this entrenched /mental lens/ runs so deep and has such a grip on the life of the people that the ((awakening teachings)) that have been brought forth to help liberate people become neutralized, distorted, undermined, and unrecognizable by the continuing dominant sway of /egomental/ forces.

We have been suggesting that these powerful /egomental forces/ also have naturally held sway over many of our great philosophers, scientists, and "cultural creatives" through the ages and impeded the full flowering of ((Rational Life)) and the maturation of our ((Humanity)). And it appears that much "academic thinking" over the centuries, far from liberating humanity from the grip of /egomental logistic/, has been engaged in articulating, theorizing, and reflecting within its /jurisdiction/ and under its /influence/. What would it take to make a successful dimensional crossing into ((Global First Philosophy))? What would it be like to enter into the missing ((First Discipline))? How would ((Science)) advance when it is no longer hampered by /egomental logistic/? What would ((Global Culture)) be like when a critical mass of ((humans)), co-awakening to the ((Hologistic)) technology of ((Consciousness)), and truly center their ((lives)) in the presiding ((Logosphere))? And how would an ((Awakened Academy)) proceed and ((reconfigure)) in the ((critical light)) of ((Global Reason))? We shall take up these and related concerns later. Everything is at stake here.

/EGOMENTALISM/: THE ROOTS OF /VIOLENCE/ AND BREAKDOWN IN HUMAN /RELATIONS/

The point, then, is that /egomentalism/ is the deep structural source and generative origin of all kinds of /disconnects/—a vast range of deep /dualisms/, entrenched patterns of /fragmentation/, systemic /polarizations/, /objectification/, /reductive thinking/, /monocentric/ self-absolutizing, and privileging of one's /worldview/ or /perspective/, so we are not just talking about certain local recurrent /dualisms/. We have been making a ((link)) between the /egomental logistic/ and all sorts of alienations, rifts, and breakdowns in ((relations)). Perhaps one of the most dangerous and devastating forms has been the breakdown of ((dialogic relations)) across and between worldviews, ideologies, religions, cultures, traditions, and even /disciplinary/ orientations and perspectives. These diverse forms of /chronic splitting/ and breakdown in ((communication)) are traceable to the dominance of the /egomental logistic/ and its /egomentalism/.

It is obviously not just /individuals/ who are caught in the /monocentric/ pattern of privileging and absolutizing their /lens/ and /worldview/ but /communities/ as well. This is ((evidenced)) by the ongoing clash of /worldviews/ and /perspectives/ through the ages—with /genocides/, /wars/, /crusades/, /holocausts/, /ethnic cleansing/, /slavery/, /colonial dominance/, /religious persecution/, and many other forms of /violence/, /hermeneutical abuse/, /gender violence/, /sexism/, /racism/, and the like.

We begin to notice now that any /culture/, /worldview/, /religion/, /scripture/, /teaching/, /ideology/, /narrative/, /perspective/, /philosophy/, /science/, or /discipline/ may be rendered within the /egomental logistic/ or may be ((lifted)) in a ((dimensional crossing)) into the ((Hologistic Rationality)) of the ((Awakened Global Mind)): It makes a world of ((difference)) whether we encounter /Jesus/ or ((Jesus)), /Buddha/ or ((Buddha)), /Yoga/ or ((Yoga)), /Descartes/ or ((Descartes)), /Physics/ or ((Physics)), /logic/ or ((Logic)), /rationality/ or ((Rationality)), /first philosophy/ or ((First Philosophy)), /logos/ or ((Logos)), /God/ or ((God)), /scripture/ or ((Scripture)), /the infinite/ or ((The Infinite)), and so on. The /egomental logistic/ can and does encompass without "discrimination" a /multitude of sins/ . . . any "worldview" or "perspective." Prior to our explicit introduction of the "dimensional differentiating signs" of / . . . / v ((. . .)), the free-floating chaotic ambiguity in "ordinary language" made it easy to capture and render any "teaching" within the /egomental lens/. But now that this primal alterity is explicitly brought into the light of day, this practice of /hermeneutical hijacking/ sets off an alarm.

Whether we "intend" it or not, when we live under the dominance of /egomental logistic/, we tend to be oblivious to our preconscious /egomental lens/, to the role our /mentation/ plays in shaping all /mental content/, and we /objectify/ our selves, /others/, and our /ecologies/ upon the /content screen/ of our /experience/; this pattern of /reductive objectification/ is already an initial step in /hermeneutical violence/ to ((Self)) and ((Others)). When we /objectify/ "Others" and process them through the privileged /lens of our worldview/, we violate their ((Otherness))—they become /objects/ for us, /contents/ on the /screen of our experience/, and this becomes a slippery slope in the precipitous fall into all forms of /violence/: we practice /monologue/ rather than respectful ((deep dialogue)). ((Persons)) are not mere /objects/, and within /egomentalism/ even our best /intentions/ to regard "others" as /persons/ are undermined by the deep, structural practice of /objectifying content/; /persons/ are not ((Persons)).

So it is not just within the endemic violence of the breakdown of human ((relations)) between /worlds/, /worldviews/, /ideologies/, and /perspectives/ in the /public space/ between /cultures/; rather, this kind of breakdown also takes place within our very Selves when I find my /self/ inhabiting multiple alter-/worlds/, and which inhabit me. Worlds and worldviews are powerful ontological and hermeneutical energy fields that tend to universalize themselves in exclusive patterns. In /egomental culture/, these /worlds/ are /worlds apart/, each defining its linguistic, epistemic, and ontological jurisdiction in their own terms, so real communication between worldviews tends to break down. Thus these breakdowns in human relations also take place /person/ to /person/ in our family life, in our workplace, in our schools, in our civic spaces, in our religious life, wherever diverse perspectives and worldviews show up. And these chronic and recurrent breakdowns are another "side effect" of /egomental life/, another symptom of the /deep dualism/ pattern.

This excursion into the depths of /egomentalism/ and the deep, structural dynamics of /egomental logistic/ may appear to have taken us a bit off course from our ((journey)) into the ((Hologistic)) dimension of the ((Logosphere)). But having this vivid and heightened sense of precisely how and why /egomentalism/ spawns deep dualisms in their many forms may serve us well in moving forward dramatically in our ((dimensional shifting)) adventure. And, of course, our ((critique of /egomental reason/)) has been proceeding here within the ((Hologistic Technology)) and through our ((Global Lens)). Indeed, this is what allows us to see into and through the futility of /egomentalism/. So let us ((resume)) our ((experimental exploration)) and enter more deeply into the ((Space of Natural Reason)) and the surrounding ((Ecology of Natural Language—The Logosphere)).

THE MISSING *FIRST DISCIPLINE*:
SOLVING THE PROBLEMS OF /EGOMENTAL DUALISM/

We are in the midst of ((experiencing)) the profound ((dimensional shift)) of crossing from /egomentalism/ into the ((sacred space)) of ((Awakened Reason)), into the ((Logosphere)) that always surrounds us. We have seen that this calls for a radical ((reorientation)) in ((rational space)) when we place ((First things First)). While the /egomental mind/ privileges its own /word/ and /lens/ and worldview/ and places its /agenda/ first, the ((awakened global mind)) recognizes that ((Infinite Presence)) is truly ((First)) in every sense, and when we honor ((First things First)) there is a profound reorientation and realignment in the ((Space of Reason)), the Hologistic Space of ((Primary Being)). As we ((recenter)) in this ((Logosphere)) through the dilation of the ((hologistic lens)), we experience the primal ((connectivity)) and ((boundless continuum)) of ((LogoSophia)).

The ((Infinite Word)) permeates and self-extends, as the ((Cosmos)), and everything in this pulsating ((Logosphere)) is a direct ((sign)) of this ((Infinite Presence)). What we usually call "signs," the written, spoken, and invisible thought ((signs)) of everyday ((language)), are now seen to be ((symptoms)) of the ((Primal Sign Continuum)). When we ((encounter)) ((First things First)), everything is radically transformed from our former /understanding/. We have seen that in this ((Primal Hologistic Continuum)), every ((item)) that appears ((. . . word, sign, consciousness, idea, concept, percept, mind, object, event, fact, world . . .)) will reflect this ((Logosphere Continuum)). ((Word)) permeates and saturates all ((things)), in every ((dimension)) . . . in ((mind)) in ((consciousness)), in ((language)), in ((thoughts)), in ((ideas)), in ((percepts)), in ((meaning)), in ((truth)), in ((object)), in ((event), in ((world)): We experience anew this ((MindWordConceptObjectEvent . . .)) continuum. ((Mind)) extends into the ((World)) into ((Matter)) into ((Nature)) and intimately touches ((Objects)); we do not begin with a presumed /dualism/ or split between /word/ v /mind/ v /world/, but with their ((mutual saturation)): We ((begin)) with the ruling ((first principle)) of ((Relativity)) rather than with the /derivative/, /divisive/, and /constructed/ /first principle/ of /Identity/.

When we begin with ((Relativity))—the infinite relational force field wherein everything ((co-arises)) and ((co-expresses)) in essential ((holo-continuum))—the chronic /dualism/, /polarization/, /mutual exclusivity/, /atomic identity/, and chaotic /fragmentation/ are left behind. It becomes clear that the true ((solution)) to the chronic /dualistic/ problems that plague /egomental reason/ cannot come forth within that inherently /broken and self-alienating space of reason/. Rather, the crossing into ((Integral Reason)), into the presiding ((context)) of the ((Logosphere)) truly ((dissolves)) those rational and ontological /pathologies/, dissolves the /egomentalism/ that is the generative cause of these dysfunctions.

It is in this ((dimensional shift)) into ((Awakened Reason)) that the old /mind/ v /matter/ chronic dualism is ((solved)) through the encounter with ((MindMatter)) as the primal ((continuum)). It is in this ((Hologistic Continuum)) that all the broken, alienated, and fragmented items—the /egomental constructs/—are ((healed)) and ((restored)) to their ((true integral and holistic form)): ((Finite and Infinite Touch)), ((Logos and Flesh meet)), ((Word and Object permeate each other)), ((Mind and Word find intimacy)), ((Space and Time co-express each other)), ((Unity and Diversity augment and need each other)), ((I and Thou find communion in deep dialogue)), ((I and Nature complement each other)), ((I and LogoSophia kiss in intimate knowledge)) . . . all of the ((primal categories)) touch, mutually embrace, and constitute each other in the ((Rational Light of Logos)); the ((diverse revelations)) of this ((Infinite First)) celebrate each other . . . ((Tao . . . Aum . . . Yahweh . . . Christ . . . Buddha . . . Krishna . . . Allah . . . Sophia . . . Nommo . . . Spirit . . . Nature . . . Gaia . . .)). All of our great ((religious paths . . . scriptures . . . teachers . . . teachings)) are disclosed in their common ((logos-code));

our diverse ((disciplinary languages and perspectives)) find their ((mutual common generative cause)) in this ((Integral Rational Continuum)) of the liberated ((liberal arts)).

DEEP ONTOLOGY OF GLOBAL FIRST PHILOSOPHY: ((HOLOGISTIC WORLDVIEW))

In our primal journey into this ((Logosphere)) . . . the missing ((First Discipline)), the Primal ((Science-Art-Philosophy)) $\Longleftrightarrow$ ((Global First Philosophy)) $\Longleftrightarrow$ the missing ((Grammar of Logos)) are mutually revealed. In this ((Space)) of ((Infinite Presence)) all ((possibilities)) are encoded . . . ((LogoSophia)) is the ((generative seed)) and ((womb)) of all possible ((worlds)), all possible forms of ((language)), all possible ((logics)), all possible ((perspectives)) and ((narratives)), all ((forms of life)), all possible ((theories)), ((hermeneutical forms)), all ((art forms)), all possible ((sciences)), the proactive source of all ((technologies)), all ((insights and breakthroughs)) . . . and encode each other. The long, deep, and relentless ((quest)) for ((*What-Is-First*)) is now seen to be the infinite call of this ultimate ((force)) . . . ((Infinite Presence)).

((HOLOGISTIC CONTINUUM OF LOGOSPHERE))

The ((Simple Truth)) of ((Infinite LogoSophia)) is that the ((Logosphere)) as the ((expression)) of this ((Infinite Presence)) is a ((Hologistic Continuum)) that could not be approached adequately without the ((. . .)) Hologistic MindProcess. The Infinite Unity of ((Logos)) implies an unbroken ((Holistic Continuum)) . . . profoundly different from /holistic/ or /continuum/: the /egomental calculus/ lacked the ((mindword technology)) to make the ((dimensional shift)) into the ((hologistic logic)) that allows us deeper ((access)) to ((Infinite Presence)). So let us journey further into this ((Holistic)) Continuum.

((RELATIVITY)) IS THE FIRST PRINCIPLE OF ((NATURAL REASON))

We have suggested that egomental /Identity/is not and cannot be the ((first principle)) of ((Natural Reason)), ((Natural Logic)), ((Natural Language)), for when /Identity/ is stripped bare of its illicit trading on the ((relational)) and ((unifying)) and ((diversifying)) resources of the ((logosphere)), this /artificial construct/ of /egomentalism/ crumbles and disintegrates into its fragmented particles. It is ((Infinite Presence)), as expressed in its ((Primal Principle of Relativity)), that makes all ((relations)), ((identities)), ((unities)), and ((differences)) possible. This ((Principle of Relativity)) expresses the ((global truth)) that every ((item)) of whatever ((sort)) or ((dimension)) ((touch, mutually permeate, or co-arise)) in boundless ((hologistic continuum)), which is the ((Logosphere)). ((Relativity)) is the source of all ((coherence)), of all ((logical relations))—entailment, implication-deduction, induction; no "logic" can arise without this genuine ((First Principle)), which is immediately funded by ((Infinite Presence)). This ((Logosphere)) is the ((space)) of ((Natural Language)) . . . of ((Natural Reason)) . . . of ((Primary Being)).

((HOLOGISTIC CONTINUUM OF MINDWORDWORLD))

Our ((dimensional shift)) from /linear thinking/ into ((Hologistic MindWord Calculus)) makes it possible to see and process the boundless ((Interconnectivity)) in all directions: We have suggested that ((. . .)) is the ((LogoSign)), hence it ((expresses)) infinite ((sign power)): when it is said in the ((First Discipline)) that ((In the Beginning is the Word)) this ((Word)) this ((Sign)) filled with boundless ((Information))—((Meaning)) . . . ((TruthForce)) . . . ((Rational Light)) . . . ((Goodness)) permeates all dimensions—this ((Infinite Sign)) touches ((Mind)) and pervades ((consciousness)), touches ((Matter)) and self-expresses in all ((objects)), ((events)), in ((Nature)) throughout the ((Logosphere)). When it is said that the ((Unified Field of Reality)) is ((Information)), the ((Akashic Field)), flowing in boundless ((Meaning)) and ((Truth-Being Force)) . . . it of course taps this ((Word)) power. This ((Logos Grammar)) . . . the ((Primal Natural Language)) situates and surrounds all items of the Universe. This is why it has been said that ((Language is the House of Being)).

Again, this crossing into the ((Hologistic)) makes clear that any primal ((words)), ((categories)), or ((concepts)), the building blocks of the ((Logosphere)) we choose, are found to ((mutually permeate)) one another, for example, ((Time)). Holistic ((Time)) expresses the ((categorical continuum)) and permeates ((Space)), ((Word)), ((Mind)), ((Matter)) . . . ((Being)), ((I am)), and all time points . . . past, present, and future . . . meet and touch in the ((Now)) . . . ((Primal Presence)), all /tenses/ arise from this ((Presence HoloTense)); so now we ((see)) that ((mindwordsign)) power . . . pervades the ((logosphere)) . . . every ((item)) is a ((sign)) of ((Logos)). And the ((Logosphere)) is the ((Event Continuum)).

When we focus on ((Mind)), here again the ((Hologistic)) power of ((Relativity)) recognizes that ((Mind)) and ((Word)) arise together in each other, ((Mind) and ((Time)) and ((Being)) are inseparable, ((Mind)),

((Space)), and ((Matter)) constitute one another, so ((MindBody)) is a primal living reality . . . ((Mind)) and ((Causation)) empower each other, ((Mind)) and ((Meaning)) . . . ((Information)) flow together, so ((Intelligence)) flows in the ((Logosphere)); it is this ((Hologistic Causation)) . . . ((causal implicature)) that explains the ((non/local/ connectivity of things and events across space-time)) . . . and the so-called ((butterfly effect)) . . . the deep ((connectivity of distant events)) throughout the ((logosphere)).

We can see at the frontier of the emerging ((new physics)) that there is an ((instinctive tapping)) of the ((Hologistic)) to cope with the ((hologistic dynamics)) of our ((Universe)) . . . "nonlocality" . . . "fractals" . . . "black holes . . . infinite density" . . . "butterfly effect" . . . "super luminary velocity" . . . "grand unified theory" . . . "chaos and complexity." It is clear that the long quest for the "Unified Field" could not be found within the old /egomental mind-space/. Rather, the dimensional shift to ((. . .)) . . . to ((Hologistic Calculus)) is the key to entering the ((Unified Field)), and what appears as /chaos/ to the /egomental lens/ reveals its deeper ((Order)) to the ((Hologistic Lens)). But this abysmal ((Order)) of the ((Logosphere)) defies all projections of /order/ and is beyond /determinacy/ or /prediction/ or /control/.

Here it should be clear that this ((Hologistic Worldview)) is not /reducible/ to "just another" /worldview/; rather, it encodes all possible "worlds" . . . filled with virtual realities, fictive worlds . . . beyond mere /fact/. ((Actuality)) is laden with ((possibilities)). The diverse "worldviews" that have emerged thus far in the ((evolution of cultures)), even the "virtual worlds" of science fiction, get their ((information potentials)) from the ((Logosphere)). In this ((light)) we can see the ((grain of truth)) in /materialism/, in /idealism/, in /dualism/, in /monism/, in /pluralism/, /theism/, /atheism/, /pantheism/, in /mysticism/, /modernism/, and /postmodernism/ . . . and of course even in /skepticism/. In a moment, as we revisit our ((fast-forward scan)) through the evolution of cultures and consciousness, this time with our explicit markers . . . ((. . .)) v / . . . / . . . for the two dimensions of mind-language-experience, we shall briefly tap these ((seeds of truth)) latent in our diverse /worldviews/, /authors/, /narratives/, and /teachings/.

((HOLOCONTINUUM MELTS AWAY ALL /DUALISMS/ AND ARTIFICIAL /DIVISIONS/))

We have been meditating on this unprecedented ((disclosure)) of the ((Hologistic Continuum)) of the ((LogoSphere)) and illustrating the ((Continuum)) power of ((Relativity)). Now let us ((focus)) for a moment on the diverse /dualisms/ and /artificial divides/ that pervade /egomental discourse/. We suggested that the intractable /mind/ v /body/ or /mind/ v /matter/ dualism arises from /egomental reason/ and its /identity/ first principle. The ((solution)) to this dualism, and the host of others that abound in /egomentalism/, cannot be found in this /dimension/ of /discourse/; rather, it is the ((dimensional shift)) to the objective continuum reality of ((Logosphere)) that dissolves the chronic /dualisms/ at all levels.

When we center in this ((holospace)) of (Natural Reason)), we find that the chasm between /finite/ v /infinite/ de/constructs/, and the ((finite $\Longleftrightarrow$ infinite)) continuum comes forth; it takes an awakened ((mind)) to become truly ((finite)) . . . to realize our abysmal ((finitude)) in its seamless interplay with ((Infinite Presence)); similarly, we find the old polar split between /inner subjectivity/ and /outer objectivity/ to ((dissolve)) in the light of ((Relativity)), where we always find the ((presence of the Other)) within the ((one)), the unbreachable ((continuum)) between my ((inner world)) and the ((external world)) of the surrounding ((ecology)); we have already suggested that ((I am)) and ((word)), and ((thought)), and ((time)), and ((space)), and ((body)), and ((world)) . . . mutually ((flow)) into one another, even as each holds its ((distinctive identity)) vis-à-vis one another.

Again, the ((global)) or ((macro)) is reflected in the ((local)) or ((micro)), and this is due to the ((consistency)) of the ((hologistic continuum)). The ((universal)) is manifested in the ((particular)), ((essence)) is ((localized)) in the ((individual)), ((form)) in the ((matter)), ((one)) in the ((many)), ((*e pluribus unum*)), ((individual)) in the ((Polis)), ((male)) in the ((female)), in the ((holistic gender continuum)); and the classic split between ((unity)) and ((diversity)) now finds a ((continuum meeting point)), as does the millennial war between /identity/ v /difference/; indeed, the ((Principle of Relativity)) is able to hold the sanctity of the ((individual)), even as it makes real the ((continuum bond)) between all ((persons)). There is no /contradiction/ or /opposition/ between the ((truth)) of my ((individuality)) and the ((truth)) of my essential common ((humanity)), since it is within the ((Logosphere)) that my ((sacred individuality)), ((unique identity)), and ((communion in community)) mutually unfold; so we begin to see that the /law of identity/ leads to /self-splitting/, /self-contradiction/, and /discoherence/, while the ((Law of Relativity)) is the genuine ((principle of non-/contradiction/)), ((inclusive middle)), ((identity-in-difference)), ((deep continuum coherence)), and ((rational consistency)).

This powerful ((hologistic dialectic)) of ((Relativity)) also melts away the classic splits between /faith/ and reason/, /reason/ and /passion/, /theory/ v /praxis/, /a priori/ v /a posteriori/, /concept/ v /percept/, /deduction/ v /induction/, /contingency/ v /necessity/, /form/ v /content/, /science/ v /spirit/, /fact/ v /value/, /nature/ v /culture/, and /is/ v /ought/.

The polar splits in the /ideologies/ of /rationalism/ v /empiricism/ that "Kant" so brilliantly sought to resolve in his "Copernican revolution" are now ((relocated)) in the ((dimensional)) shift into ((Natural Reason)). Here we find that the ((innate a priori)) of the ((Logosphere)) shows up as the abysmal ((*a posteriori*)) and ((chaotic contingency)) of the surrounding ((ecology)); we also find that /faith/ v /reason/ is burned off in the rise into ((Awakened Reason)), where ((Faith)) is a primal form of ((Rational Intuition)) and ((deep dialogic encounter)) of ((Infinite Presence)) and the ((I am)). Here too we find a seamless flow between ((sense)) and ((reason)), ((percept)) and ((concept)), and ((reason)) and ((passion)), and as the communion of ((Being)) and ((Goodness)) comes to clarity, the /split/ between /is/ and /ought/, /being/ and /value/, likewise evaporates, for the Laws of the Logosphere incorporate ((descriptive)) and ((prescriptive)) force. The ((Laws of Nature)) and the ((Global Moral Law)) meet, and so on.

THE COMMON GROUND OF CONTENDING WORLDVIEWS AND POLARIZED DISCIPLINES

In this same ((spirit)), the ((Hologistic Continuum)) is the ((dynamic common ground)) across diverse /worldviews/, /religions/, /ideologies/, and /perspectives/; in this ((powerful mediating space of global reason)), the diverse /religious worlds/ of /Judaism/, /Christianity/, and /Islam/ find their ((common origin)) in the ((Logosphere)); even the vast /alterity/ between /East/ v /West/ is bridged by ((Infinite Presence)). The ((global lens)) gives us the higher order ((rational capacity)) to bridge the /chasm/ between /Hindu wisdom/ and the teachings of /Christ/, between the insights of /Buddha/ and the teachings of /Mohammed/, for when we place the teachings of ((Jesus)) in the ((Logosphere)) and encounter the ((script of Buddha)), we are able to celebrate the ((historical uniqueness)) of both and yet find the ((global wisdom)) in the ((Buddha)) and ((the Christ)). When we enter the powerful ((rational dialectics)) of ((Deep Dialogue)), the living pulse of ((Awakened Reason)), we are able to ((mediate)) the ((alterities)) between /worlds/, discerning deeper ((unity)) in the midst of their ((diversity)), for they co-arise from ((Infinite Presence)).

The same is true, of course, of the wide-ranging diversity of the ((disciplines)) incorporated into the ((liberal arts)). When the fragmented and estranged /disciplines/ are ((situated)) in the originating ((Logosphere)) and approached in the ((Space of Integral Reason)), we can begin to find the deeper ((resonance)) between ((logic . . . music . . . mathematics . . . poetry . . . physics . . . philosophy . . .)); within the ((Hologistic Continuum)) we can begin to discern ever deeper ((analogies)) and ((co-expressions)) across the diverse ((Arts)) and ((Sciences)) in their ((multimedia)). This is the ((rational power)) of the ((First Discipline)), which brings into relief the long-dormant, hidden, or eclipsed ((common generative ground)) across widely variant ((narrative forms of life)).

It becomes clearer that ((Deep Dialogue)) and ((Awakened Critical Thinking) are the living pulse of ((Hologistic Reason)): the maturation from /egomentalism/ to ((Global Rationality)) has profound implications for addressing and redressing the diverse /crises/ facing "humanity" in the twenty-first century. Without ((Deep Dialogue)), the process of ((Peace Making)) and ((Conflict Resolution)) will be undermined and blocked. Without the awakening of genuine ((Global Citizenship)), the fabric of real ((Democracy)) will be undermined by the /fragmentation/ of our /civic space/ and /polarization/ of the /people/. A healthful ((living democracy) is based in ((Power to the People)) . . . ((We the People)) . . . and if the /People/ are /scattered/ in polarities and fragmentation, and the ((Civic Space)) is broken and polarized . . . there is no ((We)). We will pursue this theme later.

((INTEGRAL LOGIC AND THE ORIGIN OF ALL PROOFS))

We have been suggesting that in this ((dimensional shift)) into the ((Hologistic Continuum)) the awakened ((logistic)) of ((Integral Consciousness)) is inseparable from ((rational content)): ((logic)) cannot be severed from ((logistic)), and, indeed, no /rational proof/ could work without tapping the ((relational force)) of ((Relativity)). The praxis or conduct of consciousness (logistic) is directly linked to /logic/ and all of its /content/, and we earlier suggested that all /egomental systems/ are inherently ((incomplete))—((The Global Incompleteness Theorem))—of ((Integral Reason)): no /egomental /system/ based on /identity/ and severed from ((Relativity)) can stand the scrutiny of ((critical reason)): so with the crossing into ((Rational Space))—((Relational Space))—we reach a new and higher level of ((rational rigor)) and ((critical awareness)).

The ((Rationality)) of the ((Hologistic Continuum)) is bound to be different from /egomental rationality/; for example, we have suggested that no /proof/ could work without the ((rational)) resources of ((Relativity)). And since ((Words)), ((Signs)), ((Thought)), and ((Ideas)) in the ((Continuum)) behave differently from egomental /signs/, /thoughts/, or /ideas/, what might count as a ((rigorous proof)) in ((Hologistic Reason)) might be completely missed or deformed by the /egomental mind/. For example, in the power of ((Meditative Reason)), one might discover that the ((Idea)) of ((Infinite Being)), unlike any /idea/ of /infinite being/, immediately reveals the ((living truth)) and ((existential presence)) of ((Logos)) and the ((Logosphere)).

As we have seen, Descartes, in his *Meditations*, struggled with demonstrating that ((Infinite Being must be)). If his ((thought process)) is /reduced/

to /egomental logic/, then his point will be missed. And "Aristotle" already understood, in the quest for Primary Being, that not everything can be /proven/; it shows "want of education," he suggests, to ask for /proof/ of the ((rational conditions)) that make all thinking and proof possible. Perhaps ((Logos)) or ((Infinite Being)) cannot be /proven/ in /egomental logics/, but in the ((Integral Logic)) of the ((Logosphere)), the ((Idea)) of ((I am)) and my primal ((existence)) will be mutually disclosed in the ((Continuum)); so too with the ((Idea)) of ((Infinite Being)) and the primal presence of ((*What-Is-First*)). If we /reduce/ this higher order ((logic)) and ((reasoning)) to the /egomental logics/, then it would perhaps appear ludicrous. And this is what has been done. We will address this point again later.

HIGHER STANDARDS OF ((RIGOR)) AND ((CRITICAL REASON))

We have seen that /egomental reason/ tends to be blind about its own /egomental logistic/ and seeks its own form of /rigor/ and /critical thinking/ within its own presumed /rational domain/, on its own terms. But now we see that the essence of ((critical awakening)) is to become keenly aware of one's /mentation/ or /logistic mentality/ and to develop the deep dialogic ((rational skills)) of moving critically, mindfully, and sensitively across and between alternative worlds and forms of discourse. In this respect, if a /philosophical hermeneutic/ is lodged in /egomental logistic/ but is not critically aware of the nature and limits of this /rational practice/, the mental /lens/ it shapes and the fallout and implications of this minding praxis will then fall short of making the ((critical turn)) of ((awakened reason)). One may well wonder whether the current practices of "scientific method" have achieved this dimension of ((critical awakening)), and to what extent this method may be laboring under the dysfunctional ways of /egomentalism/. We suggest that the maturation of the ((scientific method)) calls forth this awakening of ((global reason)) and its ((dimensional shift)) from /science/ to ((science)).

((INTEGRAL SCIENCE AND THE MISSING FIRST DISCIPLINE))

In this ((light)) it is more apparent that the "modern" split between /science/ and /philosophy/ is an unfortunate turn (under the influence of /egomental reason/) that impeded the mutual full flowering of both ((science)) and ((philosophy)), and, of course, our common ((rational enterprise)). We have seen that careful attention to our "method of inquiry," and the "conduct of our mind," was a preoccupation that spurred on "philosophy" and gave birth to the empirical and experimental methods of inquiry that we call "modern science." But now it is clearer in the context of ((Global First Philosophy)) and the ((Hologistic Continuum)) that our methods of inquiry and minding must pay keen attention to the deeper "logistic" or technology of consciousness that shapes everything in our human condition: it makes all the difference whether our hermeneutical practices, whether in common sense, daily culture or in "science" or "philosophy" or "religious" life, are proceeding in the space of /egomental logistic/ or in the awakened consciousness of ((Hologistic Reason)).

/Scientific Method/ may be empirical, experimental, and engaged in the virtues of verification and even self-revision in the quest for "objective truth," but these important advances in the methods of inquiry, when lodged in the space of /egomental reason/, become restricted and obsessed with /content/, and they tend to be uncritical and inattentive to the deeper /logistic/ that presides and rules all /content/ and can block deeper access to ((objective reality)). We have seen that when we are uncritically lodged in /egomental reason/, the controlling /lens/ of the mind that structures and controls the /content of experience/ that appears on its screen can fall into dogmatic /ideological prejudice/ that undermines the highest ((scientific inquiry)). And here the /egomental logistic/ can become another /idol of the mind/ that impedes the maturation of the ((scientific method)).

THE MATURATION OF THE ((SCIENTIFIC METHOD))

The /egomental lens/ fixes a certain /worldview/, /categorical framework/, or /theoretical paradigm/ that also needs to be ((experimentally tested)) and revised appropriately in the feedback from the surrounding ((hologistic field)) . . . the ((Logosphere)), which is the primal field of ((objective reality)). Thus if our "science" is using the Ptolemaic lens, then the self-revision in the /theoretical framework/ to the Copernican lens brings an advance toward ((truth)). Again, when the "Newtonian" lens and its worldview or ontology were displaced with the Einsteinian lens, a new "universe" appeared—we shifted to "Einstein's universe," and of course frontier physics is now pushing the limits of this /lens/ in the quest for more powerful "concepts" and "theoretical frameworks" to cope with the mounting recalcitrant phenomena seeping through from the ((Logosphere)).

We are suggesting that the maturation in the ((scientific method)) has reached an exciting critical turning point in which the older ways of /egomental reason/ are outmoded and the ((forces)) of the ((Unified Field)) are calling us to a dimensional shift to ((hologistic reason)). ((Science)) needs to be self-critical also about its presumed /ontology/ or /ideology/ as well as its presumptions concerning the technology of mind and its "logistic" in deepening the ((rational enterprise)). This is where a ((cocreative partnership)) and ((reunion)) between ((Science)) and ((Philosophy)) would be mutually beneficial. We have been suggesting that ((First Philosophy)) is indispensable for the advancement of ((rational inquiry)) and more powerful ((hermeneutical methods)) in the encounter with ((Reality)). The clarification of ((Hologistic Reason)) and the deepening of the ((technology of consciousness)) in the encounter with the ((Logosphere)) are vital not only for cultural life in general but for all of the arts and sciences, for all the ((disciplines)) of the ((liberal arts)). And here it is more apparent that in the ((awakened rationality)) and skills of ((deep dialogue)), all ((hermeneutical arts)) practice a form of ((experimentation)) and ((self-revision)) through the interplay of ((deep dialogue)) encounters with the ((dynamic ecology)).

Every aspect of human experience is presided by the "technology of consciousness" and the "hermeneutical practices" that shape the "content" that appears on the screen of awareness. One of the great ((lessons)) of ((Global First Philosophy)) is that if our lives are ruled by /egomental logistic/, then we fall into all kinds of /rational/ and /existential/ dysfunction, whereas when we dilate the ((global lens)) and mature in critical inquiry into more ((deep dialogic)) and ((integral patterns)) of ((Hologistic Reason)), we have deeper access to the objective reality of the presiding ((Logosphere)).

((OBJECTIVE REALITY)): THE QUEST FOR ((TRUTH)) AND ((OBJECTIVITY))

The ((First Discipline)) makes clear that the primal field of ((Reality)) is the ((Logosphere)), and this is the key to ((truth)) and ((objectivity)). Every advance in the evolution of the human condition—every advance in the awakening of human reason, every advance in the evolution of cultures, every spiritual and moral insight, every advance in science and technology, every advance in the healing arts, every breakthrough to a higher form of social and political life in the quest for human flourishing and well-being—has been funded by the surrounding hologistic field of ((Infinite Presence)). We have suggested that in earlier times the chaotic fusion and confusion of the dimensions of /egomental logistic/ and the ((Hologistic Field of Reality)) facilitated the distortion and illusion that /egomental mind/ was solely responsible for important advances. Now, in light of ((Global First Philosophy)), it is clearer that any /egomental logistic/ can only appear to work by trading on the ((rational resources)) of the ever-present and presiding ((Logosphere)).

We have seen that it is the ((objectivity)) of the ((Logosphere)) that grounds ((truth)), ((knowledge)), and ((critical reason)). When /egomental life/ is severed from its grounding in the ((Logosphere)), it falls into the /dogma/ and /prejudices/ of its self /absolutized/ /lens/ and privileged /world-view/; all attempts to be /objective/ by fixating on the /content/ of /egomental experience/ naturally fail to break free of its deep /subjectivism/ and interface critically and responsibly with ((Reality)). Of course, as we have seen, it is never possible to step outside the "subjectivity" of consciousness and the "logistic" of experience to gain privileged access to ((Objective Truth and Reality)).

This is why the maturation of our deepest dimensions of awakened ((subjectivity)) through the dimensional shift to ((Hologistic Reason)) is vital for more authentic access to ((Objective Reality)). And this is why the ((technology of Deep Dialogue)) is so important in our perennial ((quest for truth)), for the rational and critical virtues of ((deep dialogue)) take us to the deeper dimension of ((awakened subjectivity)), which is open, self-reflective, transparent, and self-revising. Of course this is the true virtue of ((scientific inquiry)), but it also is the virtue of ((awakened moral consciousness))—the maturation into the ((I⟺Thou)) epistemic space in which moral, rational, and aesthetic virtues ((co-arise)). It is in this ((First Discipline) that we find the ((Integral)) meeting point of all aspects of our ((human condition)).

CONCLUDING REFLECTIONS: OUR ((EVOLUTIONARY SHIFT)) TO A HIGHER ((GLOBAL CULTURE))

It is timely to move to a concluding ((reflection)), and it would be helpful to ((revisit)) our earlier fast-forward ((scan)) through the ((evolution)) of cultures and consciousness. We have seen that in making our ((dimensional)) shift into the ((Hologistic Space of Natural Reason)) it becomes clear that ((Infinite Presence)) proactively presides in every pulse of life and existence. This ((Force Field)) is an ((Event Continuum)) that both calls and moves every ((item)) in the ((Universe)) into highest ((creative evolution)) and ((self-expression)). In this amazing ((drama)) we have suggested that this call of ((Primary Being)) has ushered the continuing ((evolution)) of our ((human condition)) to a great ((awakening)) of our true ((human form)). The ((evidence)) of this evolutionary unfolding shows itself through the ((global lens)) over millennia as our consciousness, language forms, logistic processes, rationality, discourse, and cultures ((evolve, mature, and unfold)) within the ((Logosphere)).

We saw that prior to the explicit clarification of the ((dimensional)) shift from /egomental life/ to ((awakened rational life)), the more adolescent /egomental logistic/ pre-/consciously/ traded on the boundless ((funding)) of the ((Logosphere)) to secure a (false) sense of its /independence/ and /self-sustainability/. Let us now take a quick glance again at the amazing unfolding through the centuries, this time using our logistic ((notation)) . . . the contrast and relation between ((. . .)) and / . . . / to see, perhaps ((speculate)), on how our great "thinkers" may have been, knowingly or unknowingly, touching the ((Logosphere)), tapping the resources of ((Hologistic Reason)), and moved by ((Logos)) in the powerful call of ((Primary Being)).

Through our ((Global Lens)) and with our ((dimensional shift)) into the ((Logosphere)), the space of our ((human condition)), of our ((human evolutionary drama)), is profoundly relocated and ((reorganized)). Within this ((First Discipline)) of ((Global First Philosophy)), we are able to encounter the vast development of our ((human emergence)) in our European traditions, from Heraclitus to Derrida, as ((LogoSophia)) comes into preeminence; we are able to witness the emergence of ((Biblical Scripture)) from the Judaic origins, the coming forth of ((Jesus)) as the ((Logos-made-Flesh)), to the visions of ((Mohammed)), now all sharing the ((global sacred space)) from the ((Tao)) to ((Aum)) to ((Buddha's awakening and noble truths)), the discourses and teachings of ((Krishna)), in the clarification of ((Yoga Science)), in the breakthrough of ((Shankara)) in the advance of ((Advaita Vedanta)), in the amazing ((dialectical)) advances of ((Nagarjuna)), in opening the ((Middle-Way)) into ((Sunyata)), the ((Ground of Natural Reason)), through the emergence of Chinese and Japanese ((Zen)), with ((Master Dogen)) brilliantly building on Nagarjuna and other ((Masters)) in clarifying the ((living technology)) of entering ((Now Time)), embodying ((Enlightenment)) in ((everyday life)), through the genius of ((Nishida)), twentieth-century Zen Master, founder of the Zen Kyoto School, as his distinguished career culminates in his quest for the ((Logic of Basho)), the ((Logic of Absolute Nothingness)), not to mention the remarkable maturation of the ((Vedanta teachings)) in the lifework of Aurobindo, the twentieth-century Sage, just to mention a few.

Although we may be focusing on eminent ((Male)) voices, we remember that ((Infinite Presence)) is ((LogoSophia)) and incorporates the full power of ((Feminine Energies)) and ((integral wisdom)). As the primal ((Script)) of ((Logos)) comes forth through the vast resources of ((sacred scripts)) through the ages we cross into ((Global Wisdom)) and the coming forth of the deeper ((Global Scripture)) that has been ever-present and presiding in all ((scripts)) and ((teachings)).

We are suggesting that every "thinker," "seer," "wisdom keeper," "scripture," and "first philosophy" may be processed via / . . . / or placed within the ((. . .)) hermeneutical lens and technology. And our earlier formula: ((. . . / . . . / . . .)) reminds us that all /egomental life/ and /discourse/ will proceed within the primal field of ((natural language)), so let us very briefly in this concluding moment play through our ((power scan)) of selected "scripts":

If we glance at the early Greek origins of the ((quest for Logos)), focusing for a moment on ((/Heraclitus/)), we may easily render one of his "fragments" as ((Listen not to me but to the Logos, and know that all things are One)), and it may well be that ((he)) had insights into ((Becoming)), and recognized the emptiness of /Being/.

Similarly, as ((/Parmenides/)) moves deeply into ((Primary Being)) as ((Absolute)) and ((One)) and beyond /Becoming/, ((he)) taps the space of ((First Philosophy)); ((/Socrates/)) is an embodiment of emerging ((Wisdom)) in opening ((radical inquiry)), deep ((rational dialogue)), seeing that /knowledge/ is not ((grounded in Logos)) and urging his colleagues to radically critique their everyday /beliefs/ as not genuine ((Wisdom)). There may be something to the Oracle's remark that ((Socrates is the wisest)) of all. And his brilliant student ((/Plato/)) clearly touched the ((Logos)), for example, in a high point of his *Republic* when he lays out the journey of ((reason)) and ((awakening knowledge)) to its primal source—the ((Rational Light)): he explicitly sees that this ((rational intuition)) is beyond /Being/ and /Truth/—the very source of all meaning, being, truth, and rational light, the ((Form)) of all "forms."

While Plato seems to focus on prioritizing this ((Unity)), it appears that his eminent protégé ((/Aristotle/)) accentuates ((Difference)) and ((Particularity)) and opens new dimensions into ((First Philosophy)) and the quest for ((Primary Being)); but in our journey, we saw that ((Ousia)) keeps bursting out of the /egomental box/ and any /egoized/ objectification of /predication/ as the /content of consciousness/, and this ((theme)) haunts the ((European traditions)) through the ages and into the twentieth century, as we have seen.

If we cast our ((glance)) for a moment toward the ((biblical tradition)) and focus on ((Jesus)), we can see a world of ((difference)) between ((Jesus)) as the ((Logos-made-Flesh)) and the egomental /Jesus/—in this ((Light)) we see ((Jesus)) as an ((exemplar)) of the ((Living Logos)) . . . an ((embodiment)) of the ((script)) of ((LogoSophia)) . . . and his teachings rendered via ((. . .)) come to ((Life)): ((I am the Way, the Truth, and the Life)), which ((reminds)) us that the ((Moral Law)) must be ((embodied in our Life)), that primal encounters with the ((Logosphere)) are the pulse of ((Meaning . . . Truth . . . Life . . . Primary Being . . . Goodness . . . Wholeness)), and being cut off from ((Logos)) is a form of ((ontological /death/)); and this ((Jesus)) exemplifies the ((prototype human)) . . . the ((whole integral person)) . . . ((MindMatterSpirit)) . . . rising into ((Now Time)); and the ((New Covenant)) that ((Jesus)) inaugurates and exemplifies may well be seen as the move from / . . . / to ((. . .)) . . . so ((Christ Consciousness)) calls for the letting go of /egomental/ ways.

Turning now to ((/Descartes/)), we saw earlier that his breakthrough to ((I am)) was missed by /interpreters/ who could only see /I am/ . . . the egomental /I/ . . . but if we encounter his "Meditations" as ((Meditations)) and process his "voice" via ((. . .)), his ((script)) resonates as a profound entrance into ((First Philosophy)), for his ((Methodical Doubt)) makes the classical discovery that /egomental discourse/ can be radically ((questioned)) and placed in ((Doubt)) if it is cut off from its ((foundation)); it was then that he moved out of the /predicative box/ and encountered his ((primary being)) . . . his ((Self)) in the ((I am)) . . . breaking the /egomental barrier/ and touching the depth of ((Natural Reason)), letting go of all former /narratives/ and /constructs/; this ((I am)) is pre-/predicative/ . . . and ((he)) is stunned in this ((discovery)); he then immediately advances to ((see)) that this ((I am)) is truly ((I ⟸⟹ Thou)) as he becomes clearer that the ((Idea of Infinite Being)) ((is)) ((Infinite Being)) . . . which turns on the ((uniqueness)) of this ((Idea)) . . . unlike all egomental /ideas/. . . . So the true starting point is this ((I am ⟸⟹ Thou Art)) continuum . . . his grounding and communion in ((Infinite Presence)). . . . There is so much here . . . his brilliant meditative move from ((I am)) to ((bodies are)) as he discovers that ((Mind ⟸⟹ Body)) forms an unbroken ((continuum)). Here it is apparent that this ((Descartes)) is a true ((hero)) of ((First Philosophy)) rather than the /dualistic villain/ and /dupe/ that /Descartes/ is now often taken to be.

Very quickly we might visit ((/Hume/)) and see that he is ((right)) to be skeptical about the power of /reason/ to account for our "everyday beliefs" and "logic of induction"; ((he)) rejects the long-held /mantra/ that "Humans are /rational beings/" and replaces it with ((Passion)) . . . ((Feeling)) . . . ((Sentiment)) . . . grounded in the ((Psyche)) and rooted in our ((Animal Nature)) and ((Instinct)). It is here that he finds the ((secret springs of Nature)) that fund our ((everyday beliefs)) and ((natural induction)).

((/Berkeley/)) may be seen as coming close to ((recognizing)) that /materialism/ undermines ((common sense)), which requires the ((Proactive Presence)) of ((Infinite Mind)) to fund and support our everyday ((worldview)) that is committed to an ((objective world)) that exists independently of our /ego subjectivity/; nevertheless, he clarifies that ((To be is to be Perceived)), a permutation on ((We are as we Mind)), and he sees his ((Idealism)) as echoing the truth of ((biblical Ontology)), that ((Spirit)) creates and sustains the ((World)) and all our ((experience)).

Of course ((/Kant/)) makes brilliant strides toward ((First Philosophy)) in seeing clearly the difference between /Phenomena/ and "/Noumena/," although for him the /categories/ of /experience/ cannot be applied to the ((Thing-in-Itself)). ((Noumena)) is off limits to /predicative thought/ and its /categories/, and he finds two "selves" . . . the /phenomenal self/ that can be an /object/ of /scientific study/ and the ((Noumenal Self)) . . . the ((moral self)) that is the tue ((person)) that must never be treated as an /object/ or /means to an end/ . . . but always an ((end in itself)); and he saw that /knowledge/ is of /appearance/ and off limits to /What-is-in-itself/. He found it necessary to clip the /wings of knowledge/ to open space for ((Rational Faith)).

(((/Hegel/))'s gallant attempt to surpass "Kant" and gain access to ((What Is)) opens new vistas in the ((History of Geist)), seeing all historical processes as the ((drama)) of ((Geist)) unfolding in the world, and his ingenious attempt to put aside the naïve /logic of predication/ and /identity/ to find a more powerful "logic" and "dialectic" that can reveal the deeper ((process of historical unfolding)) in the ((narrative of Geist)) opens up ((possibilities)) for ((First Philosophy)).

Needless to say, (((/Nietzsche/)), is a ((living paradox)), and his quip (((/God/ is dead, and the /Christians/ have killed him)), is a far cry from the usual way of rendering this remark. There is a world of difference between ((God)) and /God/; to objectify and reduce ((God)) to the /egomental box/ of /Infinite Being/, to /God/, is to crucify the ((Living Word)); and ((Nietzsche))'s call for a radical ((transvaluation)) of /values/ in the awakening of the ((*UberMensch*)), the empowered and morally responsible ((Human)) . . . radically ((questioning)) the /egomental culture/ and its /ethics/ of /good and evil/, and leaving the /herd mentality/ . . . all ((rings true)) in the ((Hologistic Perspectivity)) of the ((Global Lens)); we are ((perspectival beings)) . . . but the /egomental lens/ is not our only ((option)); when we mature to ((interperspectivity)), to ((hologistic perspectivity)), and learn to hold and negotiate multiple ((alter-perspectives)) in an ((awakened rational consciousness)), what we call ((global perspective)), we come closer to ((truth)); and, of course, this is not a /view/ from /nowhere/ but the ((awakened rationality)) . . . and ((Integral Perspective)) in the ((HereNow)).

The marvelous opening of (((/Husserl/)) in taking his point of departure from ((Cartesian Meditations)) finds a vital missed moment in which ((critical consciousness)) can ((bracket)) the /ego mind/ and its /ego judgment/ . . . always /prejudiced/ and lodged in /subjectivism/ to rise into a higher ((witnessing observer)) . . . which opened the new ((discipline of phenomenology)); when we suspend egomental /judgment/ = /egomentalism/ = /ego fundamentalism/, and rise into the meditative phenomenology . . . we open a higher ((lens)) of ((discernment)) beyond /judgmentalism/. ((Husserl)) saw this move as vital for the /crisis in the sciences/ and for the ((future of culture)); his gallant quest for a ((Formal and Transcendental Logic)) opens paths into ((Meditative Reason)) and the ((Logic of Logos)).

The birth of (((/Existentialism/)) through his two eminent protégés, (((/Heidegger/)) and (((/Sartre/)), is most interesting: the denouncing of naïve /essentialism/ and the encounter with (((/Nothingness/)), together with the decentering of /Being/ and /essence/, opens deeper space for ((First Philosophy)); (((/Heidegger/)) rejects the earlier prioritizing of /Sein/ or /Being/ and focuses his attention, as we have seen, on (((/Dasein/)) out of the /objectified/ and /essentialized/ /predicative box/. The "I" and "being there" of the "self," stripped of all /essence/ . . . reminiscent of the ((Cartesian ((I am)) . . .)), is rendered by ((/Sartre/)) as bare ((existence)), which is prior to /essence/ . . . and this /I/ is /No thing/ . . . /Nothingness/ . . . not quite the ((Nothingness = Sunyata)) of Buddha and Nagarjuna. We remember that ((/Heidegger/)) abandons his youthful /project/ of the /Analytic of Dasein/, and in his mature career he appears to cross over into ((Language)), the ((House of Being)), where he encounters a deeper ((Being)) and ((Dasein)), and he finds that ((humans)) are ((Meditative Beings)).

Obviously we are just getting started, and we must conclude. Had we the ((space/time)) here we would of course quickly run through the marvelous developments of certain ((Eastern traditions)) . . . from ((Buddha)) to ((Nagarjuna)) to ((Nishida)) . . . as the discourse of ((Nothingness)) or ((Emptiness)) unfolds and matures, and the ((Logic)) of Nishida begins to become explicitly articulated. We would touch upon the important breakthrough of ((/Frege/)) and witness the dramatic ((unfolding)) of the quest for the ((logic of natural language)), through the remarkable careers of ((/Wittgenstein/)), his earlier and later works. We would focus on the early ((Vedanta)) teachings as spoken by ((Krishna)) and see their dramatic unfolding through ((Shankara)), through ((Aurobindo)), again seeing the maturation of this rich tradition into its ((evolutionary)) narrative in which ((matter)) is found to be sacred, and the ((individual)) is emerging in ((creative evolution)), the ((Evolutionary Drama of Brahman)).

We would touch upon the higher possibilities of the ((meeting of diverse narrative worlds)), as in the emergence of ((Mind-Body Medicine)) and ((Integral Medicine and Healing Arts)) that can bring together in an ((Integral Art Science)) diverse alternative ((medical healing worlds)). Here we see that we need the ((Hologistic Technology)) to make a ((dimensional shift)) into ((Integral Science)), which hits limits in /egomental space/. All attempts to develop /Integral Studies/ within this /self-divisive technology/ are bound to unravel. True ((Interdisciplinary)) studies take a leap beyond egomental /interdisciplinary/ discourse that keeps hitting its own /artificial barriers/, and so on.

((FINAL TRANSITIONAL THOUGHTS))

This ((Prologue)) is meant to ((open space)) and provide vital missing ((technology)) for engaging in ((Global First Philosophy)). The rich range of themes touched upon here will be explored in greater depth in the ((chapters)) that comprise ((Part 2)). These ((themes)) also have been developed at great length in two prior volumes—*Meditative Reason: Toward Universal Grammar* (1994) and *Between Worlds: The Emergence of Global Reason* (1997); both were published by Peter Lang Press in their *Revisioning Philosophy Series*. The ((chapters)) presented here seek to open the way to ((Global First Philosophy)) and the ((Global Rationality)) of the ((Awakened Global Mind)). These themes also are developed in some detail in two sequel volumes, which will appear soon—*The Awakening of the Global Mind* and *Time, Truth, and Logos: The Quest for Global Integral Logic*. Also, these themes have been developed in diverse forms on the following Web site: http://www.awakeningmind.org.

In closing, let us echo some of the opening words of this book. We are in the midst of an amazing and exciting evolutionary shift in our ((human condition)) that has been millennia in the making. ((Humanity)) has arrived at a ((great awakening)) and ((maturation)) in its true ((Human Form)). We are in the midst of a profound ((dimensional shift)) in the ((technology of consciousness)) that opens an unprecedented advance to a higher form of ((Global Culture)), grounded in awakened ((Global Consciousness)) and ((Integral Reason)). In this ((evolutionary shift)) we see the end of the apparent /dominance/ of /egomentalism/—the end of the /age of egomental reason/ and /egomental cultures/. The growing crises faced by humanity today on a global scale are found to be rooted in rampant /egomentalism/ that has continued to dominate the /life of the people/. Nothing less than a great ((mass awakening)) across this planet will creatively meet these crises and lift our ((Human Family)) to a higher form of ((civilization)) wherein we share our ((Sacred Earth)) in collective human flourishing. This, then, is the coming forth of ((Humanity)) in our crossing together into an unprecedented ((Age of Global Reason)).

SUMMARY OVERVIEW

Meditations of Global First Philosophy:
The Quest for the Missing Grammar of Logos

The emergence of First Philosophy in its global form has been in continuing evolution on a global scale through the centuries. The ongoing globalization of discourse and the human condition over millennia has brought widely variant worldviews, ideologies, cultural patterns, and diverse forms of life into direct contact and interaction. This pattern has of course accelerated in the past century, and as we now enter the twenty-first century we have arrived at a frontier at which it is especially urgent that we learn to cope creatively with the powerful forces that emerge and erupt when very different worldviews, paradigms, ideologies, and forms of life find themselves facing one another in direct interaction. It is more evident than ever that our survival, sustainability, and possibilities for human flourishing turn upon our creative capacity to advance to more integral and dialogic habits of mind and forms of life that open space for the celebration of diversity, plurality, and individuality and at the same time foster possibilities for unity, community, and common ground.

But it may not at first be obvious that this emergence of "First Philosophy" is a global phenomenon ranging across vastly diverse philosophical worlds. This is due in large part to an almost irrepressible tendency to center our thought within a particular philosophical grammar that can inhibit and block access to a more expansive, integral, rational awareness that comes with entering a truly global perspective. If we are able to stand back from being lodged in the particularity of a given perspective and negotiate the transformations into global and dialogical habits of thought, then deeper patterns and dynamics across and between diverse worldviews come into relief.

This is because the global perspective, which comes with global habits of minding, requires a firsthand saturation in diverse worldviews, perspectives, and grammatical forms, together with the dialogical capacity to hold such multiple variant worlds together in intimate interactions. So the global perspective, the global mind, is essentially interperspectival, intergrammatical, intercultural, and interdisciplinary. This is why a global perspective opens new horizons in which deeper global patterns in the evolution of the human condition come into view.

In entering the global perspective, certain striking disclosures become evident that could not be seen before. One such finding is the recognition that there has been a perennial and relentless quest across the spectrum of philosophical and spiritual traditions to articulate and encounter that which is primordial, ultimate, first. This global phenomenon is one version of what is being called "Global First Philosophy." Of course we may be more familiar with the term *First Philosophy* in the context of classical Greek thought, in which the grammar of Logos begins to emerge in the creative thought of Socrates, Plato, and Aristotle.

In fact, it is Aristotle who explicitly speaks of First Philosophy in his powerful ontological inquiry into the fundamental grammar of Primary Being. In this version, shared with Plato, there is a guiding intuition that there must be a Primal Logos that is the foundation and source of all existence, of all names and forms, of all other disciplines. These founders of the Greek philosophical tradition rightly saw that it was of the utmost importance for human flourishing that the universal grammar of this Primal Principle be clarified and articulated. And this discipline is First Philosophy.

Others may be familiar with the term *First Philosophy* in the context of Descartes' *Meditations*, the title of which is *Meditations on First Philosophy*. Here again we find a passionate quest for tapping the universal grammar of Reason, which encodes all existence, thought, and experience. But other versions of this quest for the missing foundational grammar of Logos echo through the strivings of such pioneers as Frege, Russell, Whitehead, and Wittgenstein in their heroic attempts to uncover the fundamental logic or grammar of thought that is the generative source of all discourse, including the foundations of mathematics.

But the global perspective reveals that this deep quest to decode the Primal Word resonates in diverse ways throughout other traditions and has certainly been a primary focal point in certain "Eastern" classical traditions. Whether, for example, we enter the discourse of Lao Tzu in the articulation of the primal Tao, or encounter the Vedic scriptures in the disclosure of the Primal Infinite Word, Aum, or engage the discourse of Buddha in the *Karikas* of Nagarjuna, which explore the deep structure of Sunyata (Absolute Emptiness), or again explore the meditations of Sankara on the *Brahma Sutras*, which clarify the nondual discourse of Brahman, or fast-forward through the Zen traditions into the recent writings of Nishida in his attempt to excavate the missing primal Logic of *Basho* . . . in all of these diverse attempts we find alternative pathways into the global essence of the First Principle, the Infinite Word.

The global perspective and global way of minding or processing discourse make it possible to make significant connections across widely variant grammars of First Philosophy. But one remarkable finding in this perspective is that despite the remarkable advances, East and West, toward the articulation of *What-Is-First*, there remains something vital that is still missing. For one thing, no global Primal Name has yet emerged to bring out a striking truth of Global First Philosophy—that the Primal Principle, the Infinite Word, must be the same common source and foundation of all possible first philosophies, of all possible grammars of thought. In two earlier volumes, *Meditative Reason: Toward Universal Grammar* and *Between Worlds: The Emergence of Global Reason*, I have proposed *Logos* as a candidate for a truly global name that would help us remain mindful that the Primal Word is truly global in scope and power. It is clear that a true global name cannot be expressed in ordinary egocentric forms of language but requires the global grammar and the global form of minding.

Entering this global perspective, the global grammar of Logos, also brings out certain recurring dynamics in the evolution of thought that help clarify why it has been so difficult to cross into this global way of minding. It becomes more evident that humanity has been in a profoundly challenging struggle to move beyond the localizing forces of thought and experience that generate inveterate egocentric habits of mind and forms of life. The global perspective helps bring out how and why egocentric patterns of thought produce all sorts of fragmentation and pathologies of life. It may be said that egocentric ways of being appear to be a stage in our evolution that must be overcome as we mature into more integral, dialogic, and holistic patterns of minding that come forth as we awaken and enter global forms of thought and life. This global drama of Logos emphasizes that the emergence of Logos in the human condition has been a primary moving force in human and cultural evolution.

The chapters in this book seek to build on the earlier books and to make a contribution to the further development of Global First Philosophy.

Introduction

PART 1: THE MISSING DRAMA OF LOGOS

Perhaps the greatest lesson in the global evolution of cultures is that there is and must be something original, so profound, primordial, and infinitely universal that it must be first, originating, and unitive in scope and jurisdiction. As we reenact and inventory the vastly diverse cultural traditions of discourse and human understanding in this global context, there emerges a remarkable convergence in alternative narratives of the origin of existence, thought, and discourse. As undeniably diverse and pluralistic as these alternative accounts may be, they nevertheless bear witness to the truth that human existence is profoundly conditioned by something primal and first that makes it possible to be—to think, to experience, to exist and live in a world, to be human, and to engage in discourse.

These divergent stories, sometimes complementary, more often appearing to be competing, opposed, and even contradictory, confirm an ever-deeper primordial presence that must be countenanced for anything to work. Indeed, the more diverse and mutually incompatible divergent narratives may appear only serves to deepen the intuition of the universal and univocal presence of some ultimate or absolute condition. As we scan the vast range of cultural experiments through the ages in the global context, we may see the undeniable evidence of absolute or transcendental conditions revealed in diverse forms of life. Whether the form of life plays out in what we may call a "religious," a "philosophical," a "scientific," or a "political" worldview, there is no escaping the intuition of there being primal conditions or grounds that make the lifeworld possible. It appears that this intuition into first conditions is inscribed in existence itself and is constituted in consciousness so deeply that nothing could be or be conceived without it.

Nor does it matter whether a form of life or narrative account is explicitly about absolute conditions or not, whether it is a narrative of "*What-Is-First*," for even if it is a blatant denial or rejection of anything absolute or ultimate, it cannot but confirm the constituting conditions that make possible its voice, its thought, its speech, and its narrative. For it to be effective in denying or rejecting anything, it must engage in discourse and hence in the laws and conditions that make discourse possible. So the evidence of absolute conditions is not to be found in the content or object of what is affirmed or denied, focused upon or ignored, but in the very possibility of being there at all in the first place, of existing, of thinking, of experiencing, of being in a world, and of engaging in discourse.

This inescapability of countenancing absolute, transcendental, or constituting conditions is what orients and gives order to rational space. The place of awareness and discourse is ordered and oriented by absolute conditions that structure, prioritize, and hence open the space of natural reason. The very idea of something absolute or ultimate orders existential space by its presiding presence. This absolute condition takes the position of being First in every possible way, and this both orients and generates the space of being. This Absolute Presence, in being First, makes possible the rational force field that releases intelligible light that occasions the possibility of origins, of principle, of law and regularity, of unity and diversity, of identity and difference, of relation and relationality, and of ground and foundation. So the very idea of something being First, Absolute, or Ultimate, irrespective of how it may be characterized or named, is the universal origin of reason and the source of rational intelligibility and the possibility of thought.

Of course this means that "that which is First," however it may be named or described or even countenanced as being beyond any name or description, is profoundly "global" in scope and jurisdiction, for no matter how divergent and pluralized narratives of "*What-Is-First*" may be, the very Idea of what is Absolutely Original reveals itself in such an over-poweringly potent logos that it commands the mind to recognize and acknowledge its absolute universality, its infinite unitivity, and its abysmal originality. For this reason, competent reflection on this Absolute First entails that it must be infinitely Univocal, hence absolutely Universal in scope and power. So the depth of this First cannot but be infinite in its Presence, and this immediately entails that it is the ground and source of all possible worlds, all forms of life, of nature and culture, of evolution and history, and of religions and philosophies; it is the very origin of discourse and natural reason.

This Idea of an Infinite, Original, Universal, and Univocal Principle that is the ground and source of all that exists, the generative force of the universe, the foundation of all lifeworlds, the common ground of all religions and cultures, the active rational principle of all thought and language, is the single most important idea affecting the human condition. Our well-being essentially turns on minding this Idea rightly. It is the Infinite Word that the great world religions have sought in their irreducible diversity to express and celebrate. It is the Rational Principle that diverse philosophical traditions through the ages have sought in pluralistic grammars to articulate. And if there is a Universal Logos that is ecumenical and global and the common ground of our humanity between cultures and worlds, then it is of the utmost importance to give this question our primary attention and deepest critical scrutiny.

So let us query and interrogate this alleged Idea. Why must there be an "Absolute"? Suppose we deny that there is anything ultimate, first, infinite. What if we outright reject the idea of any "universal logos," or "primitive univocity"? Why not join those skeptics who affirm that these matters are simply off limits and beyond our human capacities? In any case, why can there not be a plurality of "absolutes," a rich diversity of "first principles," a multiplicity of "origins"? Why can there not be irreducibly diverse rationalities? Why must we favor "unity" over plurality and absolute difference? Could we not favor a rich multivocity and plurivocity over any alleged "univocity"? And why should we countenance any origin at all, any first, any foundation? Is it not best after all that we abandon once and for all the myth of origins and foundations?

Of course these queries have been raised over and over in different contexts through the ages, and it is vital both to press these challenges and to respond to them effectively. There has been an interesting diversity of strategies to establish an "Absolute First." In Judaic origins, for example, it has been hailed as one of the great advances for humanity to recognize that "God is One," to awaken to the truth that the Divine Name is One, having absolute and universal jurisdiction. The Hebrew Logos is revealed as requiring an ultimate faith to be consummated. Again, in Greek origins we find Socrates and Plato pressing rational discourse to its limits in the transcendental universal form of Goodness, the form of all forms, beyond knowledge and truth. Here in the Greek Logos it is argued that the life of reason gets its light from this ultimate and absolute condition that can be realized only through the highest rational intuition.

Further, Aristotle, in his masterful transcendental inquiry into *What-Is-First*, absolute first principles, recognized that in approaching First things it is highly naive to use mundane thinking and logic. It shows naiveté to presume that First Principles can be queried or proven in conventional logic, since the Absolute Conditions make discourse itself possible, make possible all proof, arguments, queries, and rational discourse. Any would-be skeptic who would radically question what is First always places himself or herself in a self-deconstruction or incoherence in his or her questioning and participation in discourse. Aristotle rightly observed that in order to formulate and express any intelligible thought whatsoever itself presupposes, hence confirms, the First Principle of thought, language, and being. And Plato and Aristotle broke new ground historically in inaugurating a formal science of the Universal Logos of natural reason, a birthing of First Philosophy.

As we scan diverse global traditions of First Philosophy we readily see characteristic patterns in responding to those voices that would query or deny the Absolute. In the Hindu discourse of Advaita (Nondual) Vedanta, for example, we find Sankara arguing for the immediate disclosure of Absolute Brahman, the nondual First Principle, in every thought, experience, or utterance. Here in the meditative dimension of Logos we find that Brahman is immediately revealed in every thought, and it is the egocentric mind that eclipses itself from realizing this meditative insight. Of course the diverse traditions of meditative Logos concur that how we conduct our mind is all-important in realizing the profound Unity and Infinition of *What-Is-First*. There is a certain consensus that egocentric reason is inherently pathological, self-divided, and self-eclipsed from rightly encountering the logos of awakened intelligence.

Thus in certain traditions of Buddhist dialectic, it is found that the Buddha's essential insight turns on recognizing that human existential suffering arises from egocentric minding, which eclipses natural intelligence from awakening to the Universal Law (Dharma), which is the expression of Absolute Emptiness (Sunyata), another classic face of Logos. Only by going through a profound meditative therapy, a deep and rigorous discipline of right minding, can we overcome the powerful pull of egocentric life and enter the path of right thinking and awakened living in the presence of the Law of Logos.

We can of course go on with this inventory of diverse strategies in the global evolution of Logos in dealing effectively with *What-Is-First*. The main point here is that in attempting to approach and effectively think ultimate transcendental matters it is all-important how we conduct our mind and thinking. And it cannot be presumed that our mundane or conventional habits of thought, or our egocentric ways of minding, can coherently query or deny or reject the absolute conditions that make all thinking and discourse possible. Indeed, diverse traditions of First Philosophy concur that a profound reorientation in the conduct of mind, in how we think, is essential in rigorously approaching the transcendental First. While naive, everyday thinking is out of touch with the Law of Logos that makes it possible, awakened and reflective minding centers in this Law, and every aspect of existence is thereby dramatically transformed and illumined in the presence of Logos. So the most important factor in considering Absolute conditions is to be keenly mindful of how we are conducting our thinking.

Keeping this in mind let us probe more deeply into the alleged "First." Wherever we may be situated in thought it is clear that we can never think away conditionality, being conditioned. It is true that naive, egocentric minding deludes itself into thinking that it can exist in itself absolutely, that it can be self-existing and independent, but it is immediately evident that it could not even have this illusion without the work of Unity, Difference, and Relationality. For anything to have identity, it must exhibit the power of self-unity through the ever-changing differential flow of time, it must reiterate through process, hence, it is profoundly relational. For to be a "self" in the first place, to have any thought at all, to say "I," presumes dependency on the power of unitivity, the possibility of something being self-identical, one and the same, through the differential power of time. Without this creative relational power of Unitivity, nothing could be. There would be no Univocal "I" in the first place, and hence no univocal thoughts, words, concepts, and language. "I" could not get started, nor any alleged act or production of this "I." Without the presumption of Univocity, thinking and language could not get started, could not work. Everything would pulverize and dissolve before "it" could get started. In this way we begin to see the immediate working of Absolute Unitivity in every moment.

We must remember that naive egocentric reason cannot, in its own terms, think or encounter this Absolute Unitive condition of its deepest being and thinking. As awakened reason opens to this presence of Logos, it becomes clear that this Power of Absolute Unitivity is profoundly Relational, inter-relational, and differential. This means that the Absolute condition cannot be "finitized," contained, fixated, reduced, identified, objectified, and/or reified. It is the egocentric reason that finitizes whatever it touches, including its arti-ficially constructed "infinite." This is why, repeatedly, in the global evolution of thought, competent minders of the First have discovered and insisted that it must be Infinite, Unitive, and the Univocal source of all reality. The Absolute cannot be "pluralized," because that would artificially and incoher-ently delimit it by an external and independent "other," and this is self-con-tradictory to the Univocal power of the Absolute, which makes possible the very idea of "plurality," "diversity," "difference," and "the other." Any thesis of plurality or original difference presumes Univocity. In this way the absolute condition of Unitivity immediately leads to Infinitude, which in turn implies an infinitely unified domain of reality—that reality must be a Unified interre-lational field. Logos entails a Universal Unified Field, for no field whatsoever could establish itself apart from the Logos of rational power and jurisdiction.

This is why it is naive and self-defeating to attempt to assert that absolute difference, multiplicity, and plurality are ultimate, and not unitivity or Unity. In the Hebrew Logos, when it was discovered and declared that "God is One," this was indeed a great advance in the science of the global Logos, since it recognized that *What-Is-First*, The Absolute, the Divine Word, must be Unitive and not pluralized. In the Greek Logos, when it was seen that there must be an ultimate Universal Form of all forms, the form of Goodness, as the condition of being and knowledge, also tapped the foundational power of Logos. In the Hindu Logos, when the deepest meditative insights into the Absolute First, Brahman, revealed that it must be infinitely nondual (advaita) in every way, implying a Unified Field, this also tapped and revealed vital resources of Logos. In Buddhist disclosures of ultimate reality as Absolutely

Empty, beyond all egocentric dogmatizing and ontologizing, beyond all ego-logical names and forms and descriptions, this also opened depth insights into Logos. In this breakthrough into the field of Logos, it is found that there is a Universal Law, the Law of dependent co-arising, wherein all things arise in mutual codetermination. This advance tapped the relational nature of Logos, recognizing that nondual Unity is profoundly interrelational, again implying a primordial Unified Field of Logos.

In Chinese explorations into *What-Is-First*, we find classic disclosures of the Logos of Tao, the Tao of Logos. Here too it is found that the Primordial Presence is Nameless, prior to unity and plurality, one and many, the original source of all opposites, the origin of all that exists. Here again it is confirmed that the primordial Unitivity of Absolute Logos is the ground of both unity and multiplicity, of identity and difference, the very origin of the possibility of polar oppositions. This historic development of the grammar of Tao reveals classic features in the logic of Logos, showing that the First naturally plays out as the interrelational unified field of reality.

These selected examples in the history and evolution of Logos help us see how the absolute unitivity condition leads to a higher technology of minding in which interrelationality is primitively given. We now see that the power of Unitivity is infinitely laden with multiplicity and diversity. The Absolute condition of Unitivity implies Infinition, which implies Relationality, which implies Interrelationality, hence, diversity and multiplicity. This is the original self-differential power of Unity: Infinite Unitivity implies creative differential expression; the Infinitude of Logos means irreducible diversity and plurality. So Unitivity is originally Relational, and the greater the diversity and multiplicity, the greater the presence of Unity. In this respect, Alterity is the creative power of Unitivity; this is why relationality and interrelationality are the essence of Unity. Thus multiplicity, diversity, and plurality do not compete with Unitivity but are the offspring and evidence of the play of Unitivity, the very signature of Logos.

Once we begin to awaken to this Infinition of Logos, which has been the main lesson in the global evolution of cultures, it appears silly, even trivial, to have to labor to show that Logos, *What-Is-First*, must be Infinite, Unitive, Univocal, and Universal, for it is so simple and obvious that Infinite Logos must be universal in scope and jurisdiction that it could not be ultimately multiple and pluralistic. That the Infinite Word must be "global" and holistic is such an immediately given intuition in our rational awareness that it appears tautologous and redundant to have to say it. And yet this ultimately simple truth has been deeply suppressed and repressed, the most deeply distorted and misunderstood intuition of all. The failure of egocentric cultures to see clearly that we, in all of our religious, ethnic, cultural, and ideological diversity, immediately derive from the same living source, has been at the core of continued abysmal violence and inhumanity through the ages. Becoming clear on the Infinitude of Logos is essential in recognizing that diverse religions, in their irreducible differences and plurality, arise from a common ground and express a common Truth. Logos is the very source of diverse worlds, the ground of religious and cultural pluralism, the foundation of truth, dialogue, and discourse between worlds.

PART 2: LOGOS AS THE
UNIFIED FIELD OF GLOBAL REASON

Let us reflect more deeply on Logos. We suggest that wherever we begin in thought or experience there is no getting around the immediacy of the conditionality of our thinking, that our thinking is relational, interrelational, and necessarily always under constituting conditions. Irrespective of what we may think, the content of thought, the very process and possibility of thought, implies transcendental or constituting conditions. This absolute conditionality discloses that thinking inherently arises in the play of relational difference, which entails unitivity and univocity. Thought is always situated in a dynamic process, which involves constant change, flow, and, hence, constant difference and unitivity. Thus the absolute conditionality leads to first conditions. This involves primitive alterity in the co-arising of the power of difference in unitivity, and this original relational power leads to infinition and the continuum of a unified field. It is for this reason that any attempt to find any genuine unity in thought immediately leads to the infinition of the unified domain, for this is the origin of all units, any identity, any individual, any term, concept, name, form, phenomenon.

Experience and thought could not work without unity-in-difference, without the original power of alterity, and any attempt to establish any difference or unity, any singular or plural, immediately leads to alterity, hence, to the infinition of the continuum. This implies that all units are essentially situated in the unified field of *What-Is-First*. This is the functional origin of the unity of all units, and of the differentiation of all differences. It is this originating presence in all thought and existence that we call "Logos." Logos is the infinite word, the infinite form, the originating power of alterity, of infinite unitivity, in the play of creative difference, encompassing the unitive domain of all reality.

Logos is the origin of Reason, the originating power that places diverse things in relation and order. Logos, as the Absolute First, is the intelligible light that originates the possibility of anything existing, of any identity and self-unity, of the possibility of differentiation, of predication, of things being named and being constituted in conceptual and categorial relations. It is this relational power of Logos that opens the space-time in which the world, reality, and existence may proceed. It is this infinite relational power of Logos that makes discourse possible, makes it possible for there to be an "I," a thinker, a concept, a thought, for there to be sense, signification, meaning, and truth. So all aspects of the life of reason arise in this unitive relationality of Logos.

It should now be more evident that Logos is and must be infinitely universal, and the immediate source of all possible worlds, of all names and forms, of all forms of life, of all lifeworlds, of all fields and domains. It is in this deep sense that Logos is "global," and not in any merely geographic or physical sense. Logos is global in the deeper sense that it is the functional unified field of all possible and actual realities, of all nature and evolution, of all religions and cultures, of all aspects of cultural life. Furthermore, this infinite presence of Logos entails that it is the active generative force in all things, so nothing can be or be understood apart from being immediately situated in the dynamic process of Logos. We may call this the "Logos Thesis": that all things are essentially situated in the Presence of Logos, in the universal context of the Universal Domain of Logos Law. This is the global context that situates all worlds, all religions, all philosophical grammars, all logics, all disciplinary fields or cultural forms of life, all concepts, signs, texts, and discourse.

This is the universal hermeneutical method, the analytic process of clarifying the true significance of all signs, concepts, names, and forms in any text or lifeworld. The universal philosophical method of clarifying the deeper meaning in any sign is to situate it in the universal domain of Logos Process. This is the universal context of all interpretation: the true significance of any sign, or any discourse, is explicated when it is rightly situated in the Field of Logos. And of course this requires the right technology of minding Logos. Egocentric reason is inherently disabled and incapacitated to enter into this universal hermeneutical domain of signification.

The obvious reason behind this universal principle of interpretation is the Logos Thesis itself: all things essentially arise in the dynamic infinite play of the Logos context; every text essentially arises out of the Logos context. This is an astounding and a radical thesis but one that has been confirmed over and over in the global evolution of thought. Logos is the Universal Law behind all happenings, the generative principle of evolution of all nature and culture. The Logos Thesis implies that The Absolute, as Infinite Alterity, is the dynamic process itself; reality must be a creative, dialogical, dialectical interplay of the Infinite Word. And the Universal Law governing the universe may be called the Law of Relativity, the supreme intuition that all things co-arise in the Logos field, the Logosphere. The Infinition of Logos implies that *What-Is-First* must be dynamic, creative, and an evolutionary process in itself. Whatever happens in the play of reality, in nature or culture, essentially arises in the Unified Field of Relativity.

We began with the remark that one of the greatest lessons in the global evolution of thought is that Logos is real, that Logos must be global and universal. This lesson comes forth with the recognition that egocentric reason, the conventional minding that takes egocentric consciousness as primary, is both bankrupt and pathological. When situated in the context of the evolution of Logos, it appears that egocentric discourse, egological reason, is a dialectical stage in the awakening and evolution of nature and culture. In light of the Logos Thesis, it is clear that all egocentric minding assumes in every way the Law of Relativity, the dynamic presence of the Unified Field.

The ego-constructive practice of ego culture essentially trades on the rational resources of Logos to purchase any appearance of its artificial unity and pluralities. Ego reason, in its eclipse of Logos and the Unified Field, proceeds in the illusion that it can constitute unities, identities, individuals, signs, names, forms, categories, its world, and its discourse in its own terms. One of the recurrent themes in the global evolution of first philosophies and religious worlds is that egocentric culture must be overcome in a profound existential awakening of consciousness to the presiding presence of Logos. It appears that all history is this very creative awakening to Logos, to authentically minding the Universal Law.

It is impossible to overstress the universal perennial quest in diverse cultural forms to access and express the Universal Law, the Unified Field, of Logos. It is equally impossible to exaggerate the profound disaster and pathological consequences of egocentric minding and culture making. The emergence of the Logos Thesis in the evolution of global history comes with the recognition of the bankruptcy and failure of egocentric reason—the logos of ego discourse. It is the provisional dominance of ego minding that has eclipsed the clear vision of Logos, of the Universal Law that is the common generative source of human natural reason, of ethics, of deepest religious life, of the dialectical evolution of philosophies, of the emergence and evolution of the sciences, and of all cultural forms.

As human consciousness matures and awakens beyond egocentric minding, it goes through a most profound transformation in the conduct of mind. As the powerful dialectical forces of Logos, of Natural Reason, work on egocentric consciousness, egominding is therapeutically overcome, and a higher form of reason is born. When we awaken to Logos, to the Law of Thought, to Natural Reason, to minding the Unified Field, everyday consciousness flows in a holistic and creative process that dramatically transforms our being, our experience, our everyday world, phenomena, and discourse. It is in this radical yet natural awakening that we mature into rationality and realize our true human form.

We begin to see that we humans are as we conduct our mind, and the classical thesis that we are rational beings cannot be realized in the artificiality of egocentric reason but only in the true awakening of the holistic ways of natural reason. So our very humanity turns on this rational awakening, on the realization that we are not egocentric beings but holistic beings who come to be in the right minding of the Law of Logos.

If all fields, all religions, philosophies, ideologies, cultures, and disciplines, arise out of the Universal Law of Logos, then the rich plurality of forms of life is evidence of this play of Logos. This is one of the astounding consequences of the Logos Thesis: that diverse religions, diverse forms of life, worldviews, lifeworlds, cultural forms, and disciplinary fields all immediately derive from the same Logos Law, and all are evolutes of Logos historical process—the emergence of Logos Law. It would indeed be radical to begin to demonstrate precisely how diverse religions, philosophies, logics, ontologies, cultural lifeworlds, sciences, and political and moral forms of life are all diverse evolutes and expressions of the Law of Universal Relativity.

It appears that there is a profound heretofore missing Universal Science, a truly Formal Science of all sciences, of all fields—a universal logic or logistic of all forms of life. And it appears that the diverse attempts throughout global histories to develop adequate narratives of *What-Is-First* are early excursions into this truly Formal Science of Logos, the hermeneutic of the Infinite Word.

It is, of course, the temporary dominance of egocentric minding in the human condition that has been the primary cause of the eclipse, denial, rejection, and skepticism concerning the emergence of Logos Law. This passing phase of human evolution, this egocentric reason and culture making, still serves a vital purpose in the always-superior dialectical forces of Logos. And in the past 2,000 years of global history, the plot thickens, and the dialectical drama quickens as the stakes rise higher than ever to a crisis point of no return.

Over the past 2,000 years, just to take a provisional point of departure, we may see in the evolutionary narrative of the emergence of Logos, of Global Reason, a simultaneous, twofold drama. It is clear that the egocentric paradigms of minding have ripened and played out to their pernicious consequences, for the dialectical drama of the emergence of Universal Law in the human condition has presided and worked this egocentric cultural evolution to its dysfunctional end. In this historic drama of the Logos Word it has become clear through the centuries that egocentric living has failed, and the way has been prepared for a corporate global awakening—a great paradigm shift to the higher ways of natural reason. The experiments in egocentric minding have run their course and have served the higher dialectic of Logos in the painful awakening of rational consciousness.

The fundamental advance in the emergence of global Logos is in the technology of minding, overcoming egocentric thinking and evolving to holistic minding. The holistic or dialogical turn to minding Logos, to the methods of Universal Relativity, is the key to discovering the common origin of all dimensions of culture making—of religion, philosophy, science, the arts, ethics, and political life, for in authentically minding the Law of Relativity, rational consciousness advances to a profoundly dialogical praxis that is the very essence of moral awareness, of religious awakening, of rational maturity, of the method of truth and critical thinking, of experimental inquiry and the dialogical encounter of the ecology.

1

The Quest for the
Universal Global Science

PROLOGUE

A powerful moving force in the evolution of thought has been the drive to
clarify and articulate the Primal Principle of all life and existence—the
quest for First Philosophy. Whether in the discipline of ontology, the quest
for primary being, or in the foundations of logic, the quest for the primary
laws of thought, there has persisted through the ages across diverse traditions a relentless striving to decode the ultimate grammar of *What-Is-
First*—the grammar of thought and being. Certain thinkers have suggested
that there has been an ongoing tradition of "perennial wisdom" in classical
traditions of thought, converging in a consensus of universal truth and
knowledge. It would be good to begin these meditations by reflecting critically on this narrative of perennial philosophy as one approach to this
quest for First Philosophy. Here it would be helpful to focus on the perspective of Seyyed H. Nasr, who has been an eloquent and a forceful voice
for the primordial wisdom of the perennial traditions. This will help us get
a better sense of prior attempts as well as afford us an opportunity to see
that something vital is still missing in the emergence of Global First Philosophy (GFP). In Part 1 we shall scrutinize Nasr's vision, while in Part 2
we shall suggest that the Primal First Discipline is yet to be developed in
its global form. Part 2 seeks to meditate our way more deeply into the missing GFP.

In these reflections, I focus on central themes from Nasr's *The Need for
a Sacred Science* and *Knowledge and the Sacred*. These two intimately related
works present a comprehensive, integrated vision of Nasr's mature thought. I
will focus especially on his narrative of the need for a Sacred Science. I find
here a deep convergence with findings in my own quest over the past three
decades to clarify the missing primal science of Logos.

Perhaps it would be good to begin with a summary review of some of
the main themes and concerns raised by Nasr to help set the context for this
exploration.

137

PART 1: CRITICAL REFLECTIONS ON NASR'S
VISION OF PERENNIAL PHILOSOPHY AND
THE NEED FOR A SACRED SCIENCE

Nasr's Vision of Sacred Science

Nasr's thesis in *The Need for a Sacred Science* is a unifying theme that brings together a range of insights and concerns running throughout his thought. In its most simplified form, his thesis is that there exists a Primordial Tradition that flows from an Absolute Truth that has been expressed in diverse ways through the ages. This tradition has been articulated in various formulations in the evolving school of *Philosophia Perennis* (a philosophical tradition that holds that there is a fundamental common ground of wisdom and truth recognized in a vast diversity of worldviews through the ages).

This school of Perennial Philosophy is connected to a view that there is a primal science, a sacred science, based on a universal metaphysics of this Ultimate Truth. It is held that diverse authentic cultural (religious, spiritual, philosophical) traditions through the ages have recognized, formulated, and embodied this Eternal Wisdom in diverse ways. One main point stressed by Nasr is that the diversity of these sacred traditions is important, even in recognizing that they flow from a common foundational Unity. One important common factor is that these sacred traditions are grounded in the Primordial Truth, flow from a common sacred science of metaphysics, and are thus grounded in a sacred view of reality and the possibilities for human life.

A central theme stressed by Nasr is that with the rise of the modernist worldview in Europe since the seventeenth century, there has been an increasing eclipse of the sacred traditions and a tragic loss of the Perennial Wisdom and Sacred Science that they involve. The modernist worldview, he finds, is based on a secular humanism and materialism that moves away from the Primal Spirit that is the ground of the sacred traditions and of Perennial Wisdom.

He finds that this development of secular modernism has resulted in tragic consequences for the human condition. It has resulted in all sorts of pernicious fragmentation in cultural life and has placed modern cultures on a course that he claims is not sustainable and is devastating for human flourishing and for the ecology. The secularization of modernism has severed human life from its authentic grounding and connection to reality and Primordial Spirit, which is the source of human flourishing. His main finding is that contemporary human cultures desperately need a return to the sacred traditions and to the Perennial Wisdom that flows from the power of Sacred Science. This is the most urgent priority in the human condition today.

Apparently Nasr sees this return to Sacred Science and Perennial Wisdom as vital for all aspects of human life and essential for the advancement of the sciences as well. He insists that the diversity of the wisdom traditions should be respected and honored, and that in authentically living the inner truth of an authentic sacred tradition, one lives and embodies the perennial truth being expressed differently in all sacred traditions. In this way, the return to tradition in this perennial spirit of Sacred Science can resolve one of the most profound challenges facing the modern world—that of honoring the diversity of religious and cultural forms while achieving consensus and unity in truth and reality.

Before raising some critical questions for this line of thought, it would be helpful to further texture the complex ideas expressed here by looking more closely at the actual words of Professor Nasr on these themes. The following excerpts are taken from *The Need for a Sacred Science.*

1) What Is Sacred Science?

> There is first of all the Supreme Science or metaphysics, which deals with the Divine Principle and Its manifestations in the light of that Principle. It is what one might call *scientia sacra* in the highest meaning of the term. It is the science which lies in the very center of man's being as well as at the heart of all orthodox and authentic religions and which is attainable by the intellect, that supernaturally natural faculty with which normal human beings . . . are endowed. This principal knowledge is by nature rooted in the sacred, for it issues from that Reality which constitutes the Sacred as such. It is a knowledge which is also being, a unitive knowledge which transcends ultimately the dichotomy between the object and the subject in that Unity which is the source of all that is sacred and to which the experience of the sacred leads those who are able to reach the abode of that Unity. (pp. 1–2)

Note: This key passage makes clear that there is an ultimate Reality that is sacred and is the unifying force in all humans and in diverse authentic religions and traditions. Humans are endowed with a natural capacity to overcome the fragmentation and reach the primal Unity of this Reality.

2) What Is the View of *Philosophia Perennis*?

> By *philosophia perennis*—to which should be added the adjective *universalis*—is meant a knowledge which has always been and will always be and which is of universal character both in the sense of existing among peoples of different climes and epochs and of dealing with universal principles. This knowledge which is available to the intellect, is, moreover, contained in the heart of all religions or traditions, and its realization and attainment is possible only through those traditions and by means of methods, rites, symbols, images and other means sanctified by the message from heaven or the Divine which gives birth to each tradition. (pp. 53–54)

Note: It should be noted that this tradition of universal wisdom is claimed to be situated in the heart of all religions or traditions and is theoretically attainable by individuals through the power of the intellect, although Nasr stresses that the "norm" is such that "attainment of this knowledge depends upon the grace and framework which tradition alone provides" (p. 54). This helps explain why he repeatedly emphasizes the primary importance of honoring our sacred traditions and of gaining access to perennial wisdom through the particularity of our traditions. Note also that this perennial wisdom running through our traditions is based on "universal principles" (ostensibly valid for all worldviews).

3) The Metaphysical Ground of *Philosophia Perennis*:

> The *philosophia perennis* possesses branches and ramifications pertaining to cosmology, anthropology, art and other disciplines, but at its heart lies pure metaphysics, if this latter term is understood . . . as the science of Ultimate Reality, as a *scientia sacra*. . . . Metaphysics understood in the perspective of *philosophia perennis* is a veritable "divine science" and not a purely mental construct which would change with every alternation in cultural fashions of the day or with new discoveries of a science of the material world. This traditional metaphysics, which in reality should be used in the singular as metaphysic, is a knowledge which sanctifies and illuminates; it is a gnosis if this term is shorn of its sectarian connotations going back to early Christian centuries. It is a knowledge which lies at the heart of religion, which illuminates the meaning of religious rites, doctrines and symbols and which also provides the key to the understanding of both the necessity of plurality of religions and the way to penetrate into other religious universes. (p. 54)

Note: It is clear in this passage that there is claimed to be a pure universal metaphysics—a divine science—of ultimate reality at the heart of perennial philosophy. It is noteworthy that Nasr stresses that it is a singular science, which of course suggests that it gets at the fundamental reality between diverse worlds. It should be remembered that this is a sacred science, since it is grounded in the universal Divine principle. This will be important for us in the subsequent discussion. Nasr is at pains to distinguish this "school" from other versions of "universal wisdom" by insisting that the tradition he has in mind stresses orthodoxy. "If there is one principle which all the traditional authors in question repeat incessantly, it is orthodoxy. . . . They are orthodox and the great champions of universal orthodoxy" (p. 55). We will explore this theme shortly when we take a critical look at the "tradition" of pure metaphysics and inquire into its "global" potential.

4) The Global Potential of the Sacred Science

According *to philosophia perennis*, reality is not exhausted by the psychophys-
ical world in which human beings usually function, nor is consciousness limited to the everyday level of awareness of the men and women of present-day
humanity. Ultimate Reality . . . is beyond all determination and limitation. It
is the Absolute and Infinite from which issues goodness like the rays of the
sun which of necessity emanate from it. Whether the Principle is envisioned
as Fullness or Emptiness depends upon the point of departure of the particular metaphysical interpretation in questions. (pp. 55–56)

The school of philosophia perennis speaks of tradition and traditions. It
believes that there is a Primordial Tradition which constituted original or
archetypical man's primal spiritual and intellectual heritage received through
direct revelation when Heaven and earth were still "united." This Primordial
Tradition is reflected in all later traditions. (p. 57)

Note: This passage makes an important distinction between everyday consciousness (and the everyday worldviews that flow from that level of awareness) and the direct encounter of Ultimate Reality, which is beyond all determination, and beyond the worldviews of everyday life. It also is noteworthy
that this primal Reality, expressed in the Primordial Tradition, admits of different interpretations and expressions. We will explore this "global" potential
of perennial wisdom later.

5) Ultimate Reality as Sacred: God Is Reality

God as Ultimate Reality is not only the Supreme Person but also the source
of all that is, hence at once Supra-Being, God as Person and the Godhead
or Infinite Essence of which Being is the first determination. . . . God as
Reality is at once absolute, infinite and good or perfect. In Himself He is
the Absolute which partakes of no relativity in Itself or in its Essence. The
Divine Essence cannot but be absolute and one. . . . God as Reality is also
infinite, the Infinite, as this term is to be understood metaphysically. . . .
Ultimate Reality contains the source of all cosmic possibilities and in fact
all possibilities as such even the metacosmic. . . . Metaphysically, He is the
All-Possibility. (pp. 8–9)

Note: These excerpts are striking in presenting reality as God. Here it is clear
that Nasr has entered into the perspective and language of pure universal
metaphysics. In this language of reality, pure metaphysics presumably is presenting a universally binding narrative for all worldviews. The "God as Reality" thesis would be binding even for those who do not countenance "God"

and who reject "God talk." These passages stress that whatever one's worldview, it owes its possibility to the Absolute Divine Principle. Presumably, if all people understood this "pure metaphysics," then they would recognize the global truth of this "God talk": "There would in fact be no agnostics around if only it were possible to teach metaphysics to everyone" (p. 9). Of course, this raises sensitive issues, which we will address later when we explore the "global" potential and scope of perennial wisdom and Sacred Science.

6) Sacred Science of the Self: Moving Beyond the Ego

> In order to reach the Ultimate Self through the expansion of awareness of the center of consciousness, man must reverse the cosmologic process which has crystallized both the variations and reverberations of the Self within what appears to be the cosmic veil as separate and objective existence. And this reversal must of necessity begin with the negation of the lower self. . . . The Ultimate Self in its inner infinitude is beyond all determination and cosmic polarization. (p. 16)

> The contemplative disciplines of all traditions of both East and West insist in fact on the primacy of the awareness of the self and its nature. (p. 18)

> The traditional science of the soul, along with the methods for the realization of the Self, a science which is to be found in every integral tradition, is the means whereby self-awareness expands to reach the empyrean of the Ultimate Self. This traditional science is the result of both intellectual penetration and experiment with and experience of the self by those who have been able to navigate over its vast expanses with the aid of a spiritual guide. (p. 19)

Note: These excerpts are quite important, because they stress that in the universal metaphysics/Sacred Science there is a vital difference between the everyday ego-self and the Ultimate Self, which is in direct communion with the Primal Reality. Nasr makes clear over and over that this fundamental truth has been articulated across the vast range of sacred traditions through the ages. Note here that the true inner Self has an infinite structure that is beyond all determination and polarity. In this respect, Sacred Science yields universal knowledge/realization of the Self across worldviews. We will explore this theme later.

7) Unity and Diversity in the Human Condition

> While truth is one, its expressions are many, especially for modern man who lives in a world in which the homogeneity of the traditional ambience is destroyed and in which there is on the one hand acceptance and in fact

"absolutization" of secular man and the humanism based upon man conceived in such a manner, and on the other hand the presence of diverse sacred traditions whose reality can no longer be neglected. Consequently, if one is to address the human condition today, one must not only assert the unity of the truth and the oneness of the Spirit, but also the multiple reflections of the world of the Spirit in the human ambience. (p. 45)

Note: This recurring theme stresses that truth is one, while its expressions are many. This is Nasr's archetypical model for Sacred Science, which seeks to bring out the fundamental truth while honoring the diversity of manifestations of this truth in the human situation. Here he opens the diagnosis and critique of the modern secular worldview. Nasr continues:

The one spirit somehow evades modern man, leaving in its wake a multitude of contending egos, of feuding families and of general social disintegration. (p. 47)

The oneness which people of good intention seek cannot, however, be achieved save through contact with Spirit, which is one in itself and many in its earthly reflections. . . . No contact with the Spirit is possible save through the dimension of transcendence, which stands always before man and which connects him with Ultimate Reality whether it be called the Lord, or Brahman or sunyata. (p. 47)

The human spirit as understood in the humanist sense is not sufficient unto itself to serve as basis for the unity of humanity and human understanding across cultural and religious frontiers. (p. 47)

Note: Here we see the recurrent theme of the fragmentation in modernist secular culture and the suggestion that the way to reach true Unity is through the power of Sacred Science, which brings us into true communion with the unifying power of Infinite Spirit. Nasr continues:

The great role of religions today should be not to placate the weaknesses of modern man by reducing themselves to one or more "ism" or ideology to compete with the many existing ideologies which man has spun around himself over the past few centuries. Rather their task is to hold before men the norm and the model of perfection of which they are capable and to provide the channels for that contact with the Spirit which alone can show the myriad colors and hues of the human spirit to be not sheer multiplicity and division but so many reflections of Unity. Their task is also to present to the contemporary world the sacred science and wisdom which they have guarded in their bosom and within their inward dimensions over the millennia. (p. 49)

Note: This passage further develops the diagnosis of the modernist secular worldview as broken into contending ideologies in a fragmented pluralism. We see again that the traditional wisdom traditions have guarded the seeds of Sacred Science, which the contemporary world desperately needs for its well-being.

8) The Global Scope of the Primordial Tradition

> Each tradition is marked by a fresh vertical descent from the Origin, a revelation which bestows upon each religion lying at the center of the tradition in question its spiritual genius, fresh vitality, uniqueness and the "grace" which makes its rites and practices operative. But because the Origin is One and also because of the profound unity of the human recipients despite important existing racial, ethnic and cultural differences, the fact there is both the Primordial Tradition and traditions does not destroy the perennity and universality of the *philosophia perennis*. The anonymous tradition reflects a remarkable unanimity of views concerning the meaning of human life and the fundamental dimensions of human thought in worlds as far apart as those of the Eskimos and Australian Aborigines, the Taoists and the Muslims. (p. 57)

> The conception of religion in the school of the *philosophia perennis* is vast enough to embrace the primal and the historical, the Semetic and the Indian, the mythic and the "abstract" types of religions . . . to cross frontiers as difficult to traverse as that which separates the world of Abraham from that of Krishna and Rama or the universe of the American Indians from that of traditional Christianity. (p. 58)

Note: In these revealing excerpts we see that the perennial tradition purports to be global in scope across religious worldviews. It would be interesting to inquire, as we do later, whether it finds expression in worldviews that are not religious. Does the universal metaphysic of the perennial tradition have jurisdiction over all worldviews? It also is important to note here that Nasr hints at the Primordial Tradition as "anonymous," and this raises interesting questions. Has this tradition been latent and silent and subliminal and unnamed? Is there in fact an articulated worldview or ontology running through diverse traditions, or is it an unspoken tradition that has only manifested itself in particular "authentic" traditions?

9) Traditional versus Modernist Worldviews

> For several centuries, and in fact since the Renaissance, Western man has extolled the human spirit while de-sacralizing the whole of the cosmos in the

name of the supremacy of man, only to end now in a situation which for the first time in history threatens man with truly infrahuman conditions on a scale never dreamt of before. Clearly the classical humanism which claimed to speak for man has failed, and if there is to be a future for man, there must be a profound change in the very concept of what man is and a thorough re-examination of the secular humanism of the past few centuries in the light of the vast universal and perennial spiritual traditions of mankind which this humanism has brushed aside with the claim of giving man freedom. (p. 45)

Note: In comparing and contrasting the traditional worldview with the "modernist," Nasr sees in classical humanism an increasing secularization (and hence desacrilizing) of the human condition and of our ecology. He does not explicitly call this secular humanism "egocentric," but it is clear that this ideology places the human at the center and displaces the sacred worldview, which places Infinite Reality at the center of the human condition. The farther the human condition is broken from Ultimate Reality, the greater the dysfunction and pathology. This secularized, "homocentric" worldview is found to be responsible for devastating, pernicious consequences in the human condition. He continues:

The current concept of man as a self-centered creature not responsible to any authority beyond himself and wielding infinite power over the natural environment cannot but end in the aggression of man against himself and the world of nature on a scale which now threatens his own existence. (p. 46)

Note: Here Nasr stresses that the "hierarchical" structure of the traditional worldview places the Primal Principle first and higher and the human condition as dependent and accountable to this higher reality. Again, he sees this desacralizing of human life as the primary cause of violence of all sorts.

10) Sacred versus Secular: The Need for Sacred Science

One can speak of sacred and profane science in distinguishing between the traditional and modern sciences. From the traditional point of view, there is of course no legitimate domain which can be considered as completely profane. The universe is the manifestation of the Divine Principle and there is no realm of reality that can be completely divorced from that Principle. To participate in the realm of the Real and to belong to that which is real also implies being immersed in the ocean of the sacred and being imbued with the perfume of the sacred. . . . The main difference between the traditional sciences and modern science lies in the fact that in the former the profane and purely human remain always marginal and the sacred central, whereas in modern science the profane has become central and certain intuitions and discoveries which despite everything reveal the Divine Origin of the natural world have become so peripheral that they are hardly ever recognized for what they are despite the exceptional views of certain scientists. (pp. 96–97)

Note: This contrast between traditional sacred science and modern science makes clear that from the worldview of Sacred Science, all reality is pervaded with the sacred, and all nature and the ecology are the domain of the sacred. This implies of course that modern sciences are situated in this universal field of the sacred, which contextualizes all human efforts. The "profane" is situated in the all-encompassing field of the sacred. We will pursue this point later.

> The traditional sciences of all traditional civilizations agree on certain principles of the utmost importance which need to be reiterated in this age of forgetfulness of even the most obvious truths. These sciences are based on a hierarchic vision of the universe, one which sees the physical world as the lowest domain of reality which nevertheless reflects the higher states by means of symbols which have remained an ever-open gate towards the Invisible for that traditional humanity which had not lost the "symbolist spirit." The psycho-physical world, which preoccupies modern science, is seen in the traditional perspective as a reflection of the luminous archetypes. (p. 97)

Note: Here again we see that there are certain universal principles of Sacred Science that are recognized in diverse traditional worldviews and that have vital importance for our contemporary world. We will have to look closely at Nasr's insistence that the traditional worldview expresses a "hierarchical" vision of the universe.

QUESTIONS THAT NATURALLY ARISE FOR NASR'S NARRATIVE

The aforementioned selected excerpts from Nasr's book are intended to help us focus on key themes, which we will address in Part 2. Some critical questions to keep in mind as we explore these important ideas from a global perspective follow.

1. *Philosophia Perennis* alleges that there are perennial truths that are universal, eternal, and valid for all worldviews. Or, more specifically, that there are great traditions that authentically express the Primordial Truth that holds for these traditions. If it claims to be global in scope for all possible worlds,

then what is the source of the validity for all worlds? Does this tradition establish why this must *be* so, or that it is so? Is it one united tradition, or is there diversity within in? Could there be alternative accounts of perennial truth?

Does this "school" assume or assert that "perennial" is (means) "global"—valid for all worldviews—or, rather, that certain "authentic traditions" have expressed a consensus truth from their perspective? Does it claim global scope and power? For example, Nasr insists that Ultimate Reality is God. This means of course that all worldviews, secular and sacred, must arise from this universal God. But has it been shown that worldviews that do not countenance "God" (such as the world of modern science) must come to recognize God as their true ground? How has it been established that there is global truth across vastly diverse worldviews and languages of reality? We will now critically explore the possibility of a global narrative.

2. **What is the scope of Sacred Science?** Is it a complement for what is now called "science"? Does it apply to all everyday life? Is it to be a replacement for the secular worldview in all of its forms? Must the secular or profane sciences self-revise to truly encounter the Real? Can there be a universal global science that incorporates what is valid in the modern sciences and fulfill the ideals and vision of traditional Sacred Science? Is there a universal or global worldview or "first philosophy" that grounds all worldviews—sacred and secular? Could it be that the traditional perennial philosophy itself is in evolution and development and needs to mature to full global status? Could it be that traditional wisdom is in evolution and self-development?

3. Nasr sees the modernist secular development as the main reason for the loss of this Sacred Worldview, and he envisions a return to tradition (in the appropriate spirit) as the way to recapture the sacred perennial lifeworld. He recognizes of course that the "perennial tradition" is sacred in its own right, but he emphasizes realizing the perennial truth within the particularities of each tradition. One question here is: Is there a global way, a universal praxis, that runs through the diverse traditions? Are there, for example, global norms, and a global ethic that the diverse traditions confirm and embody? Have the global scope and power of Sacred Science/*philosophia perennis* been established?

Is there an alternative account, an alternative diagnosis, that might capture the desirable ends of leading cultures into a higher form of life that is faithful to the highest and best in the sacred traditions, yet self-evolves into a global form that speaks to our future evolution? Is there a way to honor and recognize the sacred traditions of the past that would build on these by moving forward beyond modernism, postmodernism, and secularism to realize a higher global perennial way? Must perennial wisdom be lodged in the past and in tradition, or can it be in evolution and development and global maturation? We will now explore these themes in Part 2.

PART 2: MY EXPERIMENTS IN DEVELOPING THE
GLOBAL PERENNIAL LOGOS TRADITION:
THE MISSING LOGOS SCIENCE

In the spirit of creative dialogue with the themes from Nasr's narrative, I now present in a summary sketch some highlights of my journey throughout my career to clarify the Ultimate Principle of all life and experience. In my own experiments I find remarkable convergences with Nasr's findings and with the perspective of *philosophia perennis*, all the more remarkable, because in a real sense my experimental journey took an independent direction that nevertheless brought me to a profoundly analogous result. Still, as we shall see, there are possible important differences in my articulation of the Ultimate Science and of the deep diagnosis of the source of human cultural pathologies and of the preferred prescription for the most potent way to move the human condition to well-being and human flourishing.

This is where I find the greatest potential for a significant critical dialogue with Nasr's thought. As we shall soon see, I discovered early in my career that something profound and vital was still missing from human discourse. Although I instinctively gravitated to the intuition of a perennial philosophy and knew in a prearticulated way that there had to be an ultimate primal principle, an ultimate science of *What-Is-First*, I nevertheless found that the language, technology of mind, and narrative for this were still missing. The nascent perennial narrative was still semidormant and needed to be brought to mature global articulation. One remarkable disclosure was that the Primordial Truth that was seeded in diverse traditions was alive, growing, evolving, and maturing in the global evolutionary process.

It was clear in my journey through different philosophical and cultural worlds, East, West, and other, that there had to be a fundamental logic, a primal ontology, a global primordial tradition at the heart of all worldviews. However, with close critical scrutiny, I found that this was still a presumption, and in fact more deep work had to be done to tap the missing fundamental logic of natural reason, to decode the ultimate grammar of existence and experience, to bring to full global articulation the intuition of a perennial philosophical perspective, and to develop the language and narrative of the Unified Field of diverse worlds. We shall see that these innovations and results vindicate the vision of *philosophia perennis* and bring to more explicit articulation the missing Primordial Tradition in a global context. So I now review some of the highlights of my adventure, speaking directly to the central themes of Professor Nasr.

The themes and findings I summarize here have been developed in great detail in my essays and books, which present my research over the past three decades. Two companion volumes present the heart of my quest for the fundamental missing science of Logos: *Meditative Reason: Toward Universal Grammar*, and *Between Worlds: The Emergence of Global Reason*. The first appeared in 1993 in the *Revisioning Philosophy* series of Peter Lang Press, and the second appeared in 1997 in the same series. These findings are presented in a simplified narrative in a book designed for the general reader, which will appear soon, *The Awakening of the Global Mind*.

Is Perennial Philosophy Possible?: Logic and Ontology

Over three decades ago in my early career as a logician and an ontologist, I encountered polarization, fragmentation, and dualism at the deepest levels of research. As a logician, seeking the ultimate logic of reason and language, I found a primal polarization in the grammar of thought as I traced the evolution of logic from Socrates through Aristotle, Descartes, Leibniz, Kant, Hegel, Husserl, Frege, Russell, Wittgenstein, Heidegger, Quine, Sommers, and Derrida. The Aristotelian tradition of logic, which shaped the cultural space of European thought over the centuries, was in deep tension with the radical innovations introduced by Frege, Russell, Wittgenstein, Quine, and others as they developed the new mathematical paradigm for the logic of language that launched the analytical revolution in the twentieth century.

If logic is the formal science of thought itself and articulates the grammar of human reason, then the polar tension I found between the classical logical paradigm of Aristotle and the modern mathematical paradigm of Frege leads us to a split in reason itself. My early quest for the fundamental logic of thought and language led me to an apparently irreconcilable split and incoherence between the classical and modern paradigms of logic in the European tradition.

What made this a disturbing crisis is my finding that both paradigms captured fundamental features of the logic of thought and language. Neither could be dismissed, nor was there an apparent way to mediate them and bring them together. They appeared to be mutually incompatible and yet mutually complementary at the same time, but each claimed to give a comprehensive and universal account of the grammar of thought, and since the science of logic purports to articulate the deep structure of reason, if logic itself was polarized into incommensurable paradigms, this did not bode well for the ultimate coherence of human reason. So my career began with this crisis of reason. If human reason, which purports to ground in meaning, truth, and rational coherence, is itself ultimately polarized and yields dualism and incoherence, then the very foundation of the human condition appears to be fractured and unintelligible.

It was clear that in the foundation of logic something vital was missing. The long quest through the centuries to clarify the universal grammar of thought was obviously unfinished. The dream of Descartes and Leibniz, to reach the ultimate universal grammar of reason, remained unrealized, yet more vital than ever. Frege and Husserl, in very different ways, attempted to realize this dream, but their attempts fell short.

As we will see in a moment, this perennial dream to articulate the ultimate laws of thought is driven by the intuition at the heart of human reason that there must be some ultimate ground, some unifying formal structure, that is the source of rational life, that makes things intelligible and generates thought, meaning, and truth. Over the past three decades, I remained focused on attempting to resolve this ultimate problem. It is at the core of the possibility of perennial philosophy. As we shall see, the guiding intuition that there must be a fundamental grammar of thought and reason is the moving force of the Primordial Tradition.

But this polar crisis at the heart of reason in the European tradition seems to arise in all aspects of the human condition, and on a global scale. In my early research as an ontologist, concerned with the deepest explorations into the nature and structure of reality, an analogous crisis of polarization became evident. The science of ontology, like the science of logic, sought to clarify and articulate the ultimate structure of reality—the grammar of existence. It was apparent early in the game, however, that diverse philosophies and worldviews (religions, cultures, ideologies, conceptual frameworks) presented profoundly diverse ontologies or languages of experience and reality.

What made sense in one worldview failed to make sense in another. It seems that meaning and truth, and what makes sense in experience, are a function of the worldview or universe of discourse, the ontological context in which it arises. Different worlds appear to be worlds apart and incommensurable from the ontological point of view. How is it possible for human intelligence, natural reason, to move meaningfully between worlds? Is it possible to reason and communicate between worlds, across diverse ontological languages of reality? Here was another ultimate challenge for the rational enterprise, for human relations between worlds, and certainly for the possibility of perennial philosophy.

And yet nothing seemed more natural in everyday life than the possibility of all kinds of interactions, transactions, communications, and transformations between worlds. For example, someone centered in the Christian worldview (to simplify the matter) seems to be able to enter genuinely into the lifeworlds of the Buddhist or the Hindu or the Bakongo. These are very different languages of reality, and yet it appears that human intelligence has the capacity to self-transform into alternative grammars of life and to make sense of things in diverse universes that nevertheless also seem to be mutually incompatible and even incommensurable in important ways. How is it possible for us to live and move and communicate across and between diverse worlds? It was evident that this fundamental problem was not adequately formulated or resolved.

The vast differences between worldviews seem to challenge the very possibility of any perennial or global perspective, so this was another complex of challenges that I faced very early in my career, and it was apparent that these twin problems at the heart of logic and ontology were intimately linked. It seemed to me that the science of ontology was just as much in crisis as the science of logic, and both of these "sciences" purport to get to the deep structure of the human condition—the structure of thought/language and the structure of being/reality. Could there be a global or universal logic across worldviews? Was there any fundamental universal ontology that was the ground of diverse worlds? If there were not common structures or laws across or between worlds, and across paradigms of logic, then how could there be genuine communication and rational discourse between worlds? These issues get to the heart of the possibility of any alleged "perennial philosophy" or "primordial tradition."

The Perennial Quest for the Ultimate Principle

In the midst of this crisis I reached an important turning point. My philosophical journey took me into Eastern thought when in 1971 I took a special leave to spend a year studying and lecturing in India. This was my first trip to India and my first in-depth exploration of Indian traditions of philosophy. I had no idea when I went on this adventure that it would speak deeply to the impasse I had reached in my research in the foundations of reason, logic, and ontology.

My encounter with the powerful meditative traditions of Hindu and Buddhist thought enormously expanded my horizon and brought me into a deeper global perspective in the rational enterprise. And over the years, as I went more and more deeply into diverse meditative philosophies, certain unmistakable patterns across diverse worlds became clear. My journey into the meditative traditions opened deeper rational space and enabled me to see deep connections between widely variant worldviews, East, West, and other, that I could not have seen before. Therefore, meditative philosophy played a key role in my expansion into the global perspective and thus into the deeper common ground between worlds.

The Meditative Turn in Human Reason

Two remarkable breakthroughs arose together over the next two decades as my research and teaching expanded in a global context. The first great advance through the meditative experiments was the realization that there was such a thing as "egocentric" minding. In my earlier research I simply absorbed the European tradition of philosophy (logic and ontology) without reflective awareness that there was a deep pattern of thinking—a technology of mind— a way of "minding" that proceeded on the foundation of the ego. But diverse meditative traditions (in this case the diversity of approaches in the Hindu and Buddhist traditions) concurred that the single most important factor in the human condition was precisely how we were conducting our minds.

The most fundamental teaching of the meditative traditions is that ego- centric patterns of thought were the primary source of human suffering, human existential pathologies in diverse forms. Whether, for example, in the teachings of the *Bhagavadgita* or the *Dhammapada*, the core insight was that the egocentric way of being (of thinking, of interpretation, of world making, of self making) produces deep and pernicious fragmentations in all aspects of life and was the primary source of human pathologies. The great breakthrough of meditative awakening is that it is possible to overcome egocentric minding and living by advancing into more profoundly unitive, integrative, holistic, and nondual patterns of minding. The great experimental traditions of meditative living developed over millennia provided boundless evidence of the pragmatic force of these findings. The meditative turn in natural reason moves us to a more rationally integrated form of life.

Once I became aware of the patterns and dynamics and living reality of egocentric minding, my career, my research, scholarship, and teaching, indeed, my life as a whole, took a radically different turn. These meditative experi- ments opened deeper integral space in which I could see clearly why my ear- lier research had reached the crisis, the paradox, the impasse, the polarization, the fragmentation, and incommensurability. I saw clearly that egocentric rea- son was inherently incomplete, incoherent, and the source of all sorts of dualisms, fragmentations, and pathologies of life. I saw more and more clearly as I lived the meditative turn in reason that egocentric minding was an imma- ture stage in our rational and human development. I understood precisely how and why egocentric minding blocked and undermined our rational life and would always produce polarization, fragmentation, disintegration, and all sorts of violence.

Awakening the Global Perspective

At the same time, the other remarkable breakthrough that co-arose with this meditative turn was the expansion of my thought patterns into a higher global perspective. As I experimented more expansively across the spectrum of worldview—ideologies, religious and cultural worlds, political ideologies, philosophical grammars, conceptual frameworks, disciplinary languages—and diverse forms of life in the broadest global perspective I began to see deeper patterns and connections. The meditative technology of minding enabled me to experience deeper common ground across and between worlds and made it possible to hold together multiple alternative worlds in one synoptic consciousness. This global awakening of reason produced astounding results in recognizing how diverse formulations in different worldviews and language forms nevertheless expressed the same fundamental dynamics, insights, principles, and truths.

The Perennial Quest for What-Is-First

The global perspective, the capacity to hold together multiple alternative worldviews in a unifying dialogic encounter, opened a more profound dimension of Reality, for when we stand back from any one worldview processed in the egocentric way and enter the global perspective through the dialogic powers of meditative reason, certain striking perennial patterns emerge. As we scan the range of diverse worldviews across the spectrum of global cultures, it is apparent that widely diverse worlds gravitate to some primal Origin.

For example, in one classical Chinese tradition worldview, the primal origin is called Tao (the Infinite name that cannot be named); in the early Hindu tradition, "*What-Is-First*" is expressed as Aum (the infinite sacred sound) or Brahman (infinite being); in a certain Buddhist tradition, the ultimate is expressed as Sunyata (absolute emptiness beyond names and forms); in the Judaic grammar, the ultimate reality is indicated as Yahweh (the Infinite living God); in Christianity, one version of the primal principle is Logos (the infinite Word) or Christ (the Logos made flesh); in Islam, the Absolute is expressed as Allah (the one true God); certain indigenous cultures recognize the ultimate truth as the Infinite Living Spirit; in one African classical worldview, the originating force is called Nommo (the Infinite Name that generates all existence); in the grammar of physics, the ultimate reality is recognized as Energy (the ultimate stuff that can neither be created or destroyed); and so on.

Each worldview purports to be universal and all-encompassing of reality. Yet at the same time, these diverse grammars of reality (ontological languages) appear to be competing and repelling or displacing one another in their universal power, appear to be diverse universes of discourse, and this is where the meditative turn, with its global perspective and technology of processing reality, helps disclose deeper common ground and striking patterns between variant worlds.

The Missing Global Grammar

One revealing pattern is that diverse worlds in one way or another arise from a primal source or ground that is recognized to be boundless, infinite, and universal. The meditative power of the global perspective helps us see that all worldviews must co-arise from a primal source or origin, that this origin must be Infinite, and that the Infinite must be the same Primal Reality of all possible worlds. Rigorous meditation on the Infinite Origin makes evident that this Unifying Force must be Integral and One-and-the-Same Principle for all possible worlds.

Here it is vital to remember that egocentric reason inherently fails to process this Infinite Unifying force field. As we shall see shortly, the egocentric mind objectifies the "Infinite" and reduces its infinite unifying power to an artificial "unity" that levels the profound important differences between diverse worlds. At the same time it artificially "pluralizes" diverse worlds in such fragmented multiplicity and differences that they remain localized and fragmented beyond the reductive and false "unity" it constructs. It fails to understand both Unity and Difference and undermines both. Either way, the egocentric mind is unable to process the Primal Principle, hence, Reality itself.

The great enduring mystical traditions have of course recognized early in the game that the Ultimate Truth must be Infinite and, hence, must be the unifying common source of all possible worlds. But even if we have a clear intuition that the diverse mystical and spiritual traditions were expressing the "same fundamental reality," these traditions remained articulated in their own localized grammars and narratives with all of their important differences and diversity. These localizing forces, East and West, suppressed and inhibited the full maturation of the global force of the grammar of *What-Is-First*.

The intuition of a "primordial truth" or a "perennial philosophy" remained presumed and latent waiting to be activated, formulated, and realized. There was no global grammar, no open generalized space or method of minding and speaking, that brought fully into the open the global scope and power of this First Principle. The profound and pervasive influence of egocentric minding in the human condition preempted and eclipsed access to the perennial force of The First. It appears that the global turn in how we mind and in the grammar of how we formulate and express reality matters a great deal, so with all of the great advances toward expressing the Infinite Origin, East, West, and other, something vital was still missing.

The Need for a Global Grammar for the
Infinite Origin: Logos *as a Global Name*

As my experiments matured over the decades and I advanced more and more deeply into the global perspective, it became increasingly clear that a fundamental global narrative was still absent. I noticed a peculiar and striking "recursive" dialectic at work that moved me in something like a paradoxical, reflexive, yet expanding "spiral loop" that took on a life of its own. The more

I expanded in the global perspective, the more evident the dialectical patterns across and between worldviews and alternate languages of experience became. As these deeper patterns of the Primal Origin emerged, the more I found my rational awareness and experience expanding, and the more I was able to encounter deeper common ground and detect striking recursive patterns and connections between worlds that I could not see before.

I was now able to recognize how quite diverse grammars and narratives of experience were in fact alternative formulations of the same fundamental reality, and the more this primal reality was revealed, the more the global way of processing reality, the global perspective, intensified. The net effect of this recursive dialectic—the global turn in experience—was the realization that this global awakening of rational awareness was essential in detecting and tapping the missing primal field. The global way of "minding" was the key to discerning the fundamental common ground between diverse worlds, indeed, in establishing that there was in fact a primal unified field between worlds. So in this summary sketch of my experimental clarification of the missing global "science," I shall now try to replay certain key steps in the spirit of this recursive dialectic.

The fact that we can stand back from being immersed within any one worldview and rise to the global or interworld perspective is of ultimate importance in the quest for the grammar of *What-Is-First*. This power and capacity in human awareness is a primary feature of reason, which issues directly from the fundamental Infinite Force. What is strikingly noticeable when we stand back in this way and entertain the great enduring traditions through the ages is that each seeks to express and name *What-Is-First*. As we have seen, diverse languages of Reality concur that there must be some primal ultimate origin, and "it" must be Infinite. It also has been clear that this Infinite Principle must be one and the same for all realities. This follows immediately from the sacred logic of *What-Is-First*. I have suggested that in the perennial quest to express this Infinite something vital was still missing. The diverse grammars or narratives that were developed by the traditions, including modern science, each faced a boundary of localism in its grammar and narrative.

First Philosophy still lacked a universal and global grammar to name and express *What-Is-First*. The fact that we faced a vast range of alternative languages attempting to express and name the Infinite Principle—Aum, Tao, Sunyata, God, Christ, Yahweh, Allah, Nommo, Logos, Nature, First Cause, Energy (henceforth we will refer to this open-ended sequence of primal names as "the Primal Names")—is highly problematic, since these diverse languages of reality appear to be inherently incompatible, competing, and mutually exclusive. Each universalizes its discourse and purports to a "universal grammar" of The First. Each alleges to be the primary, preferred, and self-privileging grammar of The Ultimate. And although great mystic minds and intuitive geniuses know quite well that all authentic First Names must be naming the same Infinite Principle, this correct global intuition needs a global grammar to effectively formulate and express this Truth.

We need a global name for *What-Is-First*, a Name so powerful that it expresses and keeps before us the Infinite Force of the First. In seeking to uncover and tap the Universal Grammar of *What-Is-First* I proposed the word "Logos" as a working candidate to help us move in this direction. Let us experiment together with this: *Logos is the Infinite Word, the Infinite Name for the Primal Reality.* The latent global power of the genuine Primal Names just mentioned is released through the universal force of the global name *Logos*. Aum expresses *Logos*; Tao is an ultimate name for *Logos*; God is *Logos*; Allah is a direct revelation of *Logos*; Christ embodies *Logos*, and the Greco-European Logos also is a powerful expression of *Logos*; the ultimate substance of reality named in the physical sciences—Energy—expresses *Logos*, and so on. (Henceforth, for convenience and simplicity, we will express the global name *Logos* without italics or boldface, thus Logos.)

Logos as the Infinite Name has infinite alter-expressions. This is an essential feature of its infinitude. It is the Infinite Word. All names, all words, and all forms derive from and express Logos. Of course this is not to suggest that the Primal Names are "synonyms" or are "identical" or "say the same thing" or even "refer to the same thing." We must be extremely cautious to remember that each uniquely and authentically expresses Logos. We shall soon see that precisely because Logos is the Infinite Word, it has boundless unique alternative and authentic expressions.

I introduce the term *holonym* to capture this profound relation between the Primal Names—they are **holonymous** and thus **holonyms**. As holonyms, the Primal Names co-express each other in Logos and thus have a deep intimate connection. The sacred logic of Logos makes it clear that holonyms are irreducibly different, while they nevertheless co-express Logos, and of course each other. When the full global potential of the Primal Names is ignited and realized, this deep dialogic connection is brought to maturity.

Let us meditate more deeply on Logos. It should be immediately apparent that the introduction of this *global name* is of monumental significance, for this Infinite Name invokes and brings with it the universal grammar of the Infinite Word, and with this comes the global turn in minding. **The Sacred Logic** of the Infinite Name calls for a higher **logistic or technology of mind** beyond the localizing, finitizing, and fragmenting ways of egocentric minding. We mentioned earlier that the diverse meditative traditions all stressed that how we mind is all-important in the quality of life and experience. With all of the important differences in diverse meditative traditions, we may safely say in entering the global perspective that the meditative turn in minding requires breaking the egocentric barriers and crossing into the more holistic and **integral technology of nondual minding**. This is a vital step in encountering Logos, in entering the universal grammar of the Infinite Word.

The meditative turn in thinking is a key step in entering the global mind, in the authentic encounter of Logos. But something radical and unique happens with this **awakening of the global mind**, for to "think" Logos is to participate directly in the Sacred Logic or (holistic) Logistic (**hologistic**) of the Infinite Word. To process Logos is to enter into the dialectic of Infinition, wherein all things, all names, all forms, all phenomena, and all grammars or worlds are in deep mutual interaction and interrelationality. Here all things mutually permeate each other. The deepest global meditation on Logos brings us into the Primal Field, the Grand Unified Field, which is Reality itself. Let us call this Primal Field of Reality the **Logosphere**. It may be said that the global name **Logos as the Logosphere** can be thought or encountered only through the awakening of the global mind, in the hologistic of Infinition.

The great meditative and mystical traditions of the ages, in all cultures and worlds, understood that *What-Is-First* could not be approached in ordinary, egocentric ways of thinking. To think Logos is to participate directly in the Infinition process of the Logosphere. And rigorous reflection on Logos reveals that this involves the global turn, the globalization of reason as minding awakens to its highest rational coherence and integrity. In this natural expansion of awareness, the Self, the Thinker, enters a direct encounter of Logos, the Logosphere; the thought process flows in the holistic dialectic of existence, and language matures to its full integral and primal power.

So to encounter the global name—Logos—is to enter the dynamic Unified Field (Logosphere), to awaken the global mind, to live and embody the Hologistic dynamics of the Logosphere, which is to enter the universal grammar of the Infinite Word. Thus to introduce Logos as a global name brings with it the awakening of mind to the Logistic of the Unified Field and the ignition of the universal grammar of the Infinite Word. It is here that we find the source of perennial truths, the foundation of the perennial tradition, the global blossoming of Sacred Science, the source of all knowing, of all sciences, indeed, of the human condition.

Logos Is the Logosphere—The Field of Reality

To enter the global perspective, then, is to enter into the technology of global minding, the hologistic process of the Logosphere. It is not the same as holding the egocentric perspective and entertaining a plurality of worlds from this localizing pattern of minding. When we enter the boundless, yet ordered, logic of the Logosphere, there are astounding revelations of the dynamic flow of Reality. How can the Infinite Name—Logos—be Reality itself? What kind of "name" is this? How, and why, is this Infinite Word the universal and Unified Field of all realities? What is this "sacred logic" of the Logosphere? How could it be that multiple worlds, realities, coexist at once in this "unified field"? How could these diverse worlds be diverse and yet permeate one another at the same time? How do the diverse categories of existence, or Nature, arise from this Primal Word? Can human consciousness really touch and enter this dialectic of the Logosphere? How are all realities generated from this Primal Source? How is it that the awakened Self in "global minding" flows in communion with this Infinite Force? Such deep questions as these naturally arise in this context.

Logos Is Always Boundlessly Higher and First

It is vital here to look more deeply into the Logic and Logistic of Logos as the Logosphere. Meditation on Logos as *What-Is-First* reveals that Logos is Infinite in every way. We are no longer approaching Logos in the fragmented thinking of egocentric mind or "reason." We are now proceeding in the holistic and integral Logistic of the global mind. And here it is immediately evident that there must be an Infinite Source/Origin, there *must be* something Higher, First, Ultimate, and Boundless.

The Infinite Unifying Force

The global mind sees immediately that there must be a Unifying Force proactively holding things together in every way—were this not so, then thought, experience, life, and existence could not work. The thinking "self" could not be, there would be no continuity, no coherence; no language could work, no words would exist, no thoughts could be formed, no experience could arise— nothing would be. This is the simplest, most elementary point. The egocentric mind takes all of this for granted, unquestioned. The global mind is ever mindful of the boundless presence of the Unifying Force that conditions everything and makes possible self, thought, language, experience, phenomena, and world. The egocentric mind is incapable of entering into the primal Sacred Logic—the transcendental logistic—that sustains it and makes its "life" possible.

The global mind—awakened reason—sees immediately that the Unifying Force must be Infinite. Everything now turns onto processing Infinite Unity in a rigorous and competent manner. Lucid thinking here discloses that the Force that conditions all that appears must be boundless and limitless. It is this rational intuition that reveals that there is always something Higher, something First, Primal, and Originating. Were there something—anything—beyond "It," this would violate the infinite integrity of

the Unifying Force, and any such "thought" self-destructs. It is in this ultimate intuition of awakened reason into Infinite Unity that the Sacred
Logic of Logos unfolds.

Infinite Unity Means Infinite Diversity

The Unifying Force must be the originating source cause of all that exists, of
all that appears. Here it is immediately evident that Infinite Unity, being
Boundless, is Infinitely Diverse, originally generative of boundless multiplicity, diversity, and plurality. This feature of Infinite Unity—that it is already
always generative of infinite Diversity and Plurality—has not been adequately
seen and appreciated in earlier attempts at First Philosophy. Yet in Global
First Philosophy—in global minding—it is an insight of ultimate importance,
for it makes clear that Infinite Unity is ever self expressed in Infinite Diversity. This abysmal "link" (it actually is deeper than a link) reveals that Logos,
the Logosphere, is an infinitely dynamic creative process, boundless, eternal
creativity—the process of reality.

Logos as the Origin of All Grammars

This global meditation on Logos, on Infinite Unity, makes clear that there is
a primal Logic of Infinition that ignites a powerful unifying vision of Reality:
The Infinite Condition is at once the unifying source of Unity and Diversity.
From this condition, all of the fundamental Categories of existence immediately flow: It must be Infinite Word—primal infinite Language, Sign, Symbol, Name. It must be Infinite Mind, Consciousness, Cognition, Intelligence,
Experience. It must be the Boundless Cosmos, the World, Being, Phenomena, Appearance, Nature, Existence. Perhaps most remarkable of all, all of
these names and forms, all of these building blocks of Reality, must arise from
one and the same Unifying Center. Word (Language), Mind (Consciousness),
and World (the Cosmos) must co-arise from the same Infinite Origin and
hence originally permeate each other in a Unified Field. And this Unified
Field of Logos is surely the "grandest" of all—the long-sought after (and
perennially intuited) "grand unified field" of Reality.

Logos as the Logosphere—Unified Field

This is why the Infinite Name, the Primal Word, is the Logosphere—The
Infinite Cosmic Field of Reality. The Logosphere must be an Infinite Continuum of Boundless Diversity, Multiplicity, Creativity—Infinite Processing. The
Infinite Word is Being, is Mind, is Intelligence, is Nature, is the Substance of
the Universe, is Energy, is Tao, is Aum, is God, is Sunyata, is Buddhanature, is

Christ. This taps into the global significance of the biblical genesis: In the Beginning is Logos, the Word—and this Word is God.

We now see that the global name, **Logos, is boundlessly global** in scope and power. This means that nothing can be apart from It. All names and forms, all categories—Space, Time, Cause, Substance, Relation, Process, Word, Mind, World, Experience, Appearance, Meaning, Value, Cognition— arise from the same Origin. This implies of course that all of the fundamental categories or "building blocks" of Reality must be originally and profoundly Interrelational—they mutually entail and permeate each other. There is a profound Dialogic Dialectic permeating everything in the Infinite Field.

Logos/Logosphere—The Continuum of Reality

All "fields" arise from this same Origin, all grammars, narratives, worldviews, and perspectives. The very idea of a "Field," a "Force Field," arises in this Infinite Word. So the Logosphere is the Infinitely Diverse Unified Field of all possibilities, of all possible and actual worlds. All possible worlds coexist and co-arise in each other in the Logosphere. Space and Time, for example, mutually co-arise in a primal Space-Time Continuum, but so do all of the basic Categories—**Mind-Word-World-Space-Time-Matter-Cause-Energy-Cognition**—all form a **Primal Continuum** of mutual entailment. Tap into any one of these primal categories and all of the others are found to be already implanted within its inner being. Logos makes Relations possible and holds all things in primal relationality. Nothing can stand atomically apart—all things co-arise. This is the Dialogic structure of Logos. In this powerful Logic of Logos (the origin of all possible "logics"), the Rational Force of the Logosphere expresses its global unifying and diversifying power, and the implications of this are astounding for the human condition.

Logos Presides in All Evolution

The Infinite Force is Infinitely Present in every moment in the Logosphere. In the Sacred Logic of this Universal and Global Grammar, every item in the Logosphere bears the signature of Logos, every sign co-expresses Logos, every phenomenon expresses Logos—all evolution is the expression of the Cosmic Event-Continuum of Logos. It is this simple fact—that Logos presides in every moment, in every event, every phenomenon, in every being, in every act, in every historical happening—that has been noticed in diverse perennial traditions.

Logosphere—The Cosmic Continuum

Once the Infinite Force is recognized and acknowledged, it follows immediately that this Force pervades all existence, situates and constitutes all existence, and presides throughout the cosmic Unified Field. Diverse traditions of perennial philosophy have detected this truth in different formulations. It is such a simple, elementary point in the Logic of Infinition that it appears as a truism to the global mind. Once the Cosmic Event-Continuum of Logosphere is discovered, it follows immediately that all existence, all evolution and history, is the creative play of Logos. The evidence of this is overwhelming once rational intelligence awakens to the Infinite Presence of Logos. It was clear that humanity had not yet developed the technologies of mind and language for processing the Logosphere. We still lacked a Science of Logos, a science of the Logosphere—the foundation of all worldviews. This pure Formal Science was latent (and presumed) in the diverse classical perennial traditions and awaited full maturation and emergence in its explicit globalized form.

As the Logic of Logos came to increasing clarity over three decades, it was clear that we urgently needed to develop tools and technology to help us become mindful of when we were in the Grammar of Logos and when we were in the grammars of egocentric cultures. Remember in this meditation on Logos that the pathways of awakening move in a recursive loop—the deeper we encounter Logos, the more this invokes the global turn in minding, and the more, in turn, this encourages the expansion of thought and language, which enhances our capacity to process the Logosphere.

Symbolic Markers for the Two Technologies of Mind

In this recursive dialectic I found it essential over a decade ago to develop symbolic aids to help us cross over from the patterns of egocentric minding to the dynamics of global minding in the Logosphere. It became clear as I experimented across a vast range of worlds, especially in the meditative traditions, that we needed to explicitly distinguish when we are lodged in the egocentric technology of thinking/language and when we cross into the Logic and Grammar of Logos.

Two Fundamental "Logics" in the Human Condition

Here I found it vital in my teaching and research to use special markers. Whenever we think or speak in the egocentric dynamic of language, I flag that discourse with "/ . . . /" (single brackets), and when we think/speak in the Grammar of Logos, I flag that discourse with "((. . .))" (double brackets). Thus any word/sign, say, "X" in everyday language, may be processed in the egocentric technology of mind, /X/, or expressed in the Holistic Logic of Logos, ((X)). If, for example, we use the word "I," when this is uttered in the egocentric mind (whatever the worldview may be), this is specified explicitly as "/I/"; but when this word is uttered in the integral and holistic voice of the Logosphere it is rendered as "((I))."

The egocentric /I/ takes itself to be a separated, independent being—an atomic center of its life and experience. But in the global technology of Logos, the utterance ((I)) expresses a boundlessly interrelated Self in the Continuum of the Logosphere. This high-powered utterance ((I)) is the voice of the awakened Self that flows in the hologistic dynamic and Continuum of ((Logos)). In this ((Logic of Logos)), every ((X)) bears the infinite signature of ((Logos)) and is a unique meeting point of the boundless web of the Logosphere.

(*Note:* The development of this ((symbolic)) grammar of Logos played a vital role in the advancement of my experimental clarification of the Logic of Logos. It should be clear that from the beginning of these reflections in this chapter I have been attempting to speak the narrative in the ((. . .)) discourse. Now that it is explicitly introduced, we may assume that my intention is to present these reflections on Logos in the ((. . .)) logistic. However, I also use it here to flag special terms for emphasis and to mark the contrast with terms in the egocentric discourse. I have found this to be a powerful teaching device when I present these ideas in different contexts.

The Technology of ((Logos))—The Missing Science

This is an astounding result for entering the Logic and Language of the Unified Field. Once we explicitly clarify the use of signs in the egocentric voice and in the Logocentric voice, dramatic acceleration ignites. We now see, for example, the difference between /time/ versus ((Time)): egocentric /time/ is linear and separated from all other categories in egocentric worldviews—/time/ is broken into pieces of /past/, /present/, and /future/, which are somehow supposed to unite in some continuum of /time/. In contrast, in entering ((Time)) in the Logosphere, we see immediately that every ((moment)) of ((Time)), every ((now)), has an infinition structure in which all moments of time meet—((past, present, future)) meet, ((co-arise)), in every ((now)). The great mystics and meditative thinkers understood this, but we have needed a logical technology—the ((technology of Logos))—to adequately clarify, formulate, and express this global truth. To enter ((. . .)) is to awaken the ((global mind)), to cross into the ((global perspective)), where diverse worldviews ((meet and co-arise)). This, I suggest, is the emergence of the ((Primordial Tradition)) in its global form.

Testing the Two Technologies of Mind in the Human Condition

((Imagine)) if this were true—that ((Logos)) is Real, that all existence is constituted in an infinitely dynamic and interconnected Continuum—the ((Logosphere))—that all evolution is presided by the ((Infinite Presence)) of Logos, that all ((History)), across cultures and worlds, is saturated with overwhelming ((evidence)) of the ((creative and causal)) power of Logos, that all great developments in the evolution of human cultures, when seen in proper ((context)), reveal that all events in the Event-Continuum bear witness to and display the presiding ((Presence)) of Logos. This would call for a radical revisioning and recontextualizing of our present narratives and perspectives, indeed, of the ((human condition)). Entering the ((global mind)) changes everything.

The ((Global Perspective))

Let us experiment further by entering more deeply into the ((global perspective)) and crossing into the technology of the ((global mind)). When we stand back from being lodged and fixated in any one worldview and set aside the egocentric habits of mind (which of course is most difficult), the horizon of the global perspective emerges. Now we are able to gain access to multiple alternative worldviews, in their own terms and grammatical forms; we are able to entertain these diverse perspectives together in one dialogic rational consciousness. This dilates our rational capacities and takes us more deeply into the logistic structure of the Logosphere. And as we thus gain ((perspective)), Reality is disclosed in a deeper way.

In this ((context)) it is more apparent that the "postmodern" mantra, that we "humans" are inherently lodged in localized worldviews or perspectives, is nothing more than a dogma of egocentric discourse. And the self-serving suggestion that the alternative to being in a particularized (ego)-local perspective is to presume to have a "view from nowhere" betrays the egocentric prejudices against the living evidence of millennia of meditative experience and of the global perspective in natural reason. The global perspective— the power of ((interperspectivity))—is not a "view from nowhere." The choice for awakened reason is not between either an /ego perspective/ or no "perspective" at all but between the /egocentric perspective/ and the ((global perspective)).

Logos Presides in All Evolutions

As we enter this ((global perspective)) and focus on the deeper patterns and developments in the evolution of the human condition over the past 3,000 years or so (a brief moment in ((Time)), in the Logos Story of Evolution), we are now able to see that there has been a deep drive and relentless quest to express Logos across cultures and worlds. This is not surprising since, as we have seen, the Infinite Force and Presence of Logos (the Logosphere Itself) preside in every moment in all realities. The "scientific" quest to detect and name the ultimate "force" in the universe has hit all sorts of barriers and was not able to reach Logos. But the Logic of Logos makes quite evident that the Infinite Force of Logos is most real and cannot help but make its presence felt in all existence, in all events, in every stage of the dramatic unfolding of evolution. So when we scan a range of diverse worlds as we now jump in midstream, it is apparent that the moving force of ((evolution)) is the gravitation to Logos in boundless ways.

Let us scan selected cultural traditions and fast-forward through the past three millennia. In our Judaic origins we see the emergence of the breakthrough to Yahweh, the Infinite Living Spirit that must be One. The recognition that there is an ultimate primal reality that is Infinite, Living, and One is a significant moment in our common evolution that taps the Logic of Logos. It also is seen that this Infinite Spirit must be the generative first cause of all reality. This too is a classic advance. This Judaic articulation of Logos brings with it the recognition that this Living Presence, which is always infinitely higher, calls on us to reorient our lives to love and honor The First with all of our might, with our whole being.

Similarly, in the Hindu Vedic origins, it is declared in deepest meditative revelations that there is an Infinite Originating Source of all existence—Aum—the Sacred Syllable or Word. In this classic meditative articulation of The First, as a grammar of the Infinite Source is developed that reveals that all names and forms arise from Aum, which also is called Brahman, the Absolute Infinite Being, the First Cause, and the originating source of all realities. Here we find an alternative formulation of the Primal Logic of Logos.

Of course this tradition too in a different way recognizes that the global truth of Aum/Brahman reveals that the true Self is boundless and beyond the artificially constructed ego that most people confuse with the Self (which is called Atman). And here too, in tapping the Logic of Logos, this tradition sees that the key to human flourishing is overcoming the egocentric life, which is seen to be the source of diverse existential pathologies, and advancing to a higher form of life, which comes with the realization of Atman, true Self-awakening.

To accelerate, we see a similar pattern in the early Chinese traditions, for example, in the grammar of Tao. This tradition recognizes that there must be a primal Infinite Nameless Name that is the source of all names. This is the generative source and cause of all existence. In the early Greek tradition, we find an important origin of the development of philosophy and science with the recognition that there must be an Ultimate Principle, Law, Form, Origin, or Cause that explains all appearances. The First is articulated in different ways, and Heraclitus explicitly names it Logos (Word, Speech, Reason), and the grammar of Logos takes shape in the advances of Socrates, Plato, and Aristotle. So here too we find classic openings to the Logic of ((Logos)).

Again, the great awakening of the Buddha bears witness to the emerging drama of Logos in the human condition. Buddha's historic insight was that egocentric mind is the source of human suffering, and that it can be overcome in the awakening of mind beyond egocentric patterns to radical Emptiness, Sunyata, the fundamental Law or Dharma in all existence. In Buddha's teaching, ultimate Reality is a boundless Field of dynamic interrelationality of all things. All things are empty of the ego constructs of "self-existence." So here too we find another alternative formulation of classic features of Logos.

If we look at a vast range of "Indigenous" worldviews, this gravitation to some First (whether Infinite Spirit, Nature, Force) is evident. For example, in one classic African culture (Dogen), The First is called Nommo—the Infinite Name that is the Primal Force that pulsates through all of Nature—so it becomes evident that some kind of powerful pattern is at work moving human evolution, diverse cultural worlds, to alternative formulations of Logos. This is remarkable enough. What is equally remarkable is that as we fast-forward through the centuries on a global scale we also detect deep patterns of Logos emerging in the evolution of the human condition.

How the Logos Force Moves Evolution in Shaping the Human Condition

Of course it is not coincidental that diverse cultural traditions would gravitate to and express The First in the grammar of its worldview, for in the ((Logos)) perspective, it is evident that in the deepest fabric of Reality, the Logosphere, the Infinition dynamic and dialectic of Logos, is recursively and creatively playing itself out in every ((Moment)), in every ((Event)).

Let us scrutinize this more carefully. How can we be so confident that ((Logos)) is happening in every situation? The reason is as simple as it is classical—The Infinite (Force) cannot be broken down or localized in a way that reduces the Infinite Power or Presence: dividing or localizing the Ultimate "Stuff" of the Universe does not break down its Infinite structure. Every "piece" of ((Logos)) recursively iterates the Infinitude of Logos.

This is another face of the Continuum Force Field. In this pure ((Geometry)) of Logos, the ((Logosphere)) co-extends boundlessly, opening sacred ((Space)). Yet every ((point)) in the Logosphere reflects and reiterates the entire Field and thus bears the ((signature)) of Logos. In the case of humans classical traditions recognize that there is that of ((God)), Logos, in every Person; or that the Kingdom of Logos is within, or ((at hand)). Each Person, then, expresses uniquely the ((Image of Logos)), and this is the sacred origin of the ((Individuality)) of each Person. But now in ((Logos Science)) we see that all ((points)) reiterate the Logos structure, a sacred ((center)) of the Logosphere. In this way each ((item)) in the Universe is ((holonomic)), a ((holon)) expressing uniquely and differently the ((Logos Principle)). For this reason one would naturally expect to find in the dynamics of ((evolution)) the playing out of the Self-Expression of Logos in every direction.

Quest for the Ultimate ((Pattern))

To see this more clearly we need to look more deeply into the global ((pattern)) of Logos emerging in the play of evolution and the human condition. When a new "science" arises we should expect that what was taken as "given" before is now accounted for or explained—this means giving the "logos" of it. And in the primal ((Science)) of *What-Is-First*, we should expect that ultimate matters are accounted for more deeply, for as we now enter midstream to clarify the ((global perspective)) and fast-forward through the past 3,000 years or so, we are making great presumptions—we are taking as a "given"—that there are humans, with consciousness, culture, language, mind, meaning, worldviews, narratives, and perspectives. But here we are precisely attempting to place all of this in the ((context)) of the missing Story of Logos. How is the ((logos pattern)) playing out in the emergence of human reason? In consciousness? In language, mind, and world? How do worldviews arise? How are mind, word, and world mutually connected? How do diverse worldviews arise? How are diverse disciplinary languages/perspectives generated?

In reflecting deeply and rigorously on these ultimate questions, it is essential to ((remember)) that in the Logosphere ((word)), ((mind)), and ((world)) mutually permeate and pervade one another in the deepest way. This is the deep structure of ((Logos)): Logos is the Infinite ((Word)), which is ((Infinite Mind)), which is ((Reality)) itself. The egocentric mind is not able to ((process)) this primal truth. In the ((Logic)) of the Logosphere, the unified field of Existence is ((language)), is ((mind)), is ((energy)). The ultimate ((stuff)) of the Universe is ((meaning energy)), and this is the essence of ((life)). In this context of the ((Unified Field)), the Event-Continuum of Logos plays out in ((time)). Each Primal ((Name)), ((category)), or ((field)) is filled with the others. This is the original Infinition/differential structure of ((Infinite Unity)). Every ((item)) in the Logosphere reverberates with this dialectical pattern.

Evolution as the Unfolding of the ((Logos Pattern))

With this in ((mind)), let us now scrutinize some prominent patterns as the human condition takes shape over millennia. Deep in classical traditions on a global scale we see a relentless quest for *What-Is-First*. The Infinite Force is like a boundless gravitational field that both generates all items and attracts them at their core. As ((human matter)) evolves, consciousness dawns. The deepest pulse of the emergence of consciousness is the awakening of reflective self-awareness. This is the Logos impulse—the evidence of the Infinite Force in all things. But the emergence of consciousness arises with the technology of grammar, of language, of the Word finding creative expression.

The awakening of consciousness comes with the ultimate technology of Language taking form. But this mutual arising of Mind and Word is the very expression of Infinite ((Form))—of Logos, and this is ((Being)). So ((Being)) as ((Form)) is originally filled with ((Word)), ((Mind)), and ((Universe))—((Logosphere)). All through the ages it has been assumed that there is some deep link between "Form," "Word," "Meaning," "Mind," "Truth" and "Force," and "World," but now in the context of this Formal Science of ((Logos)), we see more clearly how and why these are indeed deeply connected. The assumption that "logical form" is the binding force that holds Mind, Word, and World together is now illuminated through the rational force of ((Logos)). Here we find the ultimate moving force/dynamic in the ((human condition))—the emergence of ((Logos)), the awakening of Mind, Word, and World, as ((Logos)) reflexively Self-expresses in the Logosphere.

The Great ((Quest)) in Human Life

If we now look at the evolving human condition through these ((eyes)), we see a remarkable drama unfolding on a global scale. It is now more evident that there is a deep drive in humans for "meaning," for "life," on the individual and corporate/tribal level. The primal drive in the human situation, for meaning, for well-being, for life, and even for knowledge, is evidence of the creative unfolding of the Logos dynamic—Infinite Form expressing itself in human flesh. It is little wonder, then, that diverse classical cultures would gravitate to What-Is-First ((Logos, Form, Word)) as the source of meaning, truth, value, being, and life. But this quest for ultimate meaning in life comes with the creative self-articulation of language and mind—the technology of grammar and minding. Here we see that human life becomes self-articulated in a worldview, in a grammar of life, that taps the boundless reservoir of ((meaning, being, and life)) in particular ways.

The Emergence of ((Form)) Shapes the Human Condition

Whether we look at our Judaic origin in its struggle to discern, recognize, and express ((God)), or the Vedic breakthrough to the ultimate word ((Aum)), or the Greek struggle to clarify meaning as "form," as Logos, in the philosophical lives of Socrates, Plato, and Aristotle, we see relatively early signs of the gravitation to the grammar of ((Logos)) in the human condition. It is not accidental, for example, that the Socratic quest for meaning and value would lead to the birth of "form" and "essence" and the discourse of "reason." This early gesture toward birthing the grammar of Logos unfolded over millennia into our contemporary struggles to give an account of meaning in life. But what is also revealed in these (and other) early articulations of the Infinite Word is the growing recognition that we humans are as we mind—the great perennial quest for ((Meaning)) comes with the realization that **how we mind** (the technology of minding) is all important in shaping our living realities.

We Are as We Mind

Let us go more deeply into this global truth. We just suggested that there is a holonomic, recursive, and creatively unfolding dialectic of Logos expressing itself in the Logosphere. This dynamic of the Infinite Word—Infinite Form—is ((happening)) at all times in the Logosphere. This emerging self-formulation of Infinite Form is the driving force of ((evolution)) and the key factor in understanding the continuing evolution of the human condition. In this respect the ((Logos Story)) provides the global foundation of all "evolutionary" narratives, from Genesis to the "big bang," including such diverse accounts as that of Darwin, Hegel, Marx, Teilhard, and others.

When we ((remember)) that the Logosphere is Infinite Form being formulated, and that this ((Form)), this ((Infinite Word/ Universal Grammar)), is the origin and generative meeting point of all Language, Mind, and Phenomena, of all worldviews and perspectives, it makes it easier to ((see)) that Existence itself is the unfolding of Language/Grammar/Mind and saturated with ((meaning)). It is the ((Logosphere)) that philosophy, science, religion, and common sense are trying to process and explain. But egocentric patterns of minding most often block, eclipse, deform, and repress this Primal Field of Reality.

But let us look more carefully at this. The human condition is under ongoing self-evolution, and the ((Logos Event)) is the driving force at the heart of human evolution. As the human form matures and takes shape, all of the primary features of human life mutually coshape and transform one another influenced by the Logos dialectic. **This means that Reason, Thought, Language, Meaning, Perspective, and Experience are undergoing maturation and evolution as Logos emerges.** As we now reflect on global developments over the past three millennia, it is easier to see that humans have been in a deep struggle to mature beyond the egocentric patterns of minding (language, thought, world making, experience) into the more integral, holistic, and dialogic patterns of minding the Logosphere. In this drama, as suggested earlier, we see that in diverse ways the great teachers and revolutionaries have been attempting to usher humanity beyond the dysfunctional and pathological ways of egocentric life into the higher technology of minding the Unified Field of Reality.

As the human form matures, our capacity to process and "metabolize" the Logosphere deepens. To say we are "rational" beings is to say that we are as we mind—that we arise in language, grammar, that we participate in making our worlds, shaping worldviews through forms of interpretation, that we both shape and are shaped by our grammar or worldview, that we have a voice in determining the phenomena that appear to us. To be human is to participate in world making—we are ((grammatical)) beings. All of this clarifies the global truth: ((We are as we mind)). It took millennia to clarify that humans come to be and arise in worldviews involving patterns of interpretation and making sense of things, and one of the great themes in the global ((perspective)) is that egocentric patterns of interpretation and world making have had disastrous consequences for the quality of human life.

In this ((perspective)), a striking pattern emerges: in the continuing evolution of the ((human condition)), two powerful opposing forces have been at work and play. We have seen that the egocentric mind, with its monocentric patterns, is an immature stage in human development. And every great advance in every field, in every aspect of cultural evolution, has been the overcoming of egocentric fragmentation and the painful but inexorable emergence of the holistic, dialogic, and global patterns of culture making. In this drama and living dialectic of Logos, the forces of rational awakening work in, through, and against the divisive forces of egocentric life to open an ever-higher global space for human flourishing.

This is as true of the globalizing of our inner personal space as it is true of the humanizing and civilizing of our shared corporate space in the life of the polis. It is equally true in every aspect of our cultural lives, in every field and discipline, and certainly in the evolution of the sciences. Indeed, it is now apparent that the key advance in scientific method turns not on the ego-ideologies and dogmas of empiricism but on the revisionary and dialogical patterns in the globalization of human reason and inquiry.

The highest virtues in "scientific method" are the ((dialogical virtues)) of openness to the objective alterity of Reality, the experimental spirit of being ever open to self-revision, and to the creative encounter of multiple alternative narratives and perspectives in the quest for ((truth)). The essence of the scientific disposition is the dialogic, global, or experimental attitude that deepens with the awakening of the global mind. And this is as true in our inner personal life, in our deepest spiritual, religious, and moral strivings, as it is in our ongoing attempts to open a sacred space for our shared civic and political life. In this respect, then, the awakening of the scientific spirit is at its core the awakening of the global mind in the quest to express Logos in every aspect of the human condition.

It should be clear that this is just a preliminary sketch, a beginning, of the remarkable human quest for the missing global science. This narrative is developed in a comprehensive way in the forthcoming book *The Awakening of the Global Mind* (forthcoming). Two relevant topics have been published in *PARABOLA*: "The Quest for the Primal Word" (20:3 [August 1995]) and "The Awakening of Primal Knowledge" (22:2 [Spring 1997]).

PART 3: CONCLUDING REFLECTIONS

In concluding, let us look back now at the central themes raised by Professor Nasr concerning the need for a Sacred Science. It is now more evident in light of the foregoing narrative of the great human quest for Logos that Nasr's affirmations of the tradition of *Philosophia Perennis* and of the need for Sacred Science are supported in remarkable ways. We now see that diverse great traditions in the global evolution of thought have, in importantly diverse ways, been in quest of Logos. In this respect the heart of *Philosophia Perennis* is in this global quest for Logos that embodies the sacred common ground across and between diverse worlds, narratives, disciplines, and dimensions of human cultures. It becomes clear in this transcendental quest that drives the evolution of the human condition that there has been a missing Primal Science to which ancient and classical traditions bear witness.

However, we have been suggesting that the universal grammar and technology of mind for a truly Global First Philosophy have been slowly and painfully evolving, and that *Philosophia Perennis* has been in a deep evolution and maturation. In this respect we cannot look to the past, to past traditions, for the fully developed missing Global Science of Logos and for the missing Global First Philosophy that is its vital center and ground. Nasr is, of course, correct in insisting that we honor and value the emerging Perennial Truth in our great traditions, but it also is vital to see that the missing Sacred Science and the global grammar of *Philosophia Perennis* have been undergoing self-evolution and maturation in the human condition. What is exciting is that as this sacred process matures, as Logos emerges in our evolutionary drama, this missing Global Science comes into focus with the awakening of the global mind.

2

Logos as the Infinite Primal Word: The Global Essence of Language

Let us continue our reflection on *What-Is-First* by focusing on Logos as the Infinite Word and the missing universal grammar of Primal Language.

The essence of Language begins to emerge only when we enter the primordial field in which mind, word, and world are found to be originally inseparable. At this deeper, ever-present dimension, we find that this entire world, this ecology, is Language, the infinite dynamic living process of the Word. The entire world is the play of Language, a living text, a creative dynamic script unfolding. This primal Language is saturated with mind, consciousness, thought, conceptual power, truth-force, and meaning. This living text of reality is laden with existence and expresses the world process. So what is originally given is a primal communion, a unified field, of language-mind-world. The entire natural and cultural evolution has been the creative play of this living field, the script of Logos. And the perennial lesson of the global evolution of cultures is this very disclosure and emergence of Logos.

Logos is the Infinite Word, the source and origin of all languages, of all cultural forms of life, of lifeworlds. The global evolution of cultures has reached a horizon where this global nature of Logos is more evident. This very infinitude of Logos, when rightly seen, implies the global power of the Word—global in the sense that it has always been universally presiding in natural and cultural evolution, global in the sense that no cultural grammar could exist or evolve apart from the creative unfolding of Logos. So it is the very infinition of Logos that entails its global jurisdiction and power.

Nevertheless, the localizing forces in the evolution of cultural grammars have contributed to the suppression and eclipse of the global scope and essence of the Word, so much so that we humans still lack a shared Universal Name for the Infinite Word. Our discourse across and between our cultural grammars has not yet moved us to a global consensus concerning *What-Is-First*. In our Judaic roots, the Infinite Word is disclosed as infinitely and absolutely One, and the connection is made between the infinitude of *What-Is-First* and its infinite unitivity. It is recognized that this Word is the Living God, the Living Spirit, the original cause of the universe, the ground of all existence.

In our Hindu roots, the Word is disclosed as Aum, the sacred symbol, the infinite Sound unheard, the origin of all names and forms, of language, beyond all description and predication, beyond all objectification and duality. Here the original Word cannot be thought in ordinary egocentric ways of minding but must be meditated. And this meditative thinking invokes the primal power of mind that is prior to the objectifying and dualizing ways of egocentric language. So the meditative technologies, yogas, capacitate mind to enter a nondual logos that taps into the "Aumic" powers of the Word. In this awakening of Mind, the world is revealed as Brahman, the absolute nondual, unified field of Aum.

Again, in our Buddhist origins, *What-Is-First* is revealed as Sunyata, Absolute Emptiness. Here again this tradition of Logos finds that how we conduct our mind is all-important in entering into awakened discourse and overcoming the suffering and pathologies that arise in egocentric minding. The Buddha's great insight is into the artificiality and destructiveness of ego identities and the constructs of ego existence and egocentric language. The Buddha's breakthrough, enlightenment, came with the insight that egominding generates identities and dualities that fixate on experience and breaks the spontaneous flow of life and discourse. His innovative ethics is an ethics of right minding, which overcomes the objectifying ways of ego discourse.

A new way of life is opened in realizing the emptiness of all ego constructs and thus awakening to the profoundly dialogical co-arising of all things in the dynamic space of Sunyata. In this way all of the names and forms, identities and constructs, of ego language are deconstructed, and the profoundly nondual interplay of things is revealed in the everyday workings of natural language. It becomes clear in this tradition that the primordial law, the Dharma, the ultimate truth of the co-arising of things, is the principle of language, mind, world, and experience. Thus in this disclosure Logos is revealed as radically empty of all ego constructs, yet is found, in this face of Sunyata, to be the immediate, active source and power of all discourse.

Similar disclosures of Logos are found in the Chinese Tao. Here again *What-Is-First* is revealed as Tao, the nameless absolute Presence, which shows itself in all names. This discourse on the Infinite Word concurs with other traditions that recognize that the infinitude of Logos immediately plays out into a depth of infinite or absolute unitivity that displaces all dualities and dualisms. The Tao plays out in a dynamic unified field of reality that grounds all polarities, oppositions, and pluralities. It is quite apparent here that the objectifying ways of ego thinking, which spawn fragmentations, dualities, and incommensurables, violate the Lawlike nature of Tao. So the source of life and true power comes with the rectification of discourse, with tapping into the hidden meaning in our everyday language.

In our Greek origins, too, Logos takes on a distinctive disclosure as the light of reason, as the *arche* or first principle that makes all things intelligible. In the deepest insights of Plato, for example, it is found that human intelligence, natural reason, gravitates to *What-Is-First*, to the ultimate Form, which is the generative principle of all names and forms. Here, too, Plato concurs with other traditions of Logos in recognizing that there must be an Absolute Form in whose presence all other forms arise. He calls this supreme form Goodness, and he sees that it must be beyond knowledge, truth, and being, since it is the absolute condition that makes these possible. In this discourse on Logos, it is seen that the space of reason has a telic order that originates in the presiding presence of Goodness. All intelligible discourse has inherent reference to Goodness, and this is what releases the intelligible energy or light of reason that brings meaning to language.

The evolution of Christian discourse sheds new light on Logos. Here we see a revealing confluence between the Judaic biblical grammar and the Hellenistic Logos. The Christ is seen as the Logos-becomes-flesh, and Jesus is presented as the living embodiment of the Infinite Word. Something profound happens here in the global evolution of Logos, for this discourse of the Christ as the living Logos presents a profound nondual meeting of the Infinite and finite in one being. This breakthrough concurs with other traditions of Logos in recognizing the essential nondual nature of the Infinite Word.

The Christ becomes the living embodiment of the Universal Law, which calls for overcoming the dualizing ways of egocentric living. In this context it becomes clearer that egocentric life is alienated from Logos and is the deep structure of sin. To be lodged and fixated in ego discourse is to be eclipsed from the vital power of the Living Word, the Language of Logos. It is through the surrender of the ego by recentering in Christ that a new and higher Self is born, a resurrected Self that through a higher form of minding, a new covenant of discourse, gains access to the true power of the grammar of Logos.

In this brief sketch, this partial and preliminary scan of diverse global traditions of Logos, we find both remarkable diversity of disclosures of Logos and astounding affinities and congruities. Despite a long and venerable tradition of "perennial philosophy" that instinctively knew that the diverse narratives of *What-Is-First* that emerged in the global evolution of cultures had to be about one and the same Infinite Word, there continues to be a remarkable absence of a truly global Word—not that a consensus is needed for Logos to be actually presiding through all histories, for there is more than sufficient evidence, if evidence is needed, that the Infinite Word must be Universal in scope and jurisdiction.

This is immediately evident from a competent meditation on the very meaning of Infinition. Diverse traditions have recognized in ancient times that everyday thinking and experience inherently lead to *What-Is-First*, and this in turn to Infinition. This primordial insight has been reconfirmed over and over in diverse traditions of Logos through the ages. It also has been confirmed that this Infinition of *What-Is-First* entails a primitive and an infinite Unitivity that invariably plays out to the disclosure of Logos in one way or another. And it is to be expected that the Infinite Word, in its Unitive Power, would have Universal and Univocal scope and jurisdiction.

This point is of the utmost importance in approaching the grammar of Logos. The key turns on recognizing the profound implications of the Infinition of Logos, for it is apparent that there is a most potent Logic inherent in the Infinite Word that inexorably plays out into a universal grammar of all grammars, into a primordial Unified Field that both constitutes and grounds all possible grammars. The abysmal Unitivity of the Infinite Word expresses itself in Alterity, the infinite capacity for generating alternatives, differences, diversity, plurality, multiplicity, and contingency, and this has been one of the most misunderstood and distorted features of the Infinite Word. The dominance of ego thinking, in its incapacity to competently think Logos, to process Infinition and Unitivity, has repeated the fatal mistake of not understanding that the Unity of Logos is filled with Alterity, the differential power.

True diversity, difference, and multiplicity are made possible in and through the Power of Unitivity, and they do not compete with it. The Unitive power of Logos grounds and generates alternatives, diversity, diversification, and differences. Indeed, this is the very signature of Infinite Unity. Still, ego-minding, in imposing its artificial and reductive "unity" on Logos, finds it necessary to violate real differences and diversity and plurality and reduce them to the tyranny of its ill-conceived unity. Of course this has given Unity a bad name and has led to various forms of misology and the disrepute of "logos."

Fortunately the Unitive Power of Logos is greater than all of the divisiveness of egocentric cultures and continues its perennial presiding presence in all discourse. In light of the Alterity power of Logos, it is easier to imagine that the diverse narratives of Logos that have emerged in the global evolution of cultures, in all of their rich diversity, are alter-expressions of one and the same Logos. It does not matter that humans have not yet agreed or reached a "consensus" on a shared name for Logos, for it is apparent that the Infinite Word is ever-present, always presiding in all of the happenings of natural and cultural evolution.

Indeed, I have suggested that in Light of Logos, the most revealing narrative of evolution is this very story of the continuous creative emergence of Logos in all historical proceedings, for once we begin to tap the awesome Logic of Logos, the rational power of the Word, it becomes evident that the lead story in evolution must be this creative play of Logos. At the core of all histories, all narratives, and all events, the emergence of Logos is the presiding theme.

This creative and transformative nature of The Word follows from its very Infinition and is a direct consequence of its Alterity, for Logos can never be fixated or reduced to any egological construction; it can never be objectified or predicated by egominding. The Power of Logos resists, deconstructs, and defeats all egocentric attempts to objectify, name, or capture it in any narrative. In this respect, Logos is truly Sunyata. And yet Logos is the Law, and in its Unitivity it entails the living reality of compassion. This is why diverse authentic expressions of Logos all concur in the truth of Love, and the love of Truth.

It is here that we find the universal foundation of truth and objectivity across and between diverse lifeworlds. Thus Alterity, as the differential power of infinite Unity, reveals that Otherness is an absolute feature of Logos, and it is here that we see the ultimate dialogical nature of all language. Alterity is the original force of Logos, wherein all diversity arises in Unity, and Unity expresses itself in diversity.

This is why there is no "contradiction" or "incoherence" in realizing that Logos is expressed in Yahweh, Aum, Tao, Sunyata, Brahman, and Christ. Nor is there any incompatibility between the grammatical evolution of the discourse of science and religion, for the most vital breakthrough in the evolution of scientific method is the dialogical turn to the experimental method of inquiry, of asking questions of phenomena and being truly open to listen to the experiential responses in a willingness to self-revise. At this deepest level of the conduct of mind in open scientific inquiry, religious life, moral and political discourse, and aesthetic expression, the same dialogical virtue is expressed.

In light of Alterity, it becomes possible to see that the Universal Word inherently expresses itself in a creative and an open-ended play of universal grammars. The essential Dialogical power of Logos can accommodate multiple alternative grammatical expressions in its Univocity, and the realization of this truth is of the utmost importance for the evolution and survival of human existence. Our present and future well-being turns on seeing that in the midst of all of our cultural, ethnic, religious, and ideological diversity we are nevertheless, at the core of our being, in a common dialogical origin. But this realization calls for performing the dialogical turn in the heart of our discourse.

The Alterity of Logos explains both the Unitive power of the Word as well as its infinite capacity for difference and diversity. It may be said that the core insight of "postmodern" culture is the insistence on the ultimacy of difference, diversity, plurality, and contingency. This is confirmed in the Alterity power of Logos. But all of the diversity in the world is still essentially grounded in this dialogical power of the Word and situated in the Unified Field of the Living Word.

The truth of Logos is that there is ultimate diversity and difference in the midst of the common ground of dialogical communion, which is why the ultimate Law for human life is the global ethic of dialogical love. This also is why the authentic minding of Logos calls for the deepest transformation in how we conduct our lives—the dialogical turn in the conduct of our natural reason. To mind Logos authentically, to follow the Law, to enter into the vital power of Language, requires the overcoming of the divisive and violent ways of egocentric discourse. This dialogical turn is the essence of being human and the path to realizing the essence of Language.

3

Logos and the Global Mind: The Awakening Story

Let us experiment together to see if we can find creative ways to enter more deeply into the processes of the awakening global mind. These processes surround us and are always at work in our daily lives. And it would help tremendously as we now attempt to get a rough preliminary sense of the missing story of Logos if we are ever mindful that our past and present habits of thinking are very much at issue here. We need to try wherever possible to become more aware of the ways in which we are deeply involved in egocentric habits of thinking, and as we become more mindful of this to try to stand back as best we can from egominding and experiment in the dialogical awakening of the global mind.

We shall see that the more critical distance we get from egocentric habits of mind, the greater our participation becomes in dialogical awakening or global minding. Perhaps the best way to jump-start this process and break the closed cycle is to dive in and participate experimentally in a preliminary version of the missing story of Logos, for once this story is heard, everything changes.

As we shall see, there are many ways in which the dialogical awakening of the mind may be intensified. One natural and powerful way comes as we cultivate and deepen experience between worlds. Of course we humans are always living in some degree of dialogical encounter and awakening—we are always surrounded by otherness, difference, and plurality of perspectives. This is a commonplace fact of life and everyday experience. Some of us are better at it than others, but it is rare to truly make the dialogical turn and open to the living reality of other worlds in mutual encounter. What usually happens is that we process other views, other perspectives, and other worlds from our own point of view, or if we do inhabit multiple worlds, we keep them artificially segregated and strictly separated, worlds apart. So there is always a certain degree of violence to the Other in our daily habits of mind.

The problem is that other worlds organize and process reality in ways profoundly different from our own. For example, if I am raised in a certain tradition of Christian faith, then my experience and worldview are centered in this orientation, and it is very difficult to truly encounter other worlds, such as the Hindu worlds or the Buddhist worlds or the worlds of Islam, and so on. Different worlds are worlds apart when it comes to making sense of things, to structuring and processing existence and experience. What makes sense in one world often does not make sense in another.

What is a truth or a fact in one world is often not even conceivable or thinkable in another, for worlds are patterns and habits of making sense of things. Therefore, our deepest habits of mind, our unconscious habits of interpretation and world processing, are shaped by these organizing patterns. It is one thing to converse and communicate with others who inhabit and share the same worldview and quite another to "communicate" with people who inhabit different worlds. One of the great lessons from the missing story of Logos that we are about to explore is that we humans are as we mind. The reality that we inhabit is a function of how we think. Mind and world mutually shape one another, and this is embodied in our worldviews.

It is precisely because our deepest habits of world, language, and experience processing are situated in the particular pattern of our own worldview that makes it so difficult to truly cross over and encounter from within the worldviews and perspectives of other worlds. What usually happens is that we consciously and unconsciously "translate" the language and experience of other worlds into the familiar terminology and interpretive habits of our own world.

Consequently, we humans have great difficulty truly communicating with people who inhabit different worlds.

Most often communication breaks down, we talk past one another, and it is not unusual for different levels of violence to break out at the horizon where different worlds "meet," often colliding and confronting each other. One of the great problems we face in our contemporary world, both within our culture and between cultures, and even in our everyday human relations, is the challenge of communication and coexistence between worlds.

It takes special sensitivities, skills, training, and expertise to perform effectively the dialogical turn between worlds. It takes great effort, and even courage, to step back from our deepest habits of mind, to open our selves to the lifeworlds of others, to encounter, enter, and inhabit experientially the worlds of others. This is the special challenge of the dialogical turn. Imagine how difficult it must be to step back from our own settled habits of processing reality in order to truly transform ourselves into the patterns of mind and experience of those who inhabit foreign and alien worlds. Different worlds are different ways of being, and to truly encounter and access other worlds we must be willing to transform our being to experience that world in its own terms. How is this possible?

This means that somehow we would have to stand back and get some self-critical distance from our own ways of world making and experience processing and project ourselves into the patterns of thought and of other forms of processing reality and experiencing the world. To question ourselves and the world at this depth takes courage—we make ourselves vulnerable and take risks. After all, we are questioning our very identity, our grip on reality. And this is especially hard, since it appears to be almost impossible to really step back from one's deepest settled patterns of being in the world. It is like going through a death, a loss of one's very "self," one's very "world."

It is natural to face a certain existential anxiety here, a dialogical anxiety about losing one's identity and sense of self, losing one's orientation and anchors in the world. But we will see as we enter into this process that far from losing one's true identity, our own world opens up in a deep and miraculous way. Dialogical awakening means that in opening up to the Other we open up more deeply to our Selves. Far from denying or giving up one's own tradition, one's own religion, culture, and worldview, we shall see that dialogical awakening, truly opening up to other worlds, is a twofold opening that means a deeper opening to one's Self, one's roots, one's tradition, and one's true home.

Nevertheless, it appears in our better moments that we can and do have significant breakthroughs in communicating between worlds. Through the power of empathy, sympathy, creative imagination, and a deep sense of shared humanity and compassion, we are able to perform the dialogical turn and encounter other people, other worlds, other religions, other cultures, other languages, other orientations, and other perspectives and ideologies. This too is a fact of life. We are able to open our selves, our minds, and our hearts to other worlds, and this kind of self-opening is at the core of the dialogical awakening. When we intensify and cultivate this opening of mind in ever-deeper experience between worlds, a profound change comes in our experience and mode of being in the world. This is one key to the awakening mind.

As dialogical awakening deepens, mind, experience, language, and world co-expand. This is a Dialogical Law that will become more evident as we enter the missing drama of Logos. We rise to a higher order of rational experience, feeling, and living. The power of mind functions at a deeper and higher level, and we encounter reality in a more profound way. As we gain experience and expertise in inhabiting diverse worlds, our rational capacity deepens, and we are able to experience patterns, truths, and dynamics of reality that were not as evident before. We come home to our Selves.

It is in this way that dialogical awakening between worlds opens the mind in new dimensions, cultivates a global perspective, and awakens global minding. It is in this awakening process that our true human essence as dialogical beings begins to flourish. It is in this opening of mind that the missing drama of Logos begins to show itself.

With this in mind, let us experiment further. Let us intensify this dialogical awakening between worlds and actually experiment in moving between worlds. In a sense we are always living in some degree of encounter between worlds, for our cultures have evolved through the ages in the midst of powerful forces of interaction between diverse worlds. Our cultures are inherently multicultural, intercultural in their historical evolution, and they involve a cluster of diverse worlds in complex dynamic interaction at any given time.

For example, if we focus on the evolution of the Christian world over the past two millennia, it is clear that it has been in a complex, dynamic, ongoing transformative interaction with other worlds—with its Judaic roots, with the Hellenistic world, with the Roman world, with the emergence of the worlds of the sciences, and so on. In some sense, "the Christian world" is already a complex of worlds, and the evolution of the Protestant Reformation may be seen as a schism of worlds within the earlier tradition.

Again, if we were to look at the centuries of evolution of the Buddhist tradition, we would see analogous interactions of diverse worlds as the Diaspora of the Buddhist worldview self transforms as it moves through diverse cultural context. It is well known that there was a deep schism in the tradition as it self-divided between the Hinayana and Mahayana traditions. And there was a complex interaction of worlds as Buddhist worlds differentiated themselves from the Hindu context out of which it initially arose. It is a very interesting story of how certain lineages of the Buddhist worldview transformed and adapted as they moved interactively with other cultural traditions—for example, with the Chinese cultural transformations and into the evolution of Japanese Zen life.

Again, if we were to look, say, at contemporary American culture, it is immediately evident that diverse worlds impinge on one another in a complex, dynamic, and often turbulent, chaotic, and even mysterious way. The evolving American culture is a cultural complex of diverse worlds juxtaposed in all sorts of ways—a pluralism of worlds in a multicultural context. A person may be raised in a certain sect of the Christian world complex. She also may be a practicing physicist working on problems of the origin of the cosmos. As a devout Christian, she is committed to the biblical genesis in which God is the creator of the universe. In this cosmology, God is the living infinite cause of all creation.

But as a practicing observant physicist, she also is committed to the "big bang" cosmology, which presents a very different account of origins, one that appears to be at odds with the biblical world. How does she cope with her simultaneous commitment to these very different worlds? Does she have to choose between them? Must one cosmology be the true one and the other false? Could both be true together? But how is that possible?

Take another example of living between worlds. Consider the case of a practicing Jew who is committed to the biblical account of creation. This person also is a practicing biologist who follows the Darwinian account of evolution. How can he subscribe to both worlds at the same time? Must he not choose either biblical Creation or Darwinian evolution? Are these not fundamentally incompatible, contradicting each other? Could both be true? How does he cope with his commitment to the truth of both worlds? Does he practice some sort of inner apartheid, keeping them in strict separation, switching between worlds on different occasions? What strategies do we have for coping in a healthy way with life in multiple worlds? Is it acceptable to simply segregate the diverse worlds we inhabit and switch on and off as the occasion warrants?

Take another example of a woman who is committed to the truth of the biblical world and follows the Ten Commandments and believes in the sacredness of life. She also is committed to the American philosophy, ideology, or secular "religion" that places the highest priority on the sacred value of the right to choice and self-determination. How does she reconcile her religious commitments to the biblical world with her commitments to the "secular" religious worldview of her perceived rights as a committed American citizen? How does she cope with the deep collision of worldviews—between those that encode their deepest commitments as "pro-life" versus "pro-choice"?

These are not just different "views," but they reflect different religious ideologies or worldviews. It is as if the woman is living in two competing religious worlds at once. Could both positions be true at the same time? Must we choose between them? Some people believe that the American "secular" ideology is grounded in biblical values, the very values that ground the worldview that is encoded in the "pro-life" commitment. Is there an objective truth of the matter that could decisively adjudicate between these apparently incompatible worldviews? Are these two worlds just worlds apart and beyond any comparison? Is there any common ground between apparently incompatible worldviews? How are we to cope with life between worlds? We shall see that the future sustainability of our cultures depends on answering these kinds of questions.

Examples such as these abound in all aspects of our everyday life, so it is clear that we exist and live in the midst of the encounter of diverse worlds. As we now enter the drama of Logos, we shall see that the interworld, intercultural dynamic is at the core of all human life. But it is also clear that we live under great cultural stress. There is gross confusion, ignorance, and lack of understanding in the ways of world making and multiple world encounters. Everyday people live in the midst of powerful competing forces between worlds, and it is usually the case that communication breaks down and violence on many levels erupts where diverse worlds meet and collide. We desperately need to develop rational competence here in conducting our personal and interpersonal lives.

When egocentric forces dominate a culture, people develop various strategies for coping with differences between worlds. Very often people who live in different worlds live in a kind of cultural apartheid and remain worlds apart. Communication fails, and fear, alienation, suspicion, and distrust flourish. These are hot spots where many forms of chronic violence erupt. Egominding people "translate" the worlds or worldviews of others into their own terms, into their own lifeworlds. They project their own worldviews onto the world of the Other. They do not truly encounter and enter the language-worlds of the other.

This is a "monological" way of encountering the alien worlds. Those who practice this monological strategy are not usually aware that they are projecting their own language and worldview on the other and are "reducing" the estranged lifeworld to their own egocentric view. These people usually are not aware that this "reduction" is a form of real violence to the other. This is in sharp contrast, as we shall see, to the dialogical encounter of other worlds.

When egocentric minds find themselves inhabiting multiple worlds, these same monological dynamics that arise between diverse people are played out in the inner lives of "individuals." Often one inhabiting, let us say, the biblical world and the world of physics, simply (actually, it takes real effort) keeps these alternative cosmologies strictly apart, a kind of world apartheid strategy. One treats one's two commitments as "just basically different," and never the twain shall meet.

Obviously this approach to "coping" with intrapersonal life in different worlds is unsatisfactory and has pernicious consequences. Such egocentric people live a kind of "schizoid" life, producing internal fragmentation and incoherence, leading to all sorts of existential and psychic pathologies. How can our souls be healthy? How can we truly care for our souls if real dialogue is not flourishing in our psychic life? How can we be healthy, integrated persons with personal integrity if our inner life is fragmented and alienated between different worlds, existing in multiple personal identities that are not truly in touch with each other? How can we be true "individuals" (which means undivided and whole) if we are existentially divided across multiple worlds and selves in our inner life? We shall see that the dialogical awakening in our souls is as vital for our health as it is for the health of the communities we inhabit. So the same kind of inner fragmentation and divisiveness in our psyches is reflected in the external fragmentation and alienation between persons in the polis or community, and of course between human communities as well.

Alternatively, another coping strategy is to perform some sort of "syncretism" or ego synthesis, with egocentric individuals picking and choosing what strikes their fancy, now from this worldview, now from that, a little here, and a little there, and they form a "syncretic" or composite mixture of diverse worlds to suit their taste. This strategy also is dangerous and unacceptable. It promotes the illusion of achieving a genuine encounter and synthesis of diverse worlds, when in fact a syncretic composite is highly subjective and fails to recognize the systemic integrity and wholeness of the diverse worlds being "synthesized," another form of doing violence to other worlds as well as one's own.

Our cultures have not yet provided the tools, the cultural technology, to recognize diverse worlds as "worlds." If different worlds are speaking out of different constructions or readings of reality, then this highlights the dynamics of world making and the nature of the construction of reality itself. When people inhabit different worlds that appear to be fundamentally incompatible, they often do not recognize the depth of difference in their "languages" of reality. They often act as if they are in the same "language" and disagree over the "facts." Our cultures have not yet matured to the point where we have developed basic rational and dialogical competence in negotiating life across and between worlds, and this has now become a most urgent global priority if human civilization is to survive and flourish.

If people were more aware that they are speaking from very different languages of reality, different language worlds, then this would place their attempts at communication in a different light. The first order of business would be to develop skills in truly listening to people who inhabit other worlds, learning the special dialogical skills in transforming our understanding and experience into the lifeworld of others. Our cultures still very much need more advanced rational methods for understanding how to process creatively, effectively, and humanely life between worlds. This is the depth of the dialogical awakening and cultivation of global minding that has been painfully emerging over centuries.

We shall soon see precisely how and why egocentric culture produces deep stress and violence between worlds, while the dialogical revolution in culture awakens the global mind and brings a higher technology for negotiating personal and interpersonal cultural life. This emerging technology of the global mind is the key to our survival and human flourishing.

With this as a preliminary orientation, let us now experiment further with the dialogical turn in encountering diverse worlds as we enter the missing drama of Logos. In a sense we can begin our experiment anew now that we are more mindful that egocentric habits block the dialogical turn. Ego-minding creates a barrier to a deeper encounter between worlds, and we must now experiment in breaking through and crossing the ego barrier. So let us jump in.

Let us try to cross into the rational space in which we simultaneously inhabit multiple worlds and experience them as jointly true and valid. Our challenge now is not only to experience the truth of multiple worlds, that there are multiple worlds, but also that multiple worlds share a common truth.

We now need to move beyond seeing multiple worlds apart to experiencing multiple worlds together—arising out of a common ground. This will help us move beyond the monological mind to the dialogical or global mind.

Let us select a variety of global examples of alternative worlds and encounter them together as we try sympathetically to enter them from within and experience the internal power of their language of reality. We now realize that different worlds are different ways of being, different ways of experiencing, so let us attempt to self-transform existentially and truly experience the power of alternative worlds. And let us attempt to hold these alternative forms of life together in one experience.

We will begin with our Judaic roots, with our biblical world, and move into the revolution of the Christian world. Let us then move into our Hindu roots and experience the Vedantic vision of cosmos. Then we will encounter the drama of the *Bhagavadgita* and experience the anguish of Arjuna, the warrior, as Lord Krishna opens his mind and leads him to a higher awakened consciousness. In our Buddhist roots, we will move with Gautama, the Buddha, and experience the power of his revelation and enlightenment into the roots of human suffering. Let us here notice the nature of the revolution from his Hindu roots to the birth of the world of the Buddha. We will notice striking analogies between the life of Jesus and the life of Gautama as their stories are placed in the common space of the drama of Logos.

Let us open our African origins and share certain classical visions of the origin of the cosmos. Let us enter into our classical Chinese roots and encounter the language of the Tao, the infinite nameless Name that is the origin of all things. Let us glance into the magnificent openings to the Logos in our classical Greek heritage. And let us fast-forward and remember the unprecedented openings into the origins of the cosmos that emerge in the worldview of modern science, especially in physics and astrophysics.

This preliminary sampling should give us sufficient diversity to boggle our minds and unsettle our old habits of thought. These summary sketches are intended simply to open up diverse options so that it will be easier to jump-start the missing story of Logos. At this early stage in our journey we need to lay out selected diverse models or paradigms of alternative worlds to begin to see deeper common patterns. As we proceed we will elaborate more and more deeply in stages as we encounter the diverse world paradigms in greater detail. So if these highly compressed first encounters are difficult to digest, then that is fine, is to be expected. Just keep moving through this preview and try to notice patterns across and between worlds.

As we center in our Judaic biblical roots, we remember that one great disclosure is the revelation that God is One, and we are commanded to love this one true God with all our mind and all our strength. In a way the summary force of the biblical narrative is focused right here in this primordial command to love God with all our being. This implies that we must place this Infinite Living Spirit first and foremost in our lives. God is First and comes First in all things. We are commanded to center our life in God, in Yahweh, the God of Abraham, the God of Israel.

The weight of biblical truth entails that in this recentering of our being in God, we cannot place our ego-self first. If we are to follow the foremost command of God, the Divine Law, then God must be the primary focus of our attention and the organizing principle of our lives. We are called to enter into a direct relation with this Infinite Spirit, thus implying a dialogical opening of the self to God, an I-Thou way of life. All other commandments, moral laws, depend upon our capacity and success in recentering our lives, our being, in this First Cause of all creation.

As we shift our focus to the revolutionary event of Jesus, it is revealed that a new and an unprecedented occurrence takes place in history. In our Christian roots it is affirmed that Jesus is the living embodiment of the Infinite Word, the Logos made flesh, the Infinite incarnated in finite human form. Jesus, as the Christ, the Messiah, as the Divine Living Principle, entering human history and existence, is a new and an unprecedented kind of being, the union of Infinite and finite in the flesh.

This miraculous and mysterious being, the communion of the Infinite and the finite, becomes a bridge and a crossing linking the finite, fallen world, the place of existential sin, to the Infinite Spirit, making it possible for the first time in history for fallen humans who are lodged in finitude, in sin, in separation from God, to become reconciled with God.

In this revolutionary event, Jesus is a mediating being who makes it possible for alienated humans who face the prospect of spiritual death to have the possibility of salvation and eternal life in God. Jesus, as the Logos becomes flesh, as the Infinite Word manifested in the human body, is the embodiment of the Law and brings a New Covenant to the human condition. With this new happening in history, humans, through faith in Jesus, are brought to a new and higher form of life. There is a death of the old self and a birth of a new Self through faith and love.

Jesus is taken to be the prototype of the new Human. When this story is placed in the missing drama of Logos and is processed in the global mind, it is striking that all of the key elements of the awakening of the global mind are clearly performed. Jesus as the Christ is the embodiment of the universal law, the communion of the Infinite and the finite, the communion of Spirit and flesh, the living Dialogical Principle. The essential need for Faith is precisely the letting go of the egocentric mind, rising to the higher form of Mind, which centers in Logos.

This supreme act of Faith bring us to a new and higher form of life and a higher form of minding that fulfills the awakening of the global mind. For

Christians, the event of Jesus represents an evolutionary advance that brings the God of the Old Testament to full global scope and significance. Jesus as the Christ becomes a global event that purports jurisdiction over all nations. How are we to understand and process this Global Jesus? If the Truth of Jesus is an eternal and universal truth for all humanity, then how are we to understand and maintain its global truth across cultures and religious worlds?

If we are more oriented to the biblical cosmology, then the transition into the classical Hindu worldview may tax and even strain the power of our rational and conceptual imagination. Please be patient. It will take some time and repeated exposure for these strange patterns of thought to register and sink in, for in entering this conceptual space, the structure of existence appears radically transformed. Space takes a different shape, and there is a cyclical structure to existence in Time. In this cosmology, the dominant intuition is the supreme truth of the Primal Word—Aum.

This Infinite Sacred Sound, Infinite Word, is the overwhelming presiding reality. It is the origin of all names and forms, of all that exists. But the human condition is situated in the midst of two great forces, two powerful fields. Everyday human life finds itself lodged in a beginningless and endless cycle of existence called "Samsara," and humans who find themselves existing in ego-consciousness are caught in this space-time historical cycle of endless births and rebirths.

While in the biblical world the fallen self, living in sin and alienated from God, is condemned to death, in contrast, in the Hindu Samsara the egocentric self, alienated from true Reality and its true Self, is condemned to perpetual survival in the endless cycle of ego-existence and ego-identity in the curved space-time of historical process. The existing ego-self is trapped in identity and in a particular way of thinking that keeps it entrapped in this burdensome cycle of existential suffering. The classical Vedic Scriptures—the *Upanisads*—reveal that there is a way for this bounded self to awaken and find releasement from its existential despair and bondage.

These Scriptures teach a high technology of minding, a Science of Yoga, which requires the utmost discipline in the conduct of the mind, which leads to a dissolution and releasement from egominding. The technologies of meditative thinking reveal precise, lawlike paths of the awakening of mind that break the bounds of Samsara, breaks the ego barriers, and liberate the higher Self to true Being and Freedom, to Nirvana. This higher Self, Atman, breaks all of the boundaries and constructions of the egocentric self and realizes its essential "Aumic" nature. In this cosmology, the Aumic field is an infinite Unified (Nondual) Field of Being, the Field of Brahman. In this worldview, the forms of language and thought that hold for ego-existence cannot be applied to the realm of Aum, Brahman, or Atman.

The ego mind is found to be the source of deep splits and dualities in all areas of its Samsaric existence. The ego-self comes into being in and through a deep split between the field of the ego-subject and everything else that appears as the object. It is revealed that the truth of Aum, which is beyond all of the categories and divisions of ego language and thought, is a profound Unified Field of Reality. The Primal Sacred Infinite Word is a mysterious Field in which Word, Mind, Consciousness, Knowledge, and Reality are in inseparable communion. The dualistic and fragmented language of ego-mind cannot be applied to the Unified Field of Aum.

It takes the higher methods of meditative thinking to access the Unified Field. One term used for this Aumic Field is *Brahman* (Absolute, Infinite Being, beyond the reach of ego-thinking and ego-existence). All that exists, all that appears in Samsara, is of course situated in the Infinite Field of Aum, or Brahman, and the awakened, liberated Self, the Atman, is in dialogical communion with Brahman. So in this cosmology there are two great fields or forces, the field of ego-existence, which is inherently lodged in objectification, identity, dualities, divisions, and suffering, on the one hand, and the Field of true Reality, the Infinite nondual Field of Nirvana, Atman, Aum, and Brahman, which is pure bliss, pure knowledge, freedom. When this cosmology is situated in the drama of Logos, we shall see that it follows the classic patterns of the awakening of the global mind.

Of course it is hard to relate to this high-sounding metaphysics. Let us pause and catch our breath. Almost every new term in this cosmogram will need elaboration and explanation to "translate" it into more everyday language that we can digest. And in due course we will do just that. This Vedic or Vedantic cosmology becomes much more immediately accessible through the scriptural drama of the *Bhagavadgita*. In this classical script we find a human existential situation that we can more readily enter and feel. In this epic drama we find a great warrior, Arjuna, on a battlefield in the midst of a fratricidal war, a family divided against itself in a decisive showdown for the right to rule the kingdom. Arjuna, with his brothers, represents the forces of Goodness; on the other side are the forces of evil. It so happens that Lord Krishna, the incarnation of the Divine Infinite Field of Aum, is the guide who will lead and counsel Arjuna through his crisis.

The drama intensifies as Arjuna, seeing his relatives and kin on the other side, is pierced by his conscience and moved by compassion, thus he drops his weapon and refuses to fight. He has reached the breaking point in his life as a warrior, an existential crisis in which he finds himself split in a living contradiction. His lifelong warrior ethic and worldview require him, as a warrior, to keep his honor and fight to win. But at this moment on the battlefield, he is moved by compassion and by the call from a higher ethic, a higher voice of conscience that tells him that he should not fight. The moral crisis has ripened. He is crushed, paralyzed, on the battlefield, and he drops his weapon and turns to Krishna for help.

The amazing dialogue that ensues between Krishna and Arjuna follows the classic path of the awakening of higher consciousness. Krishna takes Arjuna step by step through various yoga technologies, through various disciplines of meditative awakening, into a deeper understanding of his egocentric existence and the source of his existential despair. Arjuna embodies the human being who has been successful in his egocentric life but who has matured to the point where he is ready to awaken and face the emptiness and despair of the ego condition.

Arjuna's existential breakdown on the battlefield comes precisely because he is ready to listen to his higher consciousness, to his higher Self within. So in a real sense Arjuna is a divided "self" who at once embodies the egocentric self and the higher awakened Self that he is now ready to more fully realize. This already gives the sense that the human psyche has a dialogical ((I⟺Thou)) structure. At this stage of his awakening, Krishna is Arjuna's higher voice who teaches, guides, and dialogues with the entrapped, egocentric psyche. The therapeutic and transformative dialogue between Arjuna and Krishna is an analogue for the inner dialogical structure of the awakening self. And later, when we place this dialogical drama in the context of the global story of Logos, it will be quite evident that here too we find classic steps in the awakening of the global mind.

At this point, before we move to the revolutionary teachings of Buddha, let us refocus on some of the most relevant patterns in the Hindu cosmology. First and foremost is the revelation of a Supreme Primal Word, a First Principle, an Infinite Presence that is the ground of all that exists. Second, we see the pattern that everyday human life is lodged in an egocentric way of minding that arises out of a deep duality or split, and this way of minding itself produces all sorts of dualities, fragmentations, eclipsing it from the true Reality and actively producing existential suffering.

There is a striking contrast between the pervasive dualities and fragmentations of ego existence, on the one hand, and a higher field of Being that is harmonious, integral, and nondual—a profound Unified Field of Life. The basic challenge of life is for the egocentric self to overcome this pathological condition through an awakening process and to move out of the ego condition into the liberation of the Self, which is called Atman. I am suggesting that this passage from pathological ego-mind to liberated Awakened Mind follows the classic global pattern in the Logos drama of the awakening global mind.

Keeping this summary focus before us, we are now in a good position to make the transition to the innovations of the Buddha. This transition from the Hindu cosmology to the world of the Buddha, the Awakened One, also will test our rational capacity. The story of the Buddha's great awakening is legendary. In his youth the Hindu prince, Gautama, was deeply troubled by the pervasive suffering he observed in the human condition. He left his life of luxury and security to go off into the world to search for answers. After years of searching, going through incredible hardships and life-threatening ordeals, experimenting in the various teachings that then existed, he was still not satisfied. Finally he retreated into prolonged, deep meditations, which culminated in a great awakening that has moved the world and transformed the course of global history. What did the Buddha discover?

In his great awakening, Gautama saw more deeply than ever into the cause of human existential suffering. He simplified his revelation into Four Noble Truths, which are the core of the Buddha's teachings. In his awakening he saw that everyday human existence is suffering, that to exist is to suffer. Second, he saw the depth cause of this suffering. The basic cause of human existential suffering is ego desire, egominding. But he also saw the way out of this suffering. It all turned on letting go of the ego, letting go of the attachment to self, which comes with the right conduct of mind. One of the great lessons is that we are as we mind, that our existence and existential condition are a direct causal result of how we mind, that if we conduct our mind in the way of ego-thinking, we suffer, and if we conduct our thinking in the way of the Awakened Mind, we are liberated.

One of the most revolutionary insights of Buddha appearing to make a world of difference and opening a new cosmology is his revelation that all things are empty. It seems that Buddha sees more deeply than ever into the origins of ego-mind, into the causal origin of existence itself. We have already seen in the Hindu worldview, which is the broader context for the Buddha's innovations, that egominding arises in a primordial split between subject and object. This is the foundation of ego living, and of the existence of the ego itself. The ego takes itself to be a self-existing entity, an autonomous entity existing independently. It is this core that generates and constructs existing things that appear as objects to the ego-subject. The Buddha's great insight sees that all ego existence, the ego-subject and all objects, is artificially constructed and in this sense ultimately empty. Buddha presses beyond the Hindu cosmology in rejecting the language of Atma and insisting that there is no self: an-atma.

The Buddha rejected all substance views, and all views that held on to any kind of existent things. He was a healer who was primarily concerned with removing the arrow of suffering that pierced humans, and he rejected all metaphysical speculation with a vengeance, insisting that all views, all ego ideologies, are vacuous, empty. His great insight was that all existing things are constructed by egominding, and all views, ideologies, are the constructs of ego activity, and that egominding was based on a mistake. This is the basis of Buddha's great formula that existence is suffering. The reason is that existence is constructed and generated by ego activity.

But this is just part of the picture. If there is no self, if all existence is empty, if all views are vacuous, what then? This formula of the emptiness of all things, and of the ego, is a therapeutic first step in a remarkable life transforming awakening to a higher Life. And Buddha's supreme insight into the true nature of life comes with the recognition that all things co-arise. This is the great principle of true reality—that all things arise in a boundless network of causal interactions in an infinitely deep process of reality. Once we truly drop egominding and constructing artificial entities, and we realize that no entity can have identity unto itself, this realization opens a new horizon to a boundless Unified Field of holistically interactive processes.

This unified field of existence and experience, where all things are holistically interrelated, is the truth of nonduality. The egocentric constructions of artificial entities generate dualities and separations on all levels. The insight of nonduality is that all things are interrelational or dialogical in their being. The old substance cosmologies that act as if things had independent self-existence are displaced, and now true reality shows itself as a vast, interactive, co-arising, dynamic, ever-changing process.

When we place this awakening story in the context of the drama of Logos, we shall see how remarkably these innovations of the Buddha follow the classic pattern of the awakening of the global mind. For Buddha's great Principle of Reality—that all things co-arise—which is called the Principle of Relativity in Buddhist discourse—is also the great Moral Law, the Dharma. This Universal Principle of Relativity, that all things arise out of each other in a dynamic, interactive process, is corelative, is the Dialogical Principle itself.

The true essence of any given thing is to be found in its dialogical co-relations, its dynamic, interactive, co-arising with others in the ecological field.

The Reality Principle also is the Moral Principle, the Dharma, because the dialogical principle is the principle of compassion. The deepest level of love or compassion comes when we realize that the Other is already at the heart of one's Self. The Self and the Other inherently co-arise. The Self has no existence apart from the Other, apart from the ecology. Reality has an I-Thou structure. This is why the universal principle of ethics involves care and love for Others and for Self. The Self arises in Others, and Others in the Self. We shall see that this Dialogical Principle has global significance.

Once we truly give up a belief in independent entities, especially the illusion of ego-existence, a deeper power of minding is released, and the "self" is no longer any kind of entity but a dynamic, co-arising, interactive process. In this respect, the "no-self" is the interrelational process of Right Minding, minding the Dharma. When the Awakened Mind breaks the ego barrier and ignites to the dynamic flow of the interrelational process, it dances with the interplay of reality. This is the Dialogical or Holistic awakening of Mind.

Once the ego barrier is broken, the Awakened Mind rises to a higher order of functioning and moves in unison with the dynamic, interactive Unified Field. The great principle of co-arising, the Principle of Relativity, implies a nondual Unified Field of dynamic interrelationality. This is the secret of the dialogical nature of reality itself. It is in the new language of this Unified Field that the Buddha's great insights flow. And here it is natural to see the deep meaning of one of the great formulas of Buddha's teaching—that the Buddha is the Dharma is the Sangha or Moral Community.

Here it is seen that all things are filled with Buddha-nature. The Buddha and the Principle of Reality (Dharma) are one. The Buddha and the Polis, or Community, of beings are one. Now we begin to tap the mysterious secret of the nondual Unified Field that is implied in Hindu cosmology as well. The Principle of Relativity is the holistic principle of nonduality, for nothing can exist in dual separation. This is why it is said in Buddhist discourse that true reality is Sunyata (Emptiness). These innovations of Buddha will prove vital when we enter the drama of Logos.

This is a good point to pause and catch our breath. There is so much here to absorb and digest, but it is timely before we move on to other global paradigms of alternative cosmologies or worldviews to observe some breathtaking analogies between the being of Jesus and the being of Buddha. Let us remember that our present experiment in cultivating intensive experience between worlds is designed to help us celebrate deep differences between worlds but also to welcome striking analogies and congruities as we prepare to enter the global drama of Logos.

Here it is quite apparent that there are fundamental differences between the cosmologies of Christianity and Buddhism, but when both are situated in the common ground of Logos, powerful results begin to become evident. We have seen, for example, that the being of Jesus involved a mysterious communion between the transcendent Infinite and the immanent finite realms. And we have seen that the Buddha is one with the Dharma, the universal moral law that is the principle of reality itself. The global truth of Buddha breaks the egocentric barriers, breaks through all egocentric views and forms of discourse as Buddha becomes the Holistic embodiment of the Universal Law of Logos—the Universal Dharma. This follows the path of global awakening.

At the same time it is evident that the being of Jesus breaks the dualistic barriers and embodies a more profound nondual communion. The global truth of Jesus requires the letting go of egocentric life. Jesus becomes the Holistic living embodiment of the Universal Law of Logos. This Holistic or Dialogic turn in being opens up the new global covenant, the prototype, to all humans. This is why Jesus is the mediating being who existentially joins the separated realms of Infinite and Finite and is seen as the Logos that has become Flesh. In this way Jesus expands and fulfills biblical Script to its global signification, breaking old ethnic boundaries and identities that arise from egocentric life.

We shall see in what follows as we enter the story of Logos that in the midst of deep differences between Jesus and Buddha, it may well be that they both exemplify in uniquely creative ways the same Universal Law of Logos. Both perform a profound revolutionary expansion of their respective traditions, a globalizing awakening as the Truth of Logos becomes holistically embodied in the life of the people. The Universal Dialogical Principle of Love or Compassion may well have alternative formulations or historical embodiments. It may well turn out in light of Logos that both cosmologies may express global truth and follow similar globalizing patterns as the drama of Logos unfolds.

It may well turn out to be possible in the drama of Logos that global truth may have diverse alternative historical expressions, for we have already suggested that the truth of Jesus purports global significance for all people. And it has just been suggested that the truth of Buddha purports global significance or universal validity for all beings. Perhaps we are now on the verge of seeing that both may be universally or globally true without contradiction or diminishing one another. Indeed, we shall see as we gain momentum in entering the sphere of Logos that in dialogical interaction the life and truth of Jesus can help augment and deepen the teaching of Buddha, and the life and truth of Buddha can help support and deepen the teaching of Jesus. In the Presence of Logos, each may dialogically expand and bring each other to an even higher power of Truth. We may even begin to imagine the possibility of the Buddha-Christ. We will of course explore this in greater depth as the drama unfolds.

Meanwhile, let us continue our preliminary experimental excursion into alternative world paradigms or cosmologies as we build our repertoire of complementary global samplings. Obviously we might fruitfully take any number of alternative routes. We might for example enter into the rich array of African cosmologies as we explore the emergence of Logos in alternative African worldviews. We could go deep into Egyptian or Ethiopian roots. We might enter into Bantu cosmology. We could explore the rich cosmology of Dogen culture, which reveals a cosmogram in which the Primal Word, Nommo, is seen to be the origin of all names, a primal life force that pulses through all Nature. We would see a characteristic gravitation to some Primal Origin that is the generative source of the cosmos. The case of the Dogen-Nommo, or Primal Word, may be seen as another global prototype that resonates through many alternative African cosmologies.

Alternatively, we might enter into ancient classical Chinese cosmologies. Here in Confucian thought or in the teachings of Lao Tzu, we find rich resources for the story of Logos. Here too we find a typical quest for some primal Principle or Origin that is prototypical of the emergence of Logos. For example, in Confucian cosmology, we find the excavation of a universal Moral Law that is the Mandate of Heaven. In Lao Tzu, we find deep meditations on the Supreme Tao, the Infinite Nameless Name that is the foundation and primal cause of all names, of all existence.

As in the Indian and other traditions, it is found that everyday conventional life is lodged in ignorance and malpractice, and that it takes higher powers of thought to transform life in light of Tao. When situated in the emergence of Logos, we find classic global patterns in the technology of Tao, the move to higher dialogical consciousness, and the awakening of the global mind. It becomes clear that there is a Logos to Tao, and a Tao to Logos. We find in allied developments global resources such as the Principle of Yin and Yang—polar oppositional or complementary forces that embody the Dialogical Principle in all existence. And in the recognition of a profound and universal Life Force, Chi, that pervades all Nature, we find another prototypical principle that is grounded in Logos.

Our experiment could easily have taken still other fruitful paths. We could have focused our attention on the emergence of Islam as it arises out of the biblical roots and proceeds in a unique cultural evolution that sheds dialogical light on the unfolding of the Judaic and Christian lines of development. The development of Islam across cultures and worlds is a global event of major significance in the awakening of the global mind. This is another rich reservoir of creative developments in the drama of Logos.

Again, we could have followed the path of the spread of Buddha's teachings as it goes through powerful intercultural transformations as it evolves through Nepal and Tibet, moves through China, and emerges transformed, centuries later, in the Japanese Zen traditions. When we observe these global patterns of cultural evolutions across cultures and over centuries in the context of the emergence of Logos, we begin to see characteristic movement in the awakening of the global mind.

Of course there are numerous other rich possibilities that we might mention as we scan the spectrum of creative cosmologies and worldviews across human cultures through the ages. And as our story unfolds in stages, we shall continue to tap these fertile global resources of Logos. But let us resume our present experiment of intensifying our experience between worlds and focus our attention on two key global events that will help us open the horizon of the missing drama of Logos. Let us first review some of the spectacular advances that emerged in classical Greek openings to Logos. Then we will be in a better position to move into modern times and open up some key themes in the continuing dramatic emergence of Logos in a global context.

4

The Emergence of Logos
in Classical Greek Thought

As we now enter the rich constellation of cosmologies in early Greek thought, we find an unprecedented opening to Logos and the global emergence of reason. In our experimental journey into other worlds, we encounter here diverse cosmologies that nevertheless gravitate to classic themes in the drama of Logos. If we are able to enter into the worldviews of Thales, Democritus, Pythagoras, Parmenides, Heraclitus, Socrates, Plato, and Aristotle, we find a wonderful drama unfolding. We find through these diverse visions of reality a relentless quest for something first, for some starting point, principle, or origin that would make sense of things. We witness in these classical roots an amazing birthing of rationality, of philosophy, science, and moral consciousness.

The usual story line is that philosophy and scientific consciousness emerged in these early attempts to articulate some ultimate first cause of all existence. It appears that there is a deep intuition in human experience of there being some ultimate unifying force that embraces the vast and limitless diversity of life and existence. But it also is clear that we humans face abysmal diversity at every turn in our lives. In the amazing drama of Logos that we are preparing to encounter, we shall see that thinkers and traditions have had a tendency to stress Unity over Diversity, or Diversity over Unity, but the key to global Reason is to solve the mystery of how the Primal Intuition of Reason is at once both abysmal original Unity and boundless primal Diversity. We must understand how Eternal Being is Perpetual Becoming, how the Absolute must be a Continuous Process. It has taken centuries in the global evolution of Reason to arrive at the horizon where we may resolve this mystery: How can the Original Force of the Universe be the very source of boundless Unifying Power and boundless diversity, plurality, multiplicity, and process?

Nevertheless, as we now take a quick glance at the emergence of Reason in early Greek origins, it appears that the birth of rational consciousness has focused on clarifying and articulating the ultimate unifying power that binds existence together, that organizes the vast plurality of things into a coherent, ordered, and intelligible world. Were it not for such a unifying force organizing the field of life, nothing would make sense, nothing would work, nothing could be.

This primal twin intuition of boundless unity/diversity has been at the core of the birth of reason and the emergence of philosophy, religion, and science. The classical Greek origins that we are now previewing are truly remarkable in tapping and opening up vital themes in the global drama of Logos. The intuition or instinct of a Primal Unity generated the articulation of key forces in the life of Reason.

For one thing, it brought to light that there must be "something first," something primal and original. Contained in this intuition are the seeds of rational order—of there being something higher, of there being direction and orientation in the life of thought and experience. Were it not for this ordering force, there would be no rational space, no field of reality, no world, no universe or cosmos. In what follows we shall see that the very idea of the "space" or "field" of reason, the "unified field" of the universe, arises from this Primal Force. It is the presence of this profound ordering power that gives rise to the very idea of "law" or "principle" or "cause." And from these building blocks of Reason, all of the other allied forces emerge. For example, from the idea of "principle" (that which comes first) we already have the seeds of "law," "form," "first cause," "universe," "universal," "essence," and "identity." These are some key building blocks in the life of Reason.

It is this intuition into Primal Unity that makes it possible to think in the first place. Let us perform a simple thought-experiment on this. Imagine what would happen if there were no Unifying Force in the universe. If there were no Unifying Force, then how could there be thinking? How could there be a thinker who has some kind of continuous existence through time? How could "time" flow in any continuity without the Unifying Force binding time and holding passing moments of past, present, and future in a continuous flow?

Again, if Time were not a continuum, a continuous, unbroken flow, then how could the "thinker" have any continuity to sustain a thought? And how could a thought persist through time to retain its identity and integrity? Without the Primal Unifying Force, nothing would cohere; there would be no "relation," no "thing," to be in relation to, and nothing could make sense. The "thinker" would have no continuing identity, there would be no relation between the thinker and her or his thought, and thought could not reach out to represent and touch the world, and of course there could be no universe. Everything would dissipate, and there would be no world, no self, no consciousness, no experience, no language, no thought, no relation, no meaning, no truth or existence.

This is why the intuition into Primal Unity is so deeply inscribed and innate in all thought and experience. To be in thought is already to be lodged in the midst of this Supreme Unifying Condition, so it is little wonder that any thought and all thought would both reveal and gravitate to this Original

Unity. The moment we begin to reflect on thinking and experience the abysmal presence of the Unity Condition makes itself manifest. So it is not surprising in the Greek origins of self-conscious reflection that there would be a relentless quest for Origins, for something Primordial and First. And it is in this quest for *What-Is-First* that we find the emergence of Reason and the inseparable birthing of religious, philosophical, scientific, and moral awakenings.

It is this Universal Presence of the Unifying Condition that lights up the field of reality with the light of Reason. This Unifying Force both diversifies into the boundless multiplicity of things and at the same time holds things together in relation, order, and coherence. It is this Unifying Force that both extends or diversifies itself into the Unified Field of reality, the Universe, and holds all things under its jurisdiction and power. Without the Unifying Force, there would be no Universe, and without the Diversifying Force, there would likewise be no Universe. The great mystery in the global evolution of thought has been to tell the story of how the Original Force, *That-Which-Is-First*, can be the very source of boundless Unity and Diversity.

But this is the very power and light of Reason itself—this is why things can make sense, this is why the world is intelligible, and why thought can process the world and have meaning. Religious awareness ignites when thought and experience become mindful of this Primal Condition of Meaning. Philosophical Understanding emerges as thought awakens to this Light of Reason. Scientific life arises with the quest to know and explain things in this Space of Reason. And Moral Consciousness is born as rational life awakens to this Origin of Meaning and Truth. For it is because thought and world are saturated with Rational Light that things have Being and Value. So religious, philosophical, scientific, and moral life all have their joint origins in the awakening of rational awareness.

To see this let us glance for a moment in this preview at some of the remarkable advances in the thought of Socrates, Plato, and Aristotle. If we can get even a quick preliminary sense of the astounding developments in the thought of these teachers, then we will have a blueprint of the pattern for the subsequent evolution of European thought and of the crisis in reason and culture we face today. So let us focus attention here for a moment and try to transform our thought into the worldviews and thought processes of these teachers of Logos.

Socrates is a moral hero in the evolution of European culture, for good reason. For it is with Socrates that a profound moral revolution takes place in classical Greek thought. To appreciate this we need to remember the rational crisis that peaked as Socrates entered the scene. Prior to Socrates, the great minds envisioned alternative cosmologies that were in a quest for the Primal Origin or Cause of the universe.

Science and Philosophy arose together in brilliant attempts to grasp and articulate the intuition into Primal Unity. Some thinkers sought an ultimate natural "material" cause of the Universe, for example, seeking some primal material substance, such as Water or Air, or some primal force, such as strife and opposition, to account for the origin of things. Thales speculated that all things arose out of Primal Water, for Water obviously transformed into diverse forms—liquid, solid, vapor. And Water is essential for life. Obviously he was not only speaking of physical "water" that is perceived through the senses but of some higher kind of primal or "metaphysical" Water. In an alternative worldview, the Pythagoreans, for example, developed a cosmology in which Number was the key to the Universe. In this worldview, mathematics played a vital role in exploring reality, and the Universe was found to be filled with ratios and measures, rhythms and harmonies. In these beginnings it was clear that mathematics, music, and reason were deeply connected in the fabric of reality.

There is no question that in the diverse worldviews that were articulated there was a deep quest for *What-Is-First* and for expression of the intuition into Primal Unity. The driving force for this quest is the perception or hope that if we could truly find and name the ultimate Unifying Power of the Universe, then we would have the key to understanding the nature of things. If we could truly get at *What-Is-First*, then we would be able to make sense of things, to have a rational explanation for the Universe and for experience. This would illuminate the world with meaning.

But as we shall see in the global drama of Logos, the intuition into Primal Unity is so profound and rich that it has spawned a vast diversity of alternative, even competing, visions of reality. This is certainly the case in the unfolding story of Reason, which sets the stage for the entrance of Socrates. In fact, the emergence of Reason faced a deep crisis at its core. For two brilliant minds, Parmenides and Heraclitus, pushed the quest for *What-Is-First* to what appeared to be an ultimate contradiction.

Parmenides meditated deeply on Ultimate Reality and saw that this Reality must be Absolute, Eternal, and Unchanging. He saw deeply into Primal Unity and inaugurated a historic quest for Being. This emergence of "Being" was a monumental advance in the quest to know the Ultimate Unifying Force of reality. It now appeared that there had to be something deeper than the material "stuff" that appeared to our senses, such as Water, Air, Earth, or Fire. And it was prior to any Force of nature that could appear in experience. The Supreme Unifying Power had to be a more primordial Presence at the foundation of all experience, something that we could approach only through the meditations of rational thought.

In his visions, the supreme Idea of "Absolute Being" was born, and this was revealed as an Ultimate Unity that could not begin nor end, The Same,

Eternal, and beyond Change. Being could not change, since it was the condition that makes "change" possible. This very idea of something "Absolute," "Supreme," or "Ultimate" was inscribed in the intuition of Primal Unity. The seeds of Divine Being, Divine Form, were already given in the heart of Reason. This Being filled all Reality and was Boundless or Infininte.

We shall see as this drama further unfolds that everything turns on this insight—that *What-Is-First* must be Infinite in scope and power. The challenge is that our rational awakening essentially turns on adequately "thinking" or "processing" this Primal Infinite Power. But in the evolution of mind, it appears that our deepest habits of thought render what we think to be finitized. The global struggle of humanity through the ages turns on our capacity to cross over into encountering and processing this Infinite Unifying Force in shared human experience. We shall see that the story of this struggle, this struggle to rise to our true human form, is at the center of the drama of Logos.

But at this early stage of rational awakening in our Greek origins, the encounter of this Infinite Primal Power appeared to polarize into the alienation of Being and Non-Being. If the Primal Force is Being, then Being was Infinite and all-encompassing. Nothing could exist beyond Being. So "Non-Being" was vacuous, empty, meaningless—it could not be thought. This means that the realm of Thought and the Realm of Being coincided. Thus was born "Rationalism"—that Being and Thought were coextensive, and that the Real was Rational, and the Rational was Real. Reason pervades the world. It is this unifying power of Reason that holds together Thought and World, thus making experience and knowledge possible.

These deepest meditations on the Unifying Force revealed that it had to be Absolute and Infinite. And being Infinite, it could lack nothing, it could have no limits and negation, hence it had to be fully Actual, Eternal, and Perfect. These meditations of Reason are historic in the drama of Logos, because it is a monumental revelation of Divine Form. The foundation of religious life could be directly encountered through the power of Rational Thought.

For this reason, Being could not "become," could not change, could not be "altered," since it is the condition that makes all change possible.

It appeared that something can "change" only by becoming something else, something different. But since Being filled all Space and lacked nothing, there was no room for it to change. It appeared that this Ultimate Reality had to be Eternal, One, the Same. So all "change" at this Primal level had to be mere "appearance." And everyday experience, which constantly encountered change and process, had to be some kind of distortion or illusion, a mere superficial appearance of the true Ultimate Being.

On the other hand, Heraclitus used the same Rational Thought to penetrate deeply into Ultimate Reality, into the Unifying Condition, and he found only constant Change, perpetual Becoming, radical flux, with nothing ever remaining the same, only the flow of Difference and radical Becoming. This seems to mean that Otherness, what is radically Other, must be real. There had to be an open, empty "space" of not-being and negation and nothingness to make room for constant becoming and change. For this is the essence of change—something "becomes" what it is not, so not-being is an essential factor in all change, which opens the door to "What is Not," or "Non-Being," being in some sense real.

What is inconceivable in Parmenides' meditations on Being now appears to make perfect sense in Heraclitus' insights into the Infinite Force. The deepest reflection of Heraclitus into *What-Is-First* broke the barrier of "Substance" and "Being" and found Infinite Change and Process. If there is anything "constant" and "continuous" that could be the Unifying Principle, it was Constant Flux or Continuous Change. Now it appears that nothing was ever the same. All "things" are empty. Everything is always changing. The Ultimate Unifying Force was the Boundless Process itself.

Now it appears in this meditation on the depth of the Unifying Force that its Infinite or Boundless Power cannot be static, fixed, or eternal. Therefore, the "Being" of Parmenides could not be the Ultimate Principle, precisely because it appeared eternal, static, and nonchanging. The Primal Force, the Absolute, had to be infinitely Dynamic and Active. Somehow Heraclitus saw that the Infinite Force could not be bound by any static or eternal being. It could not be contained in any eternal substance, nor reduced to "One," but it essentially expresses itself as Many, Plural, Multiple, filled with Difference and hence in radical, perpetual Process.

It appeared in his meditations that the Unifying Force was originally filled with the power of Difference and Multiplicity, so Difference is just as primary as Unity and indeed expresses the essence of Infinite Unity. And if the Ultimate Reality or Unifying Power expresses itself in infinite, perpetual Change, then the supreme Truth is the truth of Becoming, while "being," "permanence," "sameness," and "identity" must be mere appearances. In light of this Truth, everyday experience, which seems to encounter things that endure and remain the same through time and change, must be a mere superficial appearance and distortion of the deeper underlying Reality of Infinite, Perpetual Change.

We seem to have been sucked into a deep paradox. In our thought experiment, moving with Parmenides and Heraclitus, we can feel the compelling polar insight into the depth of the Unifying Condition. We have seen that there must be a Primal Unifying Condition, but when we meditate with Parmenides on this Abysmal Unity, it seems to lead to Eternal and Infinite Being, beyond all change and becoming. And when we meditate with Heraclitus on this Primal Unity, it leads to radical Becoming, Process, and Infinite Change beyond all being and permanence.

How could Ultimate Reality be both Absolute Being and Absolute Becoming at the same time? How can the deepest rational thought on Primal Unity reveal what seems to be polar opposite truths—the truth of One versus the truth of Many, the truth of Identity versus the truth of Difference, the truth of radical Permanence versus the truth of radical Change? Clearly Primal Unity cannot be self-divided and split. Yet it appears that the ultimate reality is revealed as both Being and Becoming, as One and Many, as the power of Identity and Difference. Is reality ultimately a self-contradiction? Can this paradox of Reason and Primal Unity be resolved?

When Reason itself seems to be self-divided and appears to lead to polarized or contradictory results beyond mediation, it has the effect of opening up the floodgates for skepticism, cynicism, mysology, sophistry, and pernicious forms of relativism. If the deepest meditations of reason yield opposed views that appear to be mutually incompatible, contradictory, and beyond mediation, then how can Reason be trusted? How can there be any objective knowledge that is universally binding on all rational beings? How can there be any absolute or shared common ground between differing views? If Reason is supposed to be the mediating power that resolves conflicts and opposition and finds common ground, then what are we to do if Reason itself fragments, divides, and polarizes? Skepticism is a natural result: this is the attitude that we humans cannot really reach knowledge. Perhaps there is no knowledge. It may be that all we can have are subjective opinions.

Again, "mysology" is a hatred of Reason or Logos, a rejection and contempt for the life of Reason. And "relativism," in one simplified version, is the view that truth, if it exists, is relative to particular views or individual perspectives, which goes with the insistence that there is no objective or absolute truth binding across perspectives and views. Another simplified version of relativism is that since "truth" is universal, objective and binding across perspectives and views, there is no truth, only local, subjective opinion.

One teacher, Protagoras, who was influential in the culture at the time of Socrates, was famous for his principle that could be seen as expressing some version of relativism: "Man is the measure of what is." Of course this could be interpreted in different ways. It could mean that humans are the measure or standard of what is real, true, and meaningful. But since human interpretation or judgment is performed by individuals, it also could be taken as an opening for making truth relative to individual views: "Each person is the measure of what is." Protagoras' doctrine has the force of making relativism the only truth—that truth is relative to each person's perspective. If there is "truth," then it must be local, particular, and relative to personal views. So this doctrine of relativism favors difference and plurality over unity and universality. It rejects the possibility of any objective or universal truth across perspectives or worldviews.

As a result, this attitude of relativism, which flourishes in the crisis of Reason, opened the way for the emergence of sophistry. Sophists, supposed practitioners of "wisdom," developed certain types of relativism into an art form and practiced this form of life in their teaching. Since "truth" is relative to some perspective, and is what one makes it, the art of wisdom became the art of persuading others to become convinced of any perspective one wished to adopt, and to have others adopt as well. The sophist was a skilled rhetorician who could play with people's minds and use dialectical skills to persuade them of any perspective or line of interpretation she or he wished to present as "truth."

This is the social, political, and cultural context in which Socrates enters the scene. His deepest intuition was that there is and must be a higher Truth, that it is possible to rise to universal knowledge, that Reason is the divine power enabling humans to ask deep questions, to live a life of inquiry, to strive for Wisdom, and to enter the life of Virtue. Socrates was convinced that the attitudes of sophistry and skepticism and mysology were detrimental to the youth and to the culture. And in his passion for Wisdom, he sought to vindicate Reason and focused inquiry on Self-Knowledge. He taught that the unexamined life is not worth living. He shifted the focus from seeking external knowledge of the Universe to the deepest internal quest for Self-Understanding and Self-Knowledge.

This inner quest for personal wisdom required a deep awakening through radical self-questioning—the willingness to ask the difficult questions about the nature of the Self, the nature of knowledge, of virtue, happiness, and the life of Truth. This awakening involved a critical turn in thinking—a willingness to question one's deepest-held opinions, assumptions, and beliefs. This is one version of the dialogical awakening, the awakening of Right Reason, a vital step in the awakening of the global mind. Socrates saw this critical questioning as being essential in the art of being human and as vital for human well-being and Happiness. With this breakthrough in Socratic inquiry, a new depth of rational awakening ignited, and with this moral consciousness reached a new horizon.

This was the core of Socrates' moral and rational revolution in philosophy. It was a necessary step in the awakening of higher Reason, and it required the dialogical turn of stepping back from one's entrenched worldview and fixated patterns of thought and making the critical turn to deeper Self- Knowledge. It was not so much finding "final answers" as it was the awakening of consciousness in asking ultimate questions in the quest for Wisdom. Socrates was aware that he had not found final solutions, and yet the Oracle of Delphi proclaimed Socrates the wisest of humans. In the now-famous legend, Socrates visited the Oracle and queried her as to who was the wisest person. He knew that he did not have ultimate answers and naturally did not think of himself as having achieved wisdom.

Yet to his shock and dismay, the Oracle pronounced Socrates the wisest of all. This launched Socrates on his quest to prove the Oracle wrong and to seek out the ones who were truly wise. He visited famous sophists and began a cross-examination of their views. Soon he learned that they did not have the answers, and in fact they were characteristically confused and misguided. They were less wise than Socrates because they were convinced that they had the answers and were hence dogmatic and not truly open to rational inquiry.

Gradually Socrates began to see the wisdom in the Oracle's declaration—that true Wisdom was embodied in the critical process of opening the mind, asking radical and searching questions, and genuinely entering the path of awakening wisdom. This became one of Socrates' enduring contributions to the rational enterprise—the recognition that one is ignorant is a prerequisite for truly opening one's mind to a higher Truth and to genuine dialogical inquiry. This was a first step in philosophical awakening and entering the path of love of Wisdom.

The transition from the life of Socrates to the teachings of Plato is an intriguing one, for our primary source of knowledge of Socrates comes through the dialogical dramas of Plato, perhaps Socrates' most gifted student. Socrates himself did not produce writings, so we encounter the life and mind of Socrates through the dramatizations of Plato. It appears that the young Plato was deeply inspired by his teacher and sought throughout his brilliant career to bring to fruition Socrates' passion to vindicate Reason, to establish higher Truth and Knowledge, and to find genuine answers in the quest for Wisdom. Thus there is a natural, if an ambiguous, flow from Socrates' heroic beginnings to Plato's monumental advances in the drama of Logos.

If Socrates embodies the life of dialogue and the dialogical awakening of Reason, then Plato lifted the dialogical process to a high dramatic art and further inaugurated a great tradition in which dialogical inquiry is found to be a vital moving force in rational life. Through the dialogical transformation of mind, Plato sought to demonstrate that the apparent contradiction that emerged between the views of Parmenides and Heraclitus could be resolved by going more deeply into the foundations of Reason toward the Primal Force in experience, the origin of rational light.

In continuing Socrates' quest for Wisdom, Plato followed the path of the Primal Intuition into The First and helped open the Space of Reason in bold new ways. His keen philosophical instinct helped him see that there must be some Primordial Force that holds all things together in a Unified Field of reality. Following Socrates, it became clear to Plato that everyday, conventional experience that was centered in the senses could not enter this Unified Field of Reason. One main theme in Plato's thought is that experience must rise to a higher order of rational awareness to cross over into this unified domain of rational life.

Central to Plato's teaching is the view that the rational mind has direct access to a higher, timeless realm beyond the everyday world of changing objects in space and time. In the birth of Plato's cosmology, it became clear that behind the particular, ever-changing objects of everyday experience, there had to be rational "forms" that stabilized and grounded these fleeting entities and gave them sufficient continuity and order to enable us to make sense of them.

Thus, for example, as we encounter things in our everyday world—tables, chairs, people, stones, trees—our senses give us one impression of these things, and our rational powers can "see" and understand what they are and identify them. Plato also noticed that our sense impressions of things are fleeting and ever-changing, and yet with the power of mind, we are able to give stability and order, names and forms, to things. But Plato noticed that the entities that reason "saw" had to be in a different world or field from the fleeting impressions that appeared from the world of the senses. The forms of things encountered through our rational powers were of a different order—they were not in space or time, not changing, not directly perceivable by our senses.

This was a monumental step in the discovery and exploration of Rational Space, a world of mind or soul beyond the particular bodies in space and time. Plato opened up the philosophy of meaning by theorizing that particular things in the everyday world have names and forms that enable us to "think" them, to identify them and reidentify them, to name and process them in language, and hence to make sense of them. In the quest for the meaning of things, Socrates and Plato saw that we applied common names to classes of things, such as people or animals, or natural objects in the environment, because they must have something in common.

We call stones "stones" because all stones share some common nature that makes them stones. Plato conjectured that we call things of a given class by a common name to signify the common "form" they share, which makes them the specific objects they are. But while a given object is always particular and changing in space and time, the forms of things are of a higher realm, beyond space and time and change.

With this "discovery" of Forms or Essences in the field of Rational Space, Plato took an important step in the awakening of Reason. Forms are "universal," unchanging and common to many things in the world of change. So forms expressed the "essence" of things. While the particular things in the world of sense were always changing, the form or essence of things encountered in rational space was universal, transcendent, unchanging, and eternal.

Our senses seem to pull us to perceptual objects that are particular and changing, while our rational power appears to have access to a realm beyond the senses, encountering universal rational objects in conceptual space. If this is so, then these rational forms could function as the common ground stabilizing and unifying the fluctuating world encountered through our senses.

And if humans share a common power of Reason, then we all can have direct common access to these universal, eternal Forms. In other words, the world of forms could be the shared foundation for common truth, common meaning, the ground of communication, and a corporate reality.

This vital distinction between these two worlds or fields was a turning point in the history of thought. The world of forms or essences was beyond everyday space and time and existed in a timeless realm beyond change. Without these forms, our everyday experiences would dissolve into chaos and become amorphous, beyond meaningful thought. We have the power to think the everyday world because it is informed with the universal rational forms or essences. So the forms were the causes that made things what they were, gave them meaning, identity, essence, order, and thinkability.

The discovery of forms or essences in rational space gave Plato a powerful explanation for the nature of things, an explanation for the primary cause that makes each thing what it is. The forms also explained how "meaning" is possible—the meaning of a name or sign was precisely the form or essence that it indicated. And to define a given word is to clarify and articulate or formulate the form or essence it signified. So the being of things and the meaning of things were both explained in light of its form or essence.

This discovery of the forms of things, and the field of forms in Rational Space, was at the core of Plato's cosmology. To transform our minds into Plato's world requires us to experimentally enter this worldview in which we experience the profound difference between the world of forms and the world of everyday, common sense things. To enter into the field of forms according to Plato, we need to stand back from the powerful pull of everyday sense experience and awaken the powers of rational thought. For Plato, the philosophical life—the pursuit of Wisdom—requires us to discipline the mind, ignite our higher rational powers, and cross into the timeless world of forms.

This is the crossing into conceptual space, Rational Space, which has a life and an order of its own. When the mind or psyche awakens and "enters" this timeless domain, we become aware of the true Self, the Soul, our essence or true nature. As rational powers awaken, we become aware of our Soul, which apparently exists beyond the everyday world of space and time and changing things. So Plato's discovery of the world of eternal forms also was the discovery of the world of Soul and our higher immortal life. This rational awakening was the key to Self-Knowledge, to the art of being human. It was the key to our well-being, to human flourishing and happiness. In this respect, Plato advanced the mission of Socrates in opening the Space of Reason and charting the world of Forms.

With this "discovery" everything in everyday, commonsense experience inverts, and there is a radical revolution in perspective. We cross from one world into another. Let us focus all of our attention here for the moment and try experimentally to move with Plato from the everyday world of sense objects to the world of Forms. In everyday common sense, we are oriented to the primacy of the sensual objects and events encountered through our senses. These "physical" objects in space and time we naturally take to be the primary reality. But Plato saw that when we try to understand what is before our eyes, we go through a rational awakening, and the higher dimension of forms or essences begins to come into focus. For him our rational power has access to essences that are not in space and time, and as we struggle to see these higher objects of thought clearly, our whole sense of reality is turned around.

As our rational power of thought awakens, we begin to see that these eternal forms are the primary reality, while the objects of sense appear to be the passing and temporary copies, the secondary and derived reality. This awakening of the rational mind is nothing less than a dramatic shift in world-view. When rational consciousness awakens and we cross into the field of eternal Forms, we encounter true Reality and can see that everyday, common sense consciousness, which fixates on sense objects and sense experience, is transitory, fleeting, and hence mere "appearance."

It is in this shift in awareness that we rise to the dimension of true Knowledge and realize that our mental states in common sense experience are unstable and yield mere opinion, belief, and subjectivity. For Plato we begin to truly Know something when the rational mind is ignited and we see into the inner essences and forms of things. In this respect, everyday experience is sleeping and in the dark, while in the awakened mind we rise to a higher dimension and encounter things in the Light of Reason.

One striking example of this capacity of human reason to rise beyond the particular objects presented to our senses in naive or prereflective "common sense" is found in the mathematical sciences. In geometric thought, for example, we are able to look beyond the particular illustrations of geometric shapes such as triangles, squares, and rectangles visible to the eye to encounter the prototypes of geometric forms in rational space. Triangularity, as conceived in rational thought, is not the kind of object that can be seen with the eyes in time and space. The triangle that we draw on paper is not the same kind of object we see with our rational powers in conceptual space. Apparently in geometric reflection we are able to encounter objects of thought that are not in space and time and not subject to physical changes. So geometric insights or truths appear to have a timeless and an eternal, universal status.

It appears, then, that human reason has the power to encounter a reality beyond space and time, and for Plato this was a remarkable revelation of the true nature of human beings. We seem to live between two worlds, one in space and time, the other in the eternal realm beyond the senses. It appeared obvious to Plato that the eternal field of forms is a higher form of reality than the field of changing objects in space and time. It seems obvious that an eternal being is superior in every respect to a transitory or changing being. The Field of Being appears to be more real than the field of becoming. And since the world of eternal forms is the higher form of being, more real, then the part of us that has access to this dimension must be our true nature.

Since human rational consciousness has access to the timeless world of essences, this means that we must be akin to this dimension beyond the body, beyond space and time. If our rational consciousness can directly encounter eternal forms, then our rational energy must be similar to these eternal things. There must be something in us that has direct access to the eternal field. So the human psyche appears to have a divided or twofold nature—one aspect of psyche or "soul" is embodied in space and time, and the other aspect transcends body, space, and time and has access to the eternal world. That dimension of the psyche that is eternal, our rational mind or voice, is the Soul, the true Self.

This was the monumental discovery or clarification that humans are essentially Rational Beings. Since our rational nature is superior and closer to the Divine, this dimension of our existence must be our true essence. Our embodied life in space and time was deemed secondary and derivative. And if our true essence is our Soul or rational nature, then everything important in human life follows from this. Human ethics, how we ought to live, follows immediately. We ought to live a life of cultivation of the Soul: the moral life is the Life of Reason that values the Soul above all else. This means that the reason for life is to tend the Soul, and that everything else we do is in service of this highest goal. The Soul hungers for Knowledge, so the highest life for us is the life of striving to Know, to awaken the rational Mind. And true human happiness essentially depends upon living the kind of life that cultivates the awakening of the Soul. So ethics, and moral life, is the life of Reason.

These reflections on the classical origins of Logos in the Socratic tradition are intended to bring out the monumental advances in clarifying the grammar of Logos in the writings of Plato. Of course we have barely scratched the surface here. What is particularly noteworthy is that in Plato's thought it is clear that we begin to see global features of Logos as Plato explores the world of forms, the world of Psyche, the domain of eternal knowledge, and most of all, in his recognizing that Primal Logos, as revealed in the ultimate universal Form of Goodness, the form of all forms beyond Being and Truth, is a classical advance toward the global disclosure of Logos. Still it appears that the deep undertow of egocentric reason continues to haunt the articulation of Logos and the birth of First Philosophy in these early Greek origins. In the following meditations, we shall continue to develop this theme as we explore and excavate the global emergence of Logos.

5

Logos and the Dialogical Turn: Dialogical Awakening in the Global Evolution of Cultures

INTRODUCTION

We continue our global reflection by trying to clarify further the fundamental Logos at the heart of natural and cultural evolution. For the past thirty years my research has focused on demonstrating that there must be a primal and universal common origin for all possible cultural, religious, and philosophical worlds. It has been conjectured and stipulated as a postulate of rational faith from the dawn of religious and philosophical consciousness that there must be a primal form, an infinite, unifying principle whence all reality emerges. Diverse traditions of First Philosophy in the global spectrum of cultures have sought through the ages to give an adequate account of this primal generative form that shapes all realities.

However, in light of the vast diversity and even apparent incompatibility of alternative narratives of origins and evolution, it is not at all clear that there is a common evolutionary foundation generating these alternative accounts. We shall see as the story of Logos unfolds that there is a primal cosmic event unfolding in historical reality through diverse accounts of evolution and the process of reality.

My own efforts have focused on deepening First Philosophy to its mature global form, which makes it possible to excavate the universal common ground across cosmologies, theologies, first philosophies, and evolutionary narratives. In my books, *Meditative Reason: Toward Universal Grammar*, and *Between Worlds: The Emergence of Global Reason*, I present the findings of my efforts over the past thirty-five years. As we have seen earlier, I use the term *Logos* for the infinite primal reality in and through which all possible worlds arise. In the context of developing a global or universal First Philosophy, we find a deeper missing narrative of Logos, which makes clear that we are in the midst of a profound cosmic drama in the play of reality.

The global or cosmic story of Logos clarifies that reality is an evolutionary process playing out through nature and culture. Here we find a primal unified field of existence wherein nature and culture co-arise in a continuum.

209

We can see clearly how and why there is a universal or cosmic evolutionary event playing out in the process of reality. This unified field of Logos, together with the advanced technology of mind appropriate for processing this cosmic field, enables us to see a global narrative of evolution emerging in the human condition.

Thinkers such as Teilhard de Chardins have articulated the intuition and finding that human evolution is on the brink of a monumental evolutionary advance to a higher form of dialogical or global consciousness. But what is the evidence for this? Is this intuition validated or verified by a genuine global cosmology or first philosophy or universal ontology? What becomes of alternative accounts of evolution, such as those found in the natural sciences?

We shall now see that when this intuition of the emergence of global or dialogical consciousness is situated and clarified in the global story of Logos, we find the deeper rationale, clarification, and vindication of its meaning and truth. And we see how and why alternative accounts of natural and human evolution are localized versions of the universal Logos drama.

GLOBAL COSMOLOGY AND THE FOUNDATION OF CULTURAL AND NATURAL EVOLUTION

Central to a range of recent visionary thinkers is the insight that humanity is in the midst of a profound evolutionary change—the individual and corporate advance to a higher form of global consciousness, which ushers in a new age. This "insight" or intuition has a long perennial history and is echoed in diverse ways across the global spectrum of cultures and worldviews through the ages.

But it is difficult, to say the least, to detect significant patterns and trends across and between diverse cosmologies, for when we stand back in global perspective and scan this vast range of alternative accounts of origins and evolutions, it is truly breathtaking. In a sense, all worldviews have some story about the origin and evolution of the universe. If, for example, we scan these narratives from biblical Genesis through Darwin and the big bang account now fashionable in astrophysics; or, again, examine the unfolding drama from Heraclitus through Hegel, Marx, and Teilhard de Chardins; or still further range from Vedic narratives of Brahman and Aum through Chinese accounts of Tao (The Nameless Infinite Name), Chi (the vital living force pervading the universe), or the dialectical interplay of the primal forces of Yin-Yang; or from Buddha's cosmological insight that reality is the ever-changing dynamic process as this is developed over the centuries across cultures through the modern advances in Nishida's Zen thought; or alternatively glance at the rich array of cosmologies in the African traditions celebrating the Primal Word, Nommo, and the universal vital force that pervades the ecology, and so on, then the diversity of worldviews and cosmologies is over-whelming. These visions of origin and evolution are so disparate that it strains our imagination to detect or establish common ground.

Nevertheless, when we situate these alternative "cosmologies" in the deeper story of Logos, clear patterns and common ground begin to emerge. Indeed, we begin to see that alternative accounts of the Cosmic Event are essential in getting a deeper, more objective fix on the evolution of Logos. Far from being incompatible or even incommensurable, these profoundly diverse narratives of genesis and evolution are found to mutually augment and com-plement one another in the dialogical field of Logos. The reason for this, as we shall see, is as obvious as it is simple. Logos, as the Infinite Word, Form, or Origin, essentially invites and generates alternative narrative accounts of its cosmic play.

The Infinite Origin, being infinite, plays out infinitely in the genesis and evolution of the cosmos. Indeed, the deepest reflections on Logos reveal that all evolution is the Cosmic Event of the happening of Logos. This event of Logos must be a profound infinite Continuum embracing and generating multiple alternative stories. This is the essence of infinitude, the cosmic com-mon ground that generates such vastly diverse stories as that of biblical Gen-esis, Darwinian evolution, big bang cosmology, and the kind of cosmic evolu-tion envisioned in the narratives of Teilhard and Cousins. The infinitude of Logos implies a cosmic event-continuum, a primal Unified Field, that is the generative origin of all possible evolutionary narratives. And when these mul-tiple cosmologies are taken together in their deeper dialogical interplay, we naturally get a more profound fix on the infinite evolutionary event we are now living through.

However, the splits and dualisms between nature and culture, between natural history and human history, between matter and spirit (mind, con-sciousness), have been so deep that accounts of evolution of these polarized realms often appear to have nothing in common. Materialistic accounts of evolution of external nature appear to have no common ground with spiritual accounts of the origin and evolution of human consciousness and its cultural development. Indeed, certain narratives of "evolution" appear to be so deeply at odds that most interpreters feel forced to choose between them.

For example, biblical Genesis presents us with a narrative of divine cre-ation of the cosmos. In the beginning is Infinite Spirit, God, and through the conscious or intentional will of the Divine Mind, creation is set in motion. (In this scenario, the "cosmic event" is called "creation.") In the evolutionary accounts of Darwin or big bang cosmology, however, we are placed in a world-view that envisions the "beginning" as some primal state of material energy, and in the case of the big bang narrative, some spontaneous event erupted and the rest is history. The evolutionary process is moved in a more mechanistic way, and at some point in evolution life emerges and then consciousness and its artifacts of culture. In this account there is no Divine Intelligence or Consciousness that moves and causally directs the cosmic event of evolution.

So vastly different are the contrasting stories of Genesis and big bang that current culture reserves the term *creation* for the Genesis account of the cosmic event, and uses the term *evolution* to contrast the scenario in Darwin's account of natural and human evolution as well as the narrative in the big bang story. This terminology, which is currently fashionable, suggests that "evolution" by its nature belongs to the materialistic and mechanistic stories, not to the narratives of Infinite Spirit, Mind, and Consciousness. Of course, from the point of view of global cosmology, this is misleading, if not mistaken. Both paradigms of the cosmic event are "evolutionary," and in global cosmology or ontology, all accounts of the process of reality are evolutionary in a shared generic sense.

But any such attempt to find common terms or common ground between vastly different narratives of origins already takes us into the deeper story of Logos. Of course, this story has been sorely missing on the global scene. Shortly we will explore some of the reasons this is so. We should note in passing that this very emergence of the story of Logos and the higher technology of mind essential for adequately processing or minding the Unified Field of Logos is itself a vital step in the evolution of the human condition and the drama of Logos. The higher form of evolving consciousness, reason, discourse, and knowledge needed for advancing to the deeper cosmic event of Logos itself had to evolve in human evolution. This is already a hint of the intuition of Teilhard, Cousins, and others.

Could it be that there really is a deeper global event unfolding in human history that is a common ground across diverse narratives of evolution? Do we dare think that the Logos event is deep enough, rich enough, and powerful enough to be the common ground and missing link between such disparate stories as Genesis, the big bang, Darwin's origins, the generative power of Brahman and Aum, the Zen account of the infinite play of reality, and the dynamic process-cosmologies of Whitehead and Teilhard? This is precisely what we wish to show. And once we begin to cross into the rational space of the story of Logos, striking analogies and convergences across diverse narratives begin to come into relief.

For example, diverse narratives have converged on the theme that reality must be a perpetual dynamic process, an ongoing process of becoming, moving in some direction according to certain laws. This is certainly true in Buddhist cosmological imagination. Heraclitus, too, saw that reality must be a dynamic and perpetual process. And it is obviously true in the narratives of both Whitehead and Teilhard. These are obviously "process" cosmologies. Still, if we look at other narratives that might not at first appear to countenance existence as an evolutionary process, such as the Genesis account, or the Darwinism scenario, or the big bang cosmology, or the creative unfolding of Brahman, it emerges with deeper clarity in global cosmology that widely diverse narratives across traditions and disciplines gravitate to the consensus that reality must be some kind of primordial process. We suggest that this is both generated from and borne out by the event of Logos.

Similarly, it is no accident that widely diverse stories, such as certain Buddhist accounts of the field of existence as an infinite interactive unified field of co-arising events, or the universal field of relativity in Whitehead's cosmology, or, again, the Upanisadic accounts of the emergence of all creation from the infinite unified field of Brahman, or the emergence of the grand unified field of the cosmos in the unfolding of contemporary physics, and so on, should gravitate to the common discovery that the universe must be a profound Continuum, a universal unified field wherein all that exists is woven together in an infinitely extending interactive web of relations. This consensus, that the Universe must be a primal unified field or an interactive and interrelational web, is grounded in the missing story of Logos.

In this story it is a rather straightforward and simple truism that Infinite Logos must emerge as a primal unified field of relativity, of all things in dynamic interactive interrelationality. This "infinition" force of Logos immediately implies an infinite unifying/diversifying power, that reality must be a dynamic unified field of infinite activity expressing a continuum cosmic event. We shall see that the infinitude of Logos implies both infinite Unity and infinite Diversity. This is one of the great disclosures in the story of Logos—that infinite Unity is so great that it inherently expands in infinite diversity and multiplicity.

However great the expansion, diversity, differentiation, and individuation in the Universe, the power of Infinite Unity holds all diversity in essential interactive mutual relations. This is why Reality must be an infinite activity, a unified field, a radical process, an evolutionary development, a dialogical or an interrelational interplay or relativity, a creative, experimental self-revision, a Continuum Cosmic Event. The infinitude of Logos is that reality is essentially holistic, and evolution itself is the holistic play of the Cosmic Event of Logos emerging. This is the presiding force moving all localized stories of the evolution of reality, which is why the evolution of consciousness and rationality must take a holistic or global turn as the drama of Logos unfolds.

Logos, as the foundation of all cosmologies and narratives of reality, holds the most diversified stories of evolution in essential interrelationality. This is why, for example, such disparate narratives as the Buddhist insights into the co-arising of all things in the unified field share common ground with

Darwin's idea of mutations, adaptability to the ecology, and survival of the fittest. This insight into adaptability is a form of ecological co-arising and interrelationality. Again, despite the deep splits we have seen between Spirit and Matter, we find narratives on both sides converging on the common gravitation to the unified field of reality.

Narratives of genesis and evolution such as we find in Buddhist cosmology or in the Hindu narrative of Brahman or the Chinese discourse on Tao inherently move to existence as a unified field. But narratives such as the big bang cosmology in astrophysics, working from the starting point of material energy, likewise move to the unified field of the cosmos. So even across deep division, such as matter versus spirit, or ancient versus modern, or religion versus science, or East versus West, we find diverse accounts of evolution moving to shared insights into the Cosmic Event of Logos. As we now bring out more explicitly the missing narrative of Logos, we shall see the deeper reasons diverse narratives have developed as they have, and when seen in light of Logos, deeper affinities and patterns begin to emerge. When situated in the foundation of the Logos event, all narratives of evolution are placed under mutual self-revision, clarification, amplification, and universalization.

This is the context in which we shall now critically reflect on the intuition (thesis, finding, insight) of thinkers such as Teilhard and Cousins, that human evolution is accelerating in an epoch-making breakthrough to a higher form of individual and corporate consciousness. But it is one thing to affirm or posit this thesis and quite another to demonstrate systematically that this must be so. Are we in the midst of a historic advance to a higher form of "global consciousness"? What does this mean? In light of the wide-ranging narratives of evolution that have been formulated, and have yet to be formulated, is it a "global consensus" that evolution is moving in the direction of emerging global consciousness? Does this imply that some intelligent force is directing natural evolution? Why should human evolution move in the direction of global consciousness?

My own version of the intuition is that human evolution has been moving for centuries toward the awakening of the global mind. We shall see that this makes sense and is validated in the context of global cosmology, which clarifies the depth of the Cosmic Event of the emergence of Logos in the unified field of existence.

LOGOS AS THE FOUNDATION OF ALL COSMOLOGIES: THE COSMIC EVENT

We are in the midst of a cosmic event that has been unfolding from the beginning of time. So deep and pervasive is this event that it has been detected and expressed through the ages in profoundly diverse ways in the global evolution of cultures. This continuing historic event is so infinitely rich and ever-present that it naturally invites and admits alternative accounts. In the diverse mythologies, cosmologies, and ideologies through the ages, it becomes clear that it takes a higher form of mind to adequately approach and process this event of cosmic evolution. And through the interplay of diverse accounts of this event in a global context it is clear that this global event cannot be exhausted in any one story line but essentially calls for an open-ended interplay of alternative accounts.

In this interplay of diverse cosmic stories, it is readily seen that in the beginning there is Logos (the Infinite Word, the Infinite Presence, Infinite Being). Any authentic account of the beginning cannot escape coming to terms with this global or cosmic Logos. The Infinite Origin, the Infinite Word, the Infinite Primal Being, the First Principle, must be Infinite, and this is what immediately ensues in the cosmic event-continuum. The cosmic event is this very happening of the Infinite Word. If evolution and genesis are said to be the holistic event of Logos, then how are we to think and process this infinition event?

We shall now distill some key discoveries from our exploration of the missing Story of Logos to show how and why the cosmic event of Logos inherently leads to the awakening of the global mind.

THE PARADOX OF ADVANCING
TO THE PRIMAL BEGINNING

There is a good reason the global story of Logos has been eclipsed and missing. Since Logos is the Infinite Word, the Cosmic Event, it takes the appropriate form of thinking, the right technology of mind or logistic, to gain access to the Beginning. And this is where we face what appears to be a deep paradox, for the development of thinking, reason, language, and the technologies of mind has been in ongoing evolution as cultures matured through the ages. Indeed, cultural evolution is the expression of this ongoing evolution of mind and thinking.

So we must be keenly self-conscious of the stages of the evolution in thinking and world making, aware that our technology of thinking must be able to process the infinition dynamic of Logos in order to understand the Cosmic Beginning. Earlier premature stages in the evolution of mind and culture making cannot adequately process or express the dynamics of reality—the Logos event. The moral here is that a genuine cosmology must attend to the state of evolution of mind and discourse. In this respect, cosmology cannot afford to ignore the evolutionary state of mind, language, and world formation.

In short, only when minding has matured to its global or holistic form can it adequately express the holistic process of Logos.

Global Ontology or Cosmology, which stands back from any one cultural tradition, is able to cross beyond the bounds of the artificially finitized mind and enter the deeper holistic rational space of infinition. Global thinking in this sense enters the foundational unified field, which is the ground of all possible worlds. In this holistic technology we are able to see that cultural evolution itself has been in a deep struggle to move to a higher form of thinking and reason that is more capable of processing the infinition dynamic of existence. The paradox, then, is this: technologies of mind that are still lodged in finitized patterns cannot adequately access the process of reality, which is essentially the infinition process of Logos. So to truly reach the Beginning, to understand and articulate the evolutionary process, mind itself must evolve to its global or holistic form. This is why diverse attempts to give a viable account of cosmic beginnings and of the evolutionary process within localized forms of minding fell into various forms of incoherence and incompleteness. It takes a holistic mind to process the holistic process of Logos.

THE MISSING LOGISTIC: THE MISSING LANGUAGE AND SCIENCE OF LOGOS

Let us look at this evolution of mind, thought, and language more deeply. When we enter into global cosmology, we face the self-referential question from the start: What is the state of the evolution of our thinking and discourse in which we are now doing cosmology? Since global cosmology lives and moves between diverse cosmologies and global traditions it faces head on the primal question of the ground and foundation of all cosmologies. There are two points to notice here. First, the very idea of the Infinite Word, of Logos, immediately implies that Logos is the Infinite Field that grounds all possible narratives and realities. Logos is inherently "global" or "universal across diverse worlds." This is self-evident in the very meaning of "infinite word." When we examine a range of first philosophies across the global spectrum, we find that this primal truth of the "Infinite" is borne out. This means of course that in the "Beginning," before Genesis and before big bang, the eternal event of Logos proceeds without "beginning" and without "end." This Initial State of Logos cannot be processed by everyday conventional mind and language, as we have seen.

The second point that global cosmology realizes is that in stepping back from any one world, one tradition, or one narrative of *What-Is-First* and actually living through diverse cosmologies from within, deep patterns begin to show themselves. When we enter the deeper space between worlds, between cosmologies, mind and language are forced to expand, and we gain access to more primal patterns in the Logos event. Here we find astounding results. We begin to see that across cultures and worlds, human evolution has been in a continual, if glacial, shift from the monocentric stage of mind to holistic or dialogical or global consciousness—the emergence of the global mind. So let us now clarify this stage of the "monocentric mind."

What Cousins, following Jaspers, refers to as the "first axial period" may be seen as one version of this. Teilhard's narrative may be seen as still another version. I put it in a slightly different and perhaps more generic way. In doing global cosmology, it becomes clear that the technologies of mind have been in ongoing evolution. One stage of evolution may be called the "monocentric" or "egocentric" stage of mind and discourse. Thus when we scan the spectrum of the emergence of the world's great religions and first philosophies, we find Logos teachers in diverse ways showing that deep pathologies in the human condition arise directly from the methods of monocentric mind, and they call in different ways to a deep shift toward centering mind in Logos. The signature of the monocentric mind is that it is lodged in finitized thinking and has not yet advanced to the stage in which it can enter and negotiate the infinition process of existence. The monocentric mind by its nature eclipses the field of Logos and is not able to cope with the higher level of thought and world processing that is the unfolding event of Logos.

It appears that in our natural evolution human consciousness and culture making go through a phase that is structured around one's worldview, whether in egocentric form or in tribal or cultic form. The technology of the monocentric mind arises in a separation or logical space between the "self" or subject and the ecological field of the world that surrounds and situates it. The common structural factor is that the monocentric mind absolutizes its worldview and arises in a deep structure in which there is a primal dualism between the thinking subject and the object of thought or experience.

The point is that the logistic or technology of thinking in the monocentric stage of mind subjectifies itself and objectifies its world in a way that eclipses the Presence of Logos and enters a form of "predication" or logical process, wherein all names and things and events are vested with a certain "identity" and fixity and objectification. This is true of the "individuated" or "egocentric" self, or the experiencing "subject" that identifies with its tribe, cult, or polis or ecology. Whether the "ego" identifies itself separately from its polis/ecology or identifies itself in and through its tribal worldview, the basic technology of mind plays out in the mode of finitized duality and identity.

The egocentric mind is just one expression of the monocentric mind. The "tribal mind" or "cultic mind" is another. The field of the "subject" may be the egocentric individual, the tribe, the cult or its ecology, or the worldview as a whole. So even forms of monocentric holism are still lodged within the logistic of finitized thinking. The net effect is that this "field of the subject" is absolutized as its center of reference and universalized as its universe of discourse. Whatever the level of subjectification may be, there is always the "Other" that stands against it as an object of thought external to its lifeworld.

Global cosmology breaks free of this monocentric thinking and moves into the logical space of the dialogical mind and global thinking between worlds. In this global perspective it is able to view and review evolutionary patterns across cultures and worlds with the help of Logos teachers. Thus if we stand back and listen to these teachings, we begin to see the pattern of this awakening of consciousness beyond the monocentric life.

As we review, for example, the ancient Vedic teachings expressed in the *Upanisads* or in the teachings of Lord Krishna in the *Bhagavadgita*, or move with the Buddha in his great awakening teaching, or witness the historic advances in the teachings of Lao Tzu as the power of Tao is revealed or, again, if we open to the depth of the Judaic origins in the injunction to love God with all our heart and mind, or in the new covenant brought forth in the life of Jesus, or still in the origins of critical reason in Socrates' encounter with Logos, and so on, we find in each case a historic attempt to urge humanity onward to a higher form of consciousness.

While Cousins (following Jaspers) speaks of this global phenomenon as the "first axial age" and speaks of humanity now being on the brink of a "second axial age," it is our view that we are still in the midst of the "first axial age" (now revised in global cosmology). In our story of Logos, Cousins' second axial age is already the moving essence of the first axial age, which has been in a continuous development through the ages. We suggest, in the context of global cosmology, that over the past 3,000 years, through the continuing emergence of Logos in the human condition, humanity has been evolving beyond the monocentric age and into the corporate awakening of the global mind.

We agree with Cousins that something magnificent is now accelerating in the human condition on a global scale—the corporate birthing of the holistic or dialogical age of Logos. But this is the fruition of the continuing awakening process that was inaugurated by the Logos teachers as the "first" axial age emerged in its noticeable form. The Logos story expands and amends the idea of the "axial" age by revealing that all natural evolution has been the continuous emergence of Logos in the historical condition.

Let us reflect in greater depth on this theme for a moment. If we look at the Buddha's essential teaching, it is clear that his great awakening focused on overcoming the egocentric mind and life. Buddha's great insight turned on seeing that the monocentric mind and thinking are the source of human suffering in all of its existential forms. He had a deeper insight into the essence of existence and saw clearly that the egocentric or monocentric mind constructed names and forms and things that purported independent identity. This was especially true of the "self." Buddha saw that the classic pattern of monocentric thinking and world making dualized and objectified all aspects of its experience and existence. His great contribution was to have seen clearly and precisely how and why the technology of the monocentric mind alienated the thinking subject from the infinition flow of existence and thus generated all sorts of existential pathologies.

Buddha's great prescription, the Four Noble Truths, with its eightfold path, turned on a higher logistic or conduct of mind that flows with the infinition process of reality. At the heart of the insight into existence is that reality must be a unified field wherein all things "co-arise" in mutual dynamic interactive relationality. The primal intuition is that nothing can stand in independent self-identity or self-existence. Nothing can stand "atomically." Atomic identity is an artificial construction of the monocentric mind. This is one historic version of the breakthrough into the field of Logos—the Principle of Relativity—as the principle of reality itself. Buddha saw that true reality is an ever-changing dynamic unified field wherein all things arise in an infinite dynamic web of relations. This follows the holistic turn into the field of Logos. Buddha rightly saw that the Dharma, the universal moral law, was the dynamic law of reality itself. We have here classic ingredients in the advance to the logistic of minding Logos. It all turned on the infinition structure of Logos.

We see the same pattern in the awakening therapy administered by Lord Krishna in the dialogue of the *Bhagavadgita*. In this Vedic context, the ultimate intuition is that the ground of reality is the Infinite Word or Symbol Aum. Here again is a classic articulation of Logos. Another word for the primal principle is Brahman, the Absolute, Infinite Being, which is beyond all possible duality. Here too it is seen that Aum or Brahman entails a reality that is a unified field sustained in the infinite unifying power of Brahman. Arjuna, who embodies the egocentric or monocentric life, reaches an existential crisis, a life crisis, on the battlefield as the fratricidal battle is about to begin.

This crisis represents the inevitable split and paralysis coming from the monocentric life. In the *Bhagavadgita*, Krishna takes Arjuna through deep stages of self-awakening beyond the egocentric life. This technology of yoga is designed to help the egocentric mind cross over into the nondual unified field of Brahman. In this crossing into the meditative technology of the unified field, rational consciousness flows in harmony with the infinition structure of true existence. When the egocentric self is let go, the true nondual Self comes forth. This is the Atman, the true awakened Self, that cannot be objectified or predicated or identified in the logistic of the monocentric mind.

Again, in the context of the Judaic drama we find historic advances in the story of Logos. It is already clear that the injunction to love God with all one's heart and mind and strength involves a deep existential recentering, wherein God comes first in all things. This clearly calls for overcoming the egocentric and monocentric ways of life that privilege the subjectivity of the ego and its lifeworld and life-word. The Infinite Word inherently commands that for life to work, we must place first things first. The recognition that God is One, and the issuance of the moral commands through Moses, calls for the awakening of a higher moral consciousness that follows the laws of God. It is in this context that we find in Jesus, as the Logos become flesh, a continuing advance of the Logos in the human condition.

Jesus is a Logos teacher who embodies the Truth of Logos, the Infinite Word manifested in its awakened or true finite form. In light of Logos and global cosmology, we see that the life and teaching of Jesus as the Christ follow the classic formulas and living holistic power of the Presence of Logos. Jesus taught that unless "we" die, we cannot be born again. This global truth, echoed in various ways by diverse Logos teachers, recognizes that the egocentric self must be deconstructed, let go, must die in order that the awakened self may come forth.

The Christ is that holistic office wherein the awakened or resurrected Self crosses into the true form of finitude, which is in communion with Logos. In the missing Logos story, the "Christ" is not an egocentric individual, not a being that can be formulated in monocentric thought or language. Rather, the essence of the Christ requires the higher logistic, logic, and discourse of the field of Logos. In this missing Divine Script, the Christ is the corporate communion of the awakened human polis. And in this context it may be said that human evolution moves inexorably from the alienated and dualistic life of sin, the monocentric life, into the higher communion of life in Logos.

This is another version of the thesis that all history is the awakening of the global mind, the emergence of global or dialogical consciousness. In global cosmology/theology, it becomes clear that the deep structure of "sin" is precisely the dualistic and dualizing life of the monocentric mind. So across cultures and religious worlds, we begin to see as the "axial age" emerges through Logos teachers that the source of human pathologies traces to the ways and means of the monocentric mind. This is the deeper meaning of Jesus' formula that the "wage of sin is death." And the New Covenant of Jesus may be seen as the deeper crossing into the logistic and language and way of life of minding Logos.

Jesus insisted that the Law of Logos must be lived, embodied, that it was a living Law. And this is precisely the consensus in the higher technology of the unified field. The Law, the Dharma, cannot be objectified but must be directly embodied in the life of right minding. Thus in leaving the false and artificial "finitude" of the monocentric life, one crosses into a deeper form of authentic finitude that flows in harmony with the infinition of life in Logos. It is in this way that the Christ is a crossing from the field of sin into the life of salvation or eternal Life. And so on.

We could illustrate this awakening pattern in the life and teaching of Socrates, whose passion was for Logos. The awakening of rational life and moral awareness in the teaching of Socrates follows the axial pattern of the awakening of a higher form of life. For Socrates and Plato, this is the life that moves beyond conventional thought and experience, lodged in the objectification of the senses toward the eternal world of the Forms. This life ultimately leads to the supreme infinite form, the Form of Goodness, which is the Form of all forms. The life of the quest for wisdom is precisely the awakening of the soul to a direct intuition into Logos or Goodness. This is rational enlightenment. Put in terms of the awakening of Reason, we may say that the evolution of European culture over the centuries has been an ongoing self-revision toward realizing Logos in the human condition—the awakening of the global mind.

Let us pause for a moment and recapitulate the main point. We have been suggesting that in the missing story of Logos, which becomes more accessible through the development of global cosmology, we see global patterns in the evolution of cultures through the ages. We suggest that a primary pattern is that human cultures have been in a deep, often traumatic and painful, corporate transformation from monocentric technologies of mind to a holistic or dialogical consciousness or logistic, which moves in deeper unison with the flow of reality—the cosmic event of Logos. We suggest that there is a global tradition of Logos teachers through the ages who have played vital roles in awakening humanity to the pathological ways of the egocentric and monocentric methods of minding, bringing to humanity a higher liberating technology of mind that reveals the field of Logos, the Logosphere, the nondual unified field of reality.

One of the great lessons in the global evolution of cultures is that the monocentric mind and its culture has been devastating to the best interest of human flourishing. The Logos teachers have shown over and over through the ages that the monocentric life leads to death, violence, vice, malpractice, alienation, fragmentation, and human existential and psychic suffering in its many forms. Whatever the reasons for the evolution of monocentric cultures, it is clear that it is a stage in our birthing that must be negotiated, and that humans need to develop together in a higher form of culture in the field of Logos. As we look, for example, across the great world religions, global cosmology finds an emergent consensus of the corporate move to a higher technology of mind, which we call the awakening of the global mind. One of the great lessons from these cultural experiments is that we humans are as we mind.

When we mind in the ways of monocentric culture making, devastation results. When we advance to the logistic of the holistic or global or dialogical technology, human flourishing ensues. And human evolution has moved to the horizon in which we now awaken or perish.

Finally, we have suggested that through the centuries of global evolution brought about by the Logos teachers, we have reached a new possibility of tapping into the deeper global logic and logistic of Logos, the missing universal grammar or script of Logos, that will bring humanity together in an unprecedented dialogical corporate life. The seeds of this missing technology of Logos have been germinating over the centuries through a wealth of cultural experiments nurtured by the continuing creative energies of the Logos teachers through the ages. Human evolution, moved by the emerging Logos event, has made it possible for us now to tap into the eclipsed Logic and Logistic of the Logosphere. This higher technology of mind is the key to our future sustainability and flourishing.

THE SCIENCE OF LOGOS AND THE
LOGISTIC OF THE LOGOSPHERE

The technology of Logos is essential for gaining access to the Logosphere, the unified field of Logos. Global cosmology, by entering this logistic of Logos, is able to tap, decipher, and read the universal script or grammar of Logos. In this advanced technology of mind, we come closer to understanding the origin and dynamics of the unified field of reality. This is essential in getting a more adequate reading of "in the Beginning." What is the state of Logos in the beginning, before Genesis and before the big bang? What is the nature of the Logosphere? What is the structure of this field of reality regarding "time" and "space" and "mind" and "matter" and "cause" and "substance" and "energy"?

We have already suggested that the very structure of the Infinite Word entails infinite self-unity, infinite creative differentiation and multiplicity, and hence abysmal diversity and individuality. We have suggested also through the Logistic of Logos that the infinitude of Logos entails a radical infinite process, beyond any static constructions, and this immediately entails an infinite dynamic interplay and interrelational structure to the unified field. As Whitehead would say, all "things" are events, happenings, process. As Buddha would say, reality is the field of relational co-arising. All things are in a profound dialogical and dynamic interrelational play.

If we look more deeply into the deep structure of Logos, it is clear that its infinite unifying power entails that all names, forms, and categories must be in a holistic unifying mutual involvement. The building blocks or categories that shape existence and experience as seen in monocentric thinking— consciousness, mind, thought, word, language, relation, meaning, idea, substance, time, space, cause, individual, energy, matter, and so on—are found in the Logosphere to be in a primal union and communion.

This means that mind and consciousness infinitely pervade every point in the unified field. It means that thought and time inseparably constitute one another. It means that space and time form a continuum of space-time. It means that matter and energy, likewise, are in communion, and that in this nondual force field there must be a primal communion and continuum of energy-consciousness-word-idea-space-time-cause-matter-force-substance. In other words, the primal state of the Logosphere, understood now as Nature, as the Universal Unified Field, must be a categorial continuum wherein what is artificially divided, fragmented, finitized, and dualized in the monocentric mind is now found to be infinitely integral and interrelational and mutually constituted—nondual.

In this categorial continuum every point has an infinite holistic structure that encodes the Logosphere. This is the source of the recurrent formula that "the Kingdom of God is within," or "there is that of Christ in every man," or "Buddha Nature pervades all beings." It is impossible to process this holistic structure of every point in the Logosphere within monocentric thinking. In the Logic of Logos, the logistic of infinition, we are able to get closer to the formula that "In the Beginning is Logos, the Word." The Infinite Word is infinitely saturated with all names and forms and categories. The Word pervades Consciousness, the Word pervades Energy, the Word pervades Time and Space-Time, the Word pervades Matter and Substance, the Word is Being.

This holistic structure of the Logosphere reveals that the ultimate "stuff" of Nature (understood now as the Logosphere) must be a primal communion of mind-matter or psychomatter. For Logos, being Infinite must be infinitely conscious, as the Logos traditions have repeatedly confirmed. Equally, Logos as Nature must be infinitely extended, embodied, and this is the stuff the universe is made of. Logos Matter is PsychoMatter, MatterMind, and Nature is the extension of Divine Mind or Consciousness. Just as Space-Time is primal—Space being the extension of Time and Time being the rhythmic vibration of Space—so too Mind and Matter are originally mutually constituted as primal MindMatter.

Similarly with Mind-Matter-Space-Time-Energy—this holistic continuum of primal categories in the Logosphere helps us understand how biblical Genesis and the big bang origins can have a common ground, a common origin, for in the nondual structure of Logos, when God as Logos says ((Let there be Light)) the very speech-act, thought-act, is the very manifestation of Light. The Word, ((Light)) and the Thought, ((Light)), and the Utterance, ((Light)), and the Existence of ((Light)) are one and the same creative act. And since Logos is the universal origin of all possible worlds, cosmologies, narratives, and origins, we do not have to stretch too far to imagine that the creative act of Genesis and the big bang event may have something in common.

This finding of Global Cosmology, of course, has astounding consequences, for there has been a perennial quest through the ages to find the "ultimate stuff" of the Universe, and to decode the connection between "mind" and "matter," between "word" and "object," between "time" and "space," between "mind" and "energy," and so on. The astounding result is that in the Logosphere mind pervades matter, and matter pervades mind. Each is inherent in the other. And those native cosmologies that have insisted that Nature is alive, that consciousness and intelligence pervade Nature, are vindicated in a certain way by the structure of the Logosphere.

It also follows that in some primal sense there is intelligence moving the process of natural evolution. The inert and mechanistic view of "nature," developed in monocentric sciences, is found to be an artificial construct having no grounding in Nature as the Logosphere. It is important to add here equally that the homocentric projection on the Logosphere of "mind" and "intentional actions" and "spirit" is likewise an artificial abstraction and a construct of monocentric ideologies. Infinite Intelligence, Will, Mind, and Judgment surpass anything monocentric intelligence can come up with.

So when it is said in global cosmology and nondual logistic that Logos moves Nature, Logos moves evolution, and the Cosmic Event of Logos is historical and natural evolution, this is in a script deeper than the mechanistic materialists and the spiritualist idealism of monocentric narratives. It also follows that any future cosmology, whether of natural science or of metaphysical speculation, must pay primary attention to the missing science of the Logosphere.

It is in global cosmology and the Logistic of Logos that we find the long-sought-after missing link between First Philosophy, theology, and the natural sciences. It is in the science of the Logosphere that we find the deeper ground and vindication of the moves to ((Mind-Body)) Medicine. How can prayer and meditation have a healing effect on the body and promote physical health and well-being? When it is understood that the ultimate stuff of Nature is Mind-Matter or PsychoMatter, beyond mere "mind," "spirit", "body," and "matter," the door is opened to deeper scientific research in this emerging area of contemporary medicine. And so on.

On this note we conclude by refocusing on the main theme. We have suggested that Logos essentially plays out into the Logosphere, which is the cosmic event of Logos. Everything that happens in evolution, both natural and human, is essentially moved by this event of Logos. And it follows through the reflections of global cosmology that all evolution is the creative emergence of Logos as revealed in the historical process. It is this presiding moving force of evolution that expresses itself as the awakening of the global mind or the emergence of a shift to a higher dialogical form of life.

This direction of evolution is entailed in the structure of the Logosphere, which now makes clear the essential continuum between natural and human evolution. The emergence of human life is integral to Nature's evolution, now understood as the Logosphere. There is no dualism or split or incompatibility here between "nature" and "culture." When situated in the creative process of the Logosphere, the emergence of culture is integral to the creative unfolding of Nature. It is in this context that we see the vindication of thinkers such as Teilhard and Cousins, who saw that humanity is essentially moving to a new stage of dialogical or global consciousness. And it is the basis for our finding that through the centuries the leading event in the evolution of cultures is the awakening of the global mind.

6

The Continuing Quest
for Primal Knowledge

From the dawn of religious and philosophical awakenings there has been a perennial quest for primal knowledge. A persistent theme across cultures and worlds through the ages has been the presence of a Primal Truth out of which all existence arises, and the reality of a deep drive in human life to know this ultimate truth. In the evolution of cultures, profoundly diverse accounts have been given of this Primal Truth, as well as of human efforts to rise to an adequate realization of this truth. The awakening of primal knowledge is said to be the highest essence of human life.

For example, in our biblical roots it is declared that God is One, and that humans are to love God with all their hearts and minds. In this biblical language it is clear that God is the Primal Truth out of which all reality arises. And it is clear that this injunction to love God with all our being calls for the awakening of our deepest recognition or knowledge of God. To love God is to know God with all our hearts and minds. This heart-mind knowledge is the biblical version of primal knowledge. Primal knowledge is inscribed in our very being, and it is with our whole being that we awaken to its truth. In some sense it is always already present within us awaiting activation and actualization. When we realize primal knowledge, we realize our true Self.

This holistic knowledge is very different from the more mundane and conventional ways of knowing. When we awaken to primal or holistic knowledge, there is a radical recentering of our lives in the Divine Presence. Our being or life is transformed from being centered in the subjective ego to being centered in God. And the biblical tradition contrasts divine knowledge with mundane "knowledge" by speaking of the awakening of faith. In knowledge through faith we rise to a direct encounter with the Divine Presence and enter into an immediate relation with the Infinite Power. So in this primal knowledge we come to an awareness of the ultimate conditions making possible all life and experience. Primal knowing transforms our life and fulfills our being.

Similarly, in our Greek origins we find Socrates articulating a different version of primal knowledge. Socrates sees a deep contrast between the kind of knowledge we have when we rise to rational awareness of eternal truth, on the one hand, and the sort of transient "knowledge" we claim to have about the changing things and events in everyday life, on the other. The sort of knowledge we have about objects and events in space and time, which we gain through our senses, involves mental states that are fleeting and constantly changing.

For Socrates, genuine knowledge arises through the awakening of our power of Reason, which has access to eternal and unchanging truth beyond the realm of space and time. What people call "knowledge" in the everyday sense is for Socrates mere opinion or belief and falls far short of the kind of enlightened rational awareness of eternal truths that will come with philosophical or primal knowledge. To gain genuine or primal knowledge, humans must live a life of cultivation of the Soul, which is that part of us that has direct access to the eternal dimension of rational space. It takes a lifetime in this quest for wisdom to clarify and purify the Soul sufficiently to retrieve this primal knowledge.

The more we are able to detach and distance ourselves from the powerful pull of the changing objects of our senses, the closer we come to enlightened rational awareness of the truths of primal knowledge. When, for example, we rise to a clear vision of the pure and eternal form or essence of Justice, Equality, Piety, or Goodness, we gain absolute recollection of truth, which stands in stark contrast to the transient and imperfect "justice" that we witness in the everyday existential world. Again, when we gain mathematical knowledge, we tap into the resource of innate primal knowledge that is stored in the Soul. Mathematical truths appear to have a timeless status beyond the transient beliefs of the sensuous world. But how do we come to gain such timeless knowledge? There must be something in the knower akin to what is known.

This clarification of the Soul through rational therapy obviously involves the deepest change in our being. Socrates introduces the remarkable classical thesis that primal knowledge is eternally inscribed in the Soul, but is lost, repressed, or forgotten when the Psyche or Soul suffers the trauma of crossing from the timeless dimension of rational space into the physical dimension of embodied existence in the changing everyday world. Socrates clarifies a perennial theme in the global evolution of thought—that humans live between two profoundly contrasting worlds or dimensions. Corresponding to the eternal world and the temporal world are two basic kinds of knowledge and ways of knowing.

The natural world of the Soul is the eternal world beyond space and time, the dimension of Being, wherein the Psyche realizes its immortal Life. The reasoning behind this is quite simple. If we know eternal truths, then there must be some dimension of the knower that is likewise eternal. There must be a deep bond, intimacy, or communion between the knower and the known. This is why primal knowledge must be eternally inscribed in the Soul.

The world of the body, on the other hand, which we know through our senses, is the place of fleeting, ever-changing experience and mortality. Immortal life is the higher Life of primal knowing or rational enlightenment. Mortal life is the physical, biological life of the embodied, ever-changing psyche.

In our embodied life between these two mutually estranged worlds the primal knowledge that is innate or inborn in the Soul is forgotten, and for Socrates the primary task of human existence is to strive to remember this lost eternal knowledge. It is through the awakening of our higher rational powers that our Soul retrieves and recognizes the innate primal knowledge that is eternally inscribed within us. Socrates' eminent student, Plato, further clarifies the journey into primal knowledge by tracing the rise of rational consciousness from the lower states of transient images and beliefs to the highest direct intuition into the ultimate source of all knowledge.

For Plato there is, and must be, a supreme, originating Primal Form, the Universal Form of Goodness, which is the very source of rational light that illumines the eternal knowledge in the world of Soul. This source of rational light makes possible all knowledge and experience. The field of primal knowledge must be a holistic unity organically ordered by the infinite unifying power of the Primal Form. For Plato, it is as if everyday embodied consciousness lives in a darkened cave of shadows and appearances, and in the quest for Wisdom or primal knowledge, awakened consciousness crosses into the rational light of Goodness and sees the real eternal forms, essences, and Truth. So here, as in the biblical case, there is a Primal Truth, and through rational enlightenment humans can rise to a higher form of being through the awakening of primal or innate knowledge.

Again, if we stand back and scan the global spectrum of cultural traditions through the ages, we find a rich variety of alternative articulations of the quest for primal knowledge. In our African roots we find certain genealogies that recognize the Primal Truth and embody the primal knowledge in the corporate life of the people. In one lineage the Primal Force is called "Nommo," the original Word out of which all names and realities issue. Nommo is the Primal Vital Force, the living energy that pulsates through all existence, all nature. And the corporate life of the polis embodies the primal knowledge of this infinite life force. Here primal knowledge is expressed in primal living—living in sacred awareness and celebration of the originating Life Force that is manifested in the living ecology.

If we look to our Chinese origins, we find classic articulations of the Primal Truth in the expression of Tao—the Infinite Nameless Name that is the living source of all existence. And it is clear in this ancient tradition that primal knowledge is eternally inscribed in all manifestations of Tao. The classic pattern of primal knowing is seen in the transformation of awareness beyond all forms of duality and objectification to holistic experience in the unified field of Tao. This awakening of primal knowing involves a radical and dramatic revolution in how we think about "knowledge." In the mundane forms of egocentric knowing, the focus is on mental states of the ego subject. But in the rise to primal knowing, the awakening "knower" enters the unified field of Knowledge. It appears that the epistemic force of Tao saturates all existence with the energy of Knowledge. Where there is Tao, there is Knowledge—to awaken to Tao is to awaken to the ecology of primal knowledge.

This pattern is quite evident too in the Hindu origins of the primal Aum. In the Vedic teachings, Aum is revealed as the Infinite Sacred Symbol that generates and moves all things. The analogies to the biblical God, to Plato's Goodness, to the African Nommo, and to the Chinese Tao are evident. Aum is the Primal Truth, the Infinite Sound that is the origin of all names and forms, and yet beyond all names and designations. In this tradition we find classic disclosures of the path to primal knowledge. The meditative technologies, the various yoga sciences, developed and refined over millenia, demonstrate that everyday egocentric thinking is lodged in a deep ignorance that generates all sorts of existential pathologies and human suffering.

One symptom of egocentric minding is chronic fragmentation of experience and the dualizing of all aspects of rational life. The meditative disciplines are all designed to break the egocentric barrier and transform the knowing subject into the holistic or nondual participation in the unified field of existence. The path to genuine or primal knowledge essentially turns on awakening the knower to a direct encounter of the infinite or boundless interplay of the unified field of existence. One main lesson of the meditative traditions is that we are as we mind, that knowledge is essentially a matter of the technology of minding.

The egocentric way of minding, which is found to arise in a deep division between the "knower" and the "known," between the knowing subject and the known object, blocks access to the unified field of existence. Conversely, the meditative mind performs the holistic turn and enters into the unitive interplay of the "Aumic" field of primal knowledge. So meditative thinking is vital in the technology of knowledge. If the knower thinks or minds dualistically, then it is not possible to enter the field of Knowledge. However, if she or he enters the unitive or nondual ways of meditative minding, then she or he is dramatically transformed into a dynamic, interactive process in which the knower, the knowledge, and the known are in communion.

This communion in the dynamic web of the unified field of primal knowledge is quite evident in the Buddhist traditions as well. Here too the primary challenge in awakening to knowledge is crossing beyond the bounds of the egocentric mind, found by the Buddha to be the fundamental cause of human pathologies and suffering. It is precisely in letting go of any "object of knowledge" that genuine knowledge is realized. When the knower radically transforms into the dramatic interplay or "co-arising" of all things in the unified field of Relativity, then true knowledge flows. Ironically, it is precisely in letting go of the ego-knower and the constructed "objects of knowledge" that primal knowledge is realized.

So here too the primary lesson is that knowledge blossoms with the awakening mind, with the rational enlightenment that comes through direct encounter and participation in the boundless interplay of things. This is why in Zen experience, for example, the mutual interplay between the knower, the knowledge, and the known is so profound that the language and descriptions of the egocentric mind are totally inadequate. In the now-familiar example of Zen archery, the archer, the bow, the arrow, the action of taking aim, and the target are so deeply encountered in their mutual interplay that this becomes one holistic process. The irony is that when the "knower" and the "object of knowledge" of egocentric thinking dissolve, primal experience or knowing blossoms. Knowledge is more about the process of awakening the mind, the process of rational enlightenment or wisdom, than it is about any "content" of thought or "object" of knowledge. This is the Zen way of knowing.

What is remarkable in these diverse exemplars of primal knowledge is that we begin to see common patterns, convergences, and perhaps even emerging consensus across traditions and worlds. We see, for example, that quite diverse accounts of knowledge seem to gravitate to some kind of primordial or Primal Truth. It appears that human experience, human thought, and reason arise in a field presided by some kind of unifying power. It further appears that this primal force must be boundless or infinite. And it appears that this infinite originating power plays out into a boundless unified field of reality. If this is so, then this would explain why there have been so many diverse accounts of Primal Truth, but also why there must be a common global truth underlying and expressed in the diverse narratives that have emerged through the ages.

We have suggested elsewhere that there is, indeed, a fundamental Primal Truth at the core of diverse traditions and worlds, and we have proposed that the word "Logos" be used as a global name for this Truth. When we begin to situate the diverse traditions of Primal Truth in light of Logos, something remarkable begins to emerge. We begin to see more readily that there is a fundamental logic presiding in the global space of Logos. The infinite structure of Logos immediately implies that Primal Truth must be global in scope. This also is the direct source of the unified field of reality.

Logos implies that nothing can stand apart or exist independently, as egocentric thought would suggest. The infinite resource of Logos immediately suggests through its abysmal unifying power that all things must be interrelational and interactive in a dynamic process of reality. But it also is this infinite unifying power that spawns multiplicity and diversity and difference. And this is precisely why we should expect profoundly diverse alternative accounts of Logos or the Infinite Word. Logos, in its infinitude, generates a boundless diversity of alternative accounts that nevertheless will co-express the same fundamental pattern of primal knowledge.

It should not be surprising then that we find remarkable convergences across the global spectrum of cultures and worlds. There has been a common quest for primal knowledge through the ages because there is a common Logos being expressed in all realities. In light of the fundamental logic of Logos, we can see more clearly why diverse accounts of primal knowledge converge on a global pattern. We see in this global pattern that there are two fundamental and contrasting ways of knowing, and two kinds of knowledge.

We see that egocentric knowing inherently eclipses primal knowledge and is lodged in a chronic pattern of fragmentation and dualism. We see how diverse accounts of primal knowledge, in very different ways, diagnose the pathology in egocentric thinking. Furthermore, we see that there is a structural reason for egominding eclipsing the unified field of reality that is implied by Logos. Ego thinking cannot process the infinite structure of the unified field. In contrast, we see why in the quest for primal knowledge there is a profound transformation in the technology of knowledge, as the awakening mind breaks the egocentric barriers and crosses into the infinite nondual play of the unified field of Logos. It also is evident why primal knowledge has been thought to be inscribed or innate in our being. Indeed, it is now easier to see why as we awaken to primal knowledge we pass beyond the mental states of ego mind and actually enter into an ecology in which the infinite play of Knowledge is happening.

If we understand the unified field of Logos to be the field of Nature, then it is quite natural to think that all of Nature is saturated with Knowledge. So as we awaken to primal knowledge, we actually transform into the primal field in which thinking, language, experience, and existence find communion. This awakening of primal knowledge involves nothing less than the awakening of our being and the radical paradigm shift into the field of Knowledge.

7

Logos as the Foundation of Global Ethics: Dialogical Awakening as the Key to Global Ethics

In this chapter I focus on the essential connection between the origin of ethics, the dialogical process, and the challenge of interreligious and intercultural interchange. I try to make the essential connection between the awakening and transforming power of the dialogical process and the emergence of global ethics. We shall see that this dialogical process between religious and cultural worlds is the rational, moral, and spiritual foundation of global ethics.

In these introductory remarks I would like to try to connect two or three themes that are usually not clearly connected but that will be vital for understanding why the dialogical process, global ethics, and interreligious dialogue are profoundly and inseparably connected. It is clear that we are living in a very exciting moment in history. Something profound and wonderful is happening, and this can only be seen if we can stand back and take a look and live through the spectrum of cultures and religions evolving over the centuries. If we can do this, entering into alternative religious and cultural worlds, then something amazing begins to show itself, a deep pattern centuries in the making. It becomes clear that the different religions and cultural worlds converge in a common theme of a birth of a new level of human consciousness, a new humanity. We begin to see as we look across religious worlds that they are all deeply concerned with a stage of being human that needs to be overcome.

In one way or another, it is clear that there has been an ego-centered way of being human, and the different religious teachings converge on a consensus that egocentric life is the source of diverse human problems. The great world teachers through the ages have attempted to show that the essence of our being human turns upon awakening a dialogical consciousness that overcomes the ego-centered way of being human. This can be seen, for example, deep in the Judaic tradition with the ultimate command to love God with all our heart and all our being. That injunction calls upon humans to open themselves in the deepest way to place the Divine Presence first and foremost in all life. This calls for a deep recentering that awakens our being to dialogical ways of life. This revolutionary recentering in our innermost Self demands that we overcome an ego-centered view that places the ego-consciousness at the center of our human reality.

Clearly, if we look at the life of Jesus, the deepest concern and command to love one another, to spiritually awaken, and to really go through a profound rebirth call equally, in this tradition of the Judaic ethic, for a renovation of our being and for the move to a dialogical consciousness. So right here in our Judeo-Christian roots we find already this call for the awakening of a new awareness that centers upon God and the Presence of God as the primary concern for human beings, which in turn calls for the deepest change in our lives. So the injunction to love one another may be seen already as the essence of the dialogical principle and the dialogical turn in living.

But really if we scan across the spectrum of cultures and look, say, into the Hindu worldview, clearly here too we find in a very different scenario, but relentlessly focusing on the same point, that the essence of our awakening has to do with overcoming ego-centered consciousness. In the *Bhagavadgita*, for example, Lord Krishna takes Arjuna, who embodies the ego-consciousness, on the deep transformation and existential awakening into the higher consciousness that centers on the Divine Principle, one that really sees a profoundly interconnected reality, very different from the one shown to ego-awareness.

So also in Buddhism, the essence of Buddha's awakening (even the word "buddha" means awakened one) turns upon seeing through the emptiness and futility of living in a world that objectifies everything and creates artificial "entities," especially where the self is concerned. The Buddha's great awakening really shows that humans are not entities or objects of any kind, and that this ego-self is empty or vacuous, an artificial construction of the ego will. This ego construction of the self that seems to take itself as a separately existing entity is profoundly wrong and wrongful and is in fact the source of the deepest human suffering. So the themes of sin and suffering in our human condition are directly traced to our ego-centered way of being, and the deepest call of these religious visions moves us to dramatically awaken ourselves to a dialogical, open, interactive, unified, and holistic way of being a human.

So too if we look into the Chinese origins, for example, of the Tao or of the Confucian Mandate of Heaven, these moral origins call us equally to awaken to a higher consciousness that can see the interrelationality of humans and the Higher Law as the centering principle in human life. Equally in certain African traditions, the "Nommo," the call of the Original Word or Name in the Dogon worldview, and the Vital Force found to flow through all Nature, calls us to honor and respect the Principle of Life that pulsates through every being and all of Nature. And so on.

So when we stand back and achieve a truly global perspective, it is easier to see the deeper pattern of evolution of cultures and religions through the ages. Here we find a wealth of experimental results that have been tested. This deeper pattern reveals that what is distilled and what survives in this evolution is the convergence on this theme that human beings have been in a profound awakening of a global awareness that is nothing less than the birthing of what we are as human beings. So let us contrast these two models or two paradigms of the human being—the egocentric human and the dialogical human. It is as if all history and cultural evolution is the interplay of these two paradigms or forces in the human nature.

On the one hand, the ego-centered human takes itself to be a separately existing entity and builds its life and world and culture centered around that "reality." On the other hand, the dialogical human somehow awakens to the realization that to be human is a profoundly interrelational, interconnected, interactive way of living and being. This dialogical turn in experience means that everything in human life requires the living of this interactive, or, as the Buddhist would say "co-arising," principle of reality itself. So at this deepest level of Reality, we see this collision and contrast and tension and dialectic playing out through history between the ego-centered culture and the dialogical way of life.

This brings us then to the question of the importance of interreligious dialogue, for religions are deeply established patterns of life that have been distilled over centuries of ongoing cultural evolution and experimentation. Religious worldviews attempt to get to what is most fundamental in human culture and human reality. They are alternative, narrative, corporate expressions of what is profoundly first, the vital core of our cultural life. So as we look across the spectrum of religions, we find profoundly alternative ways of recognizing something primordial and first that is the common source of our diverse worldviews.

This Primal Reality is so profound that no one name can approach or exhaust it, so deep that no name has emerged in the evolution of global cultures presuming to name it. And yet it is important to have a word that may function as a candidate to help us focus our thoughts and attention on this deep common ground that begins to emerge out of interreligious dialogue. So the point is that the great religions in their inner roots and the awakening forces of interreligious dialogue express the ground and foundation of cultural life.

A religion is a way of life that shapes a culture. As such, if we can understand the interactions and interplay among religions, then we will begin to see that there is a profound common reality emerging from these creative encounters, a reality also found right at the core of each religion. I use the word "Logos" to indicate this profound, primordial word, from the Greek meaning "the Word, the infinite Word." We need a truly global interreligious and intercultural Primal Word to help focus our experience on the common foundation and source of all religions and cultures.

One remarkable thing that begins to emerge out of the interplay of world religions in dialogue is the recognition that there is a profound Logos, beyond any single narrative, beyond any single name, so profound in its infinitude, so deep in its Unity, that it spawns multiple infinite possibilities and diversity. So Primal Unity in its infinitude plays out in infinite diversity, plurality, multiplicity, particularity, and individuality. There is not the slightest contradiction between the Unity of Logos and the bottomless diversity and multiplicity in the unified field of Reality.

This to me is one of the greatest lessons of the centuries of interreligious dialogue and interaction—that Logos is so deep in its Unity that multiplicity, plurality, and diversity are the essence of this Unity. And right here we see the deepest seeds of the origin of dialogue and the evolution of dialogical consciousness. So if we rise to the global perspective between worlds, we more readily see this historic pattern evolving. In this historic drama of Logos, we see that human evolution inexorably moves beyond the egocentric culture to the dialogical awakening of global consciousness. This deeper story of human evolution could not be clearly seen until we advance to the global perspective that comes from creative dialogue between worlds. So what it comes down to is the ultimate principle of reality itself. The painful dialogical awakening of human life comes with this emergence of Logos in the human condition.

This Logos, this common ground at the source of all religious worlds, is the source of the dialogical. Why? Because this Primal Word in its infinite depth and presence is so deep that nothing can stand outside of its sphere of influence and jurisdiction. This profound, primordial Logos, which is at the source of all religious worlds and cultures, places all things profoundly in mutual encounter and interrelationality. The Space of Logos, the Field of Reality itself, holds all things in original interaction. Nothing can stand apart or alone. Nothing is atomic or existentially independent, as egocentric reason imagines.

Perhaps the deepest lesson we might learn from the evolution of cultures is that human beings are essentially dialogical beings. We do not stand alone. The vision of a human as an ego-centered, independently existing entity has simply been shown to be unacceptable and disastrous in the evolution of cultures, which brings us to the condition in which we are living, in what I call an exciting moment in this evolution over centuries. It appears from this that the scenario of the birthing of this dialogical consciousness is peaking more and more and accelerating in contemporary times. Yet at the same time the counter-egocentric forces of culture also are peaking—it seems something very urgent and critical is happening in our culture, putting at stake our very survival and future sustainability.

It all turns on the question of our coming to a deeper awareness and practice of this dialogical awakening and turn in our lives. In this global story of Logos, it is clear that humanity must now make the creative corporate turn to dialogical culture if we are to survive. We have arrived at a historic showdown between the two ways of being human. We must find the way to make the corporate transition from egocentric culture to awakened dialogical life. This is why the special skills that come from the creative play of global dialogue, of interreligious and intercultural dialogue, are vital now to our future flourishing.

I would like now to connect the question of this dialogical evolution coming through creative global dialogue and this new global consciousness that emerges from this process with what I will call the global mentality or the global mind. Of course when we hear the word "global" we tend first to think more of the physical dimension, the globe, the geographical sphere, and also the political sphere comprised of the different nations spread across the globe. So usually we speak of "global" in this context. But really, in the wider cultural sense, "global" means a mentality that is open to recognize the plurality of profoundly different cultures and religious worlds, worldviews, and perspectives.

So in this philosophical and cultural dimension the term *global* means having to do with the relations and differences between multiple worlds, with the mutual encounter of the plurality of diverse worldviews and cultural forms of life in human evolution. This is what we call the "'global context" and "global consciousness." It is easy to see that this "global context" is dialogical. When we speak here of "global ethics," for example, it is clearer that the essence of "global" is dialogical. And interreligious dialogue fosters global awakening.

I would like to stress that the dialogical turn is a deep change in our being. It is not simply standing where we are in our particular worldviews, speaking it out to others and listening from afar. The dialogical turn in living calls for a true risk, a willingness to let ourselves be vulnerable in our deepest being. This dialogical awakening calls upon us to open ourselves and our patterns of interpreting reality and to cultivate the willingness to question, reconsider, and revise the worldview in which we live. This of course includes all of our presumptions and assumptions that have been at the source of our way of life, and as such this is something that can feel dangerous and threatening to our very identity, to our "self," and to our most cherished habits of mind.

But it is the kind of risk that more enlightened people in the business world are already used to facing in one way or another. For example, creative entrepreneurs who have been forced by new challenges to reconsider the deepest assumptions of their business practices and business enterprises are already in touch with this dialogical risk and entrepreneurial spirit. So when I speak of the global, I mean global in the sense of a disposition to be profoundly open to others, to other persons, to other religions, to other cultures, and to other perspectives. It means a willingness to revise and experiment and self-transform in an ongoing, open-ended experimental or dialogical way.

The global is the dialogical in practice, and we should see that it does not apply only to the so-called international global scene as we are used to thinking but to our deepest inner life. This dialogical or global outlook is already at work in our personal and interpersonal relations, in the corporate life of our business, in the workplace, and in all aspects of life in society, both at the micro and macro levels.

We should think of the global as the dialogical in practice. The dialogical turn in awareness requires this open outlook—the willingness to listen to others and to encounter and enter creatively the perspectives of others, and the willingness to critically question and even overcome what one has uncritically presumed and assumed. What is remarkable in this global dialogical outlook is that this willingness to take personal risk by entering into other worldviews always deeply enriches the participant while deepening her or his roots in her or his own world. In other words, in taking this dialogical risk, the participant is graced in the deepest way.

I would like now to connect the global mind or mentality to the dialogical or global ethics. The term *global ethics* is being used in many ways right now, but for us it indicates this dialogical consciousness. If one really looks at the evolution of ethics through the religious worlds, it becomes clear that the most important advances in moral consciousness through the ages, from Moses to Jesus to Buddha to Krishna to Lao Tsu, and all the way across diverse cultures through the ages, have been movements to a deeper dialogical being. In other words, ethics points to the deepest way in which we conduct our life and our mind and our thinking.

It is not only an external behavior, but the external behavior reflects a deeper inner transformation. So the moral awakening of humanity over the past 3,000 years has been pressing to this global awakening and dialogical way of being, which is why, whether it is in the injunction to love God with all one's heart or Buddha's principle of Dharma or compassion, to love all beings and all creatures and to tend to their suffering, we get many different formulations and takes on what might be considered a principle of global ethics.

In other words, ethics is profoundly global and universal across the spectrum of cultures and religions. It is almost redundant to call it "global" ethics. Ethics is global ethics. So I would like to speak of the dialogical principle that I see as being at the heart of global ethics and all moral consciousness. For example, given the formulation that we are responsible for the well-being of all creatures, if we assert that such a formulation is a principle of global ethics, then one might ask "why?" Why should I be responsible for anyone other than myself and my immediate family? The direction of the answer is to be found in this emerging dialogical or global consciousness.

When we realize that in our deepest being we cannot stand alone, we understand that we are not human beings in isolation. On the contrary, in our deepest reality we are profoundly interactive and interconnected with those around us, not only with human beings but with all creatures, and even more

so with nature and the ecology as such. We are woven together in a dialogical, interactive principle, which we can call the Reality Principle. So the dialogical principle of global ethics really derives right at the very core of the
process of reality itself. This global ethics may be formulated in many alternative ways—it is not something new. It has been emerging for centuries under
many formulations in diverse religious and cultural worlds, and we need to see
the connections and common ground in these alternative expressions.

So the Golden Rule—for example, to do unto others as you would have
others do unto you, the injunction to love God, the injunction not to harm other
creatures, the positive injunction to take responsibility for the well-being and
care of others and the environment—is profoundly connected in the dialogical
principle. Thus in our exploration of interreligious dialogue and global ethics, I
hope it begins to become clear why global ethics is so profoundly connected to
the project of interreligious dialogue, for global ethics is inherently dialogical,
and the dialogical turn begins to emerge deeply when we see how interactions
take place and have been taking place through the centuries between alternative
religious worlds and cultures. Thus interreligious dialogue, global ethics, and
dialogical consciousness essentially co-arise in each other and in Logos.

In conclusion, I would like to say that the Global Dialogue Institute
(GDI) focuses its attention on cultivating this dialogical awakening, which is
the moral pulse of global ethics. When we look at the state of our cultures and
the present scene, I said at the beginning of this chapter that we are in a very
exciting moment in history, on the threshold of a new century and a new mil-
lennium, and some of us think a new consciousness, a new age, a new stage of
human evolution. But we also should stress the great risks and dangers we face
at this moment—it is because of those that this dialogical awakening is so
critical. If we look at our culture in America, for example, we can see the devastating evidence of the egocentric mind at work in profound violence at all
levels of society as humans abuse themselves and each other, through their
addictions and their ego-relationships, their degrading values, and their colliding ideologies.

On every level we see evidence of the egocentric culture, which always
leads to separations, divisions, and violence of all forms. So what is at stake is
our very survival, and it is in this spirit that the GDI has developed its various projects of fostering global awakening in the fundamental areas of our culture. It is clear that this awakening dialogical consciousness cannot just happen passively. It essentially requires the awakening of this human
consciousness through the very dialogical process itself. This is the wonderful
challenge—the dialogical cannot be told to anyone, and no one can passively
get it. It has to be a process in which one opens up one's being through the
dialogical process itself, and then the emergence of global ethics begins to
become a living reality.

Our future is at risk, and it is the kind of risk that certain enterprising future-oriented business persons, for example, are used to facing and negotiating. Fortunately there is a growing awareness among these corporate visionaries that we have a positive responsibility to take care of each other in the widest possible scope of our corporate ecology. It is obvious now that it is a matter of our sustainability and survival. Clearly everything is at risk, so as we prepare to engage in in-depth dialogue, we must be prepared to question at the deepest level and to stand open in the presence of others and other views; we must be ready to engage and enter into other perspectives. In the end, it will deepen our own self-understanding and open up an ethical space. The essence of global ethics comes with the awakening of the global mind.

8

Meditative Reason and the Holistic Turn to Global Philosophy

PROLOGUE

In this chapter I focus on the central themes of Meditative Reason that open up the way to the holistic turn to natural phenomenology. Perhaps the greatest lesson in the global evolution of philosophy is that *What-Is-First* situates and contextualizes all that appears, all existence, all discourse, all experience, and all phenomena. The centuries of living experiments in diverse traditions of First Philosophy reveal that there is no getting around the Absolute Presence of *What-Is-First*—that which generates and conditions all realities. These historic experiments concur that it is absolutely vital that we humans enter into an authentic way to think or mind the First Principle and to conduct our experience, ever mindful of its Presiding Presence. One of the great lessons of the global evolution of cultures is that the egocentric mind inherently eclipses *What-Is-First* and proceeds in a pathological conduct of mind that is detrimental to all aspects of human life.

This is a central finding of *Meditative Reason*—that the global evolution of cultural life has been the relentless struggle to overcome the pathological ways of egological minding with its dualizing and fragmenting dynamics and to rise and evolve into more mature ways of minding that recenter in the Universal Logos of *What-Is-First*. The work attempts to show precisely how and why egocentric minding inherently leads to pathological dualisms and incommensurable fragmentations in every aspect of human life and existence. The central narrative of the book suggests that this dramatic and historic awakening to the Universal Logos at the heart of human experience began to show itself on a global scale about 2,500 years ago in the teachings of Moses, Socrates, Buddha, Confucius, and other global teachers. The narrative suggests that there is and must be a Universal Logos at the heart of all cultures, religions, philosophies, and forms of life, and that the most potent explanatory principle of the evolution of cultures is the often traumatic awakening of consciousness as experience struggles to overcome egocentric ways and recenter in the higher technology of minding Logos. This higher technology of mind is the very emergence of natural phenomenology.

This has been equally true, for example, in the centuries of experimentation in the meditative technologies of minding found in "Eastern" philosophical traditions, as it is in the profound experimental evolution of rationality and discourse in the "Western" traditions. *Meditative Reason* attempts to reconstruct these diverse global evolutions to demonstrate and illustrate just how the story of the emergence of Logos is the most telling narrative in the global evolution of cultures.

In the story of the emergence of Logos in the Judaic and Greek origins of the European traditions, we see this awakening to the Universal Logos in the biblical injunction to love God with all your heart and mind. God, as the Infinite, Universal Word, Name, Presence, Logos, cannot be minded in the egocentric habits of mind but requires the deepest paradigm shift to recentering in the Divine Word. The Infinite Nature of the Word of God constitutively requires the sacrifice and surrender of the privileging of the egocentric mind and the recentering in the Logos. So the essence of the biblical teaching is to love and mind Logos with all one's being and life, and this means letting go of egological thinking and becoming more authentically finite. This profound paradigm shift is equally called for in the Greek origins of European cultural evolution. For instance, the pre-Socratic attempt to mind *What-Is-First*—the Universal First Principle—reached its dialectical maturity in the polar narratives of Heraclitus and Parmenides and peaked in the philosophical revolution of Socrates, Plato, and Aristotle. It is here that we see the early emergence of the Logos and the logical technology of minding the Logos in First Philosophy. Plato saw that the awakening of Reason and the realization of our true Human Form came with overcoming the egocentric ways of conventional culture and the flourishing in the paradigm shift to centering in the Universal Logos of Goodness—the Form of all forms, the origin of Being and Truth.

But the historic quest for Logos is equally evident in the centuries of meditative experiments in Eastern traditions of minding *What-Is-First*. *Meditative Reason* explores this evolution of meditative First Philosophy, focusing especially on the classical Indian traditions of Hindu and Buddhist thought. It is evident in the meditative experiment culminating in Shankara's Advaita Vedanta that the essence of Vedanta consists in the radical overcoming of egocentric minding and the awakening of nondual (advaita) phenomenological consciousness. In this tradition, minding *What-Is-First*—Aum, Brahman, Atman—essentially calls for the meditative technology of nondual thinking, and it is found that egocentric minding is inherently dualizing and pathological. The phenomenology of egocentric minding—everyday conventional experience—is found to be the very source of disorders in the human condition.

Similarly, in the Buddhist traditions, the meditative dialectic focuses on the pathologies of egocentric experience and discourse as the source of suffering. Here too various strategies are developed in the meditative dynamic for overcoming the fragmenting ways of egocentric life and the liberation of awareness in the realization of a higher form of nondual phenomenology. We can see especially in the historic innovations of Nagarjuna a perfection of the dialectic of radical deconstruction. In his founding of the Madhyamika School (The Philosophy of the Middle Way), the Buddhist "postmodern" deconstructive discourse was inaugurated, a discourse that has had a profound influence on the evolution of Buddhist hermeneutics all the way through to the contemporary flourishing of the Kyoto School of Zen founded by Nishida in this century. Nagarjuna pressed the meditative nondual dialectic all the way, thus showing that egocentric phenomenology is objectifying and reifying and constructs artificial entities (identities) that are found to be vacuous or empty upon meditative critique. So one finding that is fundamental to Buddhist phenomenology is that all egologic constructs are empty and without true reality—all ego views are vacuous, and all ego ideologies are to be deconstructed for the true vindication and liberation of consciousness and experience.

What is astounding in this philosophical therapy is that *What-Is-First*, True Reality, is nondual in nature and is inaccessible to all forms of egocentric minding. All egological metaphysics is found to be inherently inadequate, and a new potent pragmatics, which is truly "postmodern," is brought forth with the realization of the phenomenology of radical emptiness. Instead of even appearing to affirm any ultimate Being—Aum, Brahman, Atman—this tradition insists that true Reality is Sunyata—Absolute Emptiness. It is only in the perfection of the meditative dialectic that the truth of the Middle Way can be realized. We shall see shortly that this historic breakthrough is vital for the authentic encounter with the Universal Logos. In a remarkable disclosure, after the nondual therapy of deconstructing egocentric consciousness is realized, Nagarjuna teaches that there cannot be the slightest difference between the liberated phenomenology of Nirvana and the everyday world of natural experience. In other words, when the pathological ways of egominding are overcome, the spontaneity of the Natural Mind arises, and the immediacy of the everyday natural world shows itself. Thus it is found that the nonduality of meditative phenomenology is essential for the awakening of the open, natural mind and the disclosure of natural phenomena.

The narrative of Meditative Reason proceeds to suggest that despite real and apparent differences between the meditative traditions of First Philosophy, nevertheless there is and must be a Univocal and Universal Logos (Universal Law) at the heart of the diverse traditions. The text argues that it is constitutive of the Infinite Divine Word (Logos), that it be the foundation of all narratives. It is the very Logos that is disclosed as Sunyata (Absolute Emptiness) and as Aum, Brahman, and Atman, the Same Logos that is revealed as Yahweh in biblical origins and as Absolute Goodness in the deepest insights of Plato. This thesis is expanded to range experimentally over diverse cultural traditions in the global context—in the Chinese traditions of First Philosophy, which in one way or another gravitate to Tao, the Nameless Name, which is the Absolute Ground of all that exists. The diverse traditions of the Tao play out the nondual dialectic over the centuries, and here too it is found that the egological mind is self-eclipsed from minding the Tao, from direct encounter with true Reality and Natural Experience. In this way it begins to emerge that there is a Logos to Tao, and a Tao to Logos. And so on.

The work suggests that there is a Universal Logic or Grammar to the Logos that has been eclipsed by egological thinking and becomes more accessible to the nondual methods of meditative minding. But the parochial and ethnic localism of the grammars of the great traditions of First Philosophy has worked against the clear recognition of the Universal Logos in its fully revealed Universal Grammar. It takes the further innovations of a truly Global First Philosophy to develop the tools and logistics of Universal Grammar to more adequately bring forth the Logos in its universal and global disclosure. This is a central concern of the book.

As the new technology of minding Logos emerges, the innovative methods of Universal Grammar enable us to experience more clearly the Universal History and Evolution of Logos in its global unfolding. The more we overcome the atavism of egocentric minding, the more clear and evident the historical dialectic of the presiding Infinite Logos. One theme that is clear is the pervasive depth and recalcitrance of egological ways in the human condition. It is impossible to exaggerate how deeply entrenched and controlling of human culture are the divisive and fragmenting dynamics of egocentric praxis. In light of the History of Logos, it appears that the past 2,500 years have been at once a relentless process of overcoming egocentric phenomenology by the historic emergence of the Phenomenlogy of Logos, and a deeply pernicious and persistent resistance of egocentric culture to the awakening and liberative forces of the technology of Logos. It becomes clear that the primary agenda of the dramatic unfolding of global history is precisely this ongoing life-and-death struggle between the transformative and awakening forces of Logos and the opposing resistance to such change by the inertia and status quo of egocentric culture. Egocentric phenomenology or cultural hermeneutics is the old-world technology, while the technology of minding Logos, with its holistic phenomenology and cultural revolution, is the new world thinking. We suggest that the most illuminating narrative for explaining and understanding cultural evolution over the past 2,000 years is this great paradigm shift from egocentric minding to the conduct of mind in the Logic of Logos.

In light of this epic drama of Logos, it is evident that the story of Jesus—the Logos that has become Flesh—is a classic, essential breakthrough in the holistic emergence of Logos in the human condition. The Universal

Logic of Logos makes clear precisely how and why profoundly diverse disclosures of the Infinite Word—whether in the nondual advances of "Aumic" discourse in the teachings of the *Bhagavadgita* or in the Advaita of Shankara, or in the innovations of Buddha or advances of Nagarjuna, whether in the disclosures of the Tao or in the reflections of Lao Tzu or Chuang Tzu—all play out a common dialectical process of holistic emergence of the Living Word. The Infinite nature of Logos expresses itself in radical diversity or alterity, which nevertheless manifests the dialectic of nonduality and the full flourishing of the holistic turn. In this respect, the life and teaching of Jesus may be seen as a classic advance in this holistic turn in the Logic of the Word. The injunction to Love Logos with all one's heart and mind plays out through Moses and advances in the holistic emergence in Jesus, for the nondual nature of Logos requires the deconstruction of the egological split between the "finite" and the "infinite" and the manifestation of the holistic continuum between Logos and the Flesh.

The full corporate embodiment of Logos is intrinsic to the Logic of Logos and has played out in the evolution of cultures for over 2,000 years and is now the most urgent historic priority in the evolution of global culture. Thus in the global evolution of Christian discourse, we may see the creative union of the Judaic and Hellenistic cultural worlds in the grammatical innovations of Augustine and Aquinas. There is a clear historical logic of Logos being played out all the way through the Quaker innovations of the logic of the Christ in the corporate life of the Polis. This logic of embodiment—the overcoming of the egocentric practices and the centering in the Life of Logos—is the recurrent drama through the centuries. This very pattern is creatively played out in a very different scenario in the global evolution of the teachings of Buddha, so as this historical dialectic unfolds in its holistic turn in the phenomenology of Zen, we find the continued unfolding of the Logic of Logos in the paradigm shift in the human condition. The common theme is that the egocentric culture essentially blocks and eclipses the Living Word, and the paradigm shift to the holistic technology of minding Logos brings forth a higher form of Life and Experience in the full corporate embodiment of Logos.

This story is most evident in the dialectical play from Descartes' *Meditations* to the deconstructive discourse of Derrida. We suggest that the presiding factor in this chapter of the global history of Logos is precisely the deep struggle to perform the meditative turn—the nondual and holistic turn—in the conduct of mind in breaking through the historic tyranny of the egocentric culture, for the historic irony of the Cartesian meditations is that they are wonderfully classical in following the Logic of Logos in performing the nondual turn in the minding of the *Cogito*, yet the egocentric hermeneutics has continued a distorted reading that suppresses the nondual advances and saddles the

Cartesian voice with "Cartesian dualism." Meditative Reason attempts to vindicate Descartes by situating his bold meditative experiment in the context of centuries of meditative findings in the global evolution. In this context of the evolution of Logos, we find that Cartesian meditations are another historic pivot and breaking point in the hermeneutical battle between the hermeneutics of egocentric scholarship and the Phenomenology of Logos.

In reading the *Meditations*, as meditations we can see the classic moves of radical questioning of egocentric experience in Descartes' skeptical doubts concerning conventional experience in his relentless quest for absolute foundations and rational certitude in moving to Logos as the ground of his First Philosophy. We suggest that his dramatic turn to the *Cogito* must be read as the nondual turn to the meditative voice, which signals a dramatic breakthrough to the transcendental voice in human rational awareness, and the authentic existential encounter with Logos. When read in light of the Logic of Logos, the Cartesian Meditations play out in a profoundly different narrative than we typically find in the flat-footed and ego-laden interpretations that reduce Descartes' historic advances to mere pathological obsessions and neurotic anxieties that helped spawn the pernicious "modernism" and misguided and failed "enlightenment" discourse.

I am not suggesting that Descartes was always clear and lucid in performing the meditative turn in his historic experiment. Clearly he was not. He was obviously himself under the deep sway of the egocentric forces in the culture, which have continued to dominate hermeneutical practice in the unfolding dialectical drama. But I am suggesting that the one-sided egocentric readings of his experiment have grotesquely reduced and distorted the heroic advances and the delicate, if tentative, breakthrough into nondual *Cogito*. The moral of Descartes' experiment is that the nondual methods of meditative minding are essential in overcoming egocentric "reason" and in rising to the transcendental voice of ((Natural Reason)). As we shall now see, this vital nondual turn in rational consciousness would continue to haunt subsequent thinkers—Kant, Hegel, Fichte, Nietzsche, Husserl, Heidegger, Sartre, Gadamer, Derrida—for it is no accident that Husserl would pick up the theme of the transcendental turn to Phenomenology in the Cartesian meditations, and that his protégé, Heidegger, would end his career focusing our attention on the urgent need to save our humanity in cultivating the essential human form of meditative thinking. We suggest that all of this historic drama makes perfect sense in light of the unfolding dialectic of the Logic of Logos.

In a clear sense the dialectic of Logos, from Descartes to Derrida, is a grand reductio (or demonstration of the bankruptcy) of egocentric hermeneutics and phenomenology. In Kant's career, for example, we see a gallant struggle against the powerful undertow of egocentric minding and its dualistic ways. The core of Kant's contribution was to attempt to overcome the deep historic dualism between the subject (knower) and the object (known), which he found to be the common ground for the evolution of both empiricism and rationalism. His "Copernican revolution in epistemology" was designed to find a more adequate paradigm for knowledge and experience that deconstructed the "Ptolomaic" paradigm that assumed that the subject was ontologically independent of the object. Of course overcoming this subject/object dualism was a classical target for the meditative turn, and meditative traditions have provided centuries of vital experiments in performing this "Copernican revolution" in hermeneutics. Still, Kant's solution unfortunately was not radical enough—apparently he did not perform the crucial breakthrough to nondual minding but instead attempted a strategic cure within the egocentric paradigm. He attempted to show that the object was constituted in the conceptual structure of the subject, and this "revolution" was one classical way to overcome the dualism by making the object dependent on the subject. This was the "critical idealism" of Kant. It turned out to be a compromise within the egological structure that always privileges one side or the other of egocentric dualisms or polarities. We suggest that the full "Copernican revolution" sought for by Kant requires the holistic turn to true transcendental awareness required by the Logic of Logos. This transcendental turn that was so vital for Husserl in his quest for pure phenomenological consciousness could not be achieved within the egological technology and required nothing less than the full maturing to nondual minding and the overcoming of egocentric reason. It is this deep barrier that continued to plague subsequent thinkers, and all attempts to arrive at the true Phenomenology of Logos in the "transcendental ego" fell short. It is well known that Kant's compromised "solution" to the Subject/Object dualism landed him in other deep dualisms and incommensurabilities, such as the split between the noumenal and the phenomenal, and the tensions between the empirical ego and the transcendental ego and the noumenal moral self.

Hegel's magnificent innovations in the Science of Logic and the Phenomenology of Spirit pressed egological technology to its limits. His dialectical logic of identity, which moved from a static egologic identity to a dynamic dialectic, is called for by the Logic of Logos which, we shall see, proceeds on the living dynamic principle of ((Relativity)). Hegel's recognition that all historical reality is moved by Absolute Geist, Absolute Spirit, moves closer to the Presiding Presence of Universal Logos. It may be said that Hegel served the global dialectic of Logos by pressing egologic reason to its inner limits and thereby preparing the way for the more radical corporate overcoming of egocentric culture. His experimental advances, played out within the space of egocentric minding, helped ripen the recognition that a more radical holistic turn would be required to truly reach the historical dialectic of Logos that he sought.

That Hegel's important experimental advances were countered as they were by Marx, who performed a dialectical turn on Hegel's dialectic of Geist, indicates that the recurrent polar dynamic of egologic minding continued. Marx's ability to counter Hegel's dialectical idealism with a historical materialism is evidence of the repeated classical pattern of egological reason to always spawn its polar opposite. The Hegel-Marx polarity—a polarity of Idealism-Materialism—fits the inner self-polarization pattern that is the signature of the egocentric principle of identity, the principle of dualism, and self-alienation. So this ripened dialectic helped bring out the constitutive incoherence and incommensurability at the heart of egological reason. And Nietzsche's perspectivism and pluralism was another predictable development that helped expose the inevitable consequences of egocentric reason.

We shall not on this occasion discuss in any detail the importance of Husserl's historic advances in moving closer to the Phenomenology of Logos. His vital experiments, in seeking to fulfill the Cartesian dream of a pure and universal science grounded in Logos—a formal and transcendental logic—were obviously in service of the emergence of the natural phenomenology. As with Kant and Hegel, Husserl's relentless attempt to reach the universal grammar of Logos within the egological mind helped show, once and for all, the incommensurability between the Ideal of Universal Logos, with its pure phenomenological awareness, and the resources of egocentric minding. The true transcendental turn in universal reason could not be achieved in the logos of the egologic mind. And as with Kant and Hegel, Husserl's experiments helped clarify the bankruptcy of egocentric thinking and confirm the pernicious depth of ego-dualism. We find that the moral of his work is not so much the impossibility of realizing a truly universal and well-grounded phenomenological method as that the transcendental turn in truly minding Logos required a deeper "bracketing" and the more radical paradigm shift to nondual reason and holistic minding than was anticipated. The Cartesian dream of reaching the objective and universal foundation of knowledge grounded in Logos required the meditative turn and the holistic technology of minding yet to be developed. Thus Husserl's program, and his proper diagnosis of the crisis in philosophy and culture, is not discredited. Rather, his vital experiment is confirmation of the dialectic of Logos and further evidence that the transcendental turn in rational awareness could not be achieved in the "old-world" logical space of egocentric discourse.

It is here that the creative career of Heidegger, Husserl's prominent student, continued to advance the cause of the emergence of Universal Logos in the human condition. It is well known that in his earlier career he separated from Husserl's program and moved in a radical way breaking new ground in the analytic of Dasein—the existential subject. In terms of the Phenomenology of Logos, it was expected that the old metaphysics of being would be deconstructed and seen as posterior to the primacy of the existential life of Dasein, which is found to be constituted in temporality and history and the finitude of death. But something was not right with this early project. It appears that here too the deep sway of the egocentric mind continued its hegemonic power over philosophical imagination and seemed to hold Heidegger's analytic and phenomenological innovations in its domain.

We suggest that the dramatic reorientation performed by Heidegger toward the end of his career to meditative thinking is a vital, inevitable step in the emergence of Logos. Heidegger's mature voice moved to the horizon of the meditative turn, which involved the overcoming of the domination of "technological thinking" (what we call egological minding). Heidegger rightly saw that our very humanity—the essence of being human—involved our move to meditative thinking, which exhibits the classic dynamics of nondual life. The meditative turn, the awakening of our authentic existence, called for a radical opening of our selves to the Other, to the world, to phenomena. The very being of truth involved this dialogical self opening in the conduct of our mind. It appears that the shift from the hermeneutical orientation in his earlier career to the meditative orientation in the full maturity of his life follows the classical pattern of the transition from the egological phenomenology to the Phenomenology of Logos. It seems that the nondual transcendental turn in Descartes' *Cogito* (meditative voice) was being taken up and advanced by Heidegger. And in a real sense the fantastic, unfolding story of Logos from Heraclitus to Heidegger has been a continuous dialectic leading to the blossoming of Logos in the meditative turn. We suggest that this evolution of rational consciousness is inscribed in the inner life of Logos. So Heidegger's meditative turn was not a mere subjective preference but objectively required by the Logic of Logos. In a real sense he speaks as the telos of centuries of evolution of reason and helps clarify how deep the controlling power of egocentric culture is, how painful and difficult it is to truly overcome, and how much is at stake in reconstituting our hermeneutical life in consummating the transcendental turn.

Of course it is not only in the evolution of individual philosophical lives and authors that we see the evidence of the Dialectic of Logos but in the deeper cultural trends and movements as well. For the cultural movements we are now living through in our contemporary period are best illuminated in light of the Phenomenology of Logos. The earlier rise of "modernist" discourse, with its "enlightenment" and "universalist" ideals that often are associated with the Cartesian ideals and the contemporary "antimodernist" or "postmodern" backlash or rejection or dialectical reaction to the modernist ideology, is an exemplary ripening of the historical logic of Logos. Meditative Reason focuses on the recurrent pattern of polarization in ideologies through the centuries and, on a global scale, as the inevitable result of egocentric cultures, for the intention of the enlightenment ideals of universal reason, of objective knowledge well grounded in the foundations of *What-Is-First*, of universal standards and values validated by First Principles—all of this is constitutive of the Universal Logos. Likewise, the intention of the antimodernist ideologies of deconstructing the fixations of ego-identities, of rejecting naive foundationalism and essentialism, of exposing the pernicious and totalizing logocentrism that purports to be grounded in universal and objective "reason"—all this too is constitutive of the Dialectics of Logos, for the Story of Logos reveals that egological reason will always self-polarize into internal incommensurability and self-opposition, will never reach a true universal rational awareness, will never reach true foundations and universal law, and will always fall into a pernicious pluralism, localism, and self-deconstruction. Here we find that the voice of Derrida shows the full ambivalence, equivocity, confusion, and irony that reflect the hermeneutical crisis in our contemporary culture—the deep battle between the egocentric forces and the powerful, irrepressible emergence of Universal Logos.

In this global context of the evolution of Logos, Derrida's voice may be seen as equivocating between the egocentric culture, which will fall into a nihilism of mere self-deconstruction, signifying nothing, and the therapeutic deconstructive power of Logos, which will inherently call for the radical deconstruction not only of ego constructs but of the egological mind and culture itself. If read in a positive way, Derrida may be seen as making classical moves in the required radical deconstruction of ego identity, of the decentering of the presumed ego autonomy of the subject, which is vital for the healthy turn to the recentering in Logos.

If read in a negative way, that is, as a project of deconstruction within the structure of egological discourse that rejects the Logos, then this scenario must lead into a nihilistic self-defeating tailspin that undermines all that is truly good and noble in the Logic of Logos. The moral here is that the noble ideals of "modernism," of the quest for universal reason, rightly situated in the Space of Logos, are essential for the health and well-being of the human condition. It is the egocentric distortions of the Logos that should be targeted for creative deconstruction. Similarly, the noble intentions of postmodern discourse, rightly situated in the Dialectic of Logos, require the therapeutic deconstruction of egocentric phenomenology to make way for the rise to a liberated culture that accomplishes the meditative or transcendental turn to authentic corporate existence.

We have been suggesting that Infinite Logos has been the common generative principle moving all histories, all cultures and traditions, and all forms of life. The historical emergence of Logos is the common motif and common cause generating the evolution from Heraclitus, through Moses and Jesus, all the way through Descartes to Derrida. For all of the radical dialectical swings, the ebbs and flow of this Logos Word Process through history, Logos is the primary causal force. We have suggested that the presiding focus through this great dialectical drama is the true overcoming of egocentric minding in the global awakening to a higher technology of minding Logos—that Logos is the true Center of the Universe.

We have seen that the deepest drive in cultural-hermeneutical life is to express Logos, and that repeated maneuvers within the egocentric logical space have failed to perform the full holistic turn to Logos. It should now be clearer why it has been so difficult to accomplish this profound paradigm shift on a global scale. The egocentric space of minding is not just the belief in ego, in the alleged, individuated, autonomous subject, for even the antimodernist attempts to decenter this putative egocentric primary subject have remained in forms of self-deception, lodged within the egocentric form of life.

This is why even antimodernist perspectives, ideologies, and narratives, which strain to undermine ego identity and egocentric subjectivity, stressing the logic of difference and otherness in radical deconstruction, have been entrapped in the same form of minding as the modernist ideologies. The essence of the egocentric mind is its inveterate habit of fixating on "content," on objects of thought, on reifying and objectifying "what it thinks," the patho-logical habit of polar/dualistic flux between the objectified poles of "identity" and "difference." If the ego modernist has privileged ego identity, then the antimodernist naturally gravitates to privilege the opposite pole of ego differ-ence; if the former affirms ideologies of unity and universality, then the latter will invariably privilege plurality and particularity. But both sides are playing the same ego-logic dialectic of identity and difference—both polar sides are caught in the common form of minding, of attempting to represent the truth and project it as content on the "screen of consciousness." If the content-nar-ratives that privilege the ego-logic of identity fail, then likewise the content-narratives that privilege radical difference also will fail to truly express Logos. So all forms of ego representation, including the antimodernist narratives of antirepresentation, are caught in the same egocentric dialectics.

The true transcendental, meditative, holistic turn to the Logical Space of Logos cannot be accomplished in a conduct of minding that objectifies what is thought and reifies all that appears to thought as content in the ego-centric voice. That practice of mind inherently blocks the true holistic turn from entering the Presence of Logos, where natural phenomena reveal them-selves—the practice of Natural Phenomenology.

But this holistic turn in the technology of minding has been equally dif-ficult and challenging for all cultures and traditions. Meditative Reason attempts to resituate diverse philosophical, religious, and cultural traditions in this context of the historical Dialectic of Logos and to break new ground in developing a truly global perspective. Here we find that the essential struggle in the "Eastern" meditative traditions has been to cross this barrier of egological minding and advance to the technology of minding Logos. The very same challenge that faced the unfolding tradition from Heraclitus to Derrida also has played out through the unfolding historical dialectic from Buddha through Nishida. All traditions have struggled with the overcoming of egocentric malpractice and with developing the higher technology of entering into Presence, into the Space of Natural Reason, the Field of Logos.

From this global perspective of Logos History, let us explore for a moment the dialectical play of this theme through the meditative experiments of "Eastern" traditions. We shall then be in a better position to see how the experiments of East and West converge to the same holistic horizon in deeply complementary ways.

Although the centuries of Vedic and Yogic practices focused on overcoming egocentric minding, the teaching of the Universal Self, Atman, and the meditative disclosures of Aum, the Unified Field of Logos, the actual cultural practice continued to labor in the old-world logical space that appeared to objectify Self and Aum as Absolute Being, even if it could not be spoken of in ego terminology. The Buddha's great awakening was precisely in the innovation of a more effective technology of minding—a new pragmatics—that attempted to accomplish the radical crossing from egominding to the direct, living, existential encounter with Noumenality, with Natural Phenomenology. The dialectic of Sunyata, Radical Emptiness, which recognized a higher principle of Relativity, of dependent co-arising, appeared to be a step closer to the realization of nonduality and the liberation from dualized minding.

In other words, the meditative turn involved a dialectical evolution that required the practical realization of nonduality in the deepest conduct of the mind. The teaching of nonduality, rendered on the "screen" of egological discourse, is still lodged in objectification, reification, and speculation. Nothing less than the full deconstruction, not only of all ego constructs on that "screen of thought and experience" but in the deeper methods of minding that continued to objectify "objects of thought," to project content, to represent ideologies and conceptualizations, had to be pragmatically accomplished. So the meditative turn had to follow the path of nonduality rigorously and radically all the way to a higher technology of minding that truly entered the existential immediacy of the *Cogito*, of the Presence of Logos, of Sunyata, of Phenomenality.

It took centuries of continued refinement of yoga, the sciences, technologies, and experimentations to negotiate the crossing from egological minding to the full holistic turn to entering the here and now of Logos Presence. Nagarjuna, in a high point of his dialectical innovations, saw that with true Awakening of Intelligence no dualism remains between enlightened reason and everyday experience. So the full dialectical journey of nonduality must consummate in the full holistic turn to existential arrival in the here and now of everyday experience. And this is the place of Natural Reason, Natural Phenomenology.

But this ideal remained programmatic and took centuries to come to corporate realization in the evolving cultures. This holistic turn in minding required the objective development of higher logical technologies in discerning the workings of the Unified Field of Relativity—the development of new methods of minding the Continuum of Reality and actually living the First Principle of Universal Relativity, the Principle of Logos. If all ego constructs are empty—all things, phenomena, ideologies, worlds, concepts, names, and forms—then how are we to truly mind the world, nature, existence, phenomena, and conceptual life in the Place of Sunyata, the Presence of Logos? How does True Reality appear, show itself? How does Noumenality disclose itself? How must we humans mind, think, perceive, judge, interpret, evaluate, and experience beyond the artificial constructions of egominding? Obviously minding must co-arise with what is given, each codetermining the other in an infinite interrelational network of corelations. This is the technology of holistic minding of the here and now that awaited further invention and discovery.

Thus the meditative traditions excelled in the essential early stages of the Dialectic of Logos, in performing the initial phases of the nondual turn that is the signature of meditative minding. This early stage of nondual technology largely focused on the radical critique of deconstruction of ego constructs, on separating from the "everyday" conventional world of ego-cultic culture. This initial moment in the dialectic of awakening creates a divorce, distantiation, divestment, or separation between the awakening mind in transit to that higher place of true reality, of enlightenment, of Atman and Nirvana, of Tao and Allah, so a radical dualism arises between the way of nonduality and the scene of egocentric duality that is provisionally conceded to be the "everyday world." I say "provisionally" since as this dialectic matures to the full holistic flourishing of the nondual path, the old world is radically deconstructed and the real world—the world of the liberated, here and now, everyday, natural experience—can show itself. It is in this great turning when we arrive in the place of Presence, of Sunyata, of Aum, of Tao, of Logos, that we awaken to Natural Phenomenology, to true Experience. And of course it takes an advanced technology of minding to negotiate this full holistic turn to rising to this living place of true, everyday reality in Presence.

This dialectic took real strides in the creative innovations of Nishida, the founder of the Kyoto School of Zen in this century, who was steeped in the evolution of the European traditions—in the work of Aristotle, Kant, Hegel, and others. He emerged out of the living practice of Zen with its advanced methods of minding the everyday world in time and history. And it may be said that Nishida focused at exactly the right place to perform the next historical steps in the global evolution of Logos. He saw that there was a missing Universal Logic of Absolute Emptiness, of Sunyata, of Basho. Basho is this Universal Place of Absolute Emptiness, of Historical Presence, and he saw that it was vital to the advance of culture to try to more fully articulate the depth of nonduality in excavating the depth grammar of Basho, the Universal Unified Field.

It is here that we find a great dialectical convergence to a common horizon in the evolutions of East and West. The ultimate challenge is to truly overcome the old-world technologies and phenomenologies of egominding and to advance to the authentic minding of everyday reality in the holistic Place of Logos—the Universal Unified Field of Historical existence. In this Global evolution of Logos, we see that the emergence of postmodernism minding, as in the work of Derrida, is serving the radical overcoming of egocentric minding and is a clear step toward the minding of Relativity, which refuses to privilege identity over difference, or difference over identity, and which refuses to valorize unity over plurality, or plurality over unity. This therapeutic dialectic of postmodern deconstruction is a necessary stage on the way to the full holistic turn to Natural Phenomenology, which can only emerge when the egocentric habits of mind are dissolved.

This arrival at the holistic horizon of Presence, the Field of Logos, has been accomplished through diverse evolutions. We suggested earlier that Heidegger approached this horizon in the fullness of his career in his turn to meditative thinking. Naturally we find that the primary reality of this higher human place is dialogical, interactive, relational, and intersubjective. This is the sacred place of dialogical presence, or Relativity or relationality, of the disclosure of Nature and everyday phenomena. This is the space of Dialogue and co-arising that is creatively opened by Buber in his I-Thou phenomenology. It is the intended space of experimental methods, for the experimental is the praxis of dialogical minding—of asking questions of phenomena and of listening critically to the responsive speaking of natural phenomena to the open mind. Various radical critiques that have hammered away at the old-world naive splits between mind and body and attempted to rise to more authentic and full-bodied methods of human embodiment are approaching this same holistic turn to Natural Phenomenology in the Unified Field.

For example, certain creative voices in feminist critique, in ecofeminism, have been concerned to cultivate more creative forms of embodiment that play out in more radical ways of compassion and ethics of care. These important innovations may be seen as following the Logos and performing the holistic turn in the human condition. So there are alternative creative paths to the holistic turn and living the Logos. From this point of view, this genuinely Global perspective of the emergence of Logos, we see the inevitability of the overcoming of egocentric science practice as the nobility of the holistic scientific turn—the dialogical essence of the experimental minding—comes forth in the full flourishing of Relativity. For now it becomes clearer that the initial move in modern physics to "Relativity" was just a beginning of the full path to Universal Relativity, which is the living principle of Logos. So it is clear that we have only arrived at the threshold of the holistic turn, which is the telos that has been moving diverse dialectical evolutions in the global context.

Meditative Reason attempts to explore this new horizon in depth, to advance the technology of minding the Unified Field of Logos, to advance the logistic of Universal Grammar, and to help open this horizon for the next stage of the creative evolution of Natural Reason and Natural Phenomenology. In a sequel we shall review further the findings of our experiments in exploring this new technology of minding the Unified Field of Logos and its innovations for Natural Phenomenology.

9

Meditative Reason and the
Missing Logic of Logos

NISHIDA'S LOGIC AND THE QUEST
FOR THE GRAMMAR OF LOGOS

As we now proceed more deeply in these reflections on the missing primal logic of Logos it would be helpful to focus on the remarkable advances introduced by Nishida, the founder of the influential Kyoto School of Zen. Over the past thirty years there has been a dramatic flourishing of the dialogical encounter of philosophical and religious traditions in a global context. This encounter has contributed to a historic change in the hermeneutical landscape of philosophical and religious discourse. It is now more natural to enter religious studies with an interreligious sensitivity and orientation, to engage in philosophical investigations with more awareness of the presence and importance of other traditions. The face of philosophical and religious discourse has been recentering increasingly in an intercultural, intertraditional, interreligious, and intergrammatical context. In this rich and varied encounter, a new global consciousness is emerging, and this has brought into sharper focus certain perennial issues concerning the foundation of dialogical philosophy—the nature of dialogue between worlds, and the possibility of intergrammatical conversation and transformations.

I first encountered Masao Abe about twenty-five years ago. The center of my own work has been the exploration of the universal logic or grammar of discourse in a dialogical and global context. At that time I was very active in a range of dialogues in intercultural philosophy, interreligious dialogue, and interdisciplinary discourse. It was remarkable in the late seventies how many contexts for intergrammatical dialogue were emerging: the Society for Asian and Comparative Philosophy, the International Association of Buddhist Studies, and the Working Group for Cross-Cultural Philosophy of Religion of the American Academy of Religion, to mention a few. In these diverse settings I would regularly find myself participating in dialogues with him. Whether in the context of East-West philosophical dialogue or interreligious explorations, I was struck with the consistent eloquence and excellence of Abe's contributions. It was not only that he spoke well for the particular

Japanese school of philosophy and religious thought that he "represented," not only that he deepened the dialogues by articulating a certain perspective in Eastern thought, but also that he spoke in a dialogical voice and out of a dialogical mode of discourse. The more I interacted with him in various dialogical contexts the more it became apparent that he was deeply grounded in a religious and philosophical grammar that was itself profoundly dialogical and concerned essentially with performing and making manifest the foundation of dialogical encounter.

Professor Masao Abe's appearance and participation in this dialogical encounter, especially in the past fifteen years, is certainly not coincidental. He has played a central and vital role in this historical unfolding. I welcome his impressive contributions and thus the opportunity to reflect, appraise, reconsider, and assess the historical importance of his dialogical work on the scene of recent Western philosophical and religious discourse.

This was the period in which I was involved with developing the Margaret Gest Center for Cross-Cultural Study of Religions at Haverford College. Through the seventies I worked closely with colleagues at Haverford, especially Paul Desjardins (philosophy) and Wyatt MacGaffey (anthropology) to launch this newly emerging Center, which was especially concerned with cultivating interreligious inquiry and dialogue in an intercultural and interdisciplinary context. The Center featured an annual lecture series on the unity of religions and an annual interreligious dialogue that brought together diverse religious faiths in the interest of exploring common ground and honoring real diversity among the world's religions. I became the first director of this Center from 1980 to 1983 and was charged with developing a practical philosophy and dialogical strategy for the most creative launching of the activities of the Center.

Abe was a natural for the Center. In planning the early dialogues, he played a prominent role. He participated in the 1981 dialogue the "Unity of Religions," which included John Carman, Tu Wei-ming, Norbert Samuelson, Riffat Hassan, and Rita Gross. It was remarkable to see the dialogical dynamics at work in bringing out the depth of diversity of different faiths in exploring the common ground between religious worlds. I noted over and over how different religious narratives deepened and self-expanded and self-revised in and through this dialogical encounter. I invited Abe back for the 1983 dialogue "Death and Eternal Life: A Buddhist-Christian Dialogue," which included John Hick, Donald Swearer, and Victor Preller. Here again Abe's presence helped deepen the dialogue and open space for an authentic encounter of different voices and grammatical perspectives.

The Gest Center at that time also featured a Gest Visiting Professorship. The idea was that one of the best ways to educate and sensitize the community to other religious worlds, religions, and faiths was to have in residence living exemplars of diverse traditions. One of the original structures of the College—the Woodside Cottage—was converted into a residential and teaching facility and called the "Gest Meditation Center." Based on his outstanding performance in the earlier dialogues, I was successful in convincing colleagues and administrators at Haverford to appoint Abe as Gest Visiting Professor for two years (1985 to 1987). Before his arrival we had the good fortune to have three outstanding professors from different cultural and religious traditions—Valentine Mudimbe, Lobsang Lhalungpa, and Lal Mani Joshi. By the time Abe arrived, there was already momentum and high expectations at the Center. Students were increasingly responsive to the teaching presence of the resident professors, and supporting cultural events became part of the life of the Center. In addition, Abe gave public lectures to the community and was featured again in the 1986 annual dialogue "Free Will in Religious Traditions," which included Langdon Gilkey, Norbert Samuelson, and Rajeshwari Pandharipande. Abe set the context for this dialogue with his illuminating paper "Free Will and Sunyata in Buddhism." His framing of the issues helped bring out a significant dialogical encounter between the diverse religious grammars represented in the dialogue. Abe was most effective in his tenure as the Gest Professor and made a real impact introducing members of the community to the living reality of Zen thought and practice. He touched the lives of certain students who were most appreciative of their living encounter with the Zen experience.

For me the most significant and enduring impact of his work at Haverford College centered on the discussions of a distinguished group of philosophers in the greater Philadelphia area and in the Northeast. Abe and I convened the Interreligious Theology Group, which met regularly at the Gest Mediation Center over the period of his two-year residence. This group included thinkers who attended the Sunday seminars on a regular basis—Paul Desjardins, Joan Stambaugh, Douglas Steere, Steven Heine, Kenneth Kraft, Jiten Mohanty, Tom Dean, Janet Gyatso, and Michael Barnhart, some of whom traveled long distances. Some other scholars attended less frequently but nevertheless made important contributions to our discussions—David Dilworth, Richard DeMartino, Donald Swearer, Edward Casey, and others. Abe led many of these discussions and introduced us to several eminent thinkers in the Kyoto School of Zen, founded by Nishida. The quality of the discussions was high, and it was apparent that Abe embodied a living, creative understanding of the rich and deep insights of the Zen tradition.

Abe's book *Zen and Western Thought* had just appeared and provided a further resource for our dialogues and inquiry. I should mention in passing that I nominated this book to the Committee of the American Academy of Religion, which evaluates new books annually for its prestigious award. Abe's book won the academy's award for the most significant constructive/reflective

work in religious studies that year. This was another indication of the growing recognition of the importance of his dialogical philosophy for religious
studies on the American scene. His grounding in Eastern and Western
thought helped bring out the interreligious issues, and this sparked explorations at the foundation of East-West global discourse. Over the two years,
as the group became more conversant with the Kyoto School, it was apparent
that this tradition had powerful resources for deepening interreligious dialogue and East-West comparative philosophical inquiry.

The most exciting aspect of the Sunday dialogues for me was Abe's
articulate introduction of Nishida's Logic of Basho. This became the central
focus of our discussions—it was the very foundation of Nishida's life work and
the generative force of the Kyoto School. It was exciting because I found in
Nishida a creative mind of the highest order whose philosophical life culminated in the attempt to articulate the foundational logic of the Zen experience. Nishida's recognition and intuition that there is a Universal Logic of
Sunyata that needed to be excavated and formulated was deeply akin to my
own quest to articulate the Universal Grammar or Logic at the core of existence. It was a thrill to find a richly developed philosophical tradition deeply
grounded in the resources of Eastern and Western thought moving toward the
articulation of a truly global and universal logic. It was in effect an independent experiment that I could explore in relation to my own efforts to articulate the universal logic at the heart of global discourse.

As Abe introduced the group to Nishida's logic, it became clear that at
the end of his remarkable career Nishida had reached the foundations and
generative origin of his life's work. The recognition that there is a universal
logic of meditative and religious experience, logic of Sunyata or Absolute
Nothingness, is itself an important advance in global philosophical discourse.
It became clear to me that such logic helps account for the nature and possibility of interreligious dialogue and East-West comparative inquiry. But it also
was apparent that Nishida's logic of Basho had to be enacted and performed
in the living dialogical encounter that Abe exhibited so well in his life and
teaching. The more I understood the vital pulse of the Logic of Basho, the
more I recognized that Abe was performing this living logic of dialogical
encounter in his own teaching practice. While our encounter with the Logic
of Basho revealed that for Nishida the logic of Sunyata takes us to the core of
a living historical dialectic in the heart of self-consciousness, our encounter
with Abe's life work exhibited and performed this encounter or dialogical
hermeneutic in the unfolding historical scene. Abe's dialogical work, in other
words, was existentially performing and enacting the living Logic of Basho by
deepening the dialogical encounter on the global scene, by helping to open a
higher space for living dialogue between religions and philosophies. In this
respect, the historical drama we are now living through—the emergence of

global consciousness through an ever-deepening dialogical encounter—is itself the living play of the Logic of Basho. In this context, Abe's dialogical life work is the very playing out performatively of this logical dialectic. So there is a historical consistency between the foundation of Nishida's logic and the living dialogical practice of Abe at this moment of the historical unfolding of a global hermeneutical awareness. This, for me, is the significance of Abe's vital work in the West and on the global scene.

The focal point for me of Abe's life work of dialogical encounter philosophy and practice gravitated to understanding the generative Logic of Basho that gave life and foundation to the dialogical philosophy of the Kyoto School. To truly understand the significance of Abe's work and the teaching of the Kyoto School is to come to terms with the depth of the dialogical encounter—the actual historical deepening of the dialogical space of human life and discourse. To understand the possibility and depth of this interreligious dialogue and East-West philosophical encounter required coming to terms with the foundational Logic of Basho. Thus in what follows I focus on our struggle to understand Nishida's logic. In the first section I try to articulate some of the problems and barriers we encountered in making sense of the Logic of Basho. In the second section I highlight some of the relevant findings of my own thirty-year quest to articulate the Universal Grammar of global thought in an attempt to rightly situate Nishida's Logic. I attempt to bring out the historical importance of Nishida's Logic by situating it in the context of the perennial historical emergence of Universal Grammar. I suggest that when Nishida's Logic is seen as a classical and wonderful articulation of features of Universal Grammar, his work may be more readily seen to make sense, to be vindicated, and to have global historical significance.

THE PROBLEM OF NISHIDA'S LOGIC

In the full maturity of his career Nishida gravitated to the articulation of the underlying foundation of his life's work which he called the "logic of place" (Basho) or the "logic of Absolute Nothingness." His life and writings are grounded in the depth of Sunyata, and perhaps his greatest intuition is that there is a universal logic arising out of Sunyata or Absolute Nothingness. At the end of his career he focused his attention on attempting to bring this logic to articulate expression. Given his deep grounding in the evolution of Western philosophy and logics, Nishida naturally attempted to articulate the logic of Basho (universal place) in relation to certain great paradigms of logic, such as the logic of Aristotle and Hegel. In this respect he attempted to clarify what he took to be the universal logic at the foundation of Eastern and Western thought, a truly global logic. But it also is clear that in attempting to break new ground in excavating the logic of Sunyata, Nishida faced great challenges in thinking and speaking in the ways of nonduality, which is the signature of the dialectics of Absolute Nothingness.

Apparently his attempt to articulate this universal logic of awareness hit great barriers of interpretation and expression, and it is remarkable that in the last thoughts penned by him before his death he stated that his logic had not been understood by the academic world. He begins this remark as follows:

> As the result of my cogitations over these many long years, I think I have been able to clarify the form of thinking—that is, the logic—of the historically formative act from the standpoint of the historically active self itself. I have endeavored to consider as well, through my logic, various questions fundamental to the natural sciences, and to morals and religion. I think moreover, that I have succeeded in framing questions that have never been properly framed from the standpoints of previous logics. At least I think I have been able to indicate the path along which further clarification can come. (Source: "Concerning my Logic" [p. 126], Nishida's *Last Writings: Nothngness and the Religious Worldview*, Nishida Kitaro, translated with an Introduction by David Dilworth, University of Hawaii Press, Honolulu, 1978)

It is noteworthy here that his logic purports to be grounded in the historically formative act from the standpoint of the historically active self. Moreover, he stresses that he believes himself to have broken new ground in opening this logic in ways that prior logics could not. He continues:

> The reason this path has not been taken is that past logics have tended to remain without sufficient grounding. From the standpoint of abstract logic, the concrete cannot even be considered. My logic, however, has not been understood by the academic world—indeed, I may say that it has not yet been given the slightest serious consideration. Not that there hasn't been criticism. But the kind of criticism it has received has distorted my meaning—merely criticizing by objectifying my standpoint from its own. It has not been a criticism from within my own standpoint. A criticism from a different standpoint which does not truly understand what it is criticizing cannot be said to be a true criticism. I seek, above all, an understanding of what I am saying from my own standpoint. (Source: Ibid.)

This is a jolting remark. It is shocking and saddening to hear Nishida say at the end of his life that the jewel of his life's work "has not yet been given the slightest serious consideration." He obviously felt that interpreters of his logic completely misinterpreted his work from external and alien perspectives and did not make a vital transition into the paradigm of logic he developed.

Looking more closely at this remark, it appears that Nishida thinks that his standpoint is being objectified by interpreters, that his logic is of the "concrete" and cannot be rightly understood by an "abstract" logic, and that past logics remained without "sufficient grounding."

Another way to express this is that the logic of Sunyata takes us into the place (Basho) or field of the most profound existential reality—concrete reality—that is beyond all objectification or dualistic thinking. It is clear in the tradition of Sunyata that the right minding of Absolute Nothingness requires the most radical transformation of thinking into the methods of nonduality. And what Nishida is saying is that the logic of existential immediacy of Sunyata must be entered from the methods of nondual thinking and cannot be accessed through the objectifying ways of dualistic logics. Apparently Nishida is suggesting that prior logics have been lodged in objectification and dualistic thinking, which keep them abstract and not sufficiently grounded. He seems to think that logic becomes truly grounded in the ultimate grounds of Sunyata, and that only the appropriate method of minding can truly gain access to this concrete historical reality.

There are many assumptions here that need explanation. It is clear that one main problem concerning Nishida's logic is the problem of right interpretation. One question is, what is the right standpoint for justly interpreting Nishida's logic? If we can satisfactorily make the paradigm shift to rightly interpret Nishida's logic, then the next concern is, does it make sense? Does Nishida's logic qualify as a truly universal logic? Do his innovations make sense? In what sense is the logic of Sunyata a "concrete logic"? If there is a logic of Sunyata, then what is the scope and jurisdiction of such a logic—is it truly a universal and global logic? Why does Nishida think that Sunyata or Absolute Nothingness is the universal and absolute logical ground of all discourse—of all logics, East, West, and other? Most of all we focus here on the fundamental hermeneutical problem of performing the paradigm shift of moving into the standpoint of rightly minding Sunyata as the place of concrete historical reality. Of course this challenge is not unique to Nishida's discourse, but it has been a perennial challenge in the global quest to enter the place of natural reason, of universal grammar, of right minding. All traditions have had to struggle with overcoming dualistic thinking and egocentric minding, which have always been stumbling blocks for the nondual or unitive essence of reason. Within the evolution of the Buddhist tradition alone we see that the birthing of Buddha's teaching is essentially the attempt to overcome pernicious dualism and the objectifying ways of egominding to realize the liberation and flourishing of natural reason. It is clear that the continuing self-revising and evolution of the Buddhist dialectic as, for example, in the logical and dialectical innovations of Nagarjuna, have been this very attempt to articulate and live the logic of Sunyata. So we situate Nishida's quest to advance the logic of Sunyata in the global quest to articulate the universal grammar at the heart of consciousness and the human existential condition. In this respect it is not surprising that Nishida's innovations in excavating the logic of Absolute Nothingness should encounter the hermeneutical barriers it has apparently faced. But I shall suggest that this is the single most important philosophical priority in opening higher space for the cultivation of global discourse and the advancement of natural reason.

Assuming that we can accomplish this profoundly difficult task of performing the paradigm shift and transforming our thinking into the dialectical ways of Sunyata, many problems and difficulties remain in making sense of Nishida's logic, for in developing his logic of Basho, Nishida takes as his point of departure the subject-predicate logical space that is the foundation for the evolution of the science of logic, from Aristotle through Kant to Hegel. The space of predication as the space of thought and being and knowledge has been articulated in alternative paradigms through the centuries, and Nishida builds his language of logic in this context. He apparently thinks that despite the paradigm shifts in the space of predication in these major figures in the European tradition, there has been an ongoing deep pattern of dualism and objectification in these logics. So he attempts to break new ground in the space of predication, to break through the barriers and limits in the logics of Aristotle, Kant, and Hegel to resituate logic and predication in the space of Basho, Sunyata, or Absolute Nothingness.

In making this radical turn to the alleged nondual universal ground of logic, he introduces terminology and performs dramatic innovations in renovating the space of predication. He presses the logical subject and logical predicate beyond their dualistic limits all the way to their transcendental grounding in the universal place of Sunyata. He attempts to break new ground in resituating predication beyond the dualistic and dualizing or objectifying logical space or prior logics. He assumes the model of the "subsumptive judgment," wherein the logical subject is subsumed logically and ontologically by the logical predicate. He finds in the logic and ontology of Aristotle the recognition that the primitive subject—*ousia* or ontological individual—stands absolutely beyond the predicate (universal field). This paradigm apparently secures the absolute irreducibility of the object or existent thing as a ground of predication. Nishida adopts and exploits this absolute commitment to the object or being as vital in grounding objectivity.

At the same time he apparently moves with Hegel in treating the predicate position as the direction of universality, generality, and consciousness. For him the logical place of the predicate situates the field of consciousness as the most generic and all-encompassing transcendental field that subsumes all subjects or things. So in combining the alterparadigms of Aristotle and Hegel, he finds that the place of the logical subject is the place of the object, while the place of the predicate is the place of the subject—of consciousness and subjectivity. In this way the dialectic of subject and object is played out in the inner dialectic of the logical subject and predicate in the subsumptive judgment. However, Nishida presses Hegel's position beyond its limits, all the way to the place of Absolute Nothingness. While Hegel places Absolute Spirit (Geist) as the absolute transcendental predicate—the concrete universal— Nishida presses further to inquire into the grounds or place of Geist. In this way he presses the absolute predicate to its absolute ground in Sunyata or Absolute Nothingness.

By pressing the poles of dualistic predication to their absolute limits and alleged origin, Nishida attempts to reach the absolute nondual or unitive grounds of predication, where the absolute subject and absolute predicate meet and apparently co-arise. By purporting to move beyond Hegel's absolute predicate and Geist, Nishida apparently believes that he has overcome the limits of subjectivity by reaching a deeper field of Subjectivity that crosses beyond the dualism of objectivism and subjectivism. Similarly, by pressing to the absolute ground of the logical and ontological subject (object), which cannot be subsumed by any predicate, Nishida believes that he has reached the place of absolute existence—the irreducible, impredicable existent. In this way the logic of the absolute subject and absolute predicate meets in the ground of Basho or Absolute Nothingness. In a real sense, then, Basho is the absolute ground or foundation of predication (thought and being) and is thus the universal domain or unified field of the universe of discourse.

By situating predication in the nondual dialectics of Sunyata, a radically new method of minding and speaking emerges. Nishida believes that he has accomplished the ontological ideal sought for by Aristotle in preserving the absolute integrity of the primary subject, the existential individual, in all of its singularity and historical specificity. At the same time he believes that he has preserved and sublated in a deeper way the ontological ideal and telos of Hegel in moving into the truly "concrete universal"—in the field of Basho. Thus for Nishida the absolute ground of Sunyata is the place of historical existence, where the deepest transcendental subjectivity of consciousness (universal) shows itself as the infinitely deep singular and individuated historical being (particular). Apparently what is disclosed as polarized, opposite, and even contradictory in dualized logical space is found to be in a primitive union and identity in the field of Basho. And Nishida speaks of the principle of "absolutely contradictory identity" as the universal principle of all historical existence revealed in the ground of Absolute Nothingness.

In making this radical turn to the nondual foundations of logic, Nishida purports to have discovered and uncovered the true depth of the historically existing individual. In his great last essay, "The Place of Nothingness and the Religious Worldview," he brilliantly performs the discourse of the logic of

Place with its paradigm of the historical individual. This paradigm shift to the nondual understanding of the individual exhibiting the structure of absolutely contradictory identity is, in my judgment, at once his greatest contribution to the evolution of universal grammar, and at the same time the most problematic, puzzling, and difficult breakthrough to comprehend. As he performs, textures, and elucidates this discourse of the historical individual, it is clear that this individual goes beyond the Aristotelian *ousia* (primitive individual substance) to a dynamic, interactive process of historical, active self-determination. While Nishida performs articulately the speech and logic of the individual in the place of Sunyata, many questions are provoked that remain unarticulated and not theoretically addressed or explicitly thematized and explained.

To help focus on these fundamental queries to Nishida's logic, let us take some sample summary remarks from Abe's presentation of Nishida's logic:

> With this notion of Absolute Nothingness, Nishida transcends the predicative dimension of judgment and stands upon the place of the "transcendent predicate," i.e., upon the place of Absolute Nothingness in contrast to the "transcendent subject" or individual which transcends the dimension of the grammatical subject. Both the direction of the grammatical subject and the direction of the grammatical predicate are transcended, and the one unique individual as "transcendent subject" is subsumed by Absolute Nothingness as the "transcendent predicate." Nishida fully agrees with Aristotle's definition of the individual subject as that which can never become the predicate. But he does not stop at this notion and instead develops the idea of "the predicate that can never become the subject" as the "place" wherein the singular individual exists.
>
> The ideas of the "transcendent subject" as well as that of the "transcendent predicate" thoroughly radicalized. Both the transcendent subject and transcendent predicate can be transcendent with respect to each other within the non-abiding place of Absolute Nothingness. Dual transcendence of subject with respect to the predicate and of the predicate with respect to the subject is established through the boundless openness or the uncircumscribable emptiness of Absolute Nothingness.
>
> This dual transcendence is characteristic of the subsumption of interactive individuals by Absolute Nothingness. This is not a problem of mere method, but a problem of philosophical principle. We herein make immediate contact (emphasis in original) with the individual for the first time. That is, through the realization of Absolute Nothingness, the individual is fully known by us in its concrete immediacy without any conceptualization.
>
> Expressed in Nishida's terms, the individual is realized as "that which lies within" Absolute Nothingness (i.e., it rests in Absolute Nothingness, its

place), and in Absolute Nothingness determines itself without being determined from the outside by any other thing. This self-determination of the individual just as it is, is the self-determination of "place" or Absolute Nothingness and the self-determination of the world. (Source: This and the next two quotes are from Professor Abe's draft of his essay "Sunyata and the Logic of Absolute Nothingness—The Logic Expounded by the Kyoto School" which he presented to the American Philosophical Association, Eastern Division, Washington, D.C., December 27–30, 1992. Professor Abe was kind enough to share a draft of this essay with me [see p. 7]. This version was adapted by Abe from his published essay "Nishida's Philosophy of 'Place,'" *International Philosophical Quarterly*, Vol. XXVIII, No. 4, Issue No. 112 [December, 1988])

In summing up his remarks on Nishida's logic, Abe says:

The logic of place is a predicative logic in the radical sense, not a logic of the grammatical subject. Hence it stands in contrast to all forms of traditional Western "objective logic" which, strictly speaking, never fully transcend the subject-predicate structure. It is not a logic about the act of seeing or of knowing nor is it a logic about that which is seen and known objectively in terms of the grammatical subject; rather it is a logic of "place," which is prior to, and the source of, both seeing and knowing and that which is seen and known.

It is a Subjective or existential logic prior to the opposition of subject and object, a logic of totally unobjectifiable self-awakening. In comparison with the logic of place, which is Absolute Nothingness, Aristotle's logic of the grammatical subject, Kant's highly subjectified transcendental logic, and Hegel's dialectical logic are all logics of objective consciousness and in this regard do not escape objective thinking. Consequently, they fall short of the logic of truly existential self-awakening. (Source: Ibid., p. 8)

Finally, Abe stresses that Nishida's logic of this primitive existential individual moves beyond both subjectivism and objectivism to the Objective grounds of the real historical world:

The logic of place, however, neither confronts objective logic nor excludes it. Although we term it predicative logic, this does not simplify logic without a subject. As its own self-determination, place and its logic grasp all grammatical subjects without marring their uniqueness. Place reflects all individuals and their mutually determining way-of-being within itself and realizes them as its own self-determination.

In this regard, the logic of place is the logic of the self-establishment of the objective world and includes objective logic as a necessary factor or moment. The logic of place is not the form of the thinking of the subjective self. Rather, it is the form of the self-expression of true Reality in and through Absolute Nothingness. Since Nishida's philosophy of place is a logic of thoroughgoing subjective and existential self-realization, it is at the same time the logic of the establishment of the objective world. (Source: Ibid., p. 9)

Remembering that Nishida is speaking from the paradigm of the non-dual field of Sunyata, let us now raise some basic queries of his language of logic. First, given that different global traditions of logic have taken apparently different starting points, why should the place or field of Sunyata be the absolutely universal field or ground of all logics? Is the logic of place a truly universal grammar of discourse? If it is the universal foundation for logic in the global context, then why is this so?

Why is Absolute Nothingness the universal field of all predication? Why is this the existential field? Why is this the place of historical reality? How can there be real individuality in this field of Nothingness? Why is the primitive feature of this field "absolutely contradictory identity"? Is "contradictory identity" intelligible? Is it the same as absolute contradiction? How does this contradictory identity overcome the dualism of ego identity and its constitutive duality? Does contradictory identity mean that the infinite and finite are one and the same—in an absolute unity and identity? Why is this the true "concrete universal"? Does it mean that the absolute universal and the absolute particular truly meet in the structure of the historical individual? In general, do all of the opposites and polarities of the logics of identity meet in an absolute "contradictory" identity in the place of Basho? If so, then how is the singularity, determinacy, specification, and historical finitude of the individual preserved? Wherein lies the true identity of individuals?

Furthermore, if the logic of Basho brings us beyond the subjectivism of the ego to radical Subjectivity, then how and why does this preserve Objectivity? How can the grounding of logic in the direction of consciousness truly reach the objective historical reality that seems to stand beyond consciousness? If Nishida can account for the depth of Objectivity beyond ego objectivism, then how does he account for the true meeting of Subjectivity and Objectivity? Does this mean that Absolute Reality is a dynamic, historical process? Is it developing? If the feature of every moment or locus of Basho is absolutely contradictory identity, then why is this not a mere self-cancellation, signifying nothing? Why does there appear to be direction, order, priority, development, and unfolding in the place of Basho? And if his logic is spoken from the depth of religious consciousness (religious worldview), then how and why is it relevant to the natural sciences and morals as well as religion? Does Nishida mean to say that the diverse fields of the sciences and religion and ethics meet in the unified field of Basho? How so?

These and similar queries are asked in the spirit of internal questioning from within the standpoint of Nishida's discourse. They are asked in a friendly spirit of attempting to draw out further some unanswered questions that would make the logic of Basho more intelligible and help the skeptical reader make the transition into the standpoint of Nishida's grammar. In the next section I attempt to address these and related concerns by situating Nishida's logic in the context of my experiments in the development of universal grammar.

NISHIDA'S LOGIC AND UNIVERSAL GRAMMAR

In this section I sketch summarily some of the main findings of my experiments in developing a universal grammar over the past thirty-five years. I focus on the themes most relevant to our present attempt to rightly situate and make sense of Nishida's logical investigations. These themes are developed in detail in my recently published book *Meditative Reason: Toward Universal Grammar*.

Over the past thirty-five years the center of my research as a philosopher has been the excavation of the foundations of logic and ontology in a global context. As I experimented with a wide diversity of philosophical and religious grammars across the spectrum of global cultures and traditions, the guiding intuition that there is and must be a Universal Logos at the heart of diverse cultural worlds only intensified. As I attempted to reenact and live through the grammatical evolution from pre-Socratic thought through the "postmodern" dialectics now flourishing on the contemporary scene of European philosophy, it became clear that the dramatic paradigm shifts in logics and ontology already provided a rich diversity of philosophical grammars for a global perspective. As I further ranged through the unfolding dialectics in the widely variant Indian traditions of Hindu and Buddhist thought, certain global patterns confirming the presiding presence of Universal Grammar became even more pronounced.

Over the years, as I experimented further with grammatical innovations and evolution deep in classical Chinese thought, and as I explored the cultural transformations and creative innovations of certain strains of Buddhist dialectics in the unfolding of Japanese Zen traditions, the intuition into the Universal Logos deepened. In living through repeated diverse experiments in the comparative enterprise of bringing together Eastern and Western grammatical traditions in creative dialogue, the global evolution of the History of Logos emerged in ever-deepening intensity. The more I experimented in the grammatical traditions of diverse cultures, and in the diverse fields of the liberal arts, the more it became apparent that there must be a Universal Law generating the widely variant hermeneutical forms of life across the spectrum of global cultures and disciplinary fields of experience and interpretation.

Experiments across the most widely variant traditions of First Philosophy, logical and cultural grammars, and religious worldviews led to one remarkable conclusion—that there had to be an absolutely primitive Universal Principle, Law, Field, Grammar, which conditioned all possible forms of life, and that this First Principle exhibits an infinitely deep Universal Logic that must have transcendental universal jurisdiction over all possible existence, all forms of life. This Universal Logic—Logos—implies a universal Unified Field of reality itself. The supreme power of this Logic commands thought to conform to its Law and constitutively implies that it must be the primary generative force of History or Natural Evolution. The intrinsic power of this Universal Word, by whatever name it may be called, must be the very Force expressing itself throughout History—the Field of History or Reality itself.

Intergrammatical or dialogical experiments across variant traditions of First Philosophy, logic, and ontology help bring this Universal Logic to the fore. As the History of this Logos or Universal Grammar begins to emerge, certain remarkable dialectical patterns in the global evolution of thought become manifest. Most dramatic is the inescapable finding that all History is the expressive playing out of the Universal Word—the global emergence of Universal Grammar—in the history and evolution of cultures. Indeed, in light of this universal logic, it becomes apparent that over the past twenty-five centuries of evolution, just to pick an arbitrary point of departure, the most potent explanatory force of evolution of the cultures is the paradigm shift entailed in the emergence of Universal Grammar. The driving force of History is the dialectical awakening of consciousness in the self-expression of Universal Law, which calls for the deepest paradigm shift in the centering of thinking in Logos.

This is because the Infinite Word is infinitely deep in its Unitive power, so deep in fact that it expresses itself in its irreducible Diversity and Plurality. It is here that we find the origin and depth of Dialogical Form—it is the dynamic creative form of Logos itself. The Unitive Power of Logos expresses itself in Diversity and Primitive Difference, and we call this the "Alterity" of *What-Is-First*. It is this original dialogical and dialectical Alterity that grounds all language, thought, experience, discourse, and culture. This is the universal common ground of all culture making, of all hermeneutical life.

There is no lifeworld not essentially situated in Logos and constituted in its dynamic dialectic and creative expression. Thus the Hindu discourse, of Aum and Absolute Brahman and the Self as Atman, is one creative expression of the Universal Law. At the same time, the Buddhist discourse of Sunyata is another expression of Logos. The infinite depth of the Alterity of Logos generates alter-narratives of Logos as evidence of its irreducible and inexhaustible logical power. There is no incompatibility or contradiction in seeing Logos in its "Aumic" expression, or in its self-expression as Sunyata. The Alterity of Logos explains why one cultural narrative may focus on the Unitive or nondual powers of Logos, while another may celebrate the original, Differential, nondual powers of the Word. Indeed, since all cultural worlds in the global context must be constitutively situated in the Historical Evolution of Logos, it should not be surprising to find diverse traditions gravitating to Logos in one way or another. In the Judaic tradition, for example, the emergence of the Law is found in the revelation of Yahweh. This revelation is further articulated in the Laws handed down through Moses and embodied in the life of Jesus. Jesus may be seen as an exemplar of the profound Alterity of the Living Logos, the meeting of the finite in the infinite in the being of the Christ. In another context, the Tao of Chinese tradition is seen as another wonderful articulation of the Unified Field of the Universal Law.

Thus the nondual depth of Logos as the Universal Place or Unified Field of Reality tolerates, accommodates, generates, and celebrates a wealth of alternative irreducible primitive narratives or grammatical enactments of *What-Is-First*. The Unitive Alterity of Logos becomes enriched as alternative grammatical incarnations are dialogically negotiated. So the narratives of Logos as Sunyata bring out a depth dimension of Logos that the narratives of Brahman, Tao, Yahweh, Christ, and Allah may not. Similarly, the irreducible uniqueness of authentic alter-narratives of Logos are mutual correctives against any tendency to reduce or reify the essential infinition of Logos. In other words, the Infinitude of Logos essentially plays out in a plurality of alter-grammars that dialogically enrich and deepen the Historical unfolding and emergence of its Universal Grammar. This answers the ultimate concern of "postmodern" discourse, the concern to preserve primitive and irreducible difference.

One astounding pattern in the unfolding of diverse traditions is that they all struggle with the overcoming of the egocentric mind as the Universal Law emerges in its dialectical evolution, for egocentric thinking lives a logic that is essentially dualistic and objectifying and works against the Unitive Alterity of Logos. This is where the great paradigm shift of historical evolution is focused: it is the creative transformation of minding from its egocentric and dualizing ways to the holistic and nondual methods of minding the Law. While the logics of egominding work in terms of some version of the principle of ego identity, the methods of minding in Universal Grammar are holistic or nondual and conform to the Law of Relativity. This, then, is the core historical drama being played out in the evolution of cultural grammars—the dialectical overcoming of egocentric minding and the emergence of the holistic mind as a more coherent expression of Logos. The egological principle of "identity" inherently fails to preserve a coherent identity, and it fails as a principle of individuation. The nondual critique shows why ego identity is always inherently self-divisive and destroys true individuation and relationality. In contrast, the Principle of Relativity is found to be the true pragmatic principle of identity and individuation. It is clear that Nishida intuitively moved in this direction. It now becomes evident that the Principle of Relativity—the Logos Principle—is the pragmatic principle of identity and individuation. This is the ground of Nishida's insight into the nature of the historical individual.

In this context it becomes evident that Logos, as Living Dialogical Form itself, implies a Unified Field of interrelationality and diversity. There must be a Univocal, Universal Domain or Place that situates and places all existents in constitutive relationality—the being of any existent is inherently its relational and interrelational or dialogical structure. But to live relationally—in accordance with the Universal Law of Relativity—requires the overcoming of the disrelational ways of egominding. The holistic turn in minding is the more coherent way to achieve true individuality and identity. The Unified Field of Alterity cannot be thought or experienced by the egological mind, which always violates what it thinks by objectifying it. For this reason, entering the standpoint or place of the Universal, Unified Field of Historical Existence essentially calls for the nondualizing and nonobjectifying ways of holistic minding.

All of this is, of course, highly compressed and sketchy. The interested reader may pursue a more detailed development of these themes in the book, but I did want on this occasion to situate our reflections on Nishida's logic in this context of the Historic emergence of Universal Logic or Grammar, for now we can see in more transcendental form the global importance of Nishida's logic. Our experiments in Universal Grammar help show the following:

1. The Logic of Sunyata or Absolute Nothingness is a classic formulation or expression of Logos; alternative formulations of the Logic of the Unified Field are possible and desirable, and the Universal Objective Form of Logos presides and shapes any authentic philosophical logic.

2. Egocentric logics are constitutively unable to account for or adequately articulate Natural Reason or Logic; Nishida was on the right track in seeing that any logic that remained within the dualistic bounds of an egological subject/predicate logical space had to fall short of reaching the universal field of logic. Now it is clearer why the Universal Place of Logos is the ground of all predication, the meeting point and generative origin of logical subject and predicate, and of the predicative relation.

3. Egological minding is inherently blocked from thinking or encountering the Place of Existence or Historical Reality; Nishida was right in seeing that any dualistic logic was inherently abstract and eclipses itself from the

direct existential encounter of the Universal Field of "concrete existence"—the Place of History, Nature, Natural, or Pure Experience, of true Phenomena, and of Natural Mind and Language is the Place of Logos; the egocentric mind inherently blocks the expression of the Natural Mind, which is holistic and nondual in its nature.

4. The methods of nondual thinking or holistic minding are essential for entering the Place of Presence or Logos; it is not in any egological content, any reified or objectified content, that we can find the true dialogical meeting of diverse fields but in the method of minding; in the right minding in the Logos Law we find the true meeting point of the religious worldview, the deepest truth of scientific thinking and knowing, the universal ground of global ethics, and the very living pulse of philosophical wisdom; the minding process of Logos is the true ground and meeting point of religions, the foundation of interreligious dialogues.

5. The place of natural reason, natural mind, is a Unified field of relationality or interactivity and is constitutively dialogical; the Principle of Relativity is the universal ground of dialogical process, and this process is the very pulse of the living dialectic of Logos; Nishida was precisely right in performing a dialogical dynamic model of the historical individual—his logic is a valid exemplar of the grounds of dialogical encounter and provides a pragmatic hermeneutic for the conduct of dialogue.

6. True individuality is achieved only through holistic minding or dialogical praxis—in performative living, the Principle of Relativity; Nishida's focus on the self-determining creative acts of the historically existing individual makes sense within the holistic model of the individual, for the true individual is constituted in his or her conduct of minding, in holistic praxis; true self-identity and individuality can be realized only in the Place of Logos, not in the logic of egological thinking.

7. Every locus, point, or existent in the Universal Field reflects and expresses the dialogical form of Logos, exhibits the inner dialectical identity of Alterity; every item in the Unified Field, being a holistic process, realizes its identity in the open-ended, creative, infinite process of ecological interactivity. The infinite and finite essentially meet and are mutually constitutive in the heart of all moments in the Universal Place of Presence, thus egominding severs and objectifies the "finite" from the "infinite" and abstracts both in an artificial construct, whereas holistic minding in the Unified Field reveals the constitutive co-arising of the finite-infinite continuum.

8. Accordingly, every point in Logical Space is a primitive meeting point of opposites—the meeting of finite and infinite, of universal and particular, of unity and plurality, of identity and difference, and so on. True logical coherence is nondual unity, wherein what is essentially severed

into "contradiction" in the egological space finds a primitive holistic mutuality and meeting in the Universal Domain of Existence.

9. This primitive logical feature of all names, things, and phenomena may be justly rendered as "absolutely contradictory identity," which cannot be processed in egological thinking; Nishida's calling the universal dynamic Principle of the Unified Field "contradictory identity" is a barrier for the egocentric mind but is coherent and intelligible in holistic natural reason.

10. Nishida, in situating the "individual" in the Unified Field of Relativity, rightly tapped the dialogical alterity at the heart of the historical being of individuals; this Holistic model of the individual is a historic break-through that answers the needs of the "postmodern age," for the true individual cannot be reified or objectified and has a depth dialogical structure that preserves the primacy of self-unity, universality, particular-ity, historicity, temporality, embodiment, and singularity. In the inner life of the individual, "subject" is irreducibly given together with the presence of the Other—Self and Other are given together in a primitive I-Thou relationality.

11. Nishida moved in the right direction in speaking of the place of Absolute Nothingness as the place of historical existence, which is the true "con-crete universal," the primitive meeting point of universality and the sin-gularity of existential particularity; but equally one may approach this place of existence in the rhetoric or discourse of Presence or Suchness, or Fullness, in pursuing an alternative, authentic narrative of the Place of Logos—the nondual field of Brahman or Tao, for example, could gener-ate an authentic Logos Logic.

12. Nishida is right to observe that "his logic" cannot be understood from the external and alien perspective of ego thinking or objectifying logics but only in the nondual methods of holistic thinking. The awakening of con-sciousness is precisely the overcoming of egocentric objectification and the blossoming into the holistic minding of Logos Law. Nishida's Logic is a logic of awakening, a logic of dialogical encounter; the dialogical or holistic turn in minding is the very awakening to natural reason and to our true human form.

These summary remarks are meant to indicate a direction for future research in the development of Universal Logic. I am suggesting that Nishida made a magnificent advance in opening one classical path on the way to Uni-versal Grammar. His intuition into the dialogical structure of the individual provides a powerful paradigm for the next stage in the global evolution of grammar and discourse. By situating his discourse in the context of Univer-sal Grammar and the evolutionary history of Logos, I suggest that he made classic advances in the excavation of the logical space of Logos. In seeing that the Field of Sunyata, and its logic of place, is one universal opening to Logos, this further opens the horizon and invites alternative articulations of the Logic of Logos.

Finally, returning full circle back to our earlier reflections on the dialogical drama we are now living through on the global scene, we can see more readily that this is the very play of the living dialectic and unfolding of Universal Law. The teachings of Nishida and the creative development of the Kyoto School on the global scene are playing a significant role in the global emergence of Universal Grammar. The historical drama we are now living, though understood from the standpoint of the Universal Grammar of Logos, is vital evidence and confirmation of this holistic turn in logic.

10

Logos of Tao:
The Primal Logic of Translatability

In these brief reflections I attempt to resituate the philosophical concerns and challenges of interpretation and translation between worlds in the more expansive context of the global philosophy of worldviews that probes more deeply into the universal common ground of diverse worlds as they have evolved through the ages. This global space in which widely diverse world-views (cultures, religions, ideologies, cosmologies, disciplinary narratives, interpretations, translations) meet and interact opens new horizons and frontiers in exploring the hermeneutical, logical, and ontological conditions for the possibility of interpretation and translation across worldviews and traditions. How is translation possible across widely variant worlds? What are the challenges and opportunities for genuine interpretation when we approach a great classical text from a different philosophical tradition across millennia?

These summary reflections build further on an earlier work, *The Quest for the Primal Word* (*PARABOLA* 20:3 [1995]) and seek to uncover and bring to light the global foundations of human reason, which is found to be essentially integral, holistic, nondualistic, and dialogic in nature. In what follows I distill certain key themes from two of my books that present the results of research in this area over the past forty years and that have direct relevance to the present inquiry.

The first two volumes, *Meditative Reason: Toward Universal Grammar* (1994) and *Between Worlds: The Emergence of Global Reason* (1997), appeared in Peter Lang's *Revisioning Philosophy Series*. The second two volumes, *Time, Truth and Logos: Quest for a Global Integral Logic* and *The Awakening of the Global Mind*, will appear soon. These volumes seek to open global space for philosophy in general and more specifically to uncover the fundamental logic and universal grammar of natural reason that is the common generative source of diverse worldviews, of human experience, and of the shared conditions of all interpretation and translation in the human condition.

PROLOGUE ON INTERPRETATION
AND TRANSLATION BETWEEN WORLDS

It is found that when we stand back from any one cultural, philosophical, or disciplinary orientation and cross into the *global perspective*, where widely variant worldviews originate and intersect, striking patterns emerge that are not as readily seen (perhaps cannot be seen) from more localized narrative forms of life. In this global space of diverse cosmologies and grammars of reality, it is found, for example, that diverse worldviews through the ages have gravitated to some Ultimate First Principle or Presiding Reality that is the source of its form of life.

This *global transformation* taps into a deeper *interperspectival dimension* of rational consciousness, and it becomes apparent that the vast and diverse cultural and philosophical narrative attempts through the ages to name and express *What-Is-First* converge on the same Primal Infinite Source. For example, the discourse of Tao in classical Chinese thought is one magnificent attempt at "First Philosophy"—the enterprise of developing a grammar and narrative to express the most fundamental Reality. Again, the grammar of Aum in the Hindu Vedic tradition is another exemplar of this quest for the primal universal grammar.

This is certainly true of the Judaic biblical script as it seeks to name the Infinite First Principle, YAHWEH, and this tradition unfolds in the emergence of Christianity in its attempt to express an ultimate narrative in the form of The Infinite Word and Christ, and in the birth of Islam as it seeks to express the Primal Name of Allah, and so on. Ranging further, it is clear that in the development of Buddhist thought, the radical attempt to disclose ultimate truth as beyond all names and forms, as Sunyata—Absolute Emptiness, likewise qualifies as an alternative grammatical strategy in approaching *What-Is-First*.

Of course, it is no accident that a continuing deep drive throughout the birth and evolution of European philosophy since Greek origins to express the fundamental Logos, to uncover the missing primal Logic, and to tap the missing universal grammar of Logos, is yet another great chapter in this perennial and global quest to express what is Ultimate. This certainly appears in the striving of the sciences to uncover the fundamental laws and patterns of the Universe, to name and express the "Ultimate Stuff"—whether "Energy," "Force," or "First Cause"—of Nature.

For our purposes here in inquiring into the global source and resource of interpretation and translation across and between worldviews, it is essential to acknowledge that these diverse narratives of the Ultimate Ground are alternative coexpressions of *What-Is-First*. This can only become clear in entering the multiperspectival and interperspectival rational space of the *global perspective*, for in crossing into this higher-order dimension of global consciousness, there is a "dilation" of rational awareness and a profound "inversion" of perspectivity into an Integral, Nondual, and Holistic dynamic of minding (a Primal Logic) revealing that the Infinite First is and must be the same generative source of all realities—of all perspectvies, all worldviews, all cosmologies, grammars, narratives, and disciplines—of all experience.

Indeed, in crossing into this global *rational space* and technology or logistic of minding, another striking pattern becomes evident. It becomes clear that diverse First Narratives—East, West, and other—converge toward a *global consensus* that *we humans are as we mind*—our experience, our life-worlds, our cultural identities, our disciplinary narratives, the phenomena that make up our living realities, and so on are all profoundly coshaped by our thought processes, by how we conduct our minds. A potent global theme across worldviews recognizes that humans tend to become lodged, ensnared, obsessed, blocked, and locked into egocentric or monocentric patterns of minding or processing reality that have devastating consequences for the human condition and are the common sources of existential and rational pathologies of all sorts.

This profound rational theme—that we are as we mind—brings into sharp relief the method, logistic, or technology of "minding" as being of ultimate importance. It becomes clear that "egocentric" patterns of minding reality typically separate the thinking subject from the "object" of what is thought, perceived, or experienced. In thus objectifying all that appears to its consciousness, egocentric reason proceeds to "package" and "process" all phenomena, including itself, in artificially constructed language, classifications, and categorizations that inevitably deform whatever appears. Egocentric minding typically tends to be "monocentric" (rather than dialogic), processing its world from its own reductive perspective, ideology, worldview, or narrative form of life.

This is true even in (especially in) certain "postmodern" narrative forms that appear to stress multiplicility and diversity of perspectives and to insist that there is no one universal, unifying, or valid perspective. The global logistic makes quite clear that any ideology or program of discourse that is lodged in egocentric rationality is "logocentric" in this degenerate and perniciously reductive (i.e., "monocentric") way of self-absolutizing it own "logos" or narrative form of life. In this respect, both "modernist" and "postmodernist" narratives, to the extent that they are expressed in egocentric minding, stem from and share the same common rational pathology. It becomes clear that the legitimate concern to cultivate a genuine multiplicity and diversity of perspectives can only be achieved by advancing beyond egocentric "rationality" and expanding into the global rational space where multiple perspectives can truly breathe and flourish.

The trouble with /egocentric reason/ is that it has not matured to the Critical Turn in Natural Reason, to *global perspectivity* that activates the capacity to cope with multiple worldviews or perspectives in One Rational Consciousness. It suffers from a deep, precritical tendency of absolutizing its own narrative form of life, whether the logocentric/moncentric agenda of certain "modernist" programs, or the logocentric agenda of certain "postmodern" ideologies that privileges "multiplicity, plurality, and difference." So egocentric reason is not self-critically aware that it is a particular modality of Reason, a particular mentality involving deeply entrenched habits of minding that is not the only option for Natural Reason.

Certain "postmodern" narratives insist, for example, that there can be no "higher (meta) perspective" that is not situated in localized, historical, particularized, and contingent existential conditions. In this scenario, to allege to "rise" to a higher perspective inevitably falls into the "modernist" fallacy of reducing real diversity and multiplicity to a "totalizing" and therefore reductive, pernicious, "unified perspective" that inevitably violates difference. Yet in egocentric minding, egocentric modernism privileges "unity," while egocentric postmodernism privileges "difference," and the age-old dialectical war between "Unity" and "Difference" continues today with no hope for Common Rational Ground.

These postmodern voices lodged in egocentric thinking can only "imagine" that any "higher unifying narrative" must commit the "modernist" fallacy of reducing diverse perspectives to one "unified" perspective—a totalizing, hegemonic, "metanarrative" that is not healthfully situated in the human condition. It insists that any such "modernist metaperspective" must suffer the fatal error of being a "God's eye view"—a view from "nowhere"—which of course is not possible for "situated" humans. It appears in this egocentric ideology that *any good perspective must be an egocentric perspective.* So egocentric /pluralism/ is still lodged within /egocentric reason/ and thus monocentric at its core.

But of course such equally reductive postmodern complaints that insist that all legitimate perspectives must be localized in particular historical (egocentric) contexts, in particular worldviews, are uncritically dismissive of the great spiritual and philosophical traditions across cultures and through the ages that have suggested that human rational perspectives are not essentially egocentric nor localized in that way. On the contrary, such egocentric perspectives and perspectivity are found to be the originating source of diverse rational pathologies that can only be cured through the awakening power of rational enlightenment. Egocentric "perspectives" are found to lack an enlightened or a global perspective.

Indeed, the global perspective and perspectivity at the core of Natrual Reason of which we are speaking here open up space well beyond the reductive or totalizing dynamics of egocentric reason. The Global Perspective is situated in a higher-order rational space in which interperspectivity flourishes without falling into the egocentric pathologies of violating real diversity or falling into the totalizing tyranny of a reductive and subjective "unity." So the "Global Perspective" is not just another "egocentric" or "logocentric" perspective among others but involves a dramatic transformation to a more potent dimension of Natural Reason that is indeed situated in the global context and common grounding of the interperspectivity of diverse worldviews and perspectives.

The "global perspective," then, is not yet another egocentric and subjective perspective, not a grand "totalizing" metanarrative, not a self-absolutizing fictional "view from nowhere." So the only option to these postmodern portraits of a legitimate "situated" perspective is not a modernist "perspective from nowhere" or a "God's eye totalizing metaperspective." Rather, when approached beyond the polarizing and pathological dynamics of egocentric reason, other powerful, higher-order options open up that are found to be profoundly situated in a deeper historicity, specificity, and unfolding self-revising drama than could have been imagined in egocentric patterns of minding.

In this way, any and every worldview, ideology, discipline, or narrative (whatever the content) processed in egocentric thought patterns will share the same deep structural rational and existential pathologies. This global perspective also makes clear that there are diverse alternative strategies to advance beyond egocentric reason toward the integral and hologistic dynamics of global reason. Indeed, it becomes evident that the great philosophical and spiritual teachings of the ages all converge on this common rational prescription—that the key to human flourishing and to the authentic encounter with Reality comes with this overcoming of the adolescent and dysfunctional habits of egocentric minding and maturing into the integrative, nondual, and dialogical patterns of natural global reason.

In this light I have found it enormously helpful in my teaching, writing, and public presentations to introduce and make explicit a contrasting notation to help the listener more readily identify and become aware of these two great "technologies" of minding.

TWO CONTRASTING DIMENSIONS OF REASON, LANGUAGE, CONSCIOUSNESS, AND EXPERIENCE

Whenever language is used in egocentric reason (in egocentric or monocentric patterns of thought), we mark such use with "single brackets": /X/ So any utterance "X" is "enquoted," so to speak, with / . . . / to indicate and remind us that we are speaking or thinking or experiencing in the egocentric voice, mind, rational space. In contrast, whenever we use language in the hologistic dimension of global reason, we mark it with "double brackets": ((X)).

In this way, any utterance, sign, expression, phenomenon, thought, or experience expressed in this ((semantic domain)) of global reason is made explicit by these "hologistic" markers. Thus, for example, in reading the *Bhagavadgita*, it becomes clearer that the voice and speech of ((Krishna))—the voice of ((Aum)), the meditative and nondual voice that flows from the boundless Field of Aum—are in the universal grammar and narrative force of ((Aum)). Here it appears that the warrior, /Arjuna/, is lodged in an egocentric crisis that he does not yet understand, and a deep dialogue ensues between ((Krishna)) and /Arjuna/, who both embody these two ways of being and forms of consciousness.

As we shall see shortly, any sign, any word, or any utterance is *systematically ambiguous as between /X/ or ((X))*. Any word, sign, or utterance carries a certain "indeterminacy" or "multivocity" across these contrasting semantic and rational domains. This poses profound challenges in any attempt at the interpretation or translation of the human condition. Again, if the script of ((Tao)) is a primal expression of ((Logos)), it cannot be authentically appropriated in the logistic of /ego discourse/ or reduced to /Tao/. And if ((Jesus as Christ)) is the ((Logos-made-Flesh)), then his ((Living Script)) cannot be rendered in /biblical narratives/ that reduce and objectify the ((Infinite Living Word)), and so on.

Now once we have made explicit the contrast between these two great technologies of minding in human evolution, certain astounding consequences immediately follow. It becomes clear that there is a ((Primal Logic)) of *What-Is-First*, and in my earlier work in developing ((GFP)) I suggested that it would help accelerate research, understanding, the rational enterprise, and cultural advancement for planetary well-being to introduce a ((global name)) for ((*What-Is-First*)) to help humanity recognize more clearly a recurrent global insight that the ((Primal Infinite Principle)) must be one and the same generative source of all worldviews, perspectives, cultures, traditions, disciplines, narratives, and first philosophies. I proposed as well ((*Logos*)), (taken from Greek classical attempts to tap the ultimate structure and dynamics of natural reason and discourse) as such a ((global name)) to help remind us that there is, after all, a fundamental Universal Grammar or ((Logic)) of the Infinite Word that is the universal rational context for all discourse and experience.

This helps us recognize and remember that ((Logos)) cannot be approached or expressed in the egocentric habits of /minding/. In entering the global space of the ((Infinite Word)), we cross into a boundless ((Infinite Field)) of multiplicity and diversity that is nevertheless held together in profound ((Unity)). This potent ((Logic)) of ((Logos)) issues in an Infinite, Dynamic, Unified Field that is ((Integral, Hologistic, and Dialogic)). In this way, ((TAO)) is a primal expression of ((Logos)); ((Aum)) is an alternative and ((different)) expression of the ((grammar of Logos)); ((Sunyata)) is yet another articulation of the ((Infinite Logos)); the ((Infinite Word)) in its ((Infinition)) is precisely the boundless ((multiplicity and diversity)) held together in the abysmal ((Unity)); and this is well beyond the /reductive/ and /polarizing/ dynamics of /egocentric reason/.

Here it becomes clear that the ((Unified Field)) is a boundless and dynamic interplay of interrelations between all things, all signs, all being, all phenomena, and all grammatical forms of life. This is why the ((rational space)) of ((Logos)) is ((global, hologistic, integral, and dialogic, and the sacred space of irreducible individuality, multiplicity, and Diversity-in-Unity)). It should be clear that now we are well beyond the older models of /Perennial/ philosophy that are generalized within egocentric /reason/ and that inevitably have problems honoring the deepest forms of ((diversity)), ((multiplicity)), and ((individuality)) in seeking the /common universal truths/ running through all /philosophies/.

Rather, it should be more apparent that a genuine ((Perennial or Global Narrative)) is able to tap the fundamental ((Unifying Conditions)) of all forms of life without in the least requiring that they be /reduced/ to /one narrative/ or /unifying truth/. On the contrary, the ((Global Narratology)) of ((Logos)) enhances and encourages the flourishing of irreducible ((differences)) between the Narratives of ((Tao)), ((Aum)), ((Christ)), ((Sunyata)), and ((Energy)). So the ((Hermeneutic)) of ((Logos)) is able to advance beyond the /reductive/ tendencies inscribed within both /Modernist/ and /Postmodernist/ strategies that tend to be lodged in /egocentric reason/. To privilege either /Unity/ or /Multiplicity/ is to commit the same ((logical)) fallacy. The great breakthrough of the ((Logic of Logos)) is that it can truly recognize and process the simultaneous ((primacy)) of ((Unity)) and ((Multiplicity)) in the ((Infinite Dynamics of Logos)). Indeed, any and every ((item)) that ((appears)) in the ((Logosphere)) overflows with boundless ((Unity-in-Diversity)).

((REALITY IS A PRIMAL SCRIPT)): ALL EXPERIENCE IS INTERPRETATION/TRANSLATION

Another astounding consequence of this transformation into the ((Rational Space of Logos)), the ((*Logosphere*)), is to see that this ((Unified Field of Reality)) is the ((Dynamic Infinite Script)), the ((Originating and Original Text)) that is generative of all scripts, all narratives, and all grammatical forms of life. The ((recognition)) that this ((*Infinite Word*)) situates, contextualizes, and presides in all realities brings forth a radical ((inversion)) in perspectivity.

It means that any and every /egocentric narrative or perspective/ is already ((situated)) in the ((Rational Space of Logos)), which is the ((Primal Text)) that presides in all forms of discourse. There is not a word, sign, utterance, thought, experience, or phenomenon that is not situated in the ((Universal Grammar/Unified Field)), hence, under its sway and Infinite Logical/Semantic Force. This ((Logosphere)) is the primary ground and ((context)) of all hermeneutical life, of all thought, experience, interpretation, and translation. ((This)) is the ((common ground and context)) of all interpretation.

This ((hermeneutical inversion)) implies that all human life—all experience, all thought, and all language—is ((interpretation)), is a take on the ((Primal Text of Logos))—to be human, to experience, to think, is to ((interpret)); we may call this the ((Hermeneutical Thesis)), and it means that the art of being ((human)) is the ((art of interpretation))—to exist is to be situated in the hermeneutical ((force field)) of the ((Living Primal Script of the Logosphere)). And even when (especially when) we are in /egocentric minding/, we are still always situated within the presiding ((semantic force)) of the ((Logosphere)). We may formulate this global truth of discourse in the simple ((formula)):

$$((\ldots /X/ \ldots)) : ((\text{Every } /x/ \text{ is } ((x))))$$

Let us call this the fundamental ((law of universal relativity)). It expresses a global truth of all hermeneutical, rational life.

This means, of course, that any great "script"—whether of ((Tao)) or ((Aum)) or ((Yahweh)) or ((Christ)) or ((Energy))—is a rendering of the ((Original Script of Logos)). The text of Tao is an expression of the ((script of Logos)) that may to a greater or lesser extent formulate and express the ((logic of Logos)). Similarly, the Judaic biblical script may well be an authentic expression of the ((Infinite Word)), and the Gospels may well capture the ((Living Logos made Flesh)), and so too with all of the great "scripts."

The obvious point here is that if our great ((sacred scripts)) are ((expressions)) of ((Infinite Logos)), then this would suggest that all /egocentric interpretations/ or /translations/ of these ((Scripts)) would be fatally flawed. If ((Tao)) expresses the ((Grammar of Logos)), then any /interpretation/ or /translation/ that is lodged in the /hermeneutic/, /semantic/, /logic/ of /egocentric reason/ would be compromised. *((Tao)) cannot be rendered in the hermeneutic of /Tao/.* The ((Word of God)) cannot be rendered in the /egocentric word/ and is violated by reducing it to the /Word of God/, and so on.

ALL TRANSLATION IS A FORM OF INTERPRETATION

But the more ((generic)) point here is that all human experience is ((hermeneutical)), is interpretive activity, and it is more apparent that all "translation" is a form of interpretation. To "experience" is to "interpret" or "translate" within the ((Text of Logos: The Logosphere)). And the hermeneutical insights of global philosophy have made it quite clear that we humans are always situated in certain perspectives, worldviews, and conceptual ecologies that color and shape everything that appears to us. To experience is to inhabit a "lifeworld" or "worldview," which is a universal, conceptual space that makes possible phenomena. Whatever appears to me is coshaped by the conceptual ecology of my worldview (culture, ideology, religion), so this raises still another potential barrier or challenge to approaching any "text," especially one situated in a "remote" culture, tradition, or time. To allege, for example, to "translate" a great classical ((Text)), like the ((Tao)), across millennia, across worldviews, not to mention the major challenge of being mindful of the shift from /egocentric minding/ to the ((hermeneutic of Logos)), raises serious concerns, to say the least.

TWO KINDS OF FATAL FLAWS IN INTERPRETATION/TRANSLATION

The first and ultimate concern of good translation in approaching any ((Script)) is to become ((mindful)) of the ((logic and hermeneutic of Logos)), to become competent and ((literate)) in the global ((grammar of Logos)). This also requires that we become ((critical thinkers)) who are keenly mindful of the "conceptual ecologies" or "worldviews" that we inhabit and bring to this ((sacred text)). So there are two kinds of fatal flaws in approaching a ((Text)): one is the fallacy of approaching a ((Logos Script)) in the mentality of /egocentric minding/; the other is the fallacy of unwittingly imposing my own /mental ecology/, /worldview/, /ideology/ on the ((Text)), which may be rendered in a very different ((conceptual space/ecology)). Here we see that /egocentric reason/ falls into both "fallacies" in its /hermeneutical activities/. And since we humans are always in modalities of interpretation/translation—as we encounter our "Significant Other"—we are all placed under the ((Critical Review)) of ((Natural Reason)) in all of our "hermeneutical" activities.

This means, of course, that if I am to "interpret" my "Other"—whether my friend or partner, whether my "enemy" or estranged "other," whether a different worldview, religion, culture, ideology, or any ((Sacred Text)), it is imperative that I become "mindful" of not imposing my monocentric worldview on the "Text of the Other"; I must become hermeneutically sensitive in not reducing the "hermeneutic of this Other" to my habits of mind, to my worldview, to my hermeneutical ecology. This means then that I must take the ((critical turn)) in stepping back from privileging my worldview and imposing my /mentality/ on this "Other."

So the art of authentic interpretation/translation inevitably takes us into the deep dialogue of entering the ((global mentality and logistic)) in the art of interpretation—the art of being human. Indeed, this turns out to be the rational force of the great ((Texts))—and certainly of the ((Text of Tao)). But here it is easier to see that in all of our interpretive activity—from everyday, commonsense experience to the sophisticated theoria of the sciences—we are always in some degree of encounter with the ((Script of the Logosphere)).

Nor, of course, is it a matter of "translating" from contemporary "English" into ancient Chinese, Hebrew, Greek, or Sanskrit, and vice versa. That is challenging enough. Even within "English" we face the transformations from /English/ to ((English)) and of course the diverse alternative worldviews or conceptual ecologies and ideologies that morph sense and meaning within "English." It is hard enough translating across worldviews and mentalities "within" a given natural language; it is perhaps even more challenging translating across and between diverse natural languages across worldviews, across millennia, and across the dimensional divides between egocentric /reason/ and the ((Hermeneutic of Logos)).

On the other hand, although I may be situated in ((English)), I may well have more direct access to the ((Logos)) in an "ancient" ((Logos Script)), like ((Tao)), even across these distant times, places, and linguistic challenges. As we become ((literate)) in the ((logic and language of Logos)), we become more aware of the deeper dimensions of learning ((*English*)) as a qualification for competence in translatability. Thus a scholar may know /Chinese/ and not reach the ((Text of Tao)), while another might be ((literate)) in ((English)) and be in ((communion)) with ((Tao)), and be qualified to render it well.

All natural languages arise from ((Logos)) and meet in its ((Universal Grammar)) as their ((common ground)). It is through this very ((global common ground of Logos)) that authentic translation across worlds, traditions, and linguistic forms of life is possible. ((English)) has direct contact with ((Tao)), with ((Logos)); indeed, all grammars (whether ((Hebrew, Sanskrit, Arabic, Swahili, Chinese, English . . .)) . . .) are profoundly linked in the ((generative source)) of the ((Grammar of Logos)). In this respect the ((Grammar of Tao)) is directly accessible to diverse ((natural languages)) in the global space of ((natural reason)). Thus a ((thinker)) situated in ((English)) has access to ((Aum)), to ((Tao)), to ((Sunyata)), and to ((Christ)).

THE INESCAPABLE CONCLUSION: ((LOGOS OF TAO))

The foregoing reflections on the universal conditions of interpretation and translation across worlds are obviously addressed to any and every initiative in interpretation or translation. It has been suggested that we humans are always engaged in the hermeneutical arts of interpretation, inscribed in everyday experience and consciousness.

In my other writings I explore in great detail the ((hologistic dynamics)) of the ((Logic of Logos)) and attempt to show that the ((Logosphere))—the

((Primal Script of Reality))—involves a profound ((*Categorial Continuum*)), wherein all fundamental ((categories))—((space, time, cause, being, becoming, thought, mind, matter . . .))—are all immediately implicated in one another in this ((deep structure)) of any ((worldview)). Thus if the ((Text of Tao)) is an expression of ((Logos)), then it unfolds in ((*Time*)), *not in /Time/*, and any /scholarship/ that approaches the ((Narrative of Tao)) in the egocentric mentality of /time/ is bound to be *ana*((*chronistic*)) and reduce the ((temporality of Tao)) to the projection of egocentric /time/ and /scholarship/.

In sum, it should be apparent that *((literacy)) in the ((grammar of Logos))* is a qualification for the competent interpretation and translation of ((Logos Texts)). And given that all words, signs, and languages are situated in a certain indeterminacy and multivocity across the dimensions of reason and discourse, this places all of our hermeneutical activity under the ((Critical Review)) of ((Global Natural Reason)) and the ((Hermeneutic of Logos)).

11

Nagarjuna and the
End of Global Suffering

BUDDHA'S PRESCRIPTION
FOR THE END OF SUFFERING

Buddha's great awakening and depth insight into the origin of human suffering is a monumental global event that has transformed the course of our evolution. Buddha demonstrated the highest spiritual and scientific genius in distilling his discovery into four simple and powerful noble truths that have been proven to have profound global significance for all worldviews through the ages. Simply put, Buddha taught that diverse forms of human existential suffering—our individual and collective pathologies—arise from a fundamental malpractice in how we use our minds, which deforms how we shape our selves, our world, and our living realities.

Buddha's enlightenment revealed that egocentric patterns of conducting our minds are the origin of human pathologies. His profound prescription for humanity to terminate and remove the primal cause of human suffering also is summed up in his Four Noble Truths: The way to end suffering is to overcome the root cause of egocentric minding—to recognize that ego patterns of thinking directly cause our afflictions, to become aware that our living realities are caused by how we use our minds, to see clearly that our egocentric patterns and habits of mind that generate our suffering can be terminated, and that we have a direct choice to break these negative habits and regenerate and rehabilitate new integral minding patterns that bring us into alignment and harmony with our Selves, with each other, and with the flow of Reality. Buddha's eightfold path is precisely this prescription of how to break the old egocentric mind barriers and cross into a new life of awakened mind. This sums up the essence of Buddha's radical global teaching.

But this is easier said than done. Twenty-five hundred years have passed since Buddha's global awakening, and yet planetary history has shown us that we humans are still very much lodged in egocentric patterns of minding and continuing chronic patterns of pathology, violence, and existential suffering. Furthermore, Buddha's deep diagnosis of the origins of human disorders in egocentric minding has been echoed and cross-validated in an emergent global consensus through the ages in diverse spiritual technologies and world-views. For when we stand back from privileging any one worldview or cultural lens and cross into the higher global dimension, where diverse worldviews co-originate and meet, we gain a global perspective through the global lens wherein Buddha's findings are vindicated.

Through this global lens it is striking that our great spiritual, religious, and philosophical traditions, through their diverse approaches and formulations, concur that we humans cocreate our worlds through the conduct of our minds, and that egocentric patterns produce chronic fragmentations, dualisms, polarities, and existential alienation that generate all sorts of living pathologies. So if it is, indeed, a global axiom, that egocentric patterns of minding produce suffering, then the obvious question is, why has it been so difficult for us as individuals and as a species to overcome egomind addictions and rehabilitate our mind practices in more integral and healthful ways? Why do we continue to suffer individually and collectively, perhaps now more than ever? Can we break through the egomind barrier?

NAGARJUNA'S HISTORIC GLOBAL BREAKTHROUGH

This question is even more compelling in light of Nagarjuna's monumental breakthrough in bringing forth new and unprecedented spiritual technology for finding the middle way and crossing out of the bondage of the ego-mind. Nagarjuna is a second century A.D. Buddhist innovator who founded the new tradition of *The Middle Way—The Madhyamika School*, which teaches the sacred pathway beyond the egomind into the boundless open space of Buddha's *Dharma*, or Moral Law, which is the infinite uni-fied field of Reality. Nagarjuna found that even the early interpreters of Buddha's radical teaching in its first 500 or 600 years were still caught up in the tangle of egocentric reason and fatally missed the essential teaching of Buddha's liberation.

While the genius of Buddha was to have diagnosed clearly the origin of human pathologies in the egocentric habits of mind and to have prescribed the philosophical therapy essential for rehabilitating the awakened mind, Nagarjuna's spiritual and philosophical genius was to have seen precisely how and why we humans remain entrapped within deep and chronic egocentric habits and to have built on Buddha's teaching in innovating an even more potent rational therapy for breaking the ego barrier and bringing to living reality and actualization the liberating teaching of Buddha. In this respect, Nagarjuna stands out in global history as an unprecedented teacher of the highest order whose spiritual and rational innovations and technology deserve supreme acknowledgment and appropriate recognition.

Nevertheless, Nagarjuna's name remains virtually unknown on the global scene, his ingenious innovations are still not duly recognized or properly understood, and this continued eclipse of his vital contributions is not only the case for the general public but for our academic worlds as well. Still, what is most important here is not so much that Nagarjuna's name and work gain appropriate recognition but rather that his clear and decisive teaching of entering the Middle Way out of the bondage and suffering of egocentric mind is now more vital than ever for our individual and collective sustainability and flourishing as one human family caring for each other and sharing our sacred planet.

The point is that Buddha's global truths are not just for "Buddhists," any more than Nagarjuna's spiritual technology for breaking the egomind barrier is for a select few on the Buddhist path who are fortunate enough to receive it. This teaching is meant for all humans, in all walks of life, in all worldviews and perspectives, who are caught in the force fields of egomind and are suffering the consequences.

NAGARJUNA'S SPIRITUAL INNOVATIONS

The previous chapters in this book seek to take the reader into the depths of the workings of the egomind as a vital step in understanding how and why we humans become entrapped within the vice of ego-reason and its ego-logic. Nagarjuna's spiritual technology for breaking the egomind barrier requires us all to gain some literacy in this ego-logic if we are to achieve the deepest spiritual emancipation from its captivating force field. So it is of the highest importance that we pause now to gain a preliminary overview of these dynamics of egomind, to experience the key link between egominding and our existential disturbance, and thus to appreciate the global magnitude of Buddha's prescription and of Nagarjuna's breakthrough in helping us find our way beyond the egomind into the open, integral space of human flourishing.

The essence of Buddha's enlightenment is the recognition that Reality is a boundless, open, integral, holistic, unified field, wherein everything is interrelated, interconnected, in dynamic co-creativity, or co-arising. Reality is thus an infinite web of relations, and nothing can stand apart, separated, isolated, in self-identity. This depth insight means that all "things" are interrelational fields of living energy in a mutual, interconnected flow. To be "individual" (literally: undivided, undual, integral, unbroken) is to realize our intricate wovenness into this ever-changing web of relationality. We can only become Real, get Real, hence, be fully "sane," when we experience our Selves and everything in our Ecology as immediately implicated in this unified and unifying web of connectivity.

This boundless web of the ecology of existence has (is) a profound Law-like nature, which is the Dharma, the Law of Nature—the Buddha-Nature, the community of all beings. To awaken to this relational flow is to enter, discover, and mindfully hold one's place in this Unified Field, to experience one's integrity, to cross into the space of integral reason, into true knowing, into compassion and awakened emotional life and experience, to become a whole person, to flourish. Nothing has separated identity, nothing exists in separation or isolation, so to be is to be a dynamic relational and interrelational energy field intricately woven into the web of life. We are not "things," "objects," "subjects," "beings," or "entities" but ((relational force fields)).

Buddha's global insight reveals that we humans, whether through our evolution or development, tend to become ensnared in a mentality that blocks access to this primal field of integral reality, that breaks away and breaks apart from this integral relational flow and creates a primal rift and rupture that replicates itself in an endless vicious cycle, thus generating profound separations, dualities, polarities, fragmentation, alienation, dissonance, violence, and diverse forms of pathology and suffering. The core of the alienation and suffering is caused by this primal severance from the unifying, relational flow of Reality. And this separating mentality typically posits itself as a separately constituted entity, having its independent (nonrelational) identity, which we are calling the "egocentric" mind.

Buddha's fundamental breakthrough is in recognizing that the egocentric mentality is a "technology of minding," a way of processing our selves, our experience, our world, which separates us from the unifying flow of Reality. His historic and global advance was in recognizing that there is a higher, more mature "integral technology of minding"—through the awakened meditative mind—that flows with and brings us into alignment with the process of Reality itself. Our suffering ends when we become more attuned to Reality and thus leave behind the dysfunctional habits of mind that break the circuits of our intricate connectivity to the holistic fabric of the universe. Thus when our minding process itself is in sync with the process of Reality, our life flourishes and our suffering ends. When we are separated from ((Reality)), we suffer.

THIS ALIENATION FROM REALITY
IS A GLOBAL PHENOMENON

This alienation and severance from Reality is an ongoing global event for all people, across all borders and worldviews. Buddha's insight has been independently seen and confirmed through the ages on a global scale. And our diverse spiritual and philosophical traditions have recognized that this in their diverse diagnoses and unique formulations. It is at the heart of the classical Chinese insight, articulated by Lao Tzu in the *Tao te Ching*, that the Tao that is named is not the Tao. He teaches that everyday consciousness and language are not able to express the fundamental Reality, which is the primal and unifying force of Tao. It is at the heart of our Judaic founding that calls on people to place God, the Infinite Spirit, first and foremost in all life. It is recognized in the language of "sin," which sees the fallen human condition as being lodged in a primal separation from God.

It is the heart of the Vedic sciences that recognizes that our human pathologies arise from our false consciousness, which comes from deep dualism and separation from the Unifying Reality of Brahman, the Infinite Primal Field. It resonates through Christian discourse in the global advent of Jesus, whose life and sacrifice focused on healing the chasm of alienating sin and opening the way to communion with God. And, of course, it resonates in diverse ways through the Greek origins of the Logos and the human quest to rise out of the cave of ignorance into the Light of Rational awakening and to achieve our direct encounter with Reality. So in one way or another, all humans face this universal depth challenge of moving beyond the alienating ignorance and deep dualism of the egomind and into the integral and awakened consciousness of Self-realization. Our common work in becoming fully ((Human)) is to end the suffering that comes with egominding.

HOW THE EGOMIND SEPARATES US FROM REALITY AND PERPETUATES SUFFERING

The egomind, then, is first and foremost a "technology" of minding, a mental process that produces an objectifying and a fragmenting mentality, and whatever its particular worldview, it yields a "self" that remains severed from Reality. Egominding arises in and with a logical space that presents, so to speak, a "screen" of consciousness, whereupon all of our thoughts and experiences and world will appear. This logical space of egomind appearance (already separated from the unified field) implies a further deep dualism—a primal distinction—between the thinking subject, on the one hand, and the screen of appearances, on the other. This thinking subject remains on the periphery and views through its lens all that appears on its screen of awareness.

Most people live their lives as characters on this ego-screen, seen through their ego-lens, with no real critical awareness that what they encounter in their experience is, indeed, on an objectified screen or field and being viewed through their mind-lens, which has been shaped all along through their culture and worldviews. The main point is that our everyday field of awareness is already an objectified field lodged in an original deep dualism of which we are not aware. This is the situation being addressed and redressed by Buddha and Nagarjuna. Once we become identified with and are lost as characters in this objectified field of ego-mind, the harm is done, and a vicious cycle of dualism, polarization, and fragmentation is perpetuated. To help us remember when we are singling out something on this objectified screen of the egomind, let us explicitly mark it surrounded by "single strokes": / . . . /—we can think of this as marking off what is placed within it as seen through the ego lens. Making the /egosphere/, the /objectified screen/ of the ego-lens, explicit will now help us become more conscious that we are, indeed, on the field of /ego appearances/.

But let us now consciously enter this objectified ego-screen to get a better sense of how its technology of thinking works. On this ego-screen everything in our reality appears—our thoughts, our language, our culture, our worldview, our experience, our phenomena—our universe. And different cultures or philosophical traditions have given their accounts of the nature of thought, language, and world on this ego-field. In the Greek origins of European thought, for example, philosophical thinking sought to articulate the nature of language, thought, and being in this logical space. The science of logic, for example, attempted to get to the deep structure and laws of thinking, since these dynamics of thought and language would encode and shape all that appears in the world. Early attempts to initiate this science of thinking in the pioneering work of Socrates, Plato, and Aristotle recognized that all of our thinking takes place in a logical space of "predication": to think is to join logical subjects and predicates in meaningful thoughts that mirrored the world:

/S is or isn't P/ (the level of thought as expressed in language)
/Substance and Attribute/ (the level of existence reflecting the world)

So in the birth of the science of logic, the science of thought is already implied, the science of reality (ontology), and the science of language. In this context we already have some fundamental lines drawn between the domain of thinking (consciousness), the domain of signs and language, and the domain of world or existence. The idea here is that thinking is expressed in language, which mirrors the world, and all the time the ego-lens, where the "thinker" resides, remains transparently eclipsed on the edge or periphery of the "visual field" of this objectified logical space.

The idea, then, is that to think (of anything whatever) is to have already entered the space of "ego-predication"—to pick out or identify a logical subject and to affirm or deny a predicate (quality, attribute) to it: for example, /Socrates is a philosopher/, /rain is falling/, /Peter loves Mary/, and so on, and the thought

/Socrates is wise/ (expressed in a sentence)

pictures a situation "out in the world," in existence (also on the objectified screen):

/Socrates being wise/ (a "fact" in the "objective" world),

so in this way the dimension of thought/language mirrors and reflects the objective world.

This idea of thinking as predicating is not just a "Western" thing; diverse traditions, East and West, in seeking to understand and articulate the laws of everyday thinking, have in one way or another articulated these laws and dynamics of predication.

EGO-LOGIC: IDENTITY, DUALISM, SUFFERING

It is not an exaggeration to say that all ego-life and cultures will take place in this logical space of /predication/. This space of thinking is of course the very space in which my experience, events, and all phenomena show themselves. My world, my narratives and perspectives, and all of my experiences, inner and outer, are expressed in and through this logical space of /thought/ or /predication/. This is another way to appreciate the power of the thesis, that our /minding/ shapes our /living realities/—we are as we mind.

A basic operating principle of /ego-logic/ is the /Principle of Identity/, which alleges that each item or term in /thought space/, whether a /subject/ or a /predicate/, has its own inner identity, essence, or meaning. This, of course, goes for /I/, the identity of the /ego self/ as presented on the /ego screen/ in the logical space of /Predication/: for example: /I am a man/, /I am American/, /I am thinking/, and so on.

The /Law of Identity/ rules in the space of /ego thinking/, and this law has the effect of drawing a circle around each "term," alleging its own inner identity, and thus it marks it off from any other "term," excluding it from its space; so to have such inner identity is to displace all other terms in the language, thus /Identity/ is a double-edged sword that enforces /Difference/ as well. To have /identity/ is to be thus /differentiated/ from everything else.

The fundamental idea, then, in /ego thinking/, grounded on the Principle of /Identity/, is that each term or item in thought or language is differentiated from all else and has its own inner identity. This of course corresponds to the level of /existence/—so whatever the /term/ picks out in the world likewise will have its inner "signature" or "essence" or "identity"—every /thing/ has its own inner being or marker within itself that makes it /different/ from /everything else/. So in /ego consciousness/, it is presumed that everything has its own inner identity within itself. Without this presumption, thought would not work, language would not work, and of course the world would be in chaos. And this goes, first and foremost, ostensibly, for /me/, my /self/ as indicated by /I/. Thus at the fundamental ground of /ego-logic/ /I/ am an independently /existing/ /entity or being or object/ having my unique identity and differentiating essence within me. In this way the /Ego-Self/ is formed and constituted within the /objectified ego-screen/. This is how I see and experience my /self/. And this, Buddha finds, is at the core of human suffering.

This, of course, is not the place to go into technical details. What is important in this preliminary overview is to get some literacy and sense of how we unwittingly /objectify/ our selves and get caught up in an /ego drama/ that has devastating consequences if we do not become aware of how our naive, everyday thinking can entrap us in deadly dynamics and sever us from Integral Reality. This simplified introduction to /Identity/ gets right to the heart of Buddha's teaching and Nagarjuna's historic advance, for /Identity/ is already a product of a deep dualism, and the presumption of /Ego Identity/ as the absolute premise that makes all /ego thought/ and /ego experience/ work plays out in a repeating pattern of /dualism/ and /polarization/: the law of /Identity/ immediately issues in another version of mutual /exclusion/:

/S must be P or not-P/.

Or, in still another allied version of /noncontradiction/,

/S cannot be both P and not-P/.

Alternatively, the simplest form of self-identity

/S is S/ is mirrored in its counterpart:
/Either S or not-S/.

This suggests that the dynamics of /Ego Identity/ will spawn /either-or/ dualities, mutual exclusion, and ultimately will reflect the /deep dualism/ that comes with the /objectified screen/. When we live our lives in this /Ego-Thought-Space/, dominated by naive /Identity/, it has a profound, existential fallout in every aspect of our lives. This simplified introduction of how /Identity/ works in the /Ego Field/ is meant to give some hints of the magnitude of Nagarjuna's contribution to the end of suffering, for Buddha saw clearly that /Identity/ is the source of /Suffering/. Naive /Ego Identity/ leads to the illusion of independent self-existence, which brings in its wake separation, isolation, fragmentation, dualisms, pernicious polarizations, and pathologies.

NAGARJUNA'S BREAKTHROUGH

It is not possible or appropriate here to go into details about how the story of the evolution of human thought on a global scale has been hitting the walls of /Ego Identity/ and its /Objectified Field/ of experience and existence. Nagarjuna himself, who entered the scene after centuries of intensive and sophisticated philosophical developments in the classical Indian traditions, noticed the profound polar entrapment of thought within the /Objectified Field/ of /ego reason/. Even the greatest insights into the "Unified Field," when rendered in the language space of /ego reason/, become deformed, distorted, and eclipsed. This is what he found happened to Buddha's great teaching after over 500 years of its early development.

Apparently, when we are caught within the /Objectified Field/ of /ego reason/, even philosophical thought becomes ensnared in a repeating pattern of polarization from one ego extreme to another: for example, either focusing on /Being/ or /Becoming/; on /Identity/ or /Difference/; on /Unity/ or /Multiplicity/; on /Individuality/ or /Community/; on /Mind/ or /Matter/; on /Eternal/ or /Temporal/; and so on. All attempts to find a coherent, integral account of Self or Experience or Life within the /Ego Objectified Screen/ are apparently doomed to failure. This is what Nagarjuna realized—that unless we really broke through the bounds of the /egomind barrier/, beyond the /ego objectified field/, Buddha's global insight truly could not be achieved, his essential teaching truly could not be understood, and humanity would remain in its suffering condition.

Nagarjuna found that while the Hindu Schools rendered their deepest insights into the language of /Atman/, the early Buddhist teachers sought to render Buddha's teaching of the "NoSelf" in the polar opposite language of /Anatman/ = /No-Self/; but this, he felt, was incompetently rendered within the technology of /ego-thinking/, within the /objectified field/ of the /ego-field/, thus still entrapped within the /ego-lens/. Buddha's teaching cannot be rendered within the /egosphere/ of /ego-reason/.

NAGARJUNA'S MIDDLE WAY
INTO EMPTINESS (SUNYATA)

Nagarjuna saw, perhaps more keenly than any other global thinker, that as long as we are unwittingly still on the /egomind screen/, the /objectified field/, and speaking and thinking through the /ego lens/, we are doomed to continued suffering. If Buddha's great advance was to see that /Identity/ causes /Suffering/, then Nagarjuna pushed this insight further to make clear that to /Predicate/ is to /Suffer/, to think and live and experience on the /Ego Objectified Screen/

is to /Suffer/. So he devised a radical logical therapy to cure a /logical disorder/. And in his historic treatise, *Fundamentals of the Middle Way*, he demonstrated this rational therapy, chapter after chapter, to help the /ego-reader/ experience the unworkability of /ego-thinking/, the implosion of /ego-reason/, the deconstruction of /ego-identity/, and the dissolution of the /ego-logics/ into incompleteness and incoherence.

Stated in the simplest terms, Nagarjuna developed a rational therapy to help the /ego-thinker/ directly experience that if we take the principles of /ego-identity/ quite literally, then all /ego-thinking/, /ego-predication/, and ego-language/ will implode in a meltdown that reveals its emptiness and absurdity—all predications reduce to nonsense if we assume /ego-identity/ to be true and take it at face value. The core insight into Nagarjuna's therapy is that if we truly assume that all terms of thought (any and all items of /ego-language/) have their own inner identity, independent of their relations and connectivity to other terms, then all alleged /relations/ and the /connectivity/ of /ego thinking/ will fall apart and fail to connect. Since to "think" is to purport to blend and connect and weave and relate distinct "terms," "words," "categories," or "concepts" together in a "unified thought," Nagarjuna's logical therapy helps us realize that /ego predication/ cannot work under naïve /Identity/, but can only work in and through the rational resources of the Unified Field of Relationality—true Relations work in the unified field of relations, not in the artificial, constructed /ego-field/ of separated, independently constituted /information fragments/.

The main therapy is in coming to understand that /ego-identity/ is not the Rational Principle that makes language, thought, and world work. Rather, the conscientious /ego-thinker/ begins to realize that it is the primal field of Relationality, wherein all things are taken as originally interrelational and interconnected, that makes the world go round. True Language is the fabric of the Unified Field of Emptiness. True Causation is the holistic, nonlinear, intercausal nexus of the Cosmic Field, the SpaceTime Continuum flows in and through this Primal Field, and so on. So, in effect, Nagarjuna illuminates Buddha's teaching, that it is the Principle of Relativity (Relationality) that accounts for our natural intelligence, natural reason, and for the workings of the everyday world and its Natural Language, not the ego-law of /Identity/. In and through this radical therapy, the /ego-thinker/ is inverted and transformed into a direct encounter of this Primal Field of Emptiness (Relationality) and discovers the everyday world in its true, revealed form.

It is only when we realize that all possible moves in the /ego-predication game/ are bankrupt and end in absurdity do we really get it, at the mind and heart and gut level, that /egominding/ makes no sense if taken on its own terms. When the /ego-thinker/ has conscientiously worked through chapter after chapter, meditation after meditation, in Nagarjuna's radical therapy, then she or he has no place left to go but to cross into Emptiness, into Awakened Rational Awareness, into a Direct Encounter with the Unified Field of Dharma, letting go of the addiction to /egominding/, and the /ego-objectified screen/ that comes with the /ego lens/.

It is in this journey into the Field of Emptiness, Dharma, Connectivity, and Co-Arising that we experience the higher Technology of Integral Mind-ing and awaken to the boundless overflow and fecundity of Living in the Moment, in Now, in Presence, and we experience the deep dialogic intercon-nectivity of the Ecology. So the Teaching of "Emptiness" is a double-edged spiritual sword that at once deconstructs the artificial /constructions/ of the /egomind/—the constructs of /I/, of /You/, of /Mind/ of /Matter/ of /Being/ and /Becoming/ of /Space/ and /Time/—and brings us into a direct experi-ence of the fullness of Life, Nature, Self, and Reality. Awakening to this dou-ble Truth of Emptiness leaves behind all of the old, worn-out polarities of /Identity/ v /Difference/, of /Finite/ v /Infinite/ of /Mind/ v /Body, of /Unity/ v /Diversity/ and the vast range of /dualisms/ and /polarities/ that comes with the /ego-screen/ and the /ego-lens/, and it takes us into the holistic and inte-gral Space of Dharma, of Buddha-Nature, where there are no separated /things/, no /entities/, only dynamic Relations and Inter-Connectivity. This is the fundamental domain in which thought and predication and all relations can flow. This is the field of Natural Language, and of Nature. All terms of language are thus originally, mutually constituted in a boundless web of rela-tions rather than in the artificial fragments of /ego-identity/.

In this context, beyond the /egomind/, it becomes clear that we have arrived in the Open Space of Natural Language, of Natural Reason and Inte-gral Intelligence, of Natural Law or Dharma, of Compassion and Personal Wholeness. Then we may appreciate Nagarjuna's stroke of genius in noticing that in this Awakened Integral Mind, there is no longer the slightest differ-ence between Samsara (as the everyday world now experienced through the awakened mind) and Nirvana, the highest liberated freedom and joy.

Thus in crossing into this non/dual/ Field of Emptiness=Fullness, we open the awakened Integral Lens of true Knowing, of deeper Science, of Moral Freedom, and of new possibilities for global citizenship and a nonvio-lent, sustainable culture. It is in this crossing that we can experience Buddha's Truth, that the /egomind/ is the place of /suffering/, that the /egomind/ is a place of deep /Ignorance/, of /Obsessive Addiction/ to /Ego-Objects/ and to artificial /Constructions/.

To conclude on a global note, had I the time and space here I would quickly scan the centuries of the evolution of European thought from early Greek beginnings through our Judeo-Christian journeys and into the modern and postmodern dramas of recent centuries. I believe that were Nagarjuna here with us today and inspected the current state of our cultures in the East and West, North and South, in a global perspective, he would see the people of the planet still caught in deep dualisms and still repeating age-old patterns of the pendulum swing of Samsara between the recurring poles of the /ego-mind/. It would be interesting to hear his take on the megatrends in cultures through the centuries.

I believe he would see an almost tragic pattern repeating over millennia, from the polar splits faced in the early Greek origins of the narratives of Parmenides versus Heraclitus in the polarity of /Being/ versus /Becoming/, not unlike what he diagnosed in the polarity of /Atma/ versus /Anatma/ and the ongoing culture wars of /Is/ versus /Isn't/. He certainly would notice the megashift from European /Modernism/, which apparently privileged /Unity/ and /Identity/, to the recent postmodern movements that took us into privileging /Plurality/ and /Difference/ and /deconstruction/. He probably would applaud this postmodern play of /Deconstruction/, of /Identities/, since he himself practiced this.

But most certainly he would not get stuck within the old /ego-game/ of /modernism/ versus /postmodernism/, both polar extremes of /ego-reason/. And then we would see that as we now enter the twenty-first century, perhaps his teaching is more timely than ever, and humanity has arrived at a threshold where all planetary citizens may be ready to cross individually and collectively through the Middle Way, beyond the deadly forces of /egomind/ and into the Life-Affirming and Sustainable patterns of the Universal Dharma. Finally, he very likely would applaud those recent frontier scientists who now see that the key to crossing into the Unified Field requires a more radical, integral thinking beyond the /ego-boxes/, for Buddha and Nagarjuna understood that the Unified Field of Reality is a nonlocal, holistic, dynamic, ever-unfolding energetic field. At this new frontier in science is a profound convergence of the Unified Field of the Sciences and the Unified Field of Dharma, pioneered by Buddha and other spiritual geniuses.

Index

Made in the USA
Middletown, DE
28 January 2020